REALISM, ETHICS AND SECULARISM

Essays on Victorian Literature and Science

GEORGE LEVINE

CAMBRIDGE
UNIVERSITY PRESS

CAMBRIDGE UNIVERSITY PRESS
Cambridge, New York, Melbourne, Madrid, Cape Town, Singapore, São Paulo, Delhi

Cambridge University Press
The Edinburgh Building, Cambridge CB2 8RU, UK

Published in the United States of America by Cambridge University Press, New York

www.cambridge.org
Information on this title: www.cambridge.org/9780521885263

First published 2008

Printed in the United Kingdom at the University Press, Cambridge

A catalog record for this publication is available from the British Library.

Library of Congress Cataloging in Publication Data

Levine, George Lewis.
Realism, ethics and secularism : essays on Victorian literature and science / George Levine.
p. cm.
Includes index.
ISBN 978-0-521-88526-3 (hardback)
1. English literature–19th century–History and criticism. 2. Literature and science–Great Britain–
History–19th century. 3. Great Britain–Intellectual life–19th century. 4. Ethics–Great Britain–
History–19th century. 5. Knowledge, Theory of, in literature. 6. Science in literature. 7. Realism in
literature. 8. Secularism in literature. I. Title.

PR468.S34L48 2008
820.9′356–dc22   2008018926

ISBN 978-0-521-88526-3 hardback

Books are to be returned on or before
the last date below.

LIBREX-

REALISM, ETHICS AND SECULARISM

George Levine is one of the world's leading scholars of Victorian literature and culture. This collection of his essays extends and develops the key themes on which his work has centered throughout his career: the intersection of nineteenth-century British literature, culture and science and the relation of knowledge and truth to ethics. The essays offer new perspectives on George Eliot, Thackeray, the Positivists, and the Scientific Naturalists, and reassess the complex relationship between Ruskin and Darwin. In readings of Lawrence and Coetzee, Levine addresses Victorian and modern efforts to push beyond the limits of realist art by testing its aesthetic and epistemological limits in engagement with the self and the other. Some of Levine's most important contributions to the field are reprinted, in revised and updated form, alongside previously unpublished material. Together, these essays cohere into an exploration both of Victorian literature and culture and of ethical, epistemological, and aesthetic problems fundamental to our own times.

GEORGE LEVINE is Professor Emeritus at Rutgers University and Distinguished Scholar in Residence at New York University. He is the author of many books on Victorian literature and culture, and has taught at universities in the USA, UK, and Italy.

Contents

Preface

Goodness is truth, truth goodness. It is a very Victorian notion, and it runs deep. But it also runs into trouble very quickly. Looking at the Victorians from the perspective of this idea turns out to have been my life's work, although I wasn't always aware of it. And it did so, I now realize, because the idea resonates into our own moment and reverberates quite personally for many of us. The essays gathered here spin with what I now recognize as relentless tenacity around the problems related to this fundamental idea. Approaching it first with my eye primarily on the art of the Victorians, it has taken me into the dry depths of epistemology, into the study of Darwin and considerations of evolutionary biology, into that inescapable turmoil over religion that marked so much of Victorian discourse and that muddies our own intellectual waters at the start of the twenty-first century, and back again into the very heart of the Victorian ideal of art – the "realism" of its fiction, the ethical tensions of its romantic poetry, and the various and brilliant rhetorics of its prose.

I bring together in this book many of the essays with which I have explored these problems, in various forms. They were written separately, for diverse occasions at different times, and it is only recently that I realized that they might be taken for chapters of a single book. Only after many years did I come to understand how doggedly preoccupied with questions of epistemology and ethics, of selfhood and otherness, of realism and objectivity I have almost always been. Although the essays do not quite form a progressive sequence of argument, they develop into a set of closely related explorations of aspects of a single argument, always connected historically because of my continuing passion for the literature of the Victorians, most particularly its "realism," and hence for the study of Victorian culture, particularly in the light of the way these have been besieged by our contemporary criticism, and re-evaluated in the light of contemporary history. Put crudely, that argument is that questions about the possibility of knowing, epistemological questions, were for the

Victorians urgent ones, particularly so because they were always also ethical questions, and that literature takes us where philosophy cannot, answers the questions differently (if perhaps inconsistently). Both approaches among the Victorians, however, reveal a culture committed to the possibility and necessity of knowing the "real," and both approaches reveal the Victorians' remarkably creative and troubled recognition of the elusiveness of both the true and the good. Their literature, their philosophy, and their social criticism is all marked by the struggle to get it right because getting it right seemed a condition for ethics itself.

My preoccupation with the problem of "objectivity," which manifests itself repeatedly in these essays, is obviously an epistemological concern, but it takes me directly into the subject of science, the area of thought that most explicitly and demandingly seemed (and seems) to require "objectivity." And these questions take me to the heart of many of the most intense and pervasive Victorian culture wars, which were fought over questions of belief, of ethics, and of value. How might one affirm ethical norms with the "objective," merely descriptive, and "naturalistic" explanations of the world provided by science? As scientists struggled for professional (and ethical and intellectual) authority, they, particularly the scientific naturalists, set up arms against established religion. But for most Victorians religion was the sanction for morality; take religion away and they were threatened by moral anarchy and despair. These wars were fought everywhere – and the literature is largely characterized by the struggle.

Although these essays consider large cultural and sometimes philosophical issues, they tend to do so in the field of literature, or of literature in relation to science, or of science as literature. Dickens and George Eliot and Ruskin, yes, but also G. H. Lewes, and Charles Darwin, and T. H. Huxley, and Charles Lyell, and John Tyndall. All of these brilliant scientists and cultural critics and novelists (and the poets as well) were engaged in an intense and sustained debate about where the culture should be going, about what really counted, and implicitly of course, about where authority lay. In one way or other, they were obsessed with questions of knowledge and truth, and thus, while the word is normally now applied to a literary movement, "realism" was for them an overriding concern.

At the heart of this literary study, then, is my continuing concern with this "realism," primarily as it manifested itself in the Victorian novel, yet implicitly and explicitly as the questions related to it were manifest in science and in the cultural and even religious criticism of writers like

Matthew Arnold and John Henry Newman. I take realism as the literary counterpart of the epistemological/ethical question that drives so many of these essays. Realism aspires, above all, to truth-telling. But realism is also connected to the movement toward secularization that became so prominent among the Victorians despite the broad, almost culture-wide burst of religious activity at the time. Because realist literature puts to the test of narrative the possible cultural responses to the epistemological and ethical problems, it pushes – my argument is – willy-nilly toward a secular, naturalistic understanding of the world, even when the authors themselves are overtly religious and their narratives attempt to reaffirm religion. Once again, then, in the pages of the most popular fictions, the battle over moral possibility, which in these essays I focus on the epistemological/ethical question, gets fought out.

The connection of the epistemological question of "objectivity" to the work of realism is affirmed in part because of a fundamental moral/ aesthetic drive to find a way to move beyond the narrow limits of individual consciousness into a sympathetic and empathic relation to others, to the not-self. Victorian narratives are in part an answer to the question raised by so many worried Victorians as to whether it is possible to sustain the moral life without religion. Realists explore the consciousnesses and natures of a broad variety of selves, more or less strange, more or less familiar; they thrust the reader into an intimacy with possibilities well beyond the limits of the self who reads. They push the boundaries of non-self, and, as the last two essays are most concerned to emphasize, even to a recognition of the perhaps ultimate unknowability of others. And, as with all Victorian efforts at knowing, there comes the ethical concomitant, the deepest respect and reverence for that otherness.

On these matters, the ten separately conceived essays become ten chapters of one book. And while the subjects of these essays are almost all Victorians, the issues and the arguments are designed to address our contemporary conditions, for the issues with which the Victorians struggled are very much alive in current cultural debate. Obviously, the old philosophical dualism between "is" and "ought" is still alive and evoking complicated and intense debate. Obviously, the insistence that morality is and must be based upon a religious foundation is also alive and well, and the strenuous effort of secularists to insist that morality can be sustained as forcefully (or more so) in an entirely secular cultural order continues with perhaps more seriousness and, one would hope, more success than the Victorian Positivists achieved. These essays engage with contemporary critical theory, implicitly always, and from time to time explicitly; they are particularly engaged with those aspects of contemporary literary and critical theory that, by and large, reject the idea of objectivity and the possibility that the literature of Victorian realism was something other than a capitulation to the dominant ideologies of the time. I am, throughout this book, more or less unabashedly committed to representing Victorian views literally, and sympathetically, and committed as well to addressing contemporary implications of these great Victorian issues for secularism, for the idea of objectivity, for our sense of the ideological complicity of literature, and for the way our culture thinks about science and religion. If the accusation that these essays are a bit Victorian themselves is made, I won't object.

I have not tried to revise the essays extensively, but when the opportunity turned up to make connections among them, I have taken it. I have tried also to reduce the inevitable repetition that comes when one gathers separately published essays, and to include references to some more recent work (after all, the first of these essays was published at least twenty-five years ago), but I have not tried to be exhaustive in that respect. Several of the essays have never been published before, but were written for particular occasions up to this moment. Yet I hope readers will agree that while each essay has its own coherence (I hope), they really do make part of a broader argument and in effect comment on each other. It would have been disingenuous for me to try to disguise their independence and pretend by some clever work of transition that they were written with this book in mind. But in important ways, this book has always been in my mind and ideally forms part of one long argument with historical, critical, and contemporary relevance.

So I am confident after all that this book is genuinely a book, a book about profound Victorian problems of knowledge, ethics, and art, that are our own problems as well. I hope it will be clear to readers that the essays constitute a *set* of related explorations, driven by the irresistible attraction for me of the moral energy and intellectual and aesthetic power that mark Victorian realism and literature.

Introduction

I

The ravens hawking from tree to tree, not you, not you,
Is all that the world allows, and all one could wish for.
                                                    Charles Wright

That element of tragedy which lies in the very fact of frequency, has not yet wrought
itself into the coarse emotions of mankind; and perhaps our frames could hardly bear
much of it. If we had a keen vision and feeling of all ordinary human life, it would
be like hearing the grass grow and the squirrel's heart beat, and we should die of that
roar which lies on the other side of silence. As it is, the quickest of us walk about well
wadded with stupidity.

                                                    George Eliot

The hardest thing in the world is not to be you. Literature tests out the difficulty and challenges it. However self-preoccupied we become, however much our fictions call out to us as commentaries on ourselves, or as more or less fantastic reflections of the writers themselves, literature demands an exercise of the aesthetic and ethical imagination that gives us the rare opportunity not to be us. The experience of entering mentally into the strange terrain of otherness, of overhearing other selves, opens up alternatives to ourselves. It is like hearing the ravens hawking from tree to tree announcing their absolute difference, announcing a world you never made, that runs without reference to you, that is full of beings that don't know of you, who guide their lives unconcerned about whether you find them beautiful or annoying or even irrelevant. And yet, like those hawking ravens, they glimmer with a sense of independent consciousness, of awareness of the world, and in their absolute difference are therefore related to you after all.[1]

There has been much talk in recent years about the ways in which the "self" is merely a construction, no stable thing but a concoction of each moment as it is lived. In some ways this has to be right – in fact, even some distinguished Victorians, like John Stuart Mill and W. K. Clifford, believed it. Think about the difference between you then and you now, about the fact that our cells are decaying and being replaced even as we read these words, about the contradictions one discovers in one's own beliefs and actions, about how we perform ourselves differently to different people, even to ourselves, about the multiple ways in which we think of ourselves from moment to moment – say, white, Jewish, professional, lover, father, liberal, cynic, unbeliever, cheese-lover, adulterer, friend, teacher, liar, good guy, writer, critic, coward, bird-lover, duck-eater, failure, success . . . And yet with all the variations and all the contradictions, every morning we wake up being us. The "self" affirms itself in the very continuity and ordinariness of our lives.

While we are used to thinking of contemporary literature in particular as dramatizing the instability of self and the artificiality of the conception of "self," it might be argued that literature's most distinctive characteristic is its apparently non-utilitarian capacity to resist the self's demands and register the reality of otherness.[2] No literature has ever been more intent on this project than the literature of Victorian realism. The deep moral

---

[1] In his famous essay, "What is it like to be a bat?" Thomas Nagel argues that consciousness is a condition of the very question. That is, "the fact that an organism has conscious experience *at all* means, basically, that there is something it is like to *be* that organism." *Philosophical Review*, LXXXIII, 4 (October 1974): 435–50. The "relation" of that raven to us lies just in the condition of consciousness, that is, the condition that makes it necessary to imagine that there is something it is like to be that organism. Consciousness is the condition of thinking about the absolute difference between us and others, and it is the condition of aspiring somehow to overcome that difference. It may, however, be a condition of consciousness that the other cannot be really known. It can be guessed. It can be "imagined" as a fiction. It can be aspired to. The raven is probably not actually saying "not you," though it is saying something. Its unintelligibility is the sign that turns its meaning for the poet into "not you, not you." This essay is also discussed in the essays included here, "The heartbeat of the squirrel," and "Real toads in imaginary gardens."

[2] I say "apparently" here because there is an interesting school of biological criticism that sees literature as serving an evolutionary function after all, most particularly the function of creating a sense of community and connectedness. That function has, on this argument, been an indispensable condition of the evolution of the human species. See, in particular, David Sloan Wilson, *Evolution for Everyone: How Darwin's Theory Can Change the Way We Think About Our Lives* (New York: Delacorte Press, 2007). Wilson concludes a chapter on the arts in this way: "Science is often thought to rob the arts of their importance and vitality. How ironic that evolutionary theory leads to a conception of the arts as such an important part of our 'social physiology' that they can even be regarded as vital organs" (p. 193).

energy to know and to respect – maybe even love – otherness is at the heart of the enterprise of Victorian literature, which I have been studying and caring about for fifty years. Locating that energy, understanding it, has led me into the byways of epistemology, into obsessing about objectivity, into worrying the relations between knowledge and morality and between morality and faith, and into an unrelenting preoccupation with "realism" itself, and its relation to the aesthetic. The efficient and final cause of all these essays is this ethical question of self and otherness, and of the extraordinary singular qualities of literature that make possible conceptions of otherness. To think through this question in relation to the enormous field of Victorian literature, where it takes on new urgency, I have been led to consider, at times, the literary and scientific culture out of which it came – sometimes in abstract considerations of epistemology, ethics, science and objectivity, but always in concrete engagement with the literature, particular manifestations of the Victorian preoccupation with the insistence of the self and the need to engage with an otherness that transcends the self.

For the Victorians, the problem of learning to live with and understand strange and even frightening others in a world from which the God who was thought to have created all that abundance and variety of differences was being expelled was particularly urgent. Everyone recognized that encounters with difference, most particularly in urban settings, were increasing, and increasingly worrying. Even a fable as rural and apparently simple as George Eliot's *Silas Marner* focuses on the question of how to assimilate into a homogeneous community an alien and frighteningly incomprehensible figure, and dramatizes the mutual transformations that full engagement with otherness might entail.

This was the central project of Victorian realism, which managed to achieve great popularity by producing an enormous *dramatis personae* – Dickens' eccentrics, Browning's liars, hypocrites, criminals, lunatics, artists, lovers, Thackeray's vain and banal egotists, Charlotte Brontë's unbeautiful heroines, Meredith's contortedly self-conscious protagonists and Trollope's remarkably various cast of characters – politicians, clergymen, spinsters, doctors, lower nobility, clerks, artists, scoundrels. The works in which these characters figure do not normally address abstract questions of epistemology directly, but behind the particularized, elaborated personal dramas larger issues loom. Literature in general but Victorian literature in particular defies the limits implied by the dominant empiricist epistemology for which knowledge is limited by the boundaries of our selves. The novels, with few exceptions, implicitly affirm a more expansive epistemology, one in which the boundaries between epistemology and ethics, between knowing and acting, are blurred.

Dramatizing the recognition that there are ways of thinking, feeling, desiring and suffering that we haven't experienced and have trouble understanding, Victorian fiction implicitly links epistemology and ethics. Tennyson's touching adolescent self-consciousness (as in "Supposed Confessions of a Second Rate Mind"), Dickens' efforts to embrace the poor and outcast, Gaskell's focus on the working class in the early novels, Browning's dramatization of alien consciousnesses, Arnold's efforts to see the object as in itself it really is – all these are symptoms of a powerful Romantic (or post-Romantic) self-consciousness that, via Wordsworth and Shelley and Keats and Byron, had become the focus of literary attention and value and that often sought to turn against itself. They were symptoms of the intensifying realization that the insistent self was threatening, even tyrannical, and hostile to the demands of a satisfying and, indeed, moral life, particularly in a society that was quite literally transforming almost daily. So there was (and is) also a sense that we all of us are likely to have at one time or another of the great relief it would be not to be the self that we went to sleep with and that accompanies us through our days, and to see and feel with others' eyes and sensibilities. This is the ideal of Victorian realism. As an ideal, of course, it isn't always fulfilled. It was always hard to achieve, and the effort often disguised (from writers and readers alike) the degree to which the sympathy for difference was another version of the effort to assimilate difference to sameness, others to self.

The Victorians, as Matthew Arnold famously wrote, "between two worlds, one dead, the other powerless to be born," felt the threat of what Ralph Barton Perry was to name, early in the twentieth century, the "egocentric predicament." Many of them surely also felt the need in this newer world to thrust themselves beyond themselves and learn to live with the otherness that constituted the life of the metropolis and of an increasingly mobile society in which the satisfactions of feeling oneself to be part of a community or a group were inevitably challenged. If Dickens and Gaskell and George Eliot strained to make us recognize our not-selves and share their feelings and understand their desires, they were also alert to how extraordinarily difficult this was. Perhaps, in the end, it was impossible, but at one's best, in one's art, there is always the struggle to know what it is like to be the other, what it is like to be a raven even as the raven, in every dark feather, announces its difference. How not to be you but to be a raven? How to see the world as does the raven, or Tennyson's eagle, staring down at "wrinkled seas"? How to soar with unfluttering wings and call out, hawk coarsely, the fact of one's presence? And at times then, perhaps increasingly through the century, as strategies for psychological representation became more elaborate and more central, it became possible to recognize that however deep one penetrated into the being of another, one might have to stop with the simple act of recognizing it, and valuing its life even in its impenetrable difference.

These essays, then, are concerned with questions of art, particularly realist art, as, among the Victorians, questions of art were entangled with ethical questions and with questions of knowledge, what it was possible to know, *how* one might "know," whether one *could* know. Knowing, in these works, is virtually always part of a larger ethical project that entailed sympathy, empathy, and the fullest possible encounter with the not-self – the vast tangled bank of otherness that constituted both the nature Darwin described and the new, capitalist, industrial society, moving rapidly, changing ceaselessly, insisting on an individualism that separated each from each and broke down traditional communities. Thus, they are all concerned with epistemological and ethical problems as they move from abstract argument to literature, and with these problems as a means to making us feel the urgency of the not-self, its importance, even when it escapes out of the corners of our eyes into an unknowable life, but a life after all.

It is not that the new science suddenly introduced to modern consciousness the overwhelming abundance of life that composed the natural world, but that previously that abundance had by and large been domesticated by a more or less formally elaborated natural theology, which explained the abundance and those vast strange differences by reference to a divine plan and to its implications for the human. But understood in entirely naturalistic terms, and investigated so as to reveal yet more difference and variety, the abundance of life forms both estranged and embraced their curious human observers. Estranged because the strangeness of each new species seemed to have nothing to do with human interests and desires; embraced because Darwin's theory quite literally connected us all. If Christianity had long insisted that we should love our neighbor, Darwin turned our neighbors into literal family, and thus wound the bonds of connection within diversity yet tighter. "Probably," said the ever cautious Darwin, "all the organic beings which have ever lived on this earth have descended from some one primordial form, into which life was first breathed."[3]

---

[3] Charles Darwin, *On the Origin of Species* (Cambridge, MA: Harvard University Press, 1946; facsimile edition), p. 484.

But in connecting us to all other living creatures that theory also defamiliarized even the most ordinary form of life, and made the work of understanding it, sympathizing with it, becoming it, all the more difficult as it became all the more urgent. The intense scrutiny of things as they are that became the hallmark of Victorian fiction and, to a certain extent, of all its literature and art, implied a new kind of reverence for life, a recognition that radical difference was a condition of all being and that wherever one looked there was a life to be valued.

So Browning's Lippo Lippi puts the case for the realism to which much Victorian art aspired:

> The shapes of things, their colours, lights and shades,
> Changes, surprises, – and God made it all!
> –For what? Do you feel thankful, ay or no,
> For this fair town's face, yonder river's line,
> The mountain round it and the sky above,
> Much more the figures of man, woman, child,
> These are the frame to? What's it all about?
> To be passed over, despised? Or dwelt upon,
> Wondered at? Oh, this last of course! – you say.
> But why not do as well as say, – paint these
> Just as they are, careless what comes of it?
> God's works – paint anyone and count it crime
> To let a truth slip . . .
> We're made so that we love
> First when we see them painted, things we have passed
> Perhaps a hundred times nor cared to see;
> And so they are better, painted – better to us,
> Which is the same thing. Art was given for that . . .

The Victorian artist, then, is committed to report the world as he (or she) sees it, in trust that, even if not comprehensible, it becomes something beautiful and valuable simply in being seen. Behind this vision of art Lippi still has his God, and perhaps Browning does too. It is God who invests all this abundance with value and justifies Lippi's determination to record the unideal. Even Darwin, we have seen, talks about life being "breathed" into the ur-form of all organic life.

But the great Victorian trick was to be Lippi's kind of realist without God behind the veil of matter – to feel the sacredness of each individual life without invoking the sacred. Lippi's kind of vision reveals abundance and makes the ordinary thrilling. Take away from behind all that abundance a divinely intentional being, leaving only the multiple forms of life and nature, and you have much of the struggle and the interest of

Victorian literature. Victorian realism, in the very effort to affirm, as Browning has Lippi affirm, the overriding presence of a Divine Creator, takes Lippi's kind of risks to tell the truth, even when that truth is painful, distinctly unDivine, and even ugly. And the consequence of this is that the "Creator" fades increasingly into the background; characters have to be shaken into consciousness of Him, and the world described, willy-nilly, tends to be profoundly secular after all.

The Victorian practice of realism foregrounds abundance and variety; and while few of its practitioners were entirely ready to forego the designer behind the scenes, that foregrounding tended toward a pervasively secular vision. Realist writers, like the Designer behind the scenes, needed to play out their narratives on the entirely naturalistic terms that Darwin required to explain his world and upon which Lippi irreverently (and reverently) insisted. Lippi's reverence for the ordinary survives the disappearance of his God, and the literature by and large moves away from religion, making Lippi's invocation of God a last defense, and ultimately an unnecessary one, for the practice of seeing that which was traditionally ignored with clear eyes – seeing it and sympathizing with it or simply valuing its difference.

Realism plays out the struggle to come to terms with the otherness of most life without the kind of domestication that natural theology provided for students of the natural world. And realism, cast in fictional narratives which feature things and people "we have passed a hundred times" without noticing, forces on its practitioners and on its readers the epistemological problems with which Victorian scientists had to contend all the time: from what source does our knowledge derive? And how can we trust it? Literature reminds us that every narrative is related from a point of view, and therefore that even the "we" who we are is only a story, a self-story, told from some singular point of view. Although that point of view must inevitably shift as we move from place to place, from moment to moment, as we age, as our senses develop or decay, we are stuck with seeing and valuing the world *only* from the points of view available to us. There are limits to where finite consciousness can take us. There is a taste of us in our mouths and the world comes to us soaked in memories of how it has been to us before, how it is not like the before that we know. The guilts we felt the night before we feel again after consciousness returns. We are vain and want to look better than we do and recognize those old blemishes in the mirror and see, sometimes with a shock, that we do resemble our dads or mothers. We are we, and satisfied as some of us may be with that "we," with the selfness of our selves, there is certainly a part of us to which art appeals that seeks the not-self, or at least seeks to expand the self by recognizing the otherness of others, and caring about it. It is just the tension around selfness, and the passion for telling the truth about the world, devil take the hindmost, that gives to Victorian literature – for me at least – its particular and continuing attractiveness.

The "objective," third-person mode of writing novels that tended to dominate in the nineteenth century would seem to be a way of ducking the epistemological problem. But there are inescapable authorial "intrusions" even in the most objective and apparently unselfconscious rendering of narratives, and a great part of the history of Victorian fiction relates to the various efforts and devices by which narrators registered their self-consciousness about the partialness of *any* representation, about the threatened opacity (of the writing self) blocking out real entrance into otherness. The Victorian preoccupation with the egotism that writes self-aggrandizing stories is a necessary part of its realism. It is not only Meredith's "Egoist" who attempts to make the world rotate around his desires and vanity.

We may take the most cynical, the most adaptationist view of human nature and behavior and still recognize that the effort to transcend the limits of the self and of that restricting point of view derives from – or constitutes – an urgent moral sense, and is as intrinsic to our being as any strategy of survival our genes have generated. This, certainly (though perhaps described in different language) was a central motivation of Victorian literature. And it is clear that Victorian science depended on the possibility of transcending the limits of the egocentric predicament, of finding a way to register, with full confidence, an objectively constituted reality – once again, devil take the hindmost. The struggle to see from someone else's point of view is a struggle that literature enacts in almost all of its incarnations and that science, as a trustable practice, required. It is the "objectivity" of art.

The egocentric predicament reaffirms itself, or threatens to do so, in the vast body of Victorian literature and cultural commentary, as in its philosophy, and has its most famous articulation in the solipsism intimated in Walter Pater's famous "Conclusion" to *The Renaissance*, which might be taken, in one respect, as the great climax of Victorian moral realism and at the same time its antithesis: "Experience . . . is ringed round for each one of us by that thick wall of personality through which no real voice has ever pierced on its way to us, or from us to that which we can only conjecture to be without."[4] The power of this passage is, ironically, in its precise

---

[4] Walter Pater, *Renaissance* (London: Macmillan, 1888), p. 248. See Carolyn Williams' important discussion of the ways in which Pater's argument actually stops short of solipsism, *Transfigured World: Pater's Aesthetic Historicism* (Ithaca: Cornell University Press, 1990). See also my own *Dying to Know*.

representation of the emotional implications of what might seem a merely philosophical argument: our knowledge is limited by the limits of our own personality and consciousness. The passage makes readers "feel" the threat and the "isolation" of this way of thinking; it is not a way of thinking so much as a way of being and feeling. And this example can thus suggest that literature resists, even in its most dogged pursuit of the most painful kinds of experience, the very self-enclosure that its preoccupation with point of view and perspective threatens.

The struggle of Victorian literature, by and large, was the struggle to get outside those thick walls of personality, to find a way to enter the beings of others and feel what they feel, know what they know, be what they are. In this way, the practice of Victorian realism ran parallel to the dominant practices of the science that was transforming the world all around it.[5] For literature (and perhaps more widely for the culture at large) the struggle was theorized and formulated by George Eliot (and, to a certain extent, by Browning's Lippi), who made clear that for her, knowing was a moral enterprise. Knowing, and saying truthfully what one had come to know, was one of the highest moral ideals of the culture, and for nobody more than for George Eliot. She sought to combine knowing and feeling in an art that recognized, affirmed, and valued the hard unaccommodating actual and fought through the relentless appeals and limits of the self. The job was, as Matthew Arnold described the work of the critic, to see the object as in itself it truly is. The job of the artist was, as George Eliot put it movingly in *Adam Bede*, "to give no more than a faithful account of men and things as they have mirrored themselves in my mind,"[6] a formulation – whatever its commitment to rendering objective reality precisely – that must remind us of how for the most dedicated and sophisticated of realists, that thick wall of personality about which Pater wrote hovered ominously over "reality."

That faithful account, however, was not merely a report, but a means to valuing life and others ostensibly different, unsympathetic and unappealing. "Depend upon it," George Eliot wrote in her first story, "The Sad Fortunes of the Reverend Amos Barton," "you would gain unspeakably if you would learn with me some of the poetry and the pathos, the tragedy and the comedy, lying in the experience of a human soul that looks out

---

5   A classic, indispensable article describing nineteenth-century scientific practice will be alluded to frequently in the essays that follow. But it is worthwhile introducing it here: Peter Galison and Lorraine Daston, "The Image of Objectivity," *Representations*, 40 (Fall, 1992): 81–128.
6   *Adam Bede*, ch. xvii, 175 (Oxford World Classics, 1996).

through dull grey eyes, and that speaks in a voice of quite ordinary tones."[7] Knowledge is a condition of sympathy, if no guarantee of it, and epistemology links immediately to the ethical. To know the world objectively seems to require scientific detachment; but the detachment that George Eliot seeks is in the interest of – and makes possible – the valuing of the ever elusive other. The artist puts herself on the line. She will try to tell the truth as if "I were in the witness-box narrating my experience on oath." To misrepresent is to commit perjury and to be, therefore, punished by the (moral) law. Literature takes out a social contract.

It is a "social" contract. It is binding regardless of whether or not there is any transcendent force at the origins, or hovering over the workings of the world. The question of from where the moral force that makes the contract derives permeates Victorian discourse, over both science and literature. From whence does it derive and, if not from God, does it have any binding force: what is to sustain society and the many representatives of it that Victorian realism describes if there is no ultimate binding law beyond what nature itself, so devastatingly described by John Stuart Mill in his book, *Nature*, could imply? The great resurgence of religious activity among the Victorians suggests something of how enormously difficult it was for the Victorians to come to terms with that naturalistically described world that science was so successfully describing and that increasingly secularizing world that the literature was intimating. Variety, abundance, difference, otherness, in such a godless world, might well be not a great natural gift, but threatening, even terrifying.

II

Looking back over the work of a quarter of a century, I recognized that my preoccupation with these issues, though in a series of essays written independently and at different times, constructed a sustained argument, through various explorations of differents aspects of these problems. It all started with George Eliot, perhaps the most theoretical and intellectually consequent of the great imaginative writers. Her formulation of "moral realism," and her thinking about the philosophical, aesthetic, and ethical implications that I have been discussing, resonated for me well beyond the Victorians. The quiet urgency of her manifesto, quaint and unliterary as it might seem in the twenty-first century, was appropriate to

---

[7] *Scenes of Clerical Life*, "The sad Fortunes of the Reverend Amos Barton," ch. v, p. 67 (Cabinet Edition, William Blackwood and Sons) Edinburgh nd.

its moment, but is still appropriate now. She made her moral claims for art while, at the same time, she was bound to a sense that art had its own requirements and worked in its own way. No writer had a clearer sense of how extraordinarily difficult it was to tell the truth, and in particular to tell the whole truth. She was writing about epistemology, about how hard it is to know precisely, about what is entailed in valid knowing. She was writing about ethics, about how through art there develop possibilities of knowing, and how through knowing there develop possibilities of moral being and action. Art, she once wrote, "is the nearest thing to life," that is, it can move us beyond theory and argument into feeling and experience, and it is about life because it engages in the endlessly difficult and endlessly necessary activity of seeking a reality beyond the self. It is about austerity, even Paterian austerity, about the discipline of looking hard, of worrying language, of putting aside the insistent claims of desire and personality or, at least, recognizing their power and constraints.

George Eliot struggled in her narratives to reconcile the true and the good, and sometimes the marks of struggle are awkwardly evident, and the conviction that runs through her extraordinary explorations of consciousness and of social relations fades. The Victorians, after all, knew all too well that the true was not always the good. John Stuart Mill undertook to determine whether it made sense to "make nature a test of right and wrong, good and evil." Did it make sense, morally speaking, to "imitate" or "obey" nature? No being "whose attributes are justice and benevolence," said Mill, would have created nature as a model for "rational creatures" to follow. So, he famously argued, "In sober truth, nearly all the things which men are hanged or imprisoned for doing to one another are nature's everyday performances."[8]

What, morally speaking, socially speaking, could be made of that marvelously candid way of looking at things? The realist conjunction of art, aesthetics, and epistemology, understood increasingly as coming within a secular order, became the point at which the great imaginative writers of the time – and among these I include not only novelists like George Eliot, but poets, and social critics, like Arnold and Carlyle, and scientific commentators like Tyndall and Huxley – rethought, re-experienced, and recreated cultural and political authority within a newly secular society. They struggled over the question of how the ethical could sustain itself in a "nature" of the kind that Mill described. It is to understanding this conjuncture of problems and of writers that my own critical imagination

[8]   John Stuart Mill, *Nature* and *Utility of Religion* (Indianapolis: Bobbs Merrill, 1958), p. 18.

has pushed me in essay after essay, dealing with subject after subject, until I have discovered – retrospectively, of course – that in a certain sense I have been writing about the same problems, rethinking them, reformulating them, all the time.

As I looked back, then, on these essays, written over the span of twenty-five years, sometimes for immediate publication, sometimes not, I have found it easy to recognize their intricate interrelations as I have tried to understand things like how the secularists reconciled their commitment to knowledge with their commitment to ethics, or how writers so self-conscious about the difficulty of knowing could insist (did they) on the possibility of objectivity, or how literature managed both to reflect the philosophical views and resist them. These essays share a kind of background coherence around the problems implicit in George Eliot's consideration of the role of art and the possibility of knowing and the responsibility to get at the truth and to feel beyond the limits of the self. They are also, sometimes implicitly, sometimes overtly, intertwined by their interest in the pressure upon Victorian writers to re-imagine value in a context from which Lippi's ultimately sanctioning God has been withdrawn. The Victorian moral/intellectual crisis was a crisis of revaluation, manifested in various efforts to sustain traditional values without traditional social and cultural forms. Under a deluge of new knowledge, emanating most obviously from the sciences, and under the apparently moral injunction to see clearly and report with absolute honesty, the question often was whether it was possible to move from fact to moral action, from "is" to "ought," without Divine sanction. This is not a question that even today we have answered satisfactorily, but watching the Victorians struggle with it and trying to understand that struggle has always seemed to me both satisfying and moving work.

The essays are probably also united by the fact that they study these aspects of Victorian writing with an unapologetic Victorian earnestness, finding in the novels, the poetry, the scientific writing and the social commentary the most serious and important kind of engagements with the nature of knowledge and art, worrying out the question of how one lives, thinks, feels in a world subject only to naturalistic explanation. Despite their passion for Victorian literature, these are not then intended to be simply historical essays, analyzing the way the Victorians dealt with the issues. They are deliberate engagements with our own current problems and intellectual and moral combats. That the Victorians were worried about the relation between fact and value, between body and mind, between the secular and the ethical, is a commonplace, and many of the best writers and thinkers of the time believed (as I try to show in the chapter on Mallock's *Is Life Worth Living*?) that it was impossible to move from a naturalist explanation of the world to ethical conclusions: the old Humean dichotomy between "Is" and "Ought" holds tightly for many Victorians, even as many other Victorians tried to challenge it. The question was never, for the great Victorian writers, merely technical and philosophical, never merely epistemological, but always finally ethical: how might one lead a meaningful, good, and satisfying life in a world from which God has disappeared? The pervasive question echoing through novel after novel is "What can I *do*?" It is our question as well.

With extraordinary energy – intellectual, moral, affective – the Victorians brought us to the cusp of modernity, which sophisticatedly rejected them just because they so boldly and flatly insisted on the big questions and could find no way to disentangle truth from morality from beauty as they overstuffed chairs and cluttered living rooms and were so insistently, so exhaustingly (perhaps hypocritically) moral. So Ruskin, that enormous half-mad sage, passionately rejected any art that seemed indifferent to the imaginative representation of a precisely registered reality and that insisted on looking too closely at anything debased, degraded, or immoral. So Carlyle thundered on, fictionalizing history and condemning fiction, for a deep moral austerity that his culture both endorsed and flouted. But in so far as Ruskin or Carlyle could be thought of as thinking about "epistemology," they would have insisted that epistemology could not be separated from ethics, a view that only a few serious philosophers have ever endorsed.[9]

The book as a whole then takes the Victorian effort at "moral realism" not as a quaint, outdated, sentimental and even self-delusive means by which the values of the new bourgeoisie might be objectified and taught and used to affirm the new status quo, but as an extraordinarily difficult and important aesthetic, philosophical, and ethical undertaking, whose significance is still vital and whose difficulties still plague us.

The essays are united in at least one other way: while I have learned much from the dominant critical movements of my time, and have understood the efforts to demonstrate the impossibility of "realism" and

---

[9] One philosopher who has endorsed such a view is Alasdair MacIntyre, who directly addresses the question of the possibility of moving from "is" to "ought," and, on Aristotelian grounds, makes a strong case that it is possible. But his point is that it can only be made with clarity and coherence, it can only lead to a strong understanding of "virtue," if there is "some prior account of certain features of social and moral life in terms of which it has to be defined and explained." See, *The MacIntyre Reader*, ed., Kelvin Knight (Notre Dame: Notre Dame University Press, 1998), p. 82.

objectivity, the hypocrisy of "sympathy," and the middle-class complacency lying behind ostensible critiques of the new society, I have never
found those critical movements adequate to the particularity and richness
of the literature itself. Virtually all of these essays, however responsive I
have tried to be to the more recent critical movements, run against the
grain of the dominant views of contemporary critical theory and return me
to a consideration of the extraordinary Victorian effort through its art to
make of a world from which God was disappearing and the old authorities
being displaced and the fundamental epistemological and moral certitudes
challenged, something both knowable and humane.

I have consistently found that the most fruitful focal point for an understanding and valuing of this effort is at the conjunction between science and
literature, science pressing increasingly toward recognition of an objective
reality apparently incommensurate with human feelings and desires, literature pressing toward the humanizing of that knowledge. This conjunction
has taken me occasionally into the drier deeps of Victorian philosophy, but
at the heart of these critical enterprises lies always the concern with the way
art works to transform knowledge, and the way knowledge is always linked
with the ethical. Among the Victorians, the new ascendancy of science
helped move literature – and the culture – away from reliance on a transcendent reality to complete its stories satisfactorily; the movement was
difficult and halting and, as I have said, much Victorian literature remains
linked inseparably with religion, as Lippi relies on God to justify his painting of anything and everything, but it is to just the struggle and the deeply
intelligent and deeply felt tension that these essays attempt to attend.

III

Although the essays were intended to be read as free-standing, I gather
them here into something like a continuing and developing argument,
both about the way the Victorians regarded the matters and the way we
might do it. Their independent nature, however, gives to the book a
certain exploratory quality, for while the essays do, I believe, represent a
consistent set of points of view, they sometimes revisit problems from
somewhat different perspectives, and, of course, in the light of the different times in which they were written, they sometimes suggest alternative
ways to consider the problems. Nevertheless, they all point toward the
possibility of achieving something like "objectivity," even in the face of its
ultimate logical impossibility or unlikelihood; they all point toward some
reconciliation between fact and value, "is" and "ought," affirming the

Victorian effort to bring the two together; they all imply the value of engagement with otherness and the problems of trying to achieve that engagement. And, finally, they all point toward the form of realist literature that reaches toward the deepest possible understanding of the other, and the deepest possible feeling for it.

At the same time, it is important to note that each essay is, in a way, an effort of appreciation (so Victorian a word, so utterly beyond what criticism will now allow itself to be, makes me still uneasy); in other words, it is an attempt to read the various Victorian efforts, in philosophy, social action, science, and literature with sympathetic imagination, turning away from the dominant modern mode of negative hermeneutics, trying to find historically and critically why it is the Victorians wrote and argued as they did and how that critical/historical perspective throws their work into a more sympathetic light. I have attempted in most cases to get inside the sensibility and the art of the writers as they, so often, attempted to do with the characters and lives they discuss. For me, too, then, the epistemological concern has ethical implications: can we read the Victorians with understanding without having a feeling for their ways of seeing and experiencing? Without somehow knowing what they saw, understanding how that "wrinkled sea" might look wrinkled – from what perspective, under what conditions? In any case, even where the overall argument may seem to flag, the essays assert their sympathetic preoccupation with the nature of the art and the thought of the writers.

I have organized the essays around certain dominant themes, all of them growing out of the earliest of them,"George Eliot's Hypothesis of Reality," which should serve as a prologue to the arguments that follow. That I use as an epigraph the famous passage from *Middlemarch* on the heartbeat of the squirrel will have suggested already how centrally important to the arguments here are the ideas and the narratives of George Eliot. Written before any of the other chapters, this essay addresses directly that convergence of epistemology, ethics, realism, and the problem of objectivity. It shows George Eliot, with the aid of her partner, G. H. Lewes, implicitly addressing that question of whether it is possible to move from the "is" to the "ought" by making at least quasi-scientific arguments about the nature of knowledge and feeling. George Eliot and Lewes saw knowledge and feeling not as two distinct things but, psychologically and even biologically speaking, the same thing. Knowledge, for both, was a form of feeling.

Science, from this perspective, becomes a formulation not only of ideas about the order of nature but about how people think and feel and act; value and perception become aspects of each other, and there is therefore a connection between powers of sympathy, the moral power of empathizing with absolutely different beings, and the rudimental but essential capacity to get in touch with reality and to know it. Yet, like many of the great Victorians, and like most of these essays, it also considers the question of whether reality is ultimately knowable at all, and it attempts to describe a George Eliot trying to get beyond conventional epistemology and conventionally conceived reality to achieve through imaginative sympathy and desire a greater vision of human possibility.

The essay also addresses the critical problem of realism itself, pointing toward essays I came to write a quarter of a century later, about the ways in which realism aspires toward an absolute receptiveness that extends even beyond empathy, beyond the visible world, into what might seem a kind of mysticism, registering hitherto unperceived realities, and valuing them.

After this prologue, the book is organized into two separate sections and an epilogue. The first, *Ethics without God, or, can "Is" become "Ought"?*, connects the problems of epistemology and ethics with the struggles over secularism. It begins with a consideration of W. H. Mallock's question, *Is Life Worth Living?* (the title of one of his books), and his strongly held and widely shared opinion, that an ethics without a foundation in some ultimately divine sanction is ultimately no ethics at all, and leaves life utterly without purpose and meaning just because it leaves morality without sanction. A main stream of Victorian literature tends to flow around this problem, and the Victorians were, even in their moves to secularity, troubled by an inability to find a way to value life on its own terms, despite the fact that so much of Victorian literature, in particular the novel, implicitly tries to do just that. It provides another version of the paradox, that on the one hand the Victorians tried to wrench themselves free from traditional religion,[10] and on the other, as they moved toward secularity, they found it almost impossible to break out of a radical dualism between knowledge and ethics, knowledge and value.

---

[10] I do not want to overemphasize the move to secularity in Victorian culture. If among the intellectual elite there was a large exodus from conventional religion, and among the elite scientists and popularizers of science, like the scientific naturalists, there was a strong effort to displace religion from its cultural, intellectual, and even moral authority, the dominant cultural phenomenon was religion itself, which produced an enormous volume of literature, far beyond that which science produced in the same period. Nonetheless, as Bernard Lightman shows in his recent, *Victorian Popularizers of Science* (Chicago: University of Chicago Press, 2007), the balance began to shift after mid-century. Lightman shows through his study of how science was popularized through the century that the greatest effort of the popularizers was to interpret modern science as compatible with religion.

The same problem arises, in a different way, in the following chapter, on Darwin and Ruskin, where I note in detail remarkable parallels in their ways of looking at the world, and through those parallels consider again the way Victorians imagined the relation between value and fact. The essay juxtaposes Ruskin's kind of "science" to Darwin's, the one demanding a humanist and spiritual relation to the natural world and the other seeking always (with more or less success) to be "objective," to remove the human perspective – as far as possible – from our readings of nature. For Ruskin, the world was always alive with meaning, matter almost allegorical in shadowing forth fundamental values. Against the passionate, humane, and intensely moral vision of Ruskin, Darwin sets a vision that, while Darwin had his own passion for nature, requires the empirical, the rational, the detached. It was Darwin's sort of literalness, transforming metaphor and allegory to quite literal connections, that most sorely tested the idea that scientific description could serve as a basis for morality.

Ruskin, like Mallock and many other important Victorians, was convinced that such scientific description could not produce the values of either ethics or art, and thus resisted Darwinian description, which I try to show is nevertheless laden with value that Ruskin could not see or would not accept. It makes sense, however, to regard both of these most distinguished Victorians as realists, both committed to rendering in the most minute particularity the phenomena of the natural world, and both almost neuraesthenically alert to the way in which all worldly life is in motion and everything lives in time and history.

Ruskin, in his differences from Darwin, might be taken to represent Mallock's position on the question of the relation of fact to value, but the true Mallockian antithesis to Ruskin was not Darwin, but the scientific naturalists, not least of them Huxley, who did quite overtly, and in sustained ways, attempt to displace religion and occupy the cultural, moral, and social grounds traditionally thought to belong to religion. It seemed appropriate, then, that the implicit argument of this book be sustained with an extensive treatment of the arguments of Huxley and the scientific naturalists.

Although the scientific naturalists were often highly critical of Positivism, as a particular historical movement, many, like Mallock, identified them as Positivists as well. This enraged Huxley, but Mallock did have a point. For the naturalists, despite Tyndall's occasional mystic affirmations, the world was indeed adequate to itself; no transcendental reference was necessary. Huxley coined the word "Agnosticism" just to make clear that there were some issues, like whether there might be forces outside of the law-governed nature scientists explored, which could not be known. The world, Huxley believed, could be described accurately entirely in naturalist terms, but beyond the laws of nature and natural forces, Huxley was content to suggest that we remain epistemologically blocked.

My treatment of the scientific naturalists in this essay is explicitly sympathetic, resisting not only the kind of critique of them mounted by Mallock, but also the critique by modern historians of science and theorists of culture. I try to engage sympathetically with the naturalists' efforts to reconcile scientific knowledge with the ethical life, although they did not even attempt to turn their agnosticism into anything like the organized post-religion that the Positivists thought. The figures with whom this essay deals provide the perspective that both allows for an articulation of the idea of Victorian secularity and offers an alternative to the often self-contradictory or aggressively anti-science views of so many Victorians hoping to sustain the values and the traditions of an earlier age.

The issues are treated again in the following essay, "In Defense of Positivism," where I turn my attention to those "positivists" who serve explicitly as Mallock's whipping boys, the thinkers who insisted on the relevance of scientific thought to questions of morals and spirit. Positivism has not fared well, historically, and in this essay I try to emphasize its importance even to our own times and for ideas and positions normally thought to be antithetical to positivism. Although for the most part, the essay does not follow positivism into its more technical and less ethically driven twentieth-century version, it attempts to suggest how the fundamental ideas of the positivists, both Victorian and later, serve almost as a foundation for modern and postmodern forms of skepticism, and how positivism, though denigrated for its reductionist radical empiricism, lives today even in its antitheses. The essay looks at Victorian Positivism as perhaps the first large-scale effort to value life on its own terms. That is, it implicitly values life in just those terms that Mallock, and even more famously, John Balfour, in *Foundations of Belief,* rejected. This essay not only tries to defend positivism against the pervasive criticism of its history and practices, but to suggest that there is much to learn, at least from its Victorian practices and arguments.

The next essay is not in fact concerned directly with the Victorians, but can serve as a transition from this volume's early preoccupation with philosophical issues to its final focus on literary ones. "Why science isn't literature: the importance of differences" lays out the poststructuralist arguments that in effect attempt to treat science as a "text," and thus as just another text, like literature. Though sympathetic to the poststructuralist undertaking, I try to show that the position is destructive and inadequate. It does not go far enough, from my critical position at the moment, in insisting on the aspiration of science, and literature too. It may be that behind this critique there lies the Victorians' own determination to allow for the possibility of objectivity and contact with a real world beyond words, but whatever the deeper origins, the essay attempts to urge the importance of making the kinds of distinctions that allow for the possibility of something like objective representation of the "real." It is a tricky and difficult argument, probably not sustainable into its finest details, but for the purposes of this book (and certainly for me as this book represents a way of thinking about the world) the distinction between science and literature is urgent. It is urgent that we commit ourselves to the possibility of getting beyond the always insistent self far enough to register realities incompatible with the self's immediate needs. The Victorian problem of how to make epistemological virtue compatible with moral, how to infuse fact with feeling, is no dead, antiquarian problem. It is our problem.

The next section, *Literature, Secularity, and the Quest for Otherness*, rereads the issues dealt with in the first section from the point of view of literature itself. It makes sense, then, that the section begins with an extensive reconsideration of the nature of "realism." In this essay, the book devotes its fullest attention to the general problems of representation, to the difficulties of "truth-telling," and to the ethical and epistemological power that lay behind the Victorian enterprises of realism. The reading of "realism" treats it as a thoroughly mixed and sometimes self-contradictory mode, in particular as it is implicated in the ideal, first as it is initiated from an idealist conception of reality, then as empiricism drives it to self-reflexiveness about the nature of perception and of the mind doing the perceiving, but also in its ideal aspiration beyond the limits of what, theoretically, it is possible to perceive. Realism as a mode implicitly (sometimes explicitly, as with George Eliot) insists that the capacity to know the world entails both epistemological and moral openness, and that knowing the world is a condition for making it better. In its pervasive tendency toward secularity, it never loses its energy for moral growth, for the possibility of coming to know the other.

In "Dickens, secularism, and agency" I try to demonstrate, through a reading of several novels, but most particularly Dickens' *Little Dorrit*, that Victorian realist fiction is a fundamentally secular form. It builds its case around the way that "money" operates in the novel and the way in which novelists moralize it. Within the realistic tradition as it develops inside a growing bourgeois society built on capitalist principles, money is obviously a condition of success. Virtually no Victorian novelist but Trollope can imagine virtuous action designed to acquire money. I set the case against Weber's argument in *The Protestant Ethic and the "Spirit" of Capitalism*, that the virtues that are requisite to Calvinist religion are just the virtues that allow success in capitalism, and show that it was almost impossible for Victorian novelists, even as they were committed to those Calvinist virtues, to connect virtue and money, or to believe that anything but hypocrisy could connect them. The question then is how is it possible to imagine a virtuous protagonist who is also successful in the worldly way that realistic narrative at the time required. The essay thus makes another connection, via literature, between the epistemological issues and the questions of value so central to Mallock and Ruskin's way of thinking, values that they claim depend upon an ultimate transcendent power, God. And it is with brief explorations of the quest for otherness in literature that the book concludes. In "The heartbeat of the squirrel," I try to lay out two distinct efforts of the realistic imagination, the first, the one most overtly urged by the George Eliot described in the first essay (and in the essay on realism), seeks to extend our sympathies so that we come to see the world as others, very different from us, see it. This is a moral enterprise that is obviously built on an epistemological one, finding ways to come to "know" the other as science comes to know nature. George Eliot's realism was explicitly directed to this end. But given the skepticism about the possibilities of knowing with which the Victorians (and this book) are so concerned, there remains the strong possibility that actually knowing empathetically the feelings and desires of the other might not be possible. Taking the question of how the Victorians deal with animals (the ultimate "other"), I try to argue in this essay for the moral urgency of the simple recognition of otherness, and acceptance of it, without any possibility of genuinely knowing the other in the sympathetic mode for which George Eliot argues so often. And I try to argue that one of the fundamental qualities of literature is just this capacity to make us recognize otherness and value it.

Finally I take the discussion beyond Victorian realism into the twenty-first century, with a brief consideration of how J. M. Coetzee manages this question of animals as the absolute other. And thus, I conclude with a brief treatment of that aspect of Coetzee's writing that most directly addresses this last point, reconciling epistemological impasse with ethical urgency. In a short span, this essay lays out, through the example of Coetzee, a kind of ultimate ideal of realism in Coetzee's writing, and addresses the problematic of epistemology and ethics, of science and traditional values, of objectivity and feeling with which the book has been concerned throughout. Coetzee evokes a world of others, also through animals, and his work becomes, for the purposes of this book at least, the fulfillment of the realist ideal, making us believe in realities that will have nothing to do with us, that exist as they are without any reference to us, and making us feel their value and the sometimes tragic thrill of an otherness we cannot succor, we cannot fully know, but whose life we cannot ignore. In the light of Coetzee's work, I hope that this book's oscillating engagement with these large, often abstract questions, will become more fully understandable and their contemporary urgency more clear.

PART I

The subject broached: otherness, epistemology, and ethics

CHAPTER I

George Eliot's hypothesis of reality

The image of George Eliot, bending forward, listening during one of her regular Sundays with selfless and disciplined attention to her admiring visitors, corresponds precisely to the moral and intellectual ideal that informs her novels. Such an ideal, from a very modern perspective, at least, entails the denial of the libidinal energies essential to psychic health, and we point knowingly now to George Eliot's headaches and fragile health. But the denial we may abhor was, for George Eliot, an ethical and epistemological imperative. Ironically, especially from the perspective of much contemporary feminist criticism, she believed that submission of the self to the voices of external reality was a condition of real knowledge (just as, for contemporary Victorian science, objectivity was a condition of acquiring the truth).[1] The failures of Lydgate and Casaubon result primarily from the failure to submit, that is, to restrain their egoistic needs from influencing their intellectual work. It is not only that reality remains incommensurate with the desires of an aspiring self (a convention of narrative since at least *Don Quixote*), but that personality is an obstruction to perception. The common self is merely personality.

In addition, there has been a large literature in recent years that has taken that ideal with more than a grain of salt, finding in George Eliot's overt sympathy a barely disguised hostility, translating sympathy into a kind of hypocrisy that attempts to make an aggressive self-assertion look good. Such criticism is representative of a modern more or less cynical resistance to the idea of, the very possibility of a genuine altruism, a genuinely generous action that is not, in some way, an effort at

---

[1] Peter Galison and Lorraine Daston, "The Image of Objectivity," *Representations*, 40 (Fall, 1992).

self-aggrandizement.[2] Certainly, our sense of George Eliot's ethical enterprise in relation to the realities of her life has changed considerably over the last twenty years, most forcefully through the brilliant, tough, but sympathetic reading of her life and letters by Rosemarie Boden-heimer. Bodenheimer tests George Eliot's novels against her life, and vice versa, and reveals to us a woman aspiring to the authority of the voice she adopts in her novels, but deeply troubled by the potential contradictions between her ethical ideals and the clamorings of her own ego and ambition. The insistent claims of the self that she drama-tizes in her novels are clearly echoes of her own ambitious and demand-ing ego, however much she chooses to chastise both them and it. Bodenheimer argues that the strain of *Daniel Deronda*, in which she had to turn to myth to rescue her protagonist from conflicting claims on sympathy and from the power of his own authoritative voice, which inspires a trust he cannot fully satisfy, leads her to "deconstruct" sym-pathy, and to "the abandonment of the all-wise narrative voice that had promised so much to many of her readers."[3]

But in this essay, I am concerned with the narratives of sympathy and most particularly with George Eliot's struggle – a key to her writing – to enter into the realities, the consciousnesses of a wide range of diverse and often antipathetic figures. The possible failures of the project of sympathy do not at all suggest the futility of it, or that George Eliot's gestures were in any way hypocritical or even self-deceiving. She did not pretend that those gestures of openness to the other are easy. She earned the intent, listening, sympathetic expression that all who visited her Sundays at home recog-nized and valued. Nobody was more aware of the callings of the ego than she, and much of the power of her insistence sympathy depends on just that recognition, and just that understanding of how very hard it is. I don't in this essay want to claim that she always manages to bring it off, or that those unadmitted energies of selfishness aren't there. I do want to insist that the efforts at the discipline of self-denial in the face of the powerful

---

[2]   For a discussion of this criticism that is suspicious of George Eliot's claims for the importance of sympathy, see Suzy Anger, *Victorian Interpretation* (Ithaca: Cornell University Press, 2005), esp. pp. 110–13. Anger is unsympathetic to this anti-sympathy criticism and provides a complex analysis of George Eliot's own awareness of the problems and a critique of the criticism, as well. For a sample of the critique of George Eliot's "sympathy," see Laura Hinton, *Perverse Gaze of Sympathy* (Albany: State University of New York Press, 1999); Marc Redfield, *Phantom Formations: Aesthetic Ideology and the Bildungsroman* (Ithaca: Cornell University Press, 1996); Ann Cvetkovich, *Mixed Feelings: Feminism, mass Culture, and Victorian Sensationalism* (New Brunswick: Rutgers University Press, 1992).

[3]   Rosemarie Bodenheimer, *The Real Life of Mary Anne Evans: George Eliot, her Letters and Fiction* (Ithaca: Cornell University Press, 1994), p. 265.

and demanding ethical reality of the other are at the heart of George Eliot's art, and to take as fundamental the idea that the effort at such discipline is an ethical, epistemological, and aesthetic effort altogether worth the trouble, and about which we can learn much from George Eliot. She recognized that there was a profound connection between the effort of knowing and the ethic of loving; and she recognized that neither was easy. The art with which she struggled, often so painfully, was the place where the ideas and feelings could be most strenuously imagined, tested, and transformed from theory into life.

The attentive George Eliot of the Sundays at home was, we know, a deliberate fiction; to put it another way, it was an hypothesis testing the possibility of the abolition of the common self (to which, as I have suggested, George Eliot felt herself to be humiliatingly subject), to achieve the impersonality necessary both for science and the moral life. "I try," she once wrote, "to delight in the sunshine that will be when I shall never see it any more. And I think it is possible for this sort of impersonal life to attain great intensity, – possible for us to gain much more independence, than is usually believed, of the small bundle of facts that make our own personality."[4] It may well be that George Eliot's novels enact a series of implicit reprisals of submissive women against repressive men;[5] but George Eliot is not Maggie Tulliver, who turned to Thomas à Kempis in a frenzy of self denial, and whose passion returned upon her "like a savage appetite."[6] The "delight in the sunshine" she will never see can be experienced with "intensity," and comes with "independence" from personality. There is an Arnoldian buried self beyond personality, which can somehow be liberated from the distortions imposed by the "small bundle of facts."[7] That buried self is the only resource we have for getting in touch with a reality that, George Eliot had been discovering, was even more tenuous, complex, and

---

[4]   *The George Eliot Letters*, ed. Gordon S. Haight, 9 vols. (New Haven: Yale University Press, 1954–78), V, 107, cited hereafter as *GEL*.

[5]   See the discussion of George Eliot in Sandra Gilbert and Susan Gubar, *The Madwoman in the Attic* (New Haven: Yale University Press, 1979), esp. ch. 14, "George Eliot and the Angel of Destruction."

[6]   *The Mill on the Floss*, ed. Gordon S. Haight, Riverside Editions (Boston: Houghton Mifflin, 1961), Bk. 5, ch. 3.

[7]   Gilbert and Gubar, pp. 401–2, discuss the relation between Arnold's poem, "The Buried Life," and the condition of Lucy Snowe in *Villette*. They suggest that his male perspective allows him to treat the issue abstractly, without the particular anguish of a woman like Lucy. The distinction seems excessive; certainly the conception of a buried self like Arnold's is fully operative in George Eliot's moral dramas.

minutely articulated and differentiated than she had earlier thought. The ideal and the real were fused.

In her earliest important review, the young Marian Evans had counseled "earnest study" of the laws of nature and "patient obedience" to their teaching.[8] Five years later, in her review of the third volume of Ruskin's *Modern Painters*, she urged "the doctrine that all truth and beauty are to be attained by a humble and faithful study of nature, and not by substituting vague forms, bred by imagination on the mists of feeling, in place of definite, substantial reality."[9] If one thinks of Mordecai, evoking his wish from the sunset in *Daniel Deronda*, one might wonder where the "obedient" Marian Evans had gone. Surely, the commitment to externality and to faith in the identity of the "true and the good" had undergone some changes. From *Romola* through *Daniel Deronda*, her thought and art were profoundly complicated by the external truths she could not avoid, by intensified recognition of the difficulties of knowing, and by the cost of that rapt attention to visitors and to nature that true knowledge required.

Even in the drawing room – unlike Lydgate, who confined his science to the laboratory – the earnestly studious George Eliot was rigorously scientific. The method of her early realism, with its complex but confident empiricism, with its assured rendering of the surfaces of experience and faith in the power of that rendering to enlarge the sympathies of her common reader, with its movement into the disenchanting sunlight of clear perception, had become too "coarse." In *Romola*, she had reached far beyond the realist's world of Amos Barton-like dull gray eyes into a conception both epic and ideal. After *Romola*, Anthony Trollope could write to her about his own novel, *Rachel Ray*: "I have attempted to confine myself absolutely to the commonest details of commonplace life among the most ordinary people, allowing myself no incident that would be even remarkable in every day life. I have shorn my fiction of all romance." We might once have thought this George Eliot's own objective, but Trollope knew his place: "you must not suppose," he says, "that I think the little people equal as subjects to the great names. Do you, who can do it, go on" (*GEL*, VIII, 313). Between *Scenes of Clerical Life* and *Romola*, George Eliot had made herself an epic novelist, a sage, a figure above that ordinary

---

[8]   George Eliot, rev. of *The Progress of the Intellect*, by Robert William Mackay, *Westminster Review*, 54 (1851), p. 179; rpt. In *Essays of George Eliot*, ed. Thomas Pinney (New York: Columbia University Press, 1963), p. 31.

[9]   George Eliot, "Art and Belles Lettres," rev. of *Modern Painters*, vol. III, by John Ruskin, *Westminster Review*, 65 (1856), p. 343.

experience whose significance she always preached. The "ideal" had become for her an essential component of reality. As all of her scientist friends knew and were preaching, reality had become inaccessible to mere common sense.[10] Without abandoning "realism," she increasingly allied it, not with a simple empiricism, certainly not with materialism, but with what we might call a positivist idealism. "Definite substantial reality" was growing less definite, less substantial. "Forms bred on the mists of feeling" might well turn out, under the discipline of scientific control and verification, to be more true than what our common sense tells us is substantial reality.

The "ideal" for George Eliot was both a moral conception and a scientific tool. We may have failed to find in nature a perfect form, but we know, or at least usefully assume since Kepler, that were it not for the conflicting attractions of other bodies in space, the orbits of the planets would be perfect ellipses. The ellipse is the ideal toward which "definite, substantial reality" aspires, and it makes that reality comprehensible. The "undeviating law" which the young Marian Evans desired to study was a verifiable construction of the human intelligence.

The example, with some embellishment, is from G. H. Lewes' *Problems of Life and Mind*, the work that consumed him from the late 1860's until his death, and which, Casaubon-like (he made the analogy himself), he left to George Eliot to complete. Although she took the liberty to disagree with many of the ideas in it, she agreed with most of it; and it provides an important non-fictional analogue to the last two great novels.[11] Lewes' book should remind us that George Eliot wrote with sophistication about what was going on in mathematics, physics, biology, and psychology. She had observed the dissection of a brain, spoken (during Lewes' investigations) with the great scientists of the continent, and devoted her Sundays to such regulars as W. K. Clifford, that "great, great mathematician," and John Tyndall. While she was writing *Middlemarch*

---

[10] It is true that T. H. Huxley at one point called science "organized common sense" ("The Method of Zadig" in *Collected Essays* IV), but it had to be "trained and organized," and the world of post-Darwinian science was often counter-intuitive, available to "common sense" only through the accumulation of much evidence and long, complex arguments and interpretations. The raw empiricism that was implicit in scientific work had to give way to more complex inferences and arguments, while explorations of the natural world required increasingly complex instruments (which Ruskin, for example, rejected just because they belied the experience of the visible world). See below the discussion of Tyndall and Lewes on the scientific imagination.

[11] See K. K. Collins, "G. H. Lewes Revised: George Eliot and the Moral Sense," *Victorian Studies*, 21 (1978), pp. 463–92. See also Collins's useful dissertation, "Experimental Method and the Epistemology of *Middlemarch*," Diss. Vanderbilt University, 1976.

and *Daniel Deronda*, Lewes, in his healthy moments, was scratching away at his *Problems*.

"Science," Lewes announced, "is penetrating everywhere, and slowly changing men's conception of the world and of man's destiny."[12] One aspect of this penetration that we tend to forget in our current preoccupation with the dangerous effects of modern technology is the almost religious attitude required for good science. Science was not the bastion of unbelief: "The purely negative attitude of Unbelief, once regarded as philosophical," says a Carlylean Lewes, "is now generally understood to be only laudable in the face of the demonstrably incredible" (*PLM*, I, 2). Only a slight transformation changes this to Mordecai speaking to Daniel Deronda:

"What are doubts to me? In the hour when you come to me and say, 'I reject your soul: I know that I am not a Jew: we have no lot in common' – I shall not doubt. I shall be certain – certain that I have not been deluded. That hour will never come!"[13]

Mordecai has a working hypothesis: that Deronda is a Jew. Like a good scientist, he experiments as though the hypothesis were true, and he awaits a final verification. The hypothesis, meanwhile, helps create the conditions that make it true. Lewes wrote with some pride that he was the first philosopher to have "boldly generalized the observation, and proclaimed the introduction of Fiction to be a necessary procedure of Research" (*PLM*, I, 296).

Problems of Life and Mind is, as I shall be claiming for *Daniel Deronda*, an effort of reconstruction, and of reconciliation of religion and science, within a central tradition of nineteenth-century philosophy.[14] It attempts to bring to the great epistemological difficulties of the basic empirical stance a systematic, Germanic coherence. But Lewes wants to do this without slipping into the idealism of von Hartmann or Lange, or into an alternative crude "Materialism." Critics have been discovering that George Eliot's work seems to be easily assimilable to certain principles

[12] George Henry Lewes, *Problems of Life and Mind*, 2 vols. (London: Trübner, 1874), I. Cited hereafter as *PLM*.
[13] *Daniel Deronda*, ed. Barbara Hardy (Harmondsworth: Penguin Books, 1967), ch. 40. Subsequent references to this edition of the novel are given parenthetically in the text.
[14] Gillian Beer discusses the relation of Lewes' and George Eliot's work to the theories of Claude Bernard. It is surely misleading for Lewes to claim priority in asserting the importance of "fiction" to science; Bernard had discussed at great length the necessity of the hypothesis. Gillian Beer, "Plot and the Analogy with Science in Later Nineteenth-Century Novelists," *Comparative Criticism: A Yearbook*, 20 (1980).

of deconstruction. Her late novels subversively undermine traditions of narrative, history, and meaning that her culture had apparently learned to take for granted. This new emphasis on George Eliot's self-conscious disentangling of the conventions of historical process and unity and of the fictions embedded in our conventions of meaning has been salutary in that it alerts us to how far outside the conventions of Victorian narrative her art had developed. But it is entirely misleading if it also suggests that her recognition of the inevitable fictionality of language was the end rather than the beginning of her enterprise.[15] It can hardly be a surprise that George Eliot found the conventions of narrative with which she began inadequate to her developing conceptions of reality. The W. K. Clifford she so admired was, among other things, an expert in non-Euclidean geometry, which led him not only to challenge fundamental axioms of mathematics but to recognize the relativity of ideas thought to have universal application. She was deeply learned not only in the Higher Criticism, but in comparative grammar, anthropology and myth study, systems of thought that were forcing the culture out of its intellectual provincialism. And Lewes, of course, was arguing that science and language created ideal patterns that were at best abstract symbols of the feelings prompted by an assumed but indescribable reality, *"extra mentem."* "Speech," George Eliot wrote in *The Spanish Gypsy* "is but broken light upon the depth of the unspoken."[16]

But our subversive readings tend to neglect the primary object to which these self-conscious deconstructions of our common-sense traditions of order and narrative are preliminary: the reconstruction of meaning and

---

[15] The most important and persuasive argument for the subversiveness of George Eliot's enterprise is in J. Hillis Miller, "Optic and Semiotic in *Middlemarch*," in *The Worlds of Victorian Fiction*, ed. Jerome H. Buckley, *Harvard English Studies* 6 (Cambridge, MA: Harvard University Press, 1975), pp. 125–45; and Miller, "Narrative and History," *ELH*, 41 (1974), pp. 455–73. While it is part of Lewes' theory to understand the separateness between the language that constitutes the theory and the nonverbal reality beyond it, he insists (as, I would argue, did George Eliot) that "truth" is the object of theory. He and George Eliot sustain a position that, to contemporary criticism, may seem self-divided; but that they did hold the position is self-evident. Beginning with the recognition of fictionality, they proceed to argue for representation. Here is a crucial statement of Lewes': "A distinction is drawn between Art and Reality, and an antithesis is established between Realism and Idealism which would never have gained acceptance had not men in general lost sight of the fact that Art is a Representation of Reality – a Representation which, inasmuch as it is not the thing itself but only represents it, must necessarily be limited by the nature of its medium . . . while thus regulated by the necessities imposed on it by each medium of expression, Art always aims at the representation of Reality, *i.e.*, of Truth; and no departure from truth is permissible, except such as inevitably lies in the nature of the medium itself" ("Realism in Art: Recent German Fiction," *Westminster Review*, 70 (1858), p. 273).

[16] *The Spanish Gypsy*, Cabinet Edition (Edinburgh: Blackwood, n.d.), p. 104.

order that is Lewes' objective as well. The "common" must be displaced by the ideal. In reading these later books, one should attend to such remarks as those of F. W. H. Meyers after he had read *Middlemarch*: "You seem now to be the only person who can make life appear potentially noble and interesting without starting from any assumptions . . . one feels that you know the worst, and one thanks you in that you have not despaired of the republic" (*GEL*, IX, 68). While it is surely ingenuous to assume that George Eliot had no assumptions, the major characters in *Middlemarch* are notoriously on a quest for origins, and fail in part because they have assumptions of which they are not aware. George Eliot, at least, had discarded the primary religious and epistemological assumptions of her inherited culture, including the convention that a singly unitary theory of reality could be established.[17]

Middlemarch and *Daniel Deronda* are gestures beyond the written page into a reality that had become so tenuous and difficult that common sense revealed only fragments and disruption; and unitary theory – if there can be one – would have to be built out of complex hypotheses, themselves built out of experientially based intuitions. Mordecai is a type of scientist, so rigorously demanding of reality that he literally forgets himself and his body; he studies and awaits his revelation. The world of the commonplace, the seat of Trollopian realism, is demonstrably unequal to the heroic discipline and visionary power requisite for discovery of truth, creation of meaning, action for the good. The two novels extend empiricism and literary realism – trying not to break them – by assuming the ultimate unreality of the discontinuities and disruptions of order, and by tentatively affirming an intuited but largely verifiable reality. To see reality depends on the sort of intense, patient, nuanced attentiveness to the promptings of experience, to the voices of others, to the movements of nature, that is exemplified in different ways by Lydgate at his work, by Deronda at his dreaming, by Mordecai at his prophecy, and by the self Marian Evans created in the drawing room of the Priory: relentlessly compassionate, relentlessly serious and attentive, relentlessly demanding of our morality and our consciousness.

---

[17] See Elizabeth Ermarth, "Incarnations: George Eliot's Conception of 'Undeviating Law'" *NCF*, 29 (1974), pp. 273–86, for an excellent discussion of the way George Eliot resisted the notion of a single "law" governing nature and experience: "The radical relativism entailed by the law of facticity precludes the possibility of any more reductive law" (p. 285). See also Gillian Beer, "Beyond Determinism: George Eliot and Virginia Woolf," in *Women Writing and Writing about Women*, ed. Mary Jacobus (London: Croom Helm; New York: Barnes and Noble, 1979), pp. 80–99.

Lewes' attempts to reconcile empiricism to metaphysics entail a new inwardness. The shifts of perspective that are so prominent in *Middlemarch* have their analogue in Lewes' struggles with the contradictions in empiricism. For while he begins with the primary, undeniable intuition of a Not-self, he immediately breaks down the distinction between self and other by viewing them, in a Comtean light, as different aspects, objective or subjective of the same phenomenon (*PLM*, I, 194). Language creates the fiction of separate entities, but, as Lewes says, "Nothing exists in itself and for itself; everything in others and for others: *ex-ist-ens* – a standing out relation. Hence the search after the *thing in itself* is chimerical: the thing being a group of relations, it *is* what these are. Hence the highest form of existence is Altruism, or that moral and intellectual condition which is determined by the fullest consciousness – emotional and cognitive – of relations" (*PLM*, II, 26–27). In Lewes' world, there is no way to comprehend reality without examining it both objectively, as an external fact, and subjectively, as a sensation of feeling. "Perception," he says is "the assimilation of the Object by the Subject, in the same way that Nutrition is the assimilation of the Medium by the Organism" (*PLM*, I, 189).

Such a theory of perception and of the quest for scientific truth is simultaneously intellectual and moral. "Altruism," that Comtean ideal, is both a condition of organic relationship and a moral category; the discovery of the reality of that relationship – the quest for which impels the organization of novels like *Bleak House*, as well as *Middlemarch* – is a moral discovery. Lewes' world hides (and is shaped by) its Nemesis, as George Eliot's worlds hide theirs, in their elaborate, invisible network of relations. The altruism lurking behind appearances reveals the emptiness of the self apart from relation to others – a terrifying discovery made, more or less melodramatically, by Tito Melema with Baldassare, Harold Transome with the lawyer Jermyn, and Bulstrode with the revelation of Raffles.

For Lewes and George Eliot, following Darwin, the highest organism is both the most complexly differentiated from its rudimentary origins and the most integrated in other organisms. The human organism exists in a "medium" that is, quite literally, another organism – society. Lewes understands that there is no full accounting for the human organism without further understanding its medium. To encounter so completely differentiated a world, true science must be altruistic: it unravels this complexity of relationship and satisfies "the spiritual thirst for knowledge" and "the pressing desire for guidance in action: not only painting a picture of the wondrous labyrinth of Nature, but placing in our hands the Ariadne-thread to lead us through the labyrinth" (*PLM*, I, p. 26). Such images, familiar in George Eliot's novels, recur through Lewes' work: science is an ideal construction that unravels "the tangled web thread by thread. Every thread has its law; every law its general expression connecting it with all similar threads" (*PLM*, II, p. 36).

Although Lewes may have been more unqualifiedly confident about science and "law" than George Eliot, his ebullience was accompanied by a dignified scientific humility. "Every Real," he notes, "is the complex of so many relations, a conjuncture of so many events, a synthesis of so many sensations, that to know one Real thoroughly would only be possible through an intuition embracing the Universe" (*PLM*, I, pp. 342–3). George Eliot, we remember, chooses to "unravel" only a few human lots to see "how they were woven and interwoven," and refuses to disperse the "light" she can command "over that tempting range of relevancies called the universe." "The Universe," says Lewes, "is mystic to man, and must ever remain so; for he cannot transcend the limits of his Consciousness" (*PLM*, II, p. 3). Lewes' work, like George Eliot's is to unravel what can be unraveled, finding the "general expression" that might connect it with similar threads, in the vast inextricable relations of reality.

Lewes is in the paradoxical position of any empiricist who seeks systemic wholeness. Committed to common sense, he finds himself in a reality that runs counter to what common sense reveals. The "unknowable" lurks so close to the surface, the ultimate entity is so mysteriously remote, the "intuitions" required seem so remote from the methods of direct observation, that it is no wonder he urged the establishment of "Lay Sermons," or that George Eliot held her gatherings on Sundays. His language must move from appearances to realities in a rhythm that is so directly reminiscent of religious language that it is difficult to avoid the connection. One of the most striking of his passages is remarkably reminiscent of the strategies of a far more famous and impressive one, in the fifth chapter of the *Apologia pro vita sua*, in which Newman imagines the world as it must seem to common sense. Here is Lewes:

It is true that our visible Cosmos, our real world of perceptions, is one of various and isolated phenomena; most of them seeming to exist in themselves and for themselves, rising and disappearing under changing conditions ... But opposed to this continuous Cosmos perceived, there is the invisible continuous Cosmos, which is conceived as an uniform Existence, all the modes of which are inter-dependent, none permanent. The contradiction is palpable. On the one side there is ceaseless change and destruction, birth and death; on the other side destruction is only transformation, and the flux of change is the continuous manifestation of an indestructible, perdurable Existence. .... The facts of Feeling which sensation differentiates, Theory integrates. What we experience as Feeling, we systematize as Science. Hence the speculative effort, thoroughly justifiable, to reduce all phenomena to one cause, all laws to one, to see the Many in the One, and the One in the Many, as Plato divined. (*PLM*, II, 8–29)

Newman's fragmented world without God is Lewes' fragmented world without science. What our feelings offer us unsystematically ("feelings" meaning for Lewes the raw registration of reality – that is, experience), our ideas transform into the patterned, the related, the continuous. The world without earnest study is meaningless and incoherent, as it is in the late novels of George Eliot. Science, which can here be understood as, quite literally, the ideal, reveals to us a world equivalent to that nominal world in which Newman could believe only by accepting unequivocally the reality "of two and two only absolute and luminously self-evident beings, myself and my Creator."[18]

In assuming the consonance of this view with George Eliot's later fiction, I am in a sense justifying the discredited unitary enterprises of Lydgate or Casaubon, and imposing on George Eliot a position which, in her dramatic insistence on variety and particulars, she seems to be rejecting as both dangerous and untrue. But the distinction between what is available to common experience and what may be accessible to disciplined, impersonal investigation and compassion is critical. It is not necessary to assert that George Eliot believed in and could identify the unitary reality to recognize her struggles to account for the difference, the particulars, the plenitude, and reach through to an ideal of coherence and meaning. No unitary theory that fails to account for a single particular can sustain itself. Every theory must be understood as an ideal to be tested.

Lewes would have distinguished his "invisible" Cosmos from Newman's by insisting that the "invisible" was verifiable. He argued that there is not only a "sensible" world but an "extra-sensible" one, ultimately also empirical although beyond the reach of the microscope or telescope. Science had been exploring the atomic structure of the universe, and Huxley, Tyndall, and Clifford, among others, had been describing that structure although nobody had ever seen an atom. Clifford was demonstrating that every sensation we experience "is supplemented by something else which is not in it."[19]

---

[18] John Henry Cardinal Newman, *Apologia pro vita sua*, ed. Martin J. Svaglic (Oxford: Clarendon Press, 1967), pp. 216–18.
[19] William Kingdon Clifford, *Lectures and Essays*, ed. Leslie Stephen and Sir Frederick Pollock, 3rd edn., 2 vols. (London: Macmillan, 1901), I, p. 309, cited hereafter as *L&E*.

Ether has been posited as an imperceptible medium for light and electro-magnetic waves. The world itself, which had seemed so solid, stable, and irrefutably there, was becoming one infinite motion of submicroscopic particles. The invisible world constitutes far more of reality than the visible. It is not confined, says Lewes, to objects which "have never been presented to Sense": "it also comprises objects beyond even this possible range, beyond all practicable extension of Sense. It presents objects to the mind's eye such as no bodily eye could discern: molecules and waves, having their precise measurement and laws, planets and their stages of evolution before man was" (*PLM*, I, p. 261). Verifying such a reality required the most intense energy of the imagination.

Every interesting writer about science celebrated the imagination. Tyndall's important address, "Scientific Uses of the Imagination," be-comes eloquent on the topic. In that address, Tyndall argues that the microscope is itself too coarse an instrument to shed light on the ques-tion of the movement of molecules, even dangerous in its coarseness. The question, Tyndall says, is "not of the power of our instrument, for that is *nil*, but whether we ourselves possess the intellectual elements which will ever enable us to grapple with the ultimate structural energies of nature."[20] That of course is the question implicit in Lydgate's career, but his particular failure is not generally conclusive. Tyndall accepts the limits on human intellect and knowledge, rejecting only the dogmatism that assumes prematurely that it knows with certitude. The materialist Tyndall becomes positively mystical, ready to think of matter as Goethe's "Living Garment of God" (*FS*, II, p. 132), willing to risk the idea of the "Uniformity" of nature, but unwilling to talk about "*impossibilities* in nature" (*FS*, II, p. 134). Scientific imagination he sees as the condition of knowledge; the limits of that imagination he does not profess to know. When Lewes attempts to explain how he can sustain his empiricism while insisting on the reality of the extra-sensible, he argues with unsci-entific passion:

I say ideal construction, and emphasise it, with the intention of meeting the vulgar objection, iterated from all sides, against the Experiential Method, whose fol-lowers are said "to believe only in what they can see and touch;" whereas the truth is that Science mounts on the wings of imagination into regions of the Invisible

---

[20] *Fragments of Science*, 2 vols. (New York: D. Appleton, 1892), II, 126, hereafter cited as *FS*. Cf.: "Even with the microscope directed on a water-drop we find ourselves making interpretations which turn out to be rather coarse" (*Middlemarch*, ed. Gordon S. Haight, Riverside Editions [Boston: Houghton Mifflin, 1956], ch. 6. Further citations here are to this edition).

and Impalpable, peopling those regions with Fictions more remote from fact than the phantasies of the Arabian Nights are from the daily occurrences in Oxford Street. (*PLM*, I, p. 289)

In the light of such arguments, we can see how Lydgate's work, as it is described in the famous passage in *Middlemarch*, is closely connected to the scientific ideals of Lewes, George Eliot, and their entire philosophico-scientific community. This passage, so often read as a description of George Eliot's enterprise as a novelist, begins with Lydgate's dismissal as "vinous and vulgar" of the excesses of poetic imagination, even Miltonic ones, as compared with,

The imagination that reveals subtle actions inaccessible by any sort of lens, but tracked in that outer darkness through long pathways of necessary sequence by the inward light which is the last refinement of Energy, capable of bathing even the ethereal atoms in its ideally illuminated space. He for his part had tossed away all cheap inventions where ignorance finds itself able and at ease: he was enamoured of that arduous invention which is the very eye of research, provisionally framing its object and correcting it to more and more exactness of relation; he wanted to pierce the obscurity of those minute processes which prepare human misery and joy, those invisible thoroughfares which are the first lurking places of anguish, mania, and crime, that delicate poise and transition which determine the growth of happy or unhappy consciousness. (ch. 16)

Not only is Lydgate working on "The Physical Basis of Mind," the title of the third volume of Lewes' *Problems*, but he is using imagination to discover Lewes' "extra-sensible" reality. The "inward light" by which he studies the universe makes the invisible present to him as though it was a direct sensation. He is, in other words, practicing science as Ladislaw defines the poet's activity: with "a soul so quick to discern that no shade of quality escape it. . .in which knowledge passes instantaneously into feeling, and feeling flashes back as a new organ of knowledge" (ch. 22). Lydgate's science is equivalent, too, to the narrator's description of what is necessary if Dorothea is to discover Casaubon's "equivalent centre of self," conceiving "with that distinctness which is no longer reflection but feeling – an idea wrought back to the directness of sense, like the solidity of objects" (ch. 21).

Those passages suggest how central to advanced thinking on scientific study even George Eliot's ostensibly poetic passages are. In Clifford's essay, "On Some of the Conditions of Mental Development," he describes the way the scientific faculty is trained:

Men of science . . . have to deal with extremely abstract and general conceptions. By constant use and familiarity, these, and the relations between them, become just as real and external as the ordinary objects of experience; and the perception of new relations among them is so rapid, the correspondence of the mind to external circumstances so great, that a real scientific sense is developed, by which things are perceived as immediately and truly as I see you now. Poets and painters and musicians also are so accustomed to put outside of them the idea of beauty, that it becomes a real external existence, a thing which they see with spiritual eyes, and then describe to you, but by no means create, any more than we seem to create these ideas of tables and forms and light, which we put together long ago. (*L&E*, I, p. 109)

Like Lydgate, Clifford brings together invention and discovery. Like Ladislaw, he argues that scientists *and* poets share the development of senses that give to abstractions the solidity of objects. For Clifford, the faculty is developed by rigorous training; for George Eliot also. The imagination once disciplined is under the control of scientific rigor, even when it flies most free.

Such control is evident everywhere in the Lydgate passage. The "long pathways of necessary sequence" are the pathways that both Lewes and Clifford describe as "Abstraction": the analysis of the fragmented details of experience into a unifying conception by which we define "laws of nature." Gillian Beer notes accurately that such sequence "is controlled by the reasoning imagination and, as in [Claude] Bernard's analysis, there is an emphasis upon the liberty of reason first to use, and then to outgo, observation."[21] Scrupulous investigation of phenomena must be governed by an irreversible logic through which we can imagine the irreversible laws of nature. Such imaginative labor is both "arduous" and in "obedience to rigorous canons." Furthermore, the "ethereal atoms" are no mere poetic device here; they are, of course, the "extra-sensible" matter of "ether," that hypothesized matter that was indeed "illuminated" – both literally, as the conveyor of light, and figuratively, by the inward light which is human intelligence and imagination. And that intelligence is, further, quite precisely "the last refinement of Energy." Consciousness is that rarefied product of material energies, so much "refined" that it is irreducible to matter, even to so immaterial a matter as ether. Consciousness finally becomes the ultimate subject of consciousness, which penetrates through obstacles of coarser matter by virtue of its "adjustment of relation" between idea and experience and among the "minute processes" – submicroscopic and extra-sensible – that constitute the life of the organism and of the cosmos.

---

[21] Beer, "Plot and the Analogy with Science," ed. E. S. Schaffer, *Comparative Criticism: A Yearbook*, Vol. 2 (1980), 131–45.

In a world so imagined, intelligence and morality are interdependent. "The altruistic impulses," says Lewes, "have greater need of Intelligence to understand the object itself in all its relations. Hence so much immorality is sheer stupidity" (*PLM*, I, pp. 166–7). Such a passage can remind us of how morally central to George Eliot's narratives imagination has always been: Mrs. Tulliver's stolid literalness suggested not only an intellectual but a moral weakness. The most famous passage in *Middlemarch*, though it echoes Huxley,[22] is directly related to the question of the connection between imagination and morality:

If we had a keen vision and feeling of all ordinary human life, it would be like hearing the grass grow and the squirrel's heart beat, and we should die of that roar which lies on the other side of silence. As it is, the quickest of us walk about well wadded with stupidity. (ch. 20)

The "roar" is beyond the sensibilities of most people, although, as in this passage, a Lewesian scientific method can imagine it. Our common incapacity to perceive and feel more than coarsely, with anything like the minuteness and intensity of the Lydgatian researcher, is a kind of stupidity towards which the narrator sustains some ambivalence. There is evidence, as in "The Lifted Veil," that George Eliot was not always confident that the fullest knowledge is the best moral condition. In "Leaves from a Note-Book," she wrote:

Is it not conceivable that some facts as to the tendency of things affecting the final destination of the race might be more hurtful when they had entered into the human consciousness than they would have been if they had remained purely external in their activity? (Pinney, pp. 449–50)

With her primary motive that of making a difficult existence bearable, George Eliot would always step back from the more arcane intellectual pursuits to examine immediate moral consequences. Yet in her last novels she was taking the risk of knowledge in a Lewesian enterprise of projecting and testing a vision of the world that reaches beyond the fragments and discontinuities of ordinary perception to the continuous and perdurable cosmos. It is important to see that she was taking risks, that she did not imagine the discipline and restraint required of scientific investigators as entailing passivity, submission, or the absence of ego. The risk of knowledge entailed for her the "ardor" she attributes to Dorothea, to Ladislaw, and even to Lydgate when at his scientific work. The risk requires a disciplined but powerful selfhood reaching beyond the self to the ideal.

---

[22] See Ian Adam, "A Huxley Echo in *Middlemarch*," *Notes and Queries*, NS 11 (1964), p. 227.

The ideal of the continuous cosmos is, as it were, the perfect ellipse which the narratives do not quite achieve because of the influence of other bodies. The ideal is the working hypothesis, the formal and imaginative center, of the late narratives, and comes from their counterparts in the early fiction. Alexander Welsh has noted how the self-conscious and approving use of hypothesis in the late nineteenth-century scientific work was accompanied by an analogous shift in narrative mode from realism to romance.[23] "Common" begins to imply not a democratic approval but a contemptible coarseness. Lydgate fails from his spots of commonness. He is, as a social being, "stupid" and "common." The objectors to Lewes' empiricism are "vulgar," and the discontinuous cosmos is what common sense perceives. George Eliot must strain the novel beyond the limits of realism to find an ideally illuminated space.

Although *Middlemarch* is concerned with the obstacles to the ideal and the limits of knowledge, its narrator is an altruistic scientist who perceives "unapparent relations" and the continuities behind the discontinuities. Through all its questioning of history, narrative, and language, the book implies the continuous cosmos it is too wise to impose upon the common life of Middlemarch, Lowick, and Tipton Grange. The "Prelude" establishes the antinomies that will direct George Eliot to the idealizing in *Daniel Deronda* and to that book's barely disguised animosity to the merely common. The many Theresas who "found for themselves no epic life" tried "with dim lights and tangled circumstance ... to shape their thought and deed in noble agreement; but after all, to common eyes their struggles seemed mere inconsistency and formlessness." What is inconsistent and formless to "common eyes" is not so to the narrator, who seeks to find her subject in those extraordinary people who, however dimly, bear within them the light and the passion of the ideal.

Dorothea is, by the standards of even Dinah Morris or Maggie Tulliver, "extraordinary," but she must grow to that quality and is radically compromised in her Lewesian quest for a "binding theory." The true George Eliot protagonist has an intuition – often distorted and immature – of Lewes' continuous cosmos. Dorothea is driven on a quest to satisfy that intuition through a theory that would help her detect the extra-sensible world and fill in the gaps in reality which her adolescent perceptions reveal, a theory that "could bring her own life and doctrine into strict connection with that amazing past, and give the remotest sources of knowledge some bearing on her action" (ch. 10). But her attempts to

---

[23] "Theories of Science and Romance, 1870–1920," *Victorian Studies*, 17 (1973), pp. 135–54.

get beyond the common sense of Celia and the Cadwalladers are inadequately based, for she has not the accumulated experience that would give authority to her passionate imagination. In reading Casaubon's experience as a larger Miltonic reality, she moves beyond Lewes' "Extra-sensible" world into what he called the metaphysicians' "Supra-sensible" one. The mistake, however, does not invalidate either her ardor or her imagination; it provides the experience that will discipline those qualities and make her apparently unverifiable imaginative leap in favor of Lydgate a valid one. In this later instance, the ego that distorted becomes the disciplined energy of compassionate intuition. Her visit to Rome is also an experience of "stupendous fragmentariness," for she lacked what the narrator calls "the quickening power of a knowledge which breathes a growing soul into all historic shapes." In those early days, Dorothea had no "defense against deep impressions" (ch. 20); but she always has that primary intuition of a possibly unattainable coherence beyond the fragmented impressions.

Middlemarch is not, after all, about the perfect ellipse but about the way multitudinous bodies deflect planets from their orbits, as Lydgate is deflected by his "spots of commonness," as Casaubon is deterred by his moral timidity, as Dorothea is impeded by the social medium. The novel is not an intuition embracing the universe but an intuition that what we take as discontinuous will in fact be continuous, that the invisible continuous cosmos is there, and what is required is the all-embracing vision of Uriel.

Daniel Deronda is the novel in which George Eliot most directly risks establishing the conditions under which such an intuition – or hypothesis – might be affirmed and brought into accord with the harsh, unaccommodating actual. *Middlemarch* struggles, for the last time in George Eliot's career, to extend our sympathies for the common, in the sense she described it in her review of Riehl; its multiple perspectives jar us into the double vision – objective and subjective – that Lewes urges, and expands even the commonest "Real" into significance. The pettiness of Celia's or the Cadwalladers' way of seeing is, nevertheless, at least partially justified. Had Dorothea responded with Celia's revulsion from Casaubon's hairy mole, and with Mrs. Cadwallader's sensible alertness to the disparity in age, she would never have imagined Casaubon as Milton. But in *Daniel Deronda* common sense, like common life, is essentially a danger and a distortion. The world of the realist novel is irrecoverably in fragments – the church turned into a horse stable, the American Civil War commenting on Gwendolen's egoistic concerns, family ties shattered, English culture a mere façade of wealth and aristocracy. Even the best representatives of the common world endorse the villainies of its worst. Hugo Mallinger, the benevolent avuncular figure, is a malingerer who joins those failed uncles of *Middlemarch* whom U. C. Knoepflmacher has so well analyzed.[24] The Reverend Gascoigne, so generously supportive of Gwendolen and her mother, urges the marriage to Grandcourt. What is common is, at best, "well-wadded with stupidity": "It must be admitted that many well-proved facts are dark to the average man, even concerning the action of his own heart and the structure of his own retina" (*DD*, ch. 37). Even the domesticity of the Meyricks is petty and trivialized; the Cohens are indulged as exotica, although Daniel's instinctive revulsion from them has the texture of authenticity.

The narrative is uncharacteristically embittered, almost relentless in its ironies about society and the norms of social behavior. But the bitterness must be seen in the context of the almost mystically unironic Jewish section, which, as it were, describes the ellipse from which the Gwendolen sections are deflected by the fragments of reality that compose the inheritance of the culture, and by the solipsistic consciousnesses which cannot move beyond the merely "sensible" world. The Gwendolen sections are the control in an experiment designed to bridge the gap between the sensible and the exra-sensible. In moving beyond the mere raw material of feeling (which, for Lewes, constitutes experience), imposing upon it an hypothesis of the ideal, the Jewish sections move toward confirmation of the reality of Lewes' continuous cosmos.

As has often been noted, the Jewish sections contradict the whole thrust of George Eliot's art, and even of the Gwendolen sections – the idea that our dreams cannot make reality, that we must study nature scrupulously and be patiently obedient to its teaching. Gwendolen herself must learn "that her horizon was but a dipping onward of an existence with which her own was revolving" (ch. 69). Even this passage, however, reminds us of continuities and relations, of course only fragmentarily intuited by the maturing Gwendolen, but nonetheless there. Gwendolen has already been called an "insignificant thread" (ch. 11) in human history – one of those threads Lewes' science must disentangle from the full complex of reality. Having learned her insignificance by intuiting the larger world, Gwendolen, doomed to remain in the world of realism, is already alienated from it: "she was for the first time feeling the pressure of a vast mysterious movement, for the first time being dislodged from her supremacy in her own world," and in the process of this discovery she attains a feeling "deeper

---

[24] "*Middlemarch*: An Avuncular View," *Nineteenth-Century Fiction*, 30 (1975), pp. 53–81.

than personal jealousy – something spiritual and vaguely tremendous that thrust her away, and yet quelled all anger into self-humiliation" (ch. 69). She is learning to get beyond self, character, personality, and thus novels, into the "higher" condition of altruism.

We can feel here the presence of George Eliot in her drawing room – of the constructed, selfless self. In Gwendolen's transformation of anger into self-humiliation we may feel, as well, the emergence of George Eliot's headaches. But in the context of Gwendolen's narrative it is difficult to condescend to such a moral vision. Gwendolen is in the first stages of the recognition of the limits of the common self, a recognition that makes a prior condition for finding real connection with the world's "vast myste-rious movement" and allows escape from the tyranny of Grandcourt's entirely common vision. Gwendolen has become the bridge to Mordecai's "extra-sensible" world; the full power of vision requires the repression of the common self. With Mordecai, George Eliot is partly acknowledging the connection between science and what appears to be mysticism, which begins with a passionate forgetfulness of self. And it is important to recall that in Lewes' usage (and surely in George Eliot's), "ideal" does not imply a distortion of reality but an idea about reality – our only means to it. All science is ideal because it is a construction of human consciousness beyond the raw material of feeling – to which the young Gwendolen and Grand-court are confined.

Idealization and abstraction are, then, the tools of science and of the Jewish sections of *Daniel Deronda*. Daniel is almost literally abstracted from the contingencies of the sensible world, even from the contingencies of selfhood. Gwendolen learns what Daniel begins by feeling – personal insignificance in the scheme of things, the necessity of moving beyond self into the feelings and desires of others. In the character of Daniel, George Eliot suggests that the very conditions of altruistic science depend upon alienation. He is the titular hero of the book because he is alien and hence potentially beyond the limits of common desires, common vision, com-mon feelings, common sense. Recognizably a literary descendant of Adam Bede, he is yet evidence that George Eliot had become increasingly intol-erant of the old Adam in us, bearing with him unselfconsciously the unifying traditions of community and history. Sensible Adam with his skills and common sense could not reconstruct a human community so fragmented as the one in *Daniel Deronda*. Despite his uncommon affec-tion for common things, Daniel is instinctively repelled by the common almost everywhere it appears. Salvation will come from the prophetic figure who, by virtue of moral intellectual genius, is alienated from the community. That genius cannot inherit a common self but must construct a new self out of the fragments of the old, as George Eliot constructed a new self in her drawing room. "All originality," wrote Lewes, "is estrangement" (*PLM*, I, p. 174).

The excessively abstract passages that deal with Daniel's consciousness remind us even stylistically that he is made uncomfortable by his own extraordinariness – that his appearance, for example, "was of a kind to draw attention" (ch. 17). Because he feels uncommon, he begins by wanting to be unexceptional. But George Eliot carefully makes him striking in appearance, wealthy enough to be free of the economic pressures exerted on Gwendolen, leisured enough to speculate about himself without having to do anything about it, alienated enough to question even his foster father's assumptions. Thus, as he rows down the river, an act that compromised Maggie but saved Romola, his mind spins out into vast connections:

Deronda of late, in his solitary excursions, had been occupied chiefly with uncertainties about his own course; but those uncertainties, being much at their leisure, were wont to have such wide-sweeping connections with all life and history that the new image [of Mirah] of helpless sorrow easily blent itself with what seemed to him the strong array of reasons why he should shrink from getting into that routine of the world which makes men apologise for all its wrong-doing, and take opinions as mere professional equipment – why he should not draw strongly at any thread in the hopelessly-entangled scheme of things. (ch. 17)

The freedom to choose makes his narrative a romance. With the leisure to see himself in a larger context, he can avoid accepting the compromising terms of the common self and common world; but he has not yet that larger vision that would allow him to risk Lewes' sort of scientific adventure, and George Eliot's moral one, choosing a thread to draw from "the hopelessly entangled scheme of things." That risk requires a reconstructed self.

Yet the preliminary absence of that self makes Deronda the almost perfect Lewesian experimenter in life:

He was forgetting everything else in a half-speculative, half-involuntary identification of himself with the objects he was looking at, thinking how far it might be possible habitually to shift his centre till his own personality would be no less outside him than the landscape. (ch. 17)

The selflessness here is what makes the Grandcourts of this world regard him with suspicion, since their own selfhood makes it impossible to imagine the discipline of self; similarly, this selflessness makes much of

Daniel's narrative so intolerable (or merely amusing) to modern readers, "common readers." In this respect, we are no better than Grandcourt. For the novel not only implicitly rejects Grandcourt's way of perceiving; it rejects many of the conventions of novel reading, particularly the convention that characters must have common selves, "personalities" (through whose thick wall, Pater was to remind us, no human voice ever reaches), and the convention that the personalities must reflect the compromising conditions of common experience. Deronda is imagined as *almost* ideal, and the loss of selfhood is a preliminary essential to ideality.

This is not only a tenet of Positivism, but part of empiricist analysis, which, through the century, was subverting the notion of the "self." Clifford, for example, put the point forcefully: "The universe consists of feelings. A certain cable of feelings, linked together in a particular manner, constitutes me. Similar cables constitute you. That is all there is" (*L&E*, I, p. 346). Here is how Lewes puts it:

The universe to us is the universe in Feeling, and all its varieties are but varieties of Feeling. We separate these into object and subject, because we are forced to do so by the law of Relativity. With the feeling of difference or *otherness* arises the judgment of *not this*, which in turn evolves the distinction of Self and Notself. These two aspects are abstractions; in Feeling they emerge simultaneously as correlations. I can only be conscious of Self – however dimly – by detaching one group of feelings from another group, assigning a subjective unity of continuity to the one, and an objective unity to the other. (*PLM*, II, p. 19)

"Thus," he continues, "Self, the generalized abstraction of continuous Feeling, is detached from its concrete discontinuous states, and we speak of Self *and* its states as two separable terms" (*PLM*, II, p. 19).

Deronda in the boat and in his life is living out the implications of this analysis, which argues that the distinction between self and not-self is an arbitrary abstraction. He practices disassembling the self to get more fully in touch with the continuous flow of particularities and Being; and in effect, he retreats from realist fiction. Implicitly, however, the narrative suggests that a self that is arbitrarily constructed can be reconstructed in fuller accordance with the "objects" in which one re-centers. Daniel must find an external reality that will allow him to recompose the self, free, however, of the conventions of personality.

We have already seen in the character of Will Ladislaw a more trivial, or less solemn, anticipation of Deronda – the alien, abstracted, dilettante.[25]

---

[25] Jerome Beaty is one of the first to make the connection: "The Forgotten Past of Will Ladislaw," *Nineteenth-Century Fiction*, 13 (1958), pp. 159–63.

Will is imagined as an adequate partner for Dorothea *because* of his indecisiveness and receptivity to experience.[26] His failure is only of seriousness in action; but that sort of seriousness, as *Daniel Deronda* shows, must be preceded by knowledge. Indecisiveness is a crucial preliminary to knowledge. As Clifford describes it, one of the "Conditions of Mental Development" is "plasticity":

The avoidance of all crystallization as is immediately suggested by the environment. A mind that would grow must let no ideas become permanent except such as lead to action. Towards all others it must maintain an attitude of absolute receptivity; admitting all, being modified by all, but permanently biased by none. To become crystallized, fixed in opinion and mode of thought, is to lose the great characteristic of life, by which it is distinguished from inanimate nature: the power of adapting itself to circumstances. (*L&E*, I, p. 116)

One wonders if Daniel had read this passage. His problem, in any case, is to acquire the facts, fill in the gaps, so as to provide an adequate ground for decision and motive for action. Deronda, whose name, with anagrammatic play, might be forced to evoke Matthew Arnold, loves "too well the losing causes of the world" (ch. 32), and fears to draw too soon at the single thread, as Arnold feared action without "culture." But Arnold, after wearing a Ladislaw like mask and then seeking, in his poetry, for the buried self beneath the merely common, argues rather long against action. Perhaps Deronda and George Eliot were a bit more "Hebraic," as Lewes certainly was. "The highest no less than [the] lowest aim" of knowledge, Lewes argued, "is guidance in action." Feeling, which George Eliot calls "a kind of knowledge," issues in action, Lewes affirms, but it is "limited to the direct relations, and needs the guidance of a vision of relations that are not directly felt. Knowledge is simply virtual Feeling, the stored-up accumulations of previous experiences, our own and those of others: it is a vision of unapparent relations which will be apparent when the objects are presented to Sense" (*PLM*, II, p. 23). Daniel's quest for literal "unapparent relations," his mother and father, is achieved through "plasticity," urged by his need for action, and particularly for an action that might affirm the invisible continuous cosmos.

Since egolessness deprives one of a motive, Daniel needs to develop the sort of faculty Ladislaw describes in *Middlemarch*. The question is how to act in accordance with reality instead of with the dreams created by desire.

---

[26] Eugene Hollohan, "The Concept of 'Crisis' in *Middlemarch*," *Nineteenth-Century Fiction*, 28, (1974), pp. 450–7, esp. 457.

"The chief poetic energy," says the narrator, is "in the force of imagination that pierces or exalts the solid fact, instead of floating among cloud-pictures" (*DD*, ch. 33). If, as Clifford puts it, the negative condition of the scientific mind is plasticity, the positive is that it should be "creative." The mind must not "tremble before the conventionalism of one age, when its mission may be to form the whole life of the age succeeding." Rather, "it must act, create, make fresh powers, discover new facts and laws" (*L&E*, I, p. 115). Analogously, George Eliot elaborates a distinction between mere gossamer dreaming, like that of the inexperienced, egoistic Gwendolen, and creative dreaming based "in the stored up accumulation of previous experience" that will reveal the "unapparent relations" hidden in "solid fact." It is precisely the distinction that critics have refused to make. Like the vulgar characters in the novel, critics have persisted in assuming that Mordecai's visionary and creative wisdom is no more than a gossamer dream.

Lewes was aware of the problem of discriminating the two sorts of dream:

[Illusory] hypotheses are indeed a pest; but so far from their source being Imagination, it is precisely a defect of Imagination which forms their nidus. To imagine a natural process is to see the Agents or Agencies which are really operative, or which, if present, would act so as to produce the result observed. But this mental picture of the unseen process is given only to the highest minds equipped with exact knowledge. In Science, as in Art, a feeble mind can satisfy itself by vaguely supposing that something *may* in *some way or other* (not specified) determine the changes which take place; the difficulty is in precise vision. But precision is the one quality which impatient minds least appreciate; and therefore Illusory Hypotheses spring up like mushrooms in half-cultivated minds, and are readily accepted by the uncultivated, who see no difficulties because they have no vision of the requisites: marvels are not marvelous to them, for ignorance does not marvel. (*PLM*, I, p. 337)

Such is the other alien's, Klesmer's, advice to Gwendolen. Genius and precision are carefully linked through the novel, but Mordecai is the real test of this. The famous passage about "Second-sight" is an attempt to distinguish "illusory" from genuine hypotheses:

"Second-Sight" is a flag over disputed ground. But it is matter of knowledge that there are persons whose yearnings, conceptions – nay, travelled conclusions – continually take the form of images which have a foreshadowing power: the deed they would do starts up before them in complete shape, making a coercive type; the event they hunger for or dread rises into vision with a seed-like growth, feeding itself fast on unnumbered impressions. They are not always the less capable of the argumentative process, nor less sane than the commonplace calculators of the market. (ch. 38)

As we have seen, for Lewes science is a method by which what is not present to us is made ideally present, the ideal being "what is either *imaged* – that is to say, the feeling reproduced in the absence of its external object – or *conceived*, i.e., the feeling represented in a symbol." Mordecai, too, is an idealist, making present to himself "what would be Feeling, were the objective causes in direct relation with Sense" (*PLM*, I, p. 101). He tests the feeling of what is absent against the reality of Deronda. The analogy between Mordecai and the scientist is on the surface of the text. Watching Deronda rowing toward him he feels an "exultation . . . not widely different from that of the experimenter, bending over the first stirrings of change that correspond to what in the fervour of concentrated prevision his thought has foreshadowed" (ch. 40).

Daniel considers the problem directly. He wonders whether Mordecai's temper of mind is "likely to accompany that wise estimate of consequences which is the only safeguard from fatal error." Neither George Eliot nor her protagonist surrenders the tough-minded stance of the earlier novels, but she extends her considerations beyond the limits of common calculation: "Even strictly-measuring science could hardly have got on without that forecasting ardour which feels the agitations of discovery beforehand and has a faith in its preconceptions that surmounts many failures of experiment" (ch. 41). As Lewes says, "Without Hypothesis no step could be taken" (*PLM*, I, p. 317). Without imagination, true science is inconceivable, for the experimenter must sustain his energies through local defeats and leap beyond the limits of Casaubon-like pigeonholes and commonplace perceptions. Without the intense energies of feeling that allow us to experience an absent object as though it were present, there would be no science. Without faith there could be no science.

Obviously, the hypothesis I am attributing to George Eliot, that of an invisible continuous cosmos, is not "proven" by the story of *Daniel Deronda*. Romance as it may be, Daniel's story does not describe a perfect ellipse. He is forced to admit (a little too easily) that he has been "cruel" to Gwendolen. He leaves her to the world of the common and puts *his* newly constructed self to the work of national reconstruction. The ideal of a Jewish state allows for the reconstruction of the fragmented community the novel has so contemptuously dismissed, for the Jewish state was, as Comte insisted, the source of Western civilization. But Daniel is an alien in the West (as the newborn Gwendolen must be), and he leaves it to those commonplace consciousnesses who, to borrow Clifford's language, are crystallized into conventionalities which are drying up the "race."

Equally important, although the narrative implies the validity of Mordecai's hypothesis (right about Daniel, might he not be right about the Jewish state?) it leaves us yet with the empiricist's sense of the limits of human consciousness. One critic has said that the narrative surely does not share Lewes' full confidence that scientific method might "come up with objective and absolute truths for guidance of human thought and activity."[27] Lewes, in any case, was fairly certain he would not finish *Problems* and even called that work his "Key to all Mythologies" (*GEL*, V, p. 350), George Eliot his "Dorothea." Not even he could presume to think he could achieve the binding theory; but he insisted that the theory was possible, if we honor experience, require verification, and work with Lydgatian ardor, but without his spots of commonness, to bathe the "ethereal atoms" in their "ideally illuminated space." In the meantime, we must struggle to avoid crystallization and to recognize how much we must risk, how much we must trust to intuitive leaps, and reject a merely plodding accumulation of "facts."

Daniel Deronda implies the urgency of moving beyond the conventions of truth that merely dispassionate minds accept, and it tries to imagine the conditions for successful experiment – avoiding both the limits of common sense and the excesses of a demanding ego. Nothing short of heroic passion can leap beyond the limits of present consciousness, and George Eliot makes Daniel reflect that the "unemotional intellect" carries us often into a "mathematical dreamland where nothing is but what is not" while "perhaps an emotional intellect may have absorbed into its passionate vision of possibilities some truth of what will be – the more comprehensive massive life feeding theory with new material, as the sensibility of the artist seizes combinations which science explains and justifies" (ch. 41).

Daniel decides to postpone rejecting Mordecai's enthusiasms until further evidence is in because

Presumptions to the contrary are not to be trusted. We must be patient with the inevitable makeshift of our human thinking, whether in its sum total or in the separate minds that have made the sum. Columbus had some impressions about himself which we call superstitions, and used some arguments which we disapprove; but he had also some true physical conceptions, and he had the

[27] Hock Guan Tjoa, *George Henry Lewes: A Victorian Mind* (Cambridge, Mass: Harvard University Press, 1977), p. 104.

passionate patience of genius to make them tell on mankind. The world has made up its mind rather contemptuously about those who were deaf to Columbus. (ch. 41)

The attentive George Eliot of those solemn Sundays would not, she surely hoped, have been deaf to Columbus. She strained for the "plasticity" that implies "life" and precedes "creativity," and her language in this passage, as in her letters, hardly implies a denial of passion. At the risk of the deep repression she long since dramatized in Maggie Tulliver, she brought to bear her "passionate patience," as she imagined Columbus doing, on her art and her actions. The intensities of an aspiring self remained in her denial of mere personality, in her attempt to make "tell on mankind" the scientific vision that allowed her to see the arbitrariness of the selves we commonly inhabit.

Like Columbus, Deronda and Mordecai seek a new world, one that will be fulfillment of the old. Daniel evokes the Old Testament prophet whom George Eliot honored, as she wrote in her notebooks, for his intuition of a world unified, coherent, invisible, continuous: "The unknown teacher, to whom we are indebted for the Book of Daniel, is entitled to the praise that he was the first who grasped the history of the world, so far as he knew it, as one great whole, as a drama which moves onward at the will of the Eternal One."[28] *Daniel Deronda* attempts once more, in the new language of science, to confirm that ideal hypothesis of the Old Testament. George Eliot, leaning forward in her drawing room, seeks similar confirmation.

---

[28] Cited in Jane Irwin, ed., *George Eliot's "Daniel Deronda" Notebooks* (Cambridge: Cambridge University Press, 1996), p. 406.

PART II

Ethics without God, or, can "is" become "ought"?

CHAPTER 2

Is life worth living?

What do *you* think? It's hard not to take the question seriously even though it might seem to hardened scholars – and sophisticated modernists and postmodernists – a rather obvious, overserious, blunt, sophomoric Victorian sort of thing, still addressing with adolescent energy those great existential problems but not sufficiently noting the material conditions that some might say were really at stake – questions of political power, of economic want, of cultural authority. Victorian sophomoric questions usually turn out, however, to have been vital ones, and to have a post-Victorian life. Condescending to the Victorians, assuming that we have got past their questions and that their labors of thought and expense of spirit in working through them are of merely antiquarian interest, is a mistake.

The question, "Is life worth living," as the Victorians framed it, offers evidence for and anticipates that condition of "disenchantment" that Max Weber, borrowing the term from Schiller, saw as a mark of modernity.[1] I want to get Victorianly serious about this idea of *enchantment* and suggest that for the Victorians, on the whole, belonging to modernity seemed almost inevitably to entail disenchantment, in just Weber's sense. Victorian modernity was marked by the growing authority of science and by the growing "rationalization" of experience. And science, Weber argued, quoting Tolstoy, simply cannot answer the "only question important for us: 'What shall we do and how shall we live?'" That science "does not give an answer to this is indisputable" (143). The condition of

---

[1] See Weber's "Science as a Vocation," in *From Max Weber: Essays in Sociology*, ed. H. H. Gerth and C. Wright Mills (New York: Oxford University Press, 1946). It is not, Weber argues, that with the coming of science and the rationalizing of the world, everyone suddenly knew more, and mystery and meaning still presided in the world. Rather, says Weber, Disenchantment results "from the knowledge or belief that if one but wished one *could* learn . . . at any time. Hence, it means that principally there are no mysterious incalculable forces that come into play, but rather that one can, in principle, master all things by calculation. This means that the world is disenchanted" (p. 139).

disenchantment is the condition of finding no "meaning" to life, and no reason, except immediate, strictly utilitarian ones, to choose one thing rather than another.

Despite many assertions, both Victorian and contemporary, that science and religion were compatible, Weber was absolutely convinced that they were not. The same arguments for compatibility are being made today, one of them, most famously, by the late Stephen Jay Gould, who, perhaps a little ponderously, called science and religion "non-overlapping magisteria."[2] Weber was having none of that: "That science today is irreligious no one will doubt in his innermost being, even if he will not admit it to himself. Redemption from the rationalism and intellectualism of science is the fundamental presupposition of living in union with the divine" (p. 142). And for Weber, science could never be taken as "the way to happiness" (p. 143). Among the Victorians a great culture war broke out over just this question.[3] The propagandists for science, but most particularly the Comtean Positivists, sought ways to replace the kinds of emotional and spiritual satisfactions that religion had traditionally provided while denying, or questioning, all metaphysical (or as G. H. Lewes qualified it, "metempirical") reality.

Disenchantment was, Weber argued, a consequence of the new science and of the intellectualization and rationalization of the world that followed from it, across epistemology, ethics, institutions, and traditions. Rationalization, finally, provides "purely practical and technical" answers; it is utilitarian, not "spiritual." It leaves no mysteries, or rather leaves mysteries just where they were, except that they are now thought to be merely chimerical questions. Rationalization leaves life without "meaning," answering practical questions without intimating why any of these questions might be important except for resolving their local issues.

---

[2] See Stephen Jay Gould, *Rocks of Ages: Science and Religion in the Fullness of Life* (New York: Ballantine Publishing Group, 1999).

[3] The compatibility of science with religion was an intensely argued question among the Victorians, but ironically all sides wanted to claim compatibility, even when the fights were raging. For the scientists, it was important to leave open, as Tyndall did, a realm in which scientific method didn't apply while protecting the realm of science from non-scientific inroads. For each side, it was convenient to believe in something like "non-overlapping magisteria," although the reality of the engagements between the authorities in religion and the authorities in science did in fact become a battle over cultural and political authority, each side attempting to narrow the field of authority of the other. In this essay, I am concerned with a critical issue that did entail the crossing over – whether it is possible to build moral authority out of natural description or whether morality is sanctioned only by a power beyond natural description and therefore only accessible through the kinds of rituals, private and public, that marked religion.

The question, "Is the world disenchanted, as Weber thought?" might translate exactly into "Is Life Worth Living?" and though I'm certainly *not* uniquely qualified to answer the latter question, I should admit that I would not be writing this at all if my answer were not "yes," and if I did not think – or, rather, feel – that the world *can* be experienced as enchanted in spite of the authority and the threat of scientific explanation.[4] A sense of the value of all that material nature, a sense of its wonder and even mystery can survive the depredations of science. Rather, I would argue, it is the *condition* of a science that continually uncovers the extraordinary working of organisms, of their complex interrelations and mutual dependencies. The world under the eye of science can be seen as full of value, full of "meaning," almost mysteriously wonderful.

But I'm not deluded about how easy it might be to feel the enchantment of this world under entirely naturalist description, and thus to find life worth living. It is not just that there lies, philosophically, behind the question of whether one can move from science to a sense of wonder the very traditional philosophical question of whether it is possible to move from "is" to "ought." But whatever the philosophical underpinnings, among the Victorians, most commentators – if not the most voluble – could not imagine naturalist enchantment, assuming that only some extranatural force could give nature the power to enchant. The practical consequences of the disenchantment that implied that life was not worth living was, of course, suicide, and Barbara Gates has discussed at length the Victorian, particularly late-Victorian concern with suicide[5] and with what Hardy, in *Jude the Obscure*, melodramatically called "the coming universal wish not to live."

The degree to which this relatively abstract question, about the ultimate meaning of life and about the possibility of finding value in the world without God, really affects people's choices to live or die is uncertain. For William James, who addressed the question directly, choices to live or die are not philosophical, but temperamental, and he considers whether "life is worth living" with his characteristic brilliant attention to the texture of experience. He noted that "In the deepest heart of all of us there is a corner in which the ultimate mystery of things works sadly."[6] But what is particularly striking about the way *both* James and many of the English

---

4   I have explored this question at length in relation to Darwin in *Darwin Loves You: Natural Selection and the Re-enchantment of the World* (Princeton: Princeton University Press, 2007).
5   Barbara Gates, *Victorian Suicide* (Princeton: Princeton University Press, 1988).
6   William James, "Is Life Worth Living," collected in *The Will to Believe* (New York: Dover Press, 1956; 1897), p. 32.

Victorians addressed the question is that, however fundamentally different they are in attitude, temperament, and philosophical engagement, they all agree – and in this they are at one also with Weber – that a sense of the value of things, of worldly things, depends finally on belief in something beyond those things and beyond the reach of naturalist explanation. Science simply cannot produce happiness or a sense of value or a sense of the meaning of things. One cannot get from "is" to "ought," or from "is" to "good," or from "is" to "what it means." There were, of course, many different explanations for the rise in Victorian suicide rates about which Gates writes. But I will be confining myself here to this pervasive Victorian sense that one cannot move from the world of natural fact to the world of value and meaning, and that a full rationalization of the world leads to Weberian "disenchantment." Science and religion were widely felt to be incompatible. Meaning was felt to have been drained from life.

My title is taken from a very Victorian book of 1879, W. H. Mallock's *Is Life Worth Living?*, a title that William James used again for an 1895 essay. Mallock is best known for his brilliant satire on Victorian intellectual life in *The New Republic* (1877), but he was a prodigious writer, doggedly reaffirming traditional values and traditional religious views; certainly he represented a fundamentally retrograde position against the developing liberal/secular/scientific culture of mid- and late-Victorian England – the world of Mill and Arnold and George Eliot and Darwin and the scientific naturalists. But Mallock's position was central to an important line of Victorian thinking (he dedicated his book, for example, to John Ruskin), and he was there in the midst of major controversy, formalized in a symposium published in *The Nineteenth Century,* under the title, "The Influence upon Morality of a Decline in Religious Belief."

Obviously, the energy of Mallock's polemic depends upon the fact that there were indeed important Victorians who thought otherwise. Mallock's enemies, Clifford, Huxley, and Tyndall, in particular, are the most famous of them. Barbara Gates quotes L. S. Bevington's attack on Mallock. Her response is not so much theoretically but practically and politically oriented, and after all this existential worry, something of a relief: "So far as human life is worth living," she says, "so far is it worth protecting. So far as it is not worth living, so far is it needful to ameliorate it. Duty, on secular principles, consists in the summarized conduct conducive to the *permanent protection* and *progressive amelioration of* the human lot" (p. 153). This of course doesn't answer Mallock's theoretical objections – where, after all, did that secular morality come from? But it nicely implies something about the ideological implications of the Victorian debate and at the same time assumes that the answer to whether life is worth living will vary with the material conditions of the people asking the question.

Mallock, for his part, plunged into the Victorian culture wars with a sense of urgency generated by what he perceived as a radical transformation of the world:

Within less than a century, distance has been all but annihilated, and the earth has practically, and to the imagination, been reduced to a fraction of its former size. Its possible resources have become mean and narrow, set before us as matters of every-day statistics. All the old haze of wonder is melting away from it; and the old local enthusiasms, which depended so largely on ignorance and isolation, are melting likewise ... thought and feeling amongst the western nations are conforming to a single pattern: they are losing their old chivalrous character, their possibilities of isolated conquest and intellectual adventure. They are settling down into a uniform mass, that moves or stagnates like a modern army, and whose alternative lines of march have been mapped out beforehand.[7]

One can hear the coming of T. S. Eliot's "The Waste Land" in this passage, but it echoes more loudly with the kinds of arguments John Stuart Mill had made in his early essay, "Civilization."[8] However different Mallock and Mill were (it is hard to imagine a greater difference), they clearly agree about what is happening in modern society. Both feel powerfully the threat of a new aridity created by increased knowledge and increased rationalization of the organization of life. Obviously, this vision of the dreariness and aimlessness of the material world is a long way from the progressivism and enthusiastic greeting of the new and the future that has

---

[7] W. H. Mallock, *Is Life Worth Living?* (London: Chatto and Windus, 1879), pp. 150–1.

[8] See John Stuart Mill, *Essays on Politics and Culture,* ed. Gertrude Himmelfarb (New York: Doubleday and Co., 1962). In "Civilization" (1836) Mill calls the modern age, pre-eminently an era of "civilization," and argues that while civilization is a good, "there is other good, much even of the highest good, which civilization ... does not provide for, and some which has a tendency ... to impede." Mill argues similarly to Mallock, that in civilization "power passes more and more from individuals, and small knots of individuals, to masses: that the importance of the masses becomes constantly greater, that of individuals less" (p. 53). Mill asks "Are the decay of individual energy, the weakening of the influence of superior minds over the multitude, the growth of *charlatanerie*, and the diminished efficacy of public opinion as a restraining power, – are these the price we necessarily pay for the benefits of civilization, and can they only be avoided by checking the diffusion of knowledge, discouraging the spirit of combination, prohibiting improvements in the arts of life, and repressing the further increase of wealth and of production?" (p. 80). Mallock in fact leans toward a past in which such "checking," except among an elite, would in fact be desirable; Mill, of course, wants to say no; those drawbacks of civilization can be resisted. But it is striking how much agreement about the "price" of the new knowledge there is between these two ideologically opposed thinkers.

often been represented as characteristically Victorian. Such a vision
brings together thinkers as widely disparate as Mallock and Mill and
Ruskin and Carlyle and John Henry Newman and it provides a striking
confirmation of Weber's thesis. It would be hard to find a better formulation of the condition Weber was attempting to describe and analyze.
Under "positivist" description, Mallock insists, the world is radically
disenchanted.

"Positivism" is the word Mallock uses to describe scientific thinkers
who propose to extend their scientific experience and analysis into the
world of spirit and ethics. "Under the influence of positive thought," said
Mallock, "all . . . is changing" (8). "[W]ill the faith that we are so fast losing
ever again revive for us?" His one aim in the book "has been to demonstrate that the entire future tone of life, and the entire course of future
civilization, depends on the answer which this question receives" (155). But
the crucial assertion, around which I will spin my argument, is Mallock's
complaint that value for positive thinkers "is to be found in life itself, in
this earthly life, this life between the cradle and the grave . . . They have
taken everything away from life that to wise men hitherto seemed to
redeem it from vanity" (9).

It is a stunning assertion: a flat denial of the value of life in itself. Life, to
be valuable, must be understood not to be "earthly" at all. Mallock's
rhetoric makes the claim even more stunning, for it is made as if one
could simply take for granted that life has no intrinsic value. Mallock
assumes without question the impossibility of an "enchanted" relation
to life *unless* that life is a mere shell disguising some other life, some future
life, some life *not* between the cradle and the grave. Life, on this assumption, cannot validate itself. Nothing *in* life between the cradle and the
grave allows us to infer its value and meaning. Life, if it is only life, is mere
vanity and thus not worth living.

In effect, Mallock sacrifices the life we live in this world to the imagination of a life outside of it. It is the kind of move that, in another form,
the contemporary political philosopher William Connolly describes in his
"A Letter to Augustine." There Connolly mounts a dialogue with St.
Augustine about the question of "eternal life," and considers the question
of salvation as Augustine thought about it. Christian insistence on the
need for "eternal salvation," Connolly boldly tells Augustine, has created
many victims, not least Christianity itself, which "has paid a high price.
The more one looks into the depths of the human condition . . . the more
it becomes clear how much must be divested from human life and invested
in divinity if the very possibility of salvation by a sovereign god is itself

to be made secure."[9] The implication of Connolly's thrust against St. Augustine reverses Weber's argument about disenchantment, for very clearly Connolly regards the devaluing of life between the cradle and the grave in the interests of that which lies beyond life as a loss. Taking up, again implicitly, the question of the relation of the world, under scientific description, to value and meaning, Connolly is certainly suggesting that under that description value remains, enchantment is possible. His sense of the cost of the aspiration to the "eternal," if it does not explicitly reaffirm the incompatibility of science and religion, does strongly imply the value of worldly life – takes that value for granted. The cost of commitment to a life hereafter is a devaluing of the life here and now. Life, for Connolly, seems very much worth living despite the fact that any traditional philosophical analysis would leave unanswered the question, "From whence does the value of this life derive?"

Mallock leaves no space for the joys of this life. Although an admirer of Ruskin, he seems not to have shared Ruskin's own (sometimes tormenting) joy in life between the cradle and the grave. In any case, what is most striking about Mallock's argument, and about the kind of Christianity he was so aggressively defending, is, as Connolly put it, how much must be divested from human life and invested in divinity to preserve that sense of the sacred, that possibility of eternal salvation. The price of belief in the future life is a withering of this life (between the cradle and the grave).

Ironically, although Weber was insistently secular, he was to agree with Mallock's basic argument that the withdrawal of divine sanction from the world and the affirmation of the authority of rational/empirical explanation left the world disenchanted. Weber was not, of course, as was Mallock, mounting a polemic against "positive thought" but trying only to describe a cultural phenomenon. But in effect he agrees that for Western culture the exclusive focus on "this earthly life" removed whatever it was that, for most Westerners, made life worth living. Disenchantment follows from the loss of religion, but most particularly from the belief, fostered by science, that "there are no mysterious, incalculable forces" (p. 139). Everything can be explained in terms of the material conditions of earthly life. As Jane Bennett has recently put it, Weber's theory implies that enchantment depends "on a divine creator."[10] Thus, while Weber was analyzing a

---

[9]   William Connolly, *Identity/Difference* (Minneapolis: University of Minnesota Press, 1991), p. 126.
[10] Jane Bennet, *The Enchantment of Modern Life* (Princeton: Princeton University Press, 2001).

fundamental Victorian condition he was also expressing a profoundly Victorian belief.

This odd dynamic, which seemed to suggest that investment in God required withdrawal from life between the cradle and the grave, emerges in Mallock's argument almost as a summing up of an extraordinary range of Victorian literature. Mallock's polemic echoes with the dominant traditions of Victorian literature, which was pervasively at grips with disenchantment, struggling with it in an extraordinary variety of forms and styles, in an effort to re-imagine value in a modern "civilization" from which it seemed to have been banished. The new, scientifically aggressive thinkers did not for the most part address the question of whether – without religion, without teleology, without God – life were worth living; the sheer energy of their intellectual enthusiasms was, however, clear enough evidence that the world remained enchanted for them. They felt in a position to explain everything or they believed, as Weber was to describe the disenchanting power of science, that everything *might* be explained by science if it turned its full attention to it. And this of course implied that naturalistic explanation would suffice for everything.

Of course, there was that gray area to which most of the scientific naturalists came, and which is, as it were, the site of Herbert Spencer's "unknowable" as it is the source of Huxley's "agnosticism." Epistemology, these very authoritative thinkers understood, would not allow us to move beyond natural explanation. Everything beyond that was just a guess (and in the end, implicitly, barely worth the candle – who after all cares whether God was in on the very beginnings of things if science can trace us from the first spurt of life to the extraordinary achievements of the human mind). Life between the cradle and the grave was what naturalist thought strove to explain, and for the Victorians, it was clear, it was doing a remarkable job.

But everyone, from the most conservative of religious writers to the most extravagantly rebellious of scientific upstarts, like W. K. Clifford, all recognized that something in addition to the raw facts of life, or the rational explanation of natural phenomena, was essential to make life worth living. And thus the question for the positivist or scientific thinkers was whether it might be possible to achieve a condition of what I am calling, after William Connolly, non-theistic enchantment. Is it possible not merely to believe but to believe and feel that value "is to be found in life itself, in this earthly life, this life between the cradle and the grave?" Mallock said – and unequivocally – no. Somewhat more equivocally, with attention to the way the world under "naturalist" description is humanly and pragmatically oriented after all, William James said the same thing.

Comtean Positivism, half-mad in its rationality, it seems, attempts to formalize the belief that a world without god could be meaningful and enchanted. Matthew Arnold, obviously no positivist, but surely on the edges of the attitudes that Mallock condemns, fascinatingly creates a Victorian middle ground, redefining religion so as to preserve the mystery after the mystery was gone, and calling it "morality touched by emotion"[11] (*LD* 176). Critics of his religious writings complained that Arnold – who had his troubles with science but who was distinctly influenced by the new knowledge – would not overtly commit himself to the reality of a God.[12] His urgent task was to give the rationalizing and intellectualizing world – the Hellenic "light" of sweetness and light – some means to sustain the high Hebraic values that had hitherto seemed to derive from faith and could not be sustained and driven by mere this-worldly rationality. The move wouldn't satisfy the Roman Catholic Mallock or, for that matter, the politically conservative and philosophically brilliant author of one of the most forceful critiques of science's incursion into culture, Arthur Balfour, some fifteen years later in *The Foundations of Belief* (1895). And yet across the spectrum of debate it was clear that whatever sheer knowledge and intellection might do, it could not, without some heavy intervention of feeling, sustain a sense of the value of life. Everyone seemed to agree with what Weber would later say: reason and intellect and empirical knowledge were insufficient to sustain a sense of the meaningfulness of life, a sense of value, and particularly of moral value, and these finally depended absolutely on religion. The belief and fear was that without some force beyond mere natural knowledge, there could be no adequate social order.

This late-century fuss, action and reaction against the new progress of "civilization," what Weber would see the new rationalization and intellectualization of society and self, spurred largely by the developments in science, was never far from the center of the Victorians' art, its novels and its poetry. It will be useful, in trying to understand the intensity of Mallock's question and the extraordinary variety of ways in which the Victorians asked and answered it to pause to recognize the pervasiveness of the concern, even in the veriest bromides of Victorian literature, which

---

[11] Matthew Arnold, *Literature and Dogma*, ed. R. H. Super (Ann Arbor: University of Michigan Press, 1980), p. 176.

[12] It is interesting to see how R. H. Hutton treats Arnold's moves in theological arguments: "Mr Arnold is really putting Literature, – of which he is so great a master, – to shame, when he travesties the language of the prophets, and the evangelists, and of our Lord Himself, by using it to express the dwarfed convictions and religious hopes of modern rationalists who love to repeat the great words of the Bible, after they have given up the strong meaning of them as fanatical superstitions" in R. H. Hutton, *Aspects of Religious and Scientific Thought* (London: Macmillan and Co., 1899), p. 329.

bubble over with worry about whether life has meaning and is thus worth living. Even a casual anthology of more or less familiar quotations leaning toward the disenchantment that Mallock's question and arguments imply might will serve as a reminder.

I want primarily to call attention to the way virtually each of these passages implies a dualistic philosophy and sadly or angrily finds the raw experience of the world incompatible with spirit, value and feeling. Newman's famous description of the world without God is, ironically, rich with a sense of the variety and wildness of life, but it is a vision to "dizzy and appall." Ruskin remarkably opens up a vision of the horrors that lie on the other side of the wall, while we take our pleasures. George Eliot talks famously of the roar that lies on the other side of silence. Arnold, wandering between two worlds, looks back at the masters of the mind but finds no place in modernity to be at ease – the old values gone, nothing to replace them. Of course, each poem, each essay, each novel has its own complexly human (and not philosophical) engagement with the things of this world; but each registers the strain of a world from which traditional values have been banished, or in which they are being challenged. But each can be taken as implying, or directly noting, that scientific empiricism has revealed a material world that dumbly tells us nothing about value. If for Arnold, religion is required to touch morality with emotion, for Mallock, R. H. Hutton, Balfour and many others, religion is required even as a sanction for morality itself. Science, teaching us everything about the natural world, teaches us nothing, or worse than nothing, about why life might be worth living.

Deep in the fact or theory of disenchantment lies the traditional Christian *contemptus mundi.* Connolly's comment to Augustine in fact names the "price" of otherworldliness, a disinvestment from life itself, a devaluing of life between the cradle and the grave. Implicitly, natural theology's optimistic and largely failed attempt to make the natural world signify God's presence is displaced in this struggle by a religious pessimism about the world that sees it as intrinsically meaningless – only what lies behind it makes life worth living. Describing the effect of "rationalization and intellectualization" on the world, Weber claims that "the ultimate and most sublime values have retreated from public life either into the transcendental realm of mystic life or into the brotherliness of direct and personal human relations" (p.155). "Ah love, let us be true/ to one another."

Scientific skeptic and religious zealot agree. As Weber put it mockingly, "Who – aside from certain big children who are indeed found in the natural sciences – still believes that the findings of astronomy, biology, physics, or chemistry could teach us anything about the *meaning* of the world?" (142). Life can be worth living when faith seems legitimate. More emphatically, life is worth living *only* when faith is legitimate. There *must* be a realm beyond the natural if the natural itself is to have any "meaning." Meaningfulness – in the particular sense of having some significance beyond the limits of the temporal individual and within some larger moral and spiritual framework inaccessible directly to the limited human consciousness – is a condition of life's being worth living. And meaning derives from a realm of non-material perpetuity, a world of spirit unsusceptible to naturalistic investigation, and therefore from an "enchanted" world.

The battle for enchantment and the battle to believe that life is worth living has to be fought out, however odd it may seem, and against the anti-philosophical arguments of pragmatists like Richard Rorty, on the battlefield of epistemology. In his essay, "Is Life Worth Living?" James in fact reimagines a pragmatist epistemology that allows for a kind of personal knowledge of what more traditional epistemology cannot allow. Can one know anything that cannot be known in the terms of secular investigation? Secular knowledge can itself be a danger. What it is possible really to know is under dispute. Disenchantment is a function of the increased power of science to claim authority over subjects hitherto regarded as mysterious, or spiritual, or inaccessible to rational or empirical study. Knowledge is thus implicated in ethics, and there is an "Ethics of Belief" – which, significantly, became the title of a famous controversial essay by W. K. Clifford – and epistemology gets bound up in the deepest of moral and existential questions. Clifford's argument in effect affirms this fundamental Victorian dualism as it acts out the development of disenchantment. The latter is a product of an epistemology that limits all knowledge to the natural and thus in its explanatory imperialism works corrosively to remove meaning from the world. Clifford's dominant point in his essay – one taken up by virtually all participants in the culture-wide debate – is that it is immoral to believe anything on insufficient evidence. In an appendix on "Liberalism" to his *Apologia*, Newman too had confronted the matter urgently. The Liberal, he says, wrongly believes that "It is dishonest in a man to make an act of faith in what he has not had brought home to him by actual proof."[13] To which, it almost seems, Clifford responded liberally: "it is wrong always,

---

[13] John Henry Newman, *Apologia pro vita sua,* ed. Martin Svaglic (Oxford: Clarendon Press, 1967), p. 260.

everywhere, and for any one, to believe anything upon insufficient evidence."[14]

On the Victorian account, if life is to be worth living, this assertion has to be wrong. Mallock's enemy is not the devil but "Positive thought," particularly as affirmed by Huxley, and Tyndall, and Clifford, and Spencer and Stephen, for they, insisting that natural knowledge is *all* we have, and that it is authoritative everywhere, cross the boundaries between matter and spirit, by way of what is now being called reductionism. Our current battles over "reductionism," particularly as it is played out in the work of Dennett, Richard Dawkins, and Steven Weinberg, is a battle too over the explanatory range of scientific knowledge.

Dennett's most recent book, for example, is called *Breaking the Spell: Religion as a Natural Phenomenon*, and its project is to force acceptance of the idea that religion itself is a proper subject for scientific investigation and to insist that only after we have all the empirical/rational evidence can we know whether religion is a good thing. But Dennett fails to allow himself to recognize, what he surely knows, that what is at stake here is exactly whether religion is a realm for which scientific investigation is appropriate. Dennett's assumption is Clifford's, not Newman's, that it is wrong everywhere and always "to believe anything on insufficient evidence," and of course he means scientific evidence, the only acceptable kind. All of this is eerily reminiscent of the battle into which Mallock inserted himself in the 1870s, and there is no doubt that he would have found Dennett an almost perfect target as spokesman for "positive thought."

Reductionism denies dualism by claiming that phenomena normally understood to belong to the world of spirit or consciousness are subject to naturalistic investigation. The scientific naturalists were happy to recognize non-material phenomena, but simply placed them in the category of the unknowable. In his always confusing way, which Mallock satirizes in *The New Republic*, Tyndall regularly confronts the mind/body problem. At the end of his essay on "Scientific Materialism," he happily confesses that the utmost the scientist "can affirm is the association of two classes of phenomena, of whose real bond of union he is in absolute ignorance. The problem of the connection of body and soul is as insoluble, in its modern form, as it was in the prescientific ages."[15]

---

[14] W. K. Clifford, "The Ethics of Belief," in *Lectures and Essays*, ed. Leslie Stephen and Arthur Pollock (London: MacMillan and Co, 1901), 2 vols., II, p. 175.
[15] John Tyndall, *Fragments of Science* (New York: Appleton and Co., 1899), II, p. 88.

Dualism was at the center of virtually every Victorian argument. On the one hand there is the natural world, open to understanding by way of empirical study and rational analysis; on the other, there is the world behind it, a world of mystery, a world of spirit, an enchanted world. The struggle to preserve "mystery" – the place of enchantment – against science was, among the Victorians, intense. R. H. Hutton, who published weekly essays for the *Spectator*, became a learned and intelligent commentator on the relations between literature and science, and fought the fight for mystery tenaciously. He complains of science's "pretence of solving all mysteries, whereas every new department of science is rooted in mystery" (p. 118) – a point with which Tyndall would have agreed. Hutton almost sounds Darwinian although its real model is natural theology: "If the structure of the eye implies light, if the structure of the ear implies sound, then the structure of our conscience as certainly implies a spiritual presence and judgment, the access of some being to our inward thoughts and motives" (p. 133). But science then leads us to the boundaries of a realm that is not subject to science, a realm of spirit and mystery. Stephen Jay Gould's move to circumvent the growing conflicts between science and religion by describing them as two "non-overlapping magisteria" is a Tyndallian move. Each magisterium is absolutely independent of the other. Daniel Dennett, an outspoken reductionist, has denigrated that move just because it implies a firm boundary between the material and the spiritual, one that both sides reject: "in the minds of the religious it proposed abandoning all religious claims to factual truth and understanding of the natural world ... whereas in the minds of the secularists it granted too much authority to religion in matters of ethics and meaning."[16] In either case, the arguments imply a dualism – a world governed by material and explicable natural forces, and a world governed by spirit and mystery. The Victorians – particularly the non-scientists – were consistently and deeply worried by the crossing of the boundaries, in particular, by the aggressions of science into the world of spirit.

In his essay on "Science as a Vocation," Weber in effect offers his listeners the option of pursuing "science," pursuing knowledge, or, as he thought, honorably enough, returning to the church. You can't do both. Such a return entails "an intellectual sacrifice in favor of an unconditional religious devotion." Weber has no doubt that the intellectual life and faith are incompatible, and this view is in some ways consistent with

---

[16] Daniel C. Dennett, *Breaking the Spell: Religion as a Natural Phenomenon* (New York: Viking, 2006), p. 30.

the dominant Victorian account – counter to our understanding of Victorian culture as doggedly and relentlessly in pursuit of knowledge – that it might be better *not* to know. That is, it might be better not to know the mere material truth of nature, for that truth can only imply value when it is supported by faith in some force beyond nature that allows us to claim that, for example, nature is sacred (p. 117). When positive thinkers try to build morality and the virtues that are connected with enchantment from nature, when, that is, they call nature sacred and try to take it, as Mallock says, as some kind of "vast moral hieroglyph," they are secretly importing into nature values that derive from consciousness. And they are therefore secretly importing faith and a different order of knowledge into what they claim is strictly scientific. That is to say, truth, the hallowed end for "positive thought," as Mallock more or less correctly reads it, is dependent on "faith" after all. Mallock thus implicitly affirms the dualism between the natural and the spiritual by insisting that the natural is without meaning unless it is perceived through the lenses of faith. It derives meaning only from another order of life and being – the transcendent world that requires not scientific knowledge but absolute faith for which there can never be sufficient scientific evidence.

Mallock makes the dualistic point most forcefully by way of his examples. If, on the one hand, the scientific naturalists insist on the responsibilities of duty, love, and so on, how, Mallock wants to know, do they get to those values in the first place. To make his point, Mallock loads the Victorian dice and prints one of the sexiest passages I have ever read in a book by an English Victorian. From Gautier's *Mademoiselle de Maupin,* the passage opposes with delicious frank sensuality the protagonist's horniness and women's sexual splendors against the "Christ" who has "enveloped the world in his winding-sheet" (p. 88). You know things are serious when a Victorian author quotes from a French novel. Mallock's point is that under naturalistic epistemology there is no way to distinguish this sort of love, a raw sensuous celebration "but divested as far as possible of the religious element," from Christian love. While Mallock happily concedes that his enemies, like Huxley, are eminently moral men, they are so not on the naturalistic grounds they claim but because they surreptitiously borrow from the religion they reject. In his essay "Science and Theism" R. H. Hutton makes the point forcefully: "it is the suicide of a science to manufacture a theory of moral obligation out of the materials of physical necessity – a theory of vision for the blind" (p. 58).

This is a point made strongly by Arthur Balfour in *Foundations of Belief* (1895). In many ways, Balfour's is a more effective book in making the case against the idea that one can move from "is" to "ought", from science to religion. As Bernard Lightman has pointed out, Balfour is particularly shrewd in naming the enemy. For Mallock, the enemy was "positivism." For Balfour, the enemy is "naturalism."[17] The idea that everything can be explained (the Weberian idea) in terms of natural causes is the object of Balfour's brilliant polemic. That kind of naturalism, Balfour argues, is not "legitimate science," which knows its own limits. Balfour's case is lucidly, powerfully made right at the start. Considering the nature of morality and the general agreement among all factions that the moral law is "worthy of reverence," and that it "demands our ungrudging submission," he recognizes that "the persons who take a strictly naturalistic view of man and of the universe are often the loudest and not the least sincere in the homage they pay to the 'majesty of the moral law.'"[18] His point is, however, "that in the case of those holding the naturalistic creed the sentiments and the creed are antagonistic." Balfour makes a Weberian case, that the more thoroughly committed one becomes to the "naturalistic creed," "the more certain are the sentiments [of moral law] thus violently and unnaturally associated with it to languish or to die" (p. 16). It is the work of disenchantment that Balfour describes.

Yet the key in these philosophical battles was not so much to demonstrate the incoherence of the positivists' (or naturalists') arguments – although that *was* an important step – but to reclaim the authority of faith from the aggressions of science. Like most anti-science writers at the end of the century, Mallock does not deny science's importance or value, but he maneuvers to put it in its place, to keep it out of the world of values, and to separate natural knowledge from other, spiritual realities. Epistemology is so critical in these battles just because, as Weber was to suggest, the problem with science was that it was attempting to explain "everything," to exempt nothing from its intellectual and evidential rigors. Validating such explanation is Dennett's project today, as it was Clifford's and Huxley's 125 years ago. Absorbing what had traditionally been recognized as spiritual into an explanatory framework that excludes all appeal to the transcendent would seem even to undercut the dualism by which the Victorians sustained their faith in the light of the new intellection.

---

[17] Bernard Lightman, "'Fighting Even with Death': Balfour, Scientific Naturalism, and Thomas Henry Huxley's Final Battle," in *Thomas Henry Huxley's Place in Science and Letters: Centenary Essays* (Athens and London: University of Georgia Press, 1997), pp. 323–50.

[18] Arthur Balfour, *The Foundations of Belief, Being Notes Introductory to the Study of Theology* (London: Longman and Co., 1894), p. 15.

Victorian Positivism failed in part because its acolytes carried to a ritualistic extreme the views, which they shared with their more traditional contemporaries, that life was worth living only if it were infused with the kind of meaning that had traditionally been derived from religious faith. They sought, in fact, a non-theistic enchantment, although along the way they did some silly things in transforming Roman Catholic forms into secular ones and declaring sainthood for the great rationalists and thinkers of history. Huxley mocked the Positivists, but Mallock is right that on the most fundamental issues Huxley is at one with them, and most particularly on the question of the explanatory range of naturalistic knowledge. To be sure, Huxley did not propose a church, and occasionally wrote as though he did not need the sense of wonder and value that religion seemed to provide others, but he wrote with a passion and moral fervor that filled *his* world with meaning. As Adrian Desmond put it, "While Mallock and Hutton slashed at secularism for making life meaningless, Huxley put the meaning back with his essays, equating worth and purpose with duty and honesty."[19] The great moral energy of Huxley's writing is real enough, Mallock would say, but it gets no sanction from the sources Huxley allows. "The universe, as positive thought approaches it," says Mallock, "is blind and dumb . . . Science and history are sullen, and blind and dumb."

Mill said that having learnt what the sunset clouds were made of, he still found that he admired them as much as ever; *'therefore,* he said, *"I saw at once that there was nothing to be feared from analysis.'* And this is exactly what the positive school says of conscience. A shallower falsehood, however, it is not easy to conceive . . . Men of such character . . . may find conscience quite equal to giving a glow, by its approval, to their virtuous wishes; but they will find it quite unequal to sustaining them against their vicious ones; and the more vigorous the intellect of the man, the more feeble will be the power of conscience . . . In various degrees they all yield to temptation; all men in the vigour of their manhood do; and conscience still fills them with its old monitions and reproaches. But it cannot enforce obedience. They feel it to be the truth, but at the same time they know it to be a lie; and though they long to be coerced by it, they find it cannot coerce them. (146)

Where positive thought gives absolute moral dominance to truth, insisting on the heroic capacity of people to face the worst that knowledge can yield, Mallock and his religious counterparts find heroism in just the Carlylean

---

[19]   Adrian Desmond, *Huxley: From Devil's Disciple to Evolution's High Priest* (Reading, MA: Addison. Wesley, 1994; 1997), p. 631.

capacity to resist the knowledge provided by the living busy world, and to return to faith. The peroration of Mallock's book abandons the disenchanting world of science by turning away from knowledge and replaying, with more direct religious implication, the passage of Teufelsdröckh through the "Everlasting No," "The Center of Indifference," and the "Everlasting Yea," though Mallock does not directly invoke Carlyle at all. Because the world with which science is concerned gives no access to value and meaning, "It has made the question of belief or unbelief the supreme practical question for us," Mallock says. Against the corrosive effects of the new knowledge, he argues, we must have "some aims that we may still call high and holy." In this narrative, far from being the positive force that Huxley describes it to be, knowledge is morally disastrous and makes life not worth living. To make life worth living one must, Mallock argues, make an existential choice, the decision, evidence or not, to say yes or no to the question of whether "we are moral and spiritual beings." Like Teufelsdröckh in the "everlasting no," in which "my whole ME stood up, in native God-created majesty," Mallock says that the will "has to create itself by an initial exercise of itself, in an assent to its own existence" (p. 244). Only when that happens will we be able to say "Yes – to say yes without fear, and firmly, and in the face of everything."

There is a parallel movement in James' essay of the same name, for he too takes us, though explicitly, through Carlyle's everlasting no. For James, the first step toward psychological recovery from deep and suicidal pessimism is just to let go of any fantasy about a divine spirit in nature – "nature taken on her visible surface reveals no ... Spirit" (p. 43) – and recognize absolutely both the brute indifference of that nature and something of human resilience in the face of it.

It is striking to note how the battle sometimes took the shape of a contest about whether one should pursue (certain lines of) knowledge at all. From a secular point of view, one might suggest that this is a further "price," in Connolly's sense, that the aspiration to the transcendent imposes on believers. The impossibility of knowing becomes a precious idea rather than, as in science, a constant incitement to try to find out. At the end of his notorious Belfast address (1874), Tyndall warns that "it is perfectly possible for you and me to purchase intellectual peace at the price of intellectual death" (II, p. 200). But, Tyndall goes on, "I would exhort you to refuse the offered shelter, and to scorn the base repose – to accept, if the choice be forced upon you, commotion before stagnation, the breezy leap of the torrent before the foetid stillness of the swamp." But Hutton, whose life was clearly a life of learning, seems to long for the absence of knowing. In fact, he sees the work of science, as it extends into investigations of the human, as still fundamentally incapable of leading us beyond the ordinary: "in none of these separate regions can we solve the ultimate mystery, or in any true sense explain chemical affinity from force, or life ... from chemical affinity of consciousness from life, or memory from consciousness or will from memory" (p. 119).

George Eliot, it might be noted, struggled with this problem in her own work, so overtly and passionately committed to getting it right and telling the truth. When she speaks of the roar that lies on the other side of silence and of the likelihood that we would die if we heard it, she is recognizing (in the way of a great artist) that there *is* a terrifying reality out there; but she is also recognizing how extraordinarily hard and painful it is to live with that knowledge. In her now famous story, "The Lifted Veil," she gives us a protagonist, Latimer, who is gifted with second sight and can read other people's minds, and he leads a wretched life, dies a wretched death. Nonetheless, the main thrust of her work throughout, even with the full consciousness of that roar, is toward the fullest knowledge. It is a secular risk, and Tyndall's high rhetoric of defense of the pursuit of knowledge in that way is appropriate to it.

On Mallock's side of the accounting, however, the moral of this long story would seem to be that, paradoxically, only by cultivating something like *contemptus mundi* can we believe and feel that life is worth living, only by despising the world can we love it and be trusted to live in it decently. Scientific knowledge, whose whole objective is to make things comprehensible, cannot from this perspective really be reconciled to the kind of enchantment that makes us feel the wonder and the mystery of the world, that, as Jane Bennett puts us, leaves us "struck and shaken by the extraordinary amid the familiar and the everyday," that provides us with moods "of fullness, plenitude, or liveliness," that make us smile.[20] Is the moral that there is no reconciling scientific knowledge with the enchantment that gives us a sense of the deep value of life? Weber's disenchantment narrative seems to take us where Mallock ends, and then the question does become the choice between accepting the bleak news of the world – bearing "the fate of the times like a man," Weber says, or abandoning the pursuit of knowledge frankly for the comfort that comes when "the arms of the old churches are opened widely and compassionately for him" (p.155). Is life worth living only when we do not believe that its value "is to

[20]   Jane Bennett, *The Enchantment of Modern Life: Attachments, Crossings, and Ethics* (Princeton: Princeton University Press, 2001), pp. 4, 5.

be found in life itself, in this earthly life, this life between the cradle and the grave"? One of the most dazzlingly eccentric – but now recognizable as representative – arguments for non-knowledge comes from John Ruskin, to whom Mallock dedicated *Is Life Worth Living?* In *The Eagle's Nest*, Ruskin is concerned with the relation between the arts and the sciences, although he is determined to use the word "science" to mean, simply, systematic knowledge. In any case, he argues persistently through the first half of the book that true science is only the fullest possible understanding of what is known, and *not* the constant expansion of the range of knowledge. Such expansion he consistently identifies as corrupt and corrupting. "I pray you very solemnly to put that idea of knowing all things in Heaven and Earth out of your hearts and heads," he preaches. Or to translate it into Weberian terms, do not do away with "mysterious, incalculable forces." Stunningly, he claims, "He that increaseth knowledge, increaseth sorrow."[21] Almost as though he were preparing Weber's argument for him, Ruskin goes on:

Every increased possession loads us with a new weariness; every piece of new knowledge diminishes the faculty of admiration; and Death is at last appointed to take us from a scene in which, if we were to stay longer, no gift could satisfy us, and no miracle surprise. (p. 181)

It is only fair to Ruskin to note that his passion against new knowledge has to do not with the denial of life but with its affirmation. In the passage I have cited, Ruskin juxtaposes the condition of knowledge from that of the child finding in everything grounds for joy and "admiration," and pleasure. But of course, it is just this image of the child that Weber, obviously without reference to Ruskin, picks up when he argues that only a child could connect the new knowledge with affirmations of value. As with everything else, Ruskin's position is complicated and unusual, but certainly, his resistance to the extension of science's reach has to do with a fear that much that it will reveal will be ugly and unpleasant. For Ruskin, all knowledge of appearances, or almost all knowledge of appearances, is necessary. But what can't be seen, the muscles, blood vessels, and all that lies beneath the skin, should *not* be seen. There is, in life-affirming Ruskin, then, a fundamental fear of the flesh, of the ultimate realities of the material world. The more we know, the less we "admire." But against

[21] John Ruskin, *The Eagle's Nest* in *The Works of John Ruskin*, ed. E. T. Cook and Alexander Wedderburn (London: George Allen, 1906), Vol. 22, p. 181.

this sense of things there is the actual experience of many of the scientists, who, in new observations of the minute and complex workings of the natural world, fall back in awe at the intricacy, richness, and variety of the world. Ruskin's sense of the sharp divide between the material and the ideal precludes his ultimate indulgence in scientific minutiae even though his own work is marked by an astonishing attention to minutiae.

So we return to the argument with which this essay began. The strength of Mallock's philosophical demolition of "positive thought" depends in large part upon the assumption that all non-instrumental judgments of value can only derive from some transcendental consciousness, that there is nothing in the natural world that can, in itself, authorize those judgments. Authority, epistemologically, comes then from "will" and "faith" but not from the intellection that Weber takes as the mark of the disenchanted world. The split between science and value becomes virtually absolute. When William James, with a moving sensitivity to the complexities of human motives, and certainly out of his own dark psychological passages, addresses the same problem, he tries to assimilate faith and belief to truth, for, he says, "often enough our faith beforehand in an uncertified result is *the only thing that makes the result come true.*" Most of us are familiar with the kinds of examples James gives, but it is critical to notice that he takes the issues not in a broad general way but by insisting that the very question, "Is Life Worth Living," depends, as he says invoking an old joke about the title, "on the liver" (p. 60). In James' scenario, the consciousness that creates value is the individual human consciousness, and while his whole argument is meant to justify (epistemologically and morally) the possibility that there is a transcendent being, his epistemological move does not sever the spiritual from the here and now and allows human consciousness to be the determiner. His peroration lays it out clearly: "Be not afraid of life. Believe that life *is* worth living, and your belief will help create the fact."

James is peculiarly sensitive to the emotional need that has made enchantment dependent on a larger than individual human consciousness, on a meaning that derives from the possibility of the transcendent. And it is precisely here that the crux comes, as well as Mallock's and James' depreciation of the scientific naturalists. James, too, is appalled by the imperialism of the new science and its encroachment on every department of human life. "When we read . . . proclamations of the intellect bent on showing the existential conditions of absolutely everything," he asserts with something like contempt, "we feel – quite apart from our legitimate impatience at the somewhat ridiculous swagger of the program . . . menaced and negated in the springs of our innermost life."[22] The epistemological issues that Mallock labored take another shape in James, for whom the intellect itself makes only the smallest part of human experience: The "inferiority of the rationalistic level in founding belief is just as manifest when rationalism argues for religion as when it argues against it" (*Varieties*, p. 85).

For James, too – and clearly with James this was a personal reality as he engaged with his own depressive demons – meaning in life inheres in religion, "an unseen order of some kind in which the riddles of the natural order may be found explained" (p. 51). The difference between James and the Victorian commentators discussed here, most particularly Mallock, is that James wants to insist, as he puts it, that "we have a right to believe the physical order to be only a partial order; that we have a right to supplement it by an unseen spiritual order which we assume on trust, if only thereby life may seem to us better worth living again."

James' pragmatic and deeply human resolution to the problem moves some distance from the Victorian dualistic impasse. His moves here make of the essay a kind of epistemological exercise, for he wants to break down the idea that there is no connection between knowledge and value and that "scientific" method cannot be enspiriting. For James, too, of course, the critical need is the "will to believe," but instead of blocking off the worlds of affect and "meaning" from the worlds of natural science, James inserts into the very texture of his philosophy the realities and complexities of human feeling. He seeks "enchantment" after all, but achieves it, if he does, by way of the individual human consciousness and individual desire,[23] and thus along the way avoids that lapse into *contemptus mundi* that narrowed and made futile the Victorians' battle to retain some of the meaning withdrawn with religion itself. The shape of the Victorian debate over enchantment made it almost impossible for any of the participants fully to endorse the idea that Mallock so mockingly denigrates, that meaning "is to be found in life itself, in this earthly life, this life between the cradle and the grave." It is not hard to understand the Victorian resistance to the "positive thought" Mallock attacked, for it is impossible not to realize for how many people "this earthly life" is a continuous battleground of pain, deprivation, loss, and how necessary, therefore, it would

---

[22] William James, *The Varieties of Religious Experience* (New York: Modern Library, 1994; 1902), p. 12.

[23] It is valuable to consider Charles Taylor's recognition of the limitations to James' religion: that is, for James "the real locus of religion is in individual experience" and not in church or community. See Charles Taylor, *Varieties of Religion Today: William James Revisited* (Cambridge, MA: Harvard University Press, 2002).

seem to be able to find something beyond this world to compensate. It is mere superciliousness or academic arrogance to presume to argue against the views of the Victorians and even of James that this life is inadequate, even to itself.

I agree with Jane Bennett: you have to love life before you can care about anything. The question of whether life is worth living remained a live one, and unresolved, for the Victorians, in part because the moral and epistemological dualism of its terms excluded the possibility that life might be its own end, that life might be good enough, that we have world enough and time. There is something to be said for those poor mocked and denigrated Positivists (and for Feuerbach, who so inspired George Eliot), who tried to find a way to think about the world that was not built on *contemptus mundi*, and that did try to find, in the very mixed muddy often ugly condition of being human, the terms of its own validation and the possibility of re-enchantment. That famous Victorian "crisis of faith" largely put beyond the emotional range of many intellectuals the possibility that the loss of religion need not be accompanied with a loss of a sense of meaning and direction in their lives. I hope that, despite the more recent aggressions of science and further convincing demonstrations that "there are no mysterious, incalculable forces," and yet more, despite the horrors we continue to witness, it may still be possible to feel the enchantment of the material world that for Mallock remained "dumb," but that for Darwin provoked a sense of grandeur, and that for me sings every morning at my bird feeder.

CHAPTER 3

Ruskin and Darwin and the matter of matter

What profit can there be in once again juxtaposing Ruskin and Darwin? Everyone knows about Ruskin's hostility to Darwin's theory; most people think that his rejection of it was excessive, retrograde and misguided; and after all, haven't we heard enough about the science wars – culture vs. science, Arnold vs. Huxley; Leavis vs. Snow; Sokal vs. *Social Text*? In fact, virtually none of the issues over which the battles have been fought have been resolved. Stephen Jay Gould may have insisted that religion and science were two "non-overlapping magisteria,"[1] but not a lot of deeply religious or deeply secular people believe it. The issues may slide back beneath the surface, and they may even, as Gould argues, be illogical – though I'm not sure they are – but they continue to infect virtually everyone's relation to matters of "fact," and to leave in contention the matters of "value." However much we may want to argue that science/culture, science/religion are compatible, we all have at least a sneaking suspicion that they are not. The dualism can survive only because it is a dualism – one side, science, has nothing to do with religion; the other side, religion, has nothing to do with science. Theoretically, this is possible. In historical fact, the two have clashed regularly since the Renaissance.

Ruskin was one of the great aggressors in the Victorian version of these wars, in part because the ground that modern science was claiming to cover was ground that he thought he was occupying quite well himself.

---

[1] See Stephen Jay Gould, *Rocks of Ages: Science and Religion in the Fullness of Life* (New York: Ballantine Publishing, 1999). Gould starts by speaking "of the supposed conflict between science and religion, a debate that exists only in people's minds and social practices, not in the logic or proper utility of these entirely different, and equally vital, subjects." He then announces his "Principle of NOMA, or Non-Overlapping Magisteria" (pp. 3, 5). I am usually sympathetic with Gould's pleasant common-sensical take on major issues, but this seems to me fudging badly. If, as he says, the debate exists "only in people's mind and social practices," it exists in the only places that matter. Gouldian logic turns these practical differences into logical errors. Perhaps they are, but even that is debatable. One thing is certain: they will not be resolved by logical argument.

Ruskin's world, registered with the precision and the moral fervor of the ultimate Victorian realist, assimilated "science" to a kind of worldly holiness, aswarm with mythic narratives and moral values; Darwin's world was, well, Darwin's world: rigorously described, in constant motion, complex in its relationships, strenuous in life and death, and entirely material. His was a world that might provide example for Newman's claim that,

the system of physical causes is so much more tangible and satisfying than of final, that unless there be a pre-existent and independent interest in the inquirer's mind, leading him to dwell on the phenomena which betoken an intelligent Creation, he will certainly follow at those which terminate in the hypothesis of a settled order of nature and self-sustained laws. It is indeed a great question whether atheism is not as philosophically consistent with the phenomena of the physical world, taken by themselves, as the doctrine of a creative and governing power.[2]

Ruskin and Darwin, then, practiced two conflicting kinds of "science," the difference between them depending on the "pre-existent and independent interest" they brought to their work. Considering those two together, then, might help throw light on the strange inconsistencies and self-divisions evident in Ruskin's career, and also on the continuing tensions between science and religion, which had provoked Newman's arguments, and which played themselves out with particular intensity among the Victorians. It might, moreover, suggest something about the persistent philosophical (and practical) question of whether it is possible to sustain a firm ethical commitment on the strength of a strictly naturalist representation of the way the world is.

Undertaking to think again about Darwin and Ruskin, I first skimmed the index to the Cook and Wedderburn edition of Ruskin to find all of his Darwin allusions.[3] Simply put, there are a lot (friends have found a few more for me), and most of them show a Ruskin angrily, contemptuously, comically, denigrating what he takes to be Darwinism, though occasionally demonstrating respect for Darwin's naturalist work and, as Cook and Wedderburn say, being quite friendly to him personally. There is, after all, the report of Ruskin's meeting with Darwin where, according to Charles

[2] Quoted in Jack Morrell and Arnold Thackray, *Gentlemen of Science* (Oxford: Clarendon Press, 1981), pp. 240–1; "Faith and Reason, Contrasted as habits of mind," *Fifteen Sermons*, pp. 176–201.
[3] I owe an enormous debt of gratitude to the distinguished Ruskin scholar, Sharon Weltman, and to her graduate assistant, Zach Keller, both for ideas about the relation between Darwin and Ruskin and for a detailed analysis of all the Cook and Wedderburn references. All quotations from Ruskin will be cited in the text from *The Works of John Ruskin*, ed. E. T. Cook and Alexander Wedderburn (London: George Allen, 1906).

Eliot Norton, "Ruskin's gracious courtesy was matched by Darwin's charming and genial simplicity." Darwin was clearly interested in "the variety of scientific attainment which they indicated, and their animated talk afforded striking illustration of the many sympathies that underlay the divergence of their points of view and their methods of thought" (XIX, pp. xliv-xlv). However nasty some of the other allusions to Darwin might be, it is clear not only from this anecdote but from much else that, standing at opposite poles in the developing culture wars, these two giant figures of mid-Victorian culture had much in common besides Victorian gentlemanliness. The fact of their similarities makes their differences both more interesting and more intense.

Among the qualities the two men shared were deference to the realities of nature, and attention to and concern with the most minute particulars, which in turn might then be juxtaposed with enormous and sublime phenomena – worms and earthquakes, mountain heights and blades of grass. They were both, in addition, gradualists, or at least capable of comprehending how the most minute effects, multiplied, could develop into titanic geological features. Ruskin was eager to fight Tyndall – and was not above some nasty name-calling – on the question of how glaciers move, measuring for himself the rate of two inches a day; he measured as well the quantities of almost invisible silt that rush down mountain streams, noting how they can over long periods of time indicate the wearing down of the highest peaks. Yet more striking, although we associate Darwin's name with the modern conception of the world as in constant flux, it was Ruskin who said, "the truths of nature are one eternal change – one infinite variety" (III, p. 145). That sentence might well have been Darwin's.

There was even a chronological coincidence in the publication of their ideas – both achieving their greatest prominence in the 1860s, after Darwin finally finished the *Origin* and Ruskin the fifth volume of *Modern Painters*, both of them under pressure, Ruskin from his father, Darwin from Wallace's independent discovery of natural selection. And that chronological coincidence is matched by intellectual similarities, particularly in their relentless energy, their exceptional powers of observation, their skills in registering what they saw, and, even – though this gets problematic because of Ruskin's ultimate commitment to the permanence of ideals – in their sense of the changeability and constant movement of the world. Moreover, though one doesn't think about this much in relation to Darwin, they were both deeply indebted to Wordsworth's way of imagining the world (Darwin after all read the whole of *The Excursion*, and the most casual reading of his original diary of *The Beagle* voyage marks it as a Wordsworthian book).

Ironically, too, Ruskin made claims for himself as a scientist and was a member of the Geological Society (where he met Darwin), and he even – so he wrote – wanted to be its president. Despite Ruskin's apparent hostility to science, Greville MacDonald was almost right when he claimed that "The whole of Ruskin's mode of investigation and teaching was scientific. It depended upon the accurate collection of predictable facts, the arranging of them in order, and class, and the deduction there-from of the laws governing their nature, their history, their influence."[4] I don't mean to oversimplify: Ruskin's hostility to most of the science practiced in his time is self-evident; but he took the scientists on as a "scientist" himself, proposing other modes of analysis, other modes of classification. This was his turf, and he was certainly scientifically com-mitted to the finest precision of description as he wrote with the confi-dence of a true authority. He didn't hesitate to plunge into scientific disputes publicly, once to the amusement of Darwin.[5]

It is a sad but inevitable commentary on the nature of their positions that Ruskin's writing is full of Darwin; in Darwin's, even in his letters, there is no Ruskin. Ruskin, as Jonathan Smith has shown in great detail, was responding directly, almost as though in conversation with him, to Darwin's arguments in *The Descent of Man*, in *The Expression of Emotion in Man and Animals*, and in his many books on plants – orchids, climbing and insectivorous plants.[6] But Ruskin was seeking a science with a differ-ence. His was a science of the visual and felt experience of things, not of their anatomy, or hidden structures, or origins. As Diana Birch has put it, "the enduring value of Ruskin's rival venture into scientific writing lies in its dissent,"[7] in its attempt "to instill the scientific study of the world with a sense of the imaginative truths embodied in its culture" (p. 153). Some years ago, Edward Alexander argued that in the wonderful exuberance of his intellectual ambitions, Ruskin was attempting "to integrate the modes

[4]   See Derrick Leon, *Ruskin: the Great Victorian* (Hamden, CT: Archon Books, 1969; 1949), p. 276.

[5]   "I was charmed with Ruskin's folly," Darwin wrote to his good friend, the botanist Joseph Hooker. The line would surely have enraged Ruskin, who had joined "in a debate over the role of glaciers in shaping the topography of the Alps." *The Correspondence of Charles Darwin* (Cambridge: Cambridge University Press, 2001), Vol. 12, pp. 450–60.

[6]   Jonathan Smith, *Charles Darwin and Victorian Visual Culture* (Cambridge: Cambridge University Press, 2006). See in particular, chapters 3 and 4.

[7]   Diana Birch, "Ruskin and the Science of Proserpina" in Robert Hewison, ed., *New Approaches to Ruskin* (London: Routledge and Kegan Paul, 1981), p. 143.

of thinking and feeling introduced by modern science with accustomed modes of seeing, knowing, believing, and acting."[8]

Perhaps the most remarkable of all the parallels between them, and the one that most clearly suggests why they had to be opposed intellectually, was what I would call their quest for total explanation. They were among the last of the great totalizers, geniuses who sought to gather everything within their visions and systems. For Darwin, Alexander von Humboldt was a model. The author of that all-encompassing scientific description of the world, *Cosmos*, and of a travel book that became the model for the *Voyage of the Beagle*, von Humboldt was the last major scientific figure to try to hold in his head and to unify all human knowledge. In the preface to *Cosmos*, he describes his objective: "The principal impulse by which I was directed was the earnest endeavor to comprehend the phenomena of physical objects in their general connection, and to represent nature as one great whole, moved and animated by internal forces."[9] Darwin seems not to have begun with such enormous ambitions, wanting perhaps only to experience something of the wonders of the world that von Humboldt had described, particularly on tropical islands. But his theory eventually merged geology and biology and all the new sciences of the human, and entailed as well – at first, not without a struggle – the co-operation of physics. For Ruskin, no single writer provided the model and impetus, although the Bible probably stands at the root of everything he was to say and think. He was instinctively all-embracing: all of world literature, all of world science, all of mythology, all of visible nature barely sufficed. Darwin, in his modesty, and Ruskin in his modest arrogance, were both immodestly embarked on careers that aimed at world-historical significance.

If in 1872, George Eliot set the touch of emerging Victorian skepticism on such enterprises, putting to the test great totalizing ambitions in the figures of Lydgate and Casaubon, in 1860, these two titanically totalizing figures, Darwin and Ruskin, were locked in mortal combat (though Darwin didn't know it) over the fundamental issues of human knowing. Both of their enormously productive early careers moved, in certain respects, more slowly than their talents just because they were so much committed to absorbing everything, learning everything, getting it all right and precisely right. They could only achieve those great heights, echoing the Victorian instinct for compromise, by writing books inferior to their

---

[8]   Edward Alexander, "Ruskin and Science," *The Modern Language Review* 64 (1969): pp. 508–21.
[9]   Alexander von Humboldt, *Cosmos: a Sketch of a Physical Description of the Universe*, transl. E. C. Otté (New York: Harper and Brothers, 1856), p. vii.

own ideals, but masterpieces of their kind nevertheless, by being forced by external pressures to get something down. Left to his own anxious demand for full scientific proof, Darwin might have allowed Darwinism to be known, these days, as Wallaceism; left to his own digressive and omnivorous ways, Ruskin might have allowed the last volume of *Modern Painters* to remain a fragment.

What underlay their differences was not their temperamental incompatibility, certainly not professional jealousy. The difference that lies – intellectually and spiritually, at least – at the root of all the others, was their "pre-existent interest" in what underlay all the totality. For Darwin, it was matter all the way down, and he sought to go down as far as possible, and in so doing transform the significance of what one could see. For Ruskin, there was something under matter (or perhaps above it) that redeemed it from its materiality. The Victorian view (urged polemically by W. H. Mallock) that worldly life could only matter and be meaningful if there lay behind it some spiritual reality is intrinsic to the way Ruskin saw, to the way he felt and experienced everything, even in his exuberant embrace of the material world. The attitudes are manifest in the radically different modes of writing that mark the work of Darwin and Ruskin. For Ruskin, the world is valuable because everything is symbolic; for Darwin the world is valuable because everything is not symbolic, but only what it naturally is. For Darwin the relation of all living organisms does not require reference to the transcendent, nor is it symbolic; for Ruskin every living object has a symbolic relation to some human quality and manifests some link to the transcendent.

If it were matter all the way down, that didn't matter, because for Ruskin matter always signified something non-material. In accounting for everything, in being totalists, they approached matter with radically different "pre-existent interests": their works are built, in each case, on an almost reverent respect for the material world but on fundamentally different conceptions of what matter was. Everything in Ruskin's world is saturated with value; Darwin never *sees* value, even if he values what he sees, but only natural phenomena subject to secondary causes. Paul Sawyer, in discussing Ruskin's hostility to the theories of John Tyndall, has written incisively about Ruskin's revulsion from materialism.[10] But this problem of materialism is exacerbated in Ruskin's relation to Darwin because Darwin, like Ruskin, was ultimately engaged in explaining the

---

[10] See "Ruskin and Tyndall: the Poetry of Matter and the Poetry of Spirit," *Victorian Science and Victorian Values* (New York: New York Academy of Sciences, 1981), pp. 217–46.

totality, which included not only inanimate nature (if, it turns out, there is such a nature), but also all living things, including humanity.

Certainly, despite his deep love of rocks and flowers and mountains and art, Ruskin felt to his heart a ferocious hostility to materialism. But his relation to matter is more complex and variable than the ferocity of his rhetoric at any given moment suggests, and by the end of *Modern Painters* and more consistently in *Queen of the Air*, he had transformed matter into a vast mythology. Alexander has traced the way Ruskin's response to science changed as he found its apparently indiscriminate pursuit of objective knowledge incompatible with what is most vital and human in us. As science became more specialized, it seemed to lose its human connection, to grovel in the material and thus deny the joy of the experience it described. And in the '70s, with *The Eagle's Nest*, *Love's Meinie*, *Proserpina*, and *Deucalion*, Ruskin published a series of ambitious and fragmented "scientific" books, specifically anti-Darwinian, that aimed at a new kind of human-oriented systematization as it played out his aspiration to a humane and joyous science. But Ruskin's system was too unsystematic, too big and rambling and complicated, and none of these books came close to completing the jobs they were invented to perform.

So let's take for granted that despite the similarities, he truly hated what was for him Darwin's inhuman and joyless science, which he invokes gratuitously whenever he is particularly piqued about something, and sometimes when he is not. Even their friendship doesn't prevent him from describing Darwin as "a good sort of man. . .and well meaning, but with very little intellect" (XXIX, 79). The theory is a "mischievous folly," he claims (XXIII, 394). In *Fors Clavigera*, he asks, "Does not Mr. Darwin show you that you can't wash the slugs out of a lettuce without disrespect to your ancestors?" (XXVIII, 154). Gentlemanly politeness gives way as Ruskin spares no rhetoric in his hostility: "All these materialisms, in their unclean stupidity, are essentially the work of human bats; men of semi-faculty or semi-education, who are more or less incapable of so much as seeing, much less thinking about, colour, among whom, for one-sided intensity, even Mr Darwin must be often ranked, as in his vespertilian treatise on the ocelli of the Argus pheasant which he imagines to be artistically gradated, and perfectly imitative of a ball and socket" (XXV, p. 263). Next to the political economists, Darwin's is the name that comes most readily to his pen when he sets out against the culture of the moment, against the degradation of landscape, and art, and human relations, and Christianity. Among the often uproariously funny and gratuitously nasty allusions to Darwin, there is a familiar one over which I want to pause:

we might sufficiently represent the general manner of conclusion in the Darwin-ian system by the statement that if you fasten a hair-brush to a mill-wheel, with the handle forward, so as to develop itself into a neck by moving always in the same direction, and within continual hearing of a steam-whistle, after a certain number of revolutions the hair-brush will fall in love with the whistle; they will marry, lay an egg, and the product will be a nightingale. (XXV, p. 36)

Even in a less parodic form this would have little to do with "natural selection," or Darwin's evolution. While Jonathan Smith has shown just how the language here mirrors some of Darwin's own language in the *Descent* (pp. 130–1), the passage willfully (or not) misrepresents Darwin's argument and is at best a parody of Lamarckianism. Both Darwin and Ruskin are more interesting than this, if not always funnier. What this comic sequence emphasizes, however, and in this respect Ruskin wouldn't have cared about a difference between Darwin and Lamarck, is that the theory of evolution seems to suggest that mere objects, mere things, things without consciousness or feeling can be seen in ways that are appropriate *only* to conscious and spiritual beings. The preoccupation of Darwin with reproduction and the plant organs that do the work is for Ruskin both prurient and obscene; the hairbrush and the whistle are Ruskin's parody of the sexual courting that Darwin emphasized. Ruskin's analogy suggests that Darwinism is utterly mad.

That's actually a serious point, the kind of point made, in less satirical, more solemn ways, by a host of Victorian cultural commentators. So it isn't sufficient, in looking at the relation between these two dominant mid-Victorian figures, simply to dismiss Ruskin's hostility as a retrograde mistake. They were both too smart to be reduced to the kinds of carica-tures Ruskin loved to play with. More interesting is why such very deep hostility. In their implicit battle over the matter of matter, Darwin and Ruskin represent an absolutely central tension in Victorian culture, one which manifests itself in the extremes of Ruskin's brilliant rhetoric, and in the quiet refusal of cultural engagement in Darwin's dogged representa-tion of the way things are – and were.

Jonathan Smith offers one of the most original and insightful explora-tions of this kind of difference, as it manifests itself in the writing and illustrations of the books of Ruskin and Darwin. Smith's basic argument is that Ruskin recognized that Darwin's theory, especially as, in *The Descent of Man*, he tries to argue that our ethical and aesthetic senses were natural-istically derived, challenges absolutely Ruskin's own sense of what art is or should be. The naturalistic alternative that Darwin offered, most particularly in deriving the aesthetic sense from sexual desire, implied for Ruskin aesthetic and moral degradation. If beauty is "ultimately about physical sensation and sexual reproduction rather than morality and character, then it becomes just another form of Victorian escapism, a retreat from commodity culture rather than a confrontation with it. The stakes could not have been higher" (p. 156). Smith's diagnosis, which has the virtue also of not dismissing Ruskin's rejection of Darwin as mere retrograde intellectual failure, is certainly correct. It is Darwin's *way* of looking at the world – his "pre-existent interest," as it were – that is so disturbing to Ruskin. In its scientific detachment from the felt experience of the natural world in order to understand its origins or its hidden structures, it wallows in the material. This kind of scientific objectivity, the detachment of knowledge from a human context, is for Ruskin deadly. It simply misses, and absolutely misses, everything that gives the world value.

At one point in *Proserpina*, Ruskin tells us what's wrong with Darwin's kind of observation:

When therefore I said that Mr. Darwin, and his school, had no conception of the real meaning of the word "proper," I meant that they conceived the qualities of things only as their "properties," but not as their "becomingness"; and seeing that dirt is proper to a swine, malice to a monkey, poison to a nettle, and folly to a fool, they called a nettle *but* a nettle, and the faults of fools but folly; and never saw the difference between ugliness and beauty absolute, decency, and indecency absolute, glory or shame absolute, and folly or sense absolute. Whereas the perception of beauty, and the power of defining physical character, are based on moral instinct, and on the power of defining animal or human character. Nor is it possible to say that one flower is more highly developed, or one animal of a higher order, than another without the assumption of a divine law of perfection to which the one more conforms than the other. (XXV, pp. 268–9)

Insofar as this kind of procedure would even have been comprehensible to Darwin, it would have seemed utterly beside the point of science. Though inconsistently, Darwin resisted the idea of "higher" and "lower" organisms, which might have been for Ruskin even worse than pretending to identify ranks without reference to "a divine law of perfection." For Ruskin, clear vision entailed a preliminary moral condition. Without that moral precondition, one cannot see and one cannot know in any way that truly matters. That is one of the reasons that seeing, for Ruskin, was a prophetic act; not merely science (though including science) but also visionary, literally and metaphorically; and this is one of the reasons that art, for Ruskin, is always revelatory of the culture's (not to speak of the artist's) moral condition. But then, so too is science. And a science that sees nettles only as nettles, swine only as swine, snakes only as snakes, and matter only as matter is a degraded and a degrading science. It is not seeing what really matters.

It might be worth pausing over at least one of Ruskin's pieces of "science," to get a sense of how he was a remarkable observer of the natural world and at the same time brought to bear upon that world the "pre-existent" moral dispositions that, on his accounting, make seeing possible in the first place. As Alexander points out, the transition to the new science comes most forcefully in *Modern Painters, V*, and let me quote from there an ostensibly realist discussion of leaves, but one that is entirely dependent on metaphors and analogies as it sees in the very formations of the natural world moral fables:

The mineral crystals group themselves neither in succession, nor in sympathy; but great and small recklessly strive for place, and face or distort each other as they gather into opponent asperities. The confused crowd fills the rock cavity, hanging together in a glittering, yet sordid heap, in which nearly every crystal, owing to their vain contention, is imperfect, or impure. Here and there one, at the cost and in defiance of the rest, rises into unwarped shape or unstained clearness. But the order of the leaves is one of soft and subdued concession. Patiently each awaits its appointed time, accepts its prepared place, yields its required observance. Under every oppression of external accident, the group yet follows a law laid down in its own heart; and all the members of it, whether in sickness or health, in strength or languor, combine to carry out this first and last heart law; receiving, and seeming to desire for themselves and for each other, only life which they may communicate, and loveliness which they reflect. (VII, pp. 49–50)

The passage earns its implicit metaphors, its moral judgments, by virtue of its relation to the meticulous analysis of leaf-shapes and textures which precede it. Moreover, it is precisely descriptive in spite of its extravagance, offering a convincing image of both rocks and leaves. Science and moral parable become one. Inorganic stones are instantly recognizable as individuals within a laissez-faire economy; the inference that political economy is modeled on inorganic nature and therefore means death is hard to avoid. Similarly, leaves demonstrate the priority of life, and the necessary connection of life with community, love, and self-sacrifice. Ruskin's biological laws are in effect sermons: "So soon as there is life at all, there are these four conditions of it, – harmony, obedience, distress, and delight-some inequality" (V, p. 82). Read for this the theory of evolution by natural selection and one can see how the same ideas are transferred into a new set of metaphors – organic interdependence, the struggle for existence, and survival of the fittest – which obviously require a totally different set of intellectual and cultural priorities, but most strikingly also derive from a pre-existent moral condition that allows Darwin to interpret the material world without an allusion to moral law. The only law is physical law. Ironically, of course, in the long run Darwin wants to blur the boundaries between plant and animal so that while here Ruskin gives what seems metaphorical animation to the leaves, Darwin will give them just the kinds of qualities – particularly in his discussions of climbing and insectivorous plants – that indicate non-metaphorical, literally material connection with the human.

From *Modern Painters*, Ruskin goes on to what he later calls the safer guidance of primal mythology, the myths, for example, of "Proserpina and Deucalion are at least as true as Eve or Noah; and all four together incomparably truer than Darwinian theory." "In general," he claims, at the start of *Deucalion*,

The reader may take it for a first principle, both in science and literature, that the feeblest myth is better than the strongest theory: the one recording a natural impression on the imaginations of great men, and of unpretending multitudes; the other, an unnatural exertion of the wits of little men, and half-wits of impertinent multitudes. (XXVI, pp. 98–99)

Later, in *The Queen of the Air*, Ruskin explicitly affirms the natural theology implicitly initiated in *Modern Painters, V*. Attempting, as ever, to impose order on an endlessly proliferating reality (and thus, even in the throes of his mythological mission, he feels the pull of a Darwinian world), Ruskin finds his subject running out from under him. The discriminations multiply, related stories fill footnotes: the queen of the air comes to preside over all of nature, but in ways that defy system. At last, examining Athena, this time as "a Spirit of Creation and Volition," Ruskin confronts Darwin once more: "whatever the origin of species may be, or however those species, once formed, may be influenced by external accident, the groups into which birth or accident reduce them have distinct relation to the spirit of man" (XIX, p. 358). It is a pre-condition of all Ruskin's science that the world, inorganic, organic, beautiful, hideous, bear a "distinct relation to the spirit of man." "Where man is not, nature is barren," says Blake, and so too does Ruskin. Without that relation it is meaningless; with it, all that is important is explained. However deferential to the natural world he may be, Ruskin's world is radically anthropocentric.

There is another irony in Ruskin's relation to Darwin. He advises his readers to ignore "origins." We have no need to know origins, he says, and he is appalled by the preoccupation with the grubby materiality involved in knowing those origins or in lingering over courtship and conception as opposed to seeing the thing as it is.[11] But in dealing with these larger issues Ruskin's, strategy is to retreat outside the range of Darwin's theory – to the very origin of matter, the origin of the materials that Darwin would take as given for his own naturalistic explanation of species development. That origin, of course, is not material, and the move allows language, with Biblical resonances, to generate metaphysical agencies – "a power which creates that calcareous earth itself." Affirm any reality in language and one implies a prior reality, and an identity separate from any manifestation of it. The "power" creates the calcareous earth,

separately, and quartz, separately, and gold, separately, and charcoal, separately; and then so directs the relations of these elements that the gold may destroy the souls of men by being yellow, and charcoal destroy their souls by being hard and bright; and quartz represent to them an ideal purity; and calcareous earth, soft, may beget crocodiles and, dry and hard, sheep; and the aspects and qualities of these two products, crocodiles and lambs, may be, the one repellent to the spirit of men, the other attractive to it, in a quite inevitable way, representing to him states of moral evil and good, and becoming myths to him of destruction, redemption, and, in the most literal sense, 'word' of God. (XIX, p. 359)

This too, it seems, is science, but it is obviously science that depends absolutely on the relation of matter to the human, to human perception, and on the ultimately unmaterial sources and nature of matter. Ruskin's science challenged a science that deferred absolutely to matter, that was visible and tangible and subject entirely to laws of matter, and that would not define nature by its relation to the human. Ruskin's science is his way of confronting the crisis of the new secularity that is one of the distinctive marks of Victorian culture. If matter is not *only* matter, then the authority of science and the scientific naturalists has to be reconsidered, particularly in the light of the spiritual and moral and historic elements that are inwoven with mere matter. The new rationality, the new science, this further geometrically multiplied assertion of the values of the Enlightenment, required of science and economics and the new human sciences total, rationally coherent and fully naturalistic explanations for everything. (This is the condition that Max Weber would later argue was the cause of the disenchantment of modernity.) Alexander von Humboldt's all embracing Enlightenment enterprise was to co-ordinate and encompass everything and thus make the world known. And although most of the

---

[11] In considering the illustrations that Darwin and Ruskin use for flowers, for example, Jonathan Smith points out that Darwin is concerned with the functional, inseminating features of the flowers, but Ruskin will usually not even draw in those features, looking at the flowers from angles that disguise them.

people we think of as "scientists" in those earlier years of the nineteenth century were also highly cultured students of literature and myth and the ancients, they tended to seek exclusively secular answers to their fundamental questions about origins or ends – no vestige of a beginning, no prospect of an end; only continuing analyses of the world we know now. *On the Origin of Species* was, in fact, not about ultimate origins, but only about the process that began after the Origin. While Ruskin insisted that we do not need to know anything about our origins and that the quest to study origins was in fact degrading, it is Darwin who refuses to worry about ultimate origins; it is Ruskin who looks back to the ultimate origin, to the "power" that created the calcareous earth.

One can see why, for the Victorians, how one feels about matter here and now becomes a matter of life and death. In his *Is Life Worth Living?*, which he dedicated to Ruskin, W. H. Mallock in effect asked whether life would matter if there were only matter. The simple answer was "no." His explanation is distinctly Ruskinian. If life is *only* life, if it is all about the material world in which we are embodied, it has no value at all. Mallock criticizes those whom he calls "positive thinkers," like Huxley, Tyndall, Lewes, Stephen, Spencer, for affirming that value "is to be found in life itself, in this earthly life, this life between the cradle and the grave." The consequence of this, Mallock claims, is that "they have taken everything away from life everything that to wise men hitherto seemed to redeem it from vanity."[12] Ruskin found Mallock's arguments "faultlessly logical" (XXIX, p. 216). "Vanity," a word with Biblical resonance, is precisely what Ruskin recognized in the contemporary science that required of its acolytes a radical objectivity, a turning away from the human needs, human desires, human interests, in order to get as close as possible to the matter that was its subject.

Ironically, then, Ruskin, who sought another kind of selflessness before art and before the natural world, saw scientific selflessness as a form of self-interest and degradation, rather like the vanity displayed, from Ruskin's point of view, in the realistic representations of seventeenth-century Dutch painting. In considering the two kinds of science, we tend to give the palm of precise and meticulous observation to Ruskin, however fine Darwin's perceptions might be. But Ruskin, in the end, could only see what he could transform into myth and morality. And it is a genuine question whether Darwin, who would not moralize ichneumenidae or other kinds of parasites, who described the sexual organs of barnacles,

---

[12] W. H. Mallock, *Is Life Worth Living?* (London: Chatto and Windus, 1879), p. 9.

who spent years worrying about the defecation of worms, euphemistically called "castings," was not in the end even more precise than Ruskin in his observations of the visible world, and whether the relentless precision and pursuit of "fact" that marked his life's work was not, in some ways, worthy of rather high moral marks, even in the Ruskinian scheme of things.[13]

And thus, although one of the things that most absolutely distinguished Ruskin from the austere and Calvinist-minded Carlyle, his most immediate prophetic antecedent, was his love of the visible world, there was yet something that divided him permanently, something in him that shared Carlyle's revulsion from mere matter, as, for example, it is expressed in Teufelsdröckh's condition as he plunges toward the everlasting no: "To me the Universe was all void of Life, of Purpose, of Volition, even of Hostility: it was one huge, dead immeasurable Steam-engine, rolling on, in its dead indifference, to grind me limb from limb."[14] The fundamental argument against the attempt to substitute modern science for traditional religious thought was that there was no way to build a morality or an ideal from mere matter. Mallock makes this case repeatedly. A. J. Balfour, in *Foundations of Belief,* makes it forcefully: "If naturalism be true, or, rather, if it be the whole truth, then is morality but a bare catalogue of utilitarian precepts; beauty but the chance occasion of a passing pleasure; reason but the dim passage from one set of unthinking habits to another. All that gives dignity to life, all that gives value to effort, shrinks and fades under the pitiless glare of a creed like this."[15] These are Ruskinian sentiments, almost at the level of Ruskinian rhetoric.

Thus, despite Ruskin's obvious passion for the natural world, manifested not only in explicit reverence for some of its aspects but in the almost mad precision of his observation of the texture of flowers and clouds and the movements of water and glaciers, he retained, even in the days when he had fallen away from his parents' rigorous religiosity, something of the deep Christian distrust of materiality. Naturalism simply could not be "the whole truth." We have already seen examples of how Ruskin is never satisfied to describe the physical object without some sense that the object is more than itself, that is, more than matter. His realism, about which he writes with such passion in the third volume of *Modern Painters*, is visionary, and he saves matter by, in effect, refusing it and

---

[13] For a sustained argument that Darwin's way of viewing the world provides a model for moral engagement despite its disinterestedness, see my *Darwin Loves You: Natural Selection and the Disenchantment of the World* (Princeton: Princeton University Press, 2006).
[14] Thomas Carlyle, *Sartor Resartus* (New York: Odyssey Press, 1937), p. 164.
[15] A. J. Balfour, *The Foundations of Belief* (New York: Longmans, Green, and Co., 1895), p. 77.

turning it into allegory. So his gorgeous love of the physical world issues in that astonishing rhetoric that humanizes everything, crystals, leaves, clouds, water. Remember the distinction he establishes between the Dutch painters, who attend only to "literal truth," and the Italian, "who attend only to the invariable, the great and general ideas which are fixed and inherent in universal Nature" (V, pp. 23–24). The literal truth is a "lower" one, and in fact Ruskin right from the start tries to theorize the virtues, particularly in his early treatments of Turner, of an ideal truth that is nevertheless as literally true as one can be in a world that is always changing and moving.[16] His admiration of Turner, in fact, seems to me an aspect of his divided attitude toward matter itself. He despises the Dutch truth-tellers, who give us, as he perceives them, merely the literal condition, freezing figures from ordinary life in clearly defined moments that are anything but beautiful – on his "theoretic" accounting. He admires the ideal, which he sees Turner attaining, in part because his paintings seem on first view so unrealistic but in fact capture better than any one before the changeableness and motion of clouds and sky and water and nature itself.

But in the end, even with Turner, nature must be something other than what we literally see, must derive its very physical beauty from a non-material condition: the changeableness that Turner so brilliantly captures becomes an emblem of modernity, and despite Turner's greatness, therefore, a sign of a falling away from the ideal serenity of earlier landscapes, earlier ways of being. Even in his earliest superb descriptions of Turner paintings, Ruskin fills them with significance and movement and moral strength that the ordinary viewer can only see, as most of them see them now, because Ruskin has told us a story that there is every possibility Turner never imagined. Ruskin, as Charlotte Brontë says, teaches us how to see, but seeing is seeing beyond the visible, recognizing the visible as something like an allegory of the ideal. While there are long sequences in his work that seem, indeed, to be disquisitions in the science of the material world, Ruskin's science will always, immediately or eventually, turn into both a moral screed and a kind of mythology. The science of

---

[16] For a thorough discussion of Ruskin's attitude toward the Dutch Painters, see Ruth Yeazell's *The Art of the Everyday: Dutch Painting and the Realist Novel in Britain and France* (Princeton: Princeton University Press, 2007). Yeazell argues that "Ruskin's contempt for Dutch art is impossible to separate from his disapproval of its subject matter." I would suggest that the merely material, without possible mythological or moral interpretation, is anathema to Ruskin. The "carnal" without redemption; the "ale-house and the card-table" are the equivalent in Ruskin's moral scheme to the sheer sexual material that points to our Darwinian origins.

aspects, the visionary science, is in the long run freed from the touch of matter even as it manages to describe, sometimes in breathtaking and gorgeous ways, the sensations that the visualized object might produce. That, at least, was the direction of his career from *Modern Painters, V* onward. The material world is a vehicle for spiritual conditions that can be seen and understood best as they are allegorized in myth.

The world of Enlightenment, entirely secular matter, for a whole culture that had largely been raised within some form of Christian tradition, immediately raised the question of value. What does matter matter if it is *only* matter? There is no space in such a world for any value but use value. In Darwin's theory, the driving value is always functional: what works to make for reproduction? Darwin's theory, no matter what apparently non-utilitarian excitements Darwin himself felt, reads the world as though it can be explained almost entirely in terms of how organisms devise ways to reproduce – not only the species themselves are dependent on this, but the particular qualities of the species, including morality and art. What is missing from matter is just non-utilitarian value. As Smith points out, the non-utilitarian is the province of the art that Ruskin defended as some might defend a church. If all value were utilitarian, art would be nothing but another form of matter, worthy only in so far as it makes something happen.

How might the new culture resolve this tension between secularity and the religious traditions that had in earlier ages presided over morals? How might Ruskin reconcile his almost physical thrill at the colors of the world and of art, at the shapes of mountains and landscape, with the saturated readings of the Bible that occupied him every day of his childhood? Ruskin's passionate differences from Darwin and from contemporary science, which surely threatened to turn those landscapes to dust, had little to do with this or that particular reading of nature – no matter how furious he got with Tyndall's glacier theory, or how angry he got about Darwin's evolution theory. What mattered was the focus on matter and the mode of that focus. On this the two were absolutely and temperamentally divided. On this, the heaviest load of cultural and moral significance lay.

Take, for example, Ruskin's view of flowers. In *Proserpina*, he claims, "The flower exists for its own sake, – not for the fruit's sake. The production of the fruit is an added honour to it – is a granted consolation to us for its death. But the flower is the end of the seed" (XXV, p. 350). Here, boldly and unapologetically, is the assertion of a value other than use value – an aesthetic value. But of course, in the end for Ruskin everything valuable is valuable only insofar as it relates to the human, and the "non-utilitarian" beauty of the flower is an aspect of the possible moral redemption of man that art (and correct observation) can offer. The end product is for us.

Darwin's books about plants, like *The Different Forms of Flowers on Plants of the Same Species*, or *The Various Contrivances by which Orchids are Fertilised by Insects*, are even in their titles unremittingly specialized and unremittingly focused on modes of reproduction. He looks at and measures stamen and pistils and pollen, and follows the various transformations of flowers as the plants find better ways to reproduce. One can sympathize with Ruskin's hostility, in particular if the point of his work is to make the plants and their moral significances knowable to the lay reader. Unlike the writing in his more famous books, Darwin's writing in these technical elaborations of points in support of his overall theory makes no concessions to ordinary perceiving and insists on looking at things that might undermine the mythic significances Ruskin always finds. The entire subject is sex. Sex determines the length of the pistils and stamens, the fact that certain flowers "exist under two or three forms," and are thus "heterostyled," the fact that some flowers have remained self-pollinating, hermaphroditic, in parts but are more "perfectly fertile" when they have been fertilized with pollen from another form.[17] One can virtually feel Ruskin's shudder of aversion, from the language adopted, the subjects described, and the utilitarian values implied.

It is, then, a little difficult to be disturbed by Ruskin's bowdlerized botany, in particular when it leads to such extraordinary imaginations of the world as he gives us in his allegorical looking. His energies are directed to the visible joys of the material world, to its vitality, while Darwin's is directed toward its function. Note, for example, how in *The Queen of the Air* Ruskin talks about these flowers: "The main fact, then, about a flower is that it is the part of the plant's form developed at the moment of its intensest life; and this inner rapture is usually marked externally for us by the flush of one or more of the primary colours ... in all cases, the presence of the strongest life is asserted by characters in which the human sight takes pleasure, and which seem prepared with distinct reference to us, or rather, bear, in being delightful, evidence of having been produced by the power of the same spirit as our own" (XIX, p. 358). The compensation of the fruit for the loss of the flower is *our*

---

[17] Charles Darwin, *The Different Forms of Flowers on Plants of the Same Species* (Chicago: Chicago University Press, 1986; 1877), pp. 2–3.

compensation. But in making the flowers ours to perceive Ruskin misses the other kind of moral implications of Darwin's materialist rigor. The wonderful "rapture" of the flower that Ruskin describes, implying a deep imaginative sympathy (mutedly sexual even) for the flower, is less about the flower than about Ruskin.

Darwin's rigorous prose (like the more available prose of his more famous books) is also, however, dependent on "a feeling for the organism," but one that makes material science possible: that is, he tries to understand what the organisms are doing from the point of view of the organisms. The pistils of some flowers are shaped in ways that make them peculiarly receptive to pollen from other plants, and thus guarantee more robust offspring. Darwin writes, then, as he tries to understand, he tries to imagine, what the organism gets out of it, regardless of the subsidiary pleasures it might also offer man. And he can do this only because he does not begin with the assumption that the world is designed for humans, that matter unmythologized is contemptible. Inhuman matter, for Darwin, has its own intrinsic value. That it is not pretty, that Darwin doesn't, as Ruskin rightly argues, recognize the "beautiful" or the "good" in the natural world he describes, is partly a function of that primary, preliminary commitment to value the material for its own sake and to look at it as intensely.

So Ruskin's view of flowers suggests another way in which he produces a kind of natural theology, in which organisms do not flourish so much for their own sakes, but for ours. And they do so under the guidance of an overriding moral law. Here, even before the publication of Darwin's *Origin*, Ruskin is asserting an anti-Darwinian botany. The flower is the jewel of the plant, "each bud more beautiful itself, than perfect jewel . . . the glory is in the purity, the serenity, the radiance – not in the mere continuance of the creature." So that when Darwin worries the question of "continuance" he is looking at the wrong thing, in the wrong place. For Ruskin, even here, it doesn't theoretically matter whether Darwin's theory is right about how from generation to generation characteristics are inherited. What matters is the flower itself, and "it is because of its beauty that its continuance is worth Heaven's while" (XXV, p. 250). As Sharon Weltman has put it, for Ruskin Darwin simply misses the point. "The origin of the plant is irrelevant. What matters is the aesthetic and spiritual significance."[18]

---

[18]   Much of my thought about Ruskin has been influenced by Sharon Weltman, who in a letter to me made these points.

And yet it is a pity that Ruskin resisted so furiously Darwinian insights and talents that absolutely parallel his own. Ruskin's "negative capability" in relation to the flower makes him feel the "internal" rapture, although he sees the beauty emerging from that rapture as designed for human aesthetic appreciation not for the flower's fulfillment. The vision is an indication that the flower and the man are united under the creative power that has the "same spirit as our own." But this is just the insight that the imaginative Darwin has as he looks at orchids, or at the Argus pheasant's magnificent tail. He recognizes that the female pheasant (whom Ruskin was to mock) shares human aesthetic appreciation, and her attraction to the beauty of the tail leads through long generations to those pheasants with the most remarkable tails having the greatest success in breeding. But in the end, this kind of imagination leads Darwin to see the bird and the flower sharing "the same spirit as our own," in the most literal sense. It is Darwin's fundamental argument – that we are literally, not metaphorically, all one family. And though Ruskin will want us to feel all supported by a single spirit, he cannot bear that we should be bound materially.

Darwin's anthropomorphic instincts allowed him to develop this fundamental insight of his work; but his anthropomorphism does not turn into anthropocentrism. Rather, it allows him to reject anthropocentrism as a distorting egoism. Ironically, then, Ruskin's way of looking at the world suffers from precisely the egoism he condemned in Darwin, science, and Dutch art. He sees the flower, gets close to imagining what a flower feels like, and ends by imagining not what this does for the flower but what it does for humans. It is an ironic twist in the implicit moral war between Darwin and Ruskin.

One can imagine Ruskin wincing as Darwin explains why flowers often grow so as to expose their sensitive and vulnerable anthers to the weather, unprotected. "The fullest freedom for the entrance of pollen from another individual will explain this state of exposure" (*Origin*, p. 97). The shapes and colors of flowers, in Darwin's world, are dependent on their function in reproduction, the spreading of seed. And this, for Ruskin, who will impose his culture's most rigorous moral codes on nature, is just a kind of pornography.

We don't need to know our "origins," Ruskin insists: "it is not necessary for any young persons, nor for many old ones, to know, even if they *can* know, anything about the origin of species." But he says, "it is vitally necessary that they should know what a species *is*" (XXVI, p. 304). Here again is an impulse that drives Darwin himself, except that for Darwin, what one *is* must be understood as something in history, whose very nature is dependent on its past and likely to transform in the future. This would, in the first instance, seem to be utterly Ruskinian, too, for as we have seen Ruskin knows all too well that the world is in constant flux.

But it is not. "The first thing that will strike us, or that ought to strike us, in modern landscapes, is their *cloudiness*" (V, p. 317). They ask us to triumph in "mutability; to lay the foundation of happiness in things which momentarily change or fade; and to expect the utmost satisfaction and instruction from what it is impossible to arrest, and difficult to comprehend." The vision is positively Darwinian, except that there is the implication that these cloudy and mutating spaces are laden with moral significance. Nevertheless, Ruskin claims that "attention to the real form of clouds, and careful drawing of effects of mist" produces a new "subject of science," as we learn the real form of clouds, "the effects of mist on vision," and "aerial perspective." Here is Ruskinian mutability to be set against the Darwinian version, which blurs the sharp outlines of difference everywhere, and destabilizes the concept of species entirely.

But this is a kind of mutability and instability that Ruskin couldn't abide, even if it were accurate. As we have seen, while he is not interested in the origin of species, he is adamant that students should know what a species is. And while it is likely that Ruskin is being playful as he proceeds in that remarkable performance, "The Living Wave," he is implicitly serious when he allows that yes, "between the ... species, or families, there are invariable links – mongrel creatures, neither one thing nor another, but clumsy, blundering, hobbling, misshapen things" (XXVI, p. 304). Aren't we thankful, he asks, "that we're not one of those, a penguin, for example, who lies somewhere on the genealogical scale between a windhover and a trout" (p. 305).

With his profound sense of mutability, it is not odd that Ruskin probably was a believer in evolution, of some kind or other. In *Love's Meinie*, there is a passage that suggests that he does accept evolution. Noting the difference between the forces that work on inorganic matter and on "life," he argues that "the infinitely more exalted powers of life must exercise more intimate influence over matter than the reckless forces of cohesion; – and that the loves and hatreds of the now conscious creatures would modify their forms into parallel beauty and degradation, we might have anticipated by reason, and we ought long since to have known by observation." But there is contempt for Darwinian theory even in this, because any fool might have known before Darwin that living creatures "would modify their forms"! But once again, the evolution he implies is Lamarckian, rather than Darwinian, a much less "self-evident" and less humanly attractive idea. Characteristically he emerges from this recognition of mutability with an implicit assertion of moral strength. The "wonder," he says, is not that species should sometimes be confused, but that "the greater number of them remain so splendidly, so manifestly, so eternally distinct, and that the vile industries and vicious curiosities of modern science, while they have robbed the fields of England of a thousand living creatures, have not created in them one" (XXV, p. 56). Finally, in his characteristically self-divided way, he thinks of species as absolute identities, subject as they may be to the fluctuations of time and history. When he says we must know what a species *is*, he surely believes that there *is* some permanent ideal condition of the species.

It is, finally, the dogged refusal to take matter for anything but matter that makes Ruskin and Darwin irreconcilable. Bowing to Lamarckian evolution – a rather quick bow, one would have to say – Ruskin allows into the world he will believe in a process that depends on will, intention, love, and hate. It is a humanly recognizable process, one which, by the end of the century, Samuel Butler and George Bernard Shaw were fighting for with considerable contempt for Darwin's theory. Ruskin, surely, could never accept Darwin's summary of the material world he has described: "there is grandeur in this view of life." Without reference to the human, the world of matter lay for Ruskin as Balfour and Mallock describe it, without meaning, without value. Driven by a passion for the world that made him reject Carlyle's Calvinist austerity, Ruskin could not take it on its own terms. Matter could never merely be matter. Nettles could never merely be nettles. So we return again to Ruskin's primary predisposition in his scientific and artistic study: "All true landscape, whether simple or exalted," he claims, "depends primarily for its interest on connection with humanity, or with spiritual powers" (VII, p. 255).

In Ruskin's science, finally, the ideal trumps the particular; the particular matters insofar as it images forth the ideal. As the famous passages in "The Nature of Gothic" make clear, Ruskin's attitude toward the individual and particular are complex. He wants to encourage the work of individual craftsmen contributing to the irregularity and vitality of Venetian buildings, and he is appalled by the mechanical "perfection" of modern machine production. But for him, as well, the particular and individual mark a step away from the ideal. His hostility to modern capitalist individualism is both moral and aesthetic: moral in that it indicates a refusal of community, sharing, compassion; and aesthetic in that it leads to a disorder that violates the ideal. His developing appreciation of Italian art was opposed not only to the Northern art of the Flemish painters but even, implicitly, to the extraordinary "realism" of Turner with which his career started. For Darwin, too, the material entailed imperfection (but in this world, that is all there is). The nature of his science was to deal thoroughly, unrelentingly with the material and the imperfect. Imperfection was no invitation for Darwin to seek the ideal but a means to recognize real material history and a demonstration that the ideal readings of earlier scientists and theologians had caused them to misunderstand how nature really worked, and to recognize that it was the very engine of imperfection and change that drove the transformation of species.

With all that it is important to admit that when it comes to the quality and power of writing, Darwin does not belong in the same league with Ruskin. It was, as Ruskin might have said, a strictly utilitarian prose, and yet in its work of reimagining the world and finding the forms that might best represent the way things are against the long tradition of language and scientific description that found little means for the mutability and mindlessness of matter in unceasing process, Darwin's writing requires attention and admiration too. He wrote for the nineteenth century a new and coherent narrative of ultimate (or almost) origins that, ironically, far more powerfully influenced the way most people think and feel than any of the wonderful myths that Ruskin wrote.

The differences in style properly sum up the irreconcilable differences that underlay their passion for the natural world. Darwin's project was enormously difficult, for part of his labor was to *resist* the tug of language toward the ideal. He had to locate and invalidate the fundamental figure by which all language – depending on abstraction for its power to transcend the limits of any particular time and place – implies an ideal reality underlying phenomena, and may, by virtue of its intrinsic character, as naturally create fictions as it does represent a non-verbal reality. Often, as Ruskin clearly thought, Darwin's prose was anything but "beautiful," and that absence of beauty Ruskin surely would have found indicative of his being hopelessly mired in matter. But being mired in matter was, to play with paradox, just Darwin's ideal.

The whole argument of the *Origin* hangs on Darwin's ability to break free of the constraints of language, to make nouns flexible and put them in motion, so that the concept of self-identical species is broken down and the possibility of recognizing every species as an historical form opens up. "No clear line of demarcation," he says," has as yet been drawn between species and sub-species; varieties and individual differences. These differences blend into each other in an insensible series; and a series impresses the mind with the idea of an actual passage."[19] Ruskin was not the first to recognize that Darwin trapped himself in a paradox in that he had to write about species while in effect denying their reality (in any but an historical, practical, material sense). But the trap is a linguistic one, for language can only affirm by implying categories and classes. It had no form to affirm the irrevocability of change and variation without metaphor, and Ruskin's gorgeously rich manner of registering a world in flux depends, finally, on the substratum of the ideal. So here, Darwin uses the metaphor of "passage" to connect organisms that have hitherto been connected only through timeless similarities of structure. And Ruskin's scientific systematics, we have seen, entail mythic and moral and non-literal connection among organisms, making those connections by way of the life of the organisms in myth, beyond matter. But as Gillian Beer has put it, "In the process of Darwin's thought, one movement is constantly repeated: the impulse to substantiate metaphor and particularly to find a real place in the material order for older mythological expression."[20]

For the most part, Ruskin's brilliant use of metaphor and his application of myth to the material world works in a reverse way – that is, to transform the material into the metaphor, into the mythic. And it is in this ultimate respect, working its way down to the very use of language, that Darwin and Ruskin's science stand utterly opposed. It is not that Ruskin doesn't believe in "evolution." It is not that he doesn't believe in sexual selection (although like most of his even more expert contemporaries, he had his doubts). It is not that he disagrees with Darwin about the nature of the pheasant's ocelli (though he does). The difference is that Darwin's work – even, and particularly, his metaphors – drags us back relentlessly to the material, to matter; Ruskin's work struggles in the most extraordinary variety of forms and linguistic manipulations, to pry us free of it. Although the subject is secular, it reverberates in Ruskin's prose with the resonances of religion. "Desert," he claims, " – whether of leaf or sand – true desertness is not in the want of leaves, but of life. Where humanity is not, and was not, the best natural beauty is more than vain. It is even terrible; not as the dress cast aside from the body; but as an embroidered shroud hiding a skeleton" (VII, p. 258).

19 Charles Darwin, *On the Origin of Species* (Cambridge, MA: Harvard University Press, 1964; facsimile of the first edition), p. 107.
20 Gillian Beer, *Darwin's Plots: Evolutionary Narrative in Darwin, George Eliot and Nineteenth-century Fiction* (Cambridge: Cambridge University Press, 2000), 2nd edn (original 1983), p. 74. This book is the *locus classicus* for study of Darwin's language and style. Chapter Three, "Analogy, Metaphor, and Narrative in *The Origin*," remains the best single analysis of Darwin's prose.

In perhaps a final irony, the work of both Darwin and Ruskin allies them with the project of the realist novel that so dominated Victorian literature. George Eliot invoked Ruskin in her review of the third volume of *Modern Painters* as a great theorist of realism. But much of the power of Victorian science was in its return to the ordinary, familiar, material world to make it explicable – though in material terms. In Darwin's case, part of the work was, by looking very closely at the familiar (like, for example, worms) to defamiliarize it by making us recognize that it is not as stable as it looks, that it has a history belied by its current appearance, that it is moving off into a future where further transformations are possible. Ruskin too was defamiliarizing the familiar, making us see narrative and moral significance in unmoving objects. In their very different modes, they were both engaged in a romantic enterprise. But romanticism can encompass the excesses of Byron, the gorgeous exoticism of Keats and Shelley, *and* the deliberate low-keyed realism of Wordsworth, a poet to whom both men owed a great deal. Darwin doesn't turn to the leach-gatherer, but nothing could better demonstrate the importance of the ordinary than the worm, which certainly, like the nature that Darwin inherited from Newton and Bacon and Lyell and Herschel and von Humboldt, never made leaps. Nothing could more quietly annihilate the ideal space between man and the unintelligent brute than evidence of the intelligence of the worm.

Ruskin, of course, found this Darwinian strategy reductionist and even obscene. It left the world disenchanted. Darwinian explanations do not exalt humanity, but lead it down into worm-burrow. "We will assume," says Ruskin, "that science has done its utmost; and that every chemical or animal force is demonstrably resolvable into heat or motion, reciprocally changing into each other" (XIX, p. 356). We are still left with the question of the initiating force: "we can show no scientific proof of its not being personal, and coinciding with the ordinary conception of a supporting spirit in all things" (XIX, p. 356). The Victorian myth of the ordinary that issued in the great works of Victorian realism became to the ever self-contradictory Ruskin another version of the wormlike reductionism he found in science. Although George Eliot's enterprise was to re-infuse the ordinary with the emotions and significance formerly attributed only to the powerful, and thus to do what she thought Ruskin was doing in his deep attentiveness to the minutiae of nature, he fought her art to the last. An art that lingers on the low, the ordinary, the base, is a corrupt art, and the influence of that art (like its source) is morally dangerous. To the last, he fought against worms and the wormlike, and insisted on finding in language and nature (in etymologies and landscape) the spirit that he believed was being driven out of matter by the new knowledge. "Of the forces that act on matter," he said, "the noblest we can know is the energy which imagines or perceives, the existence of a living power greater than its own" (XXII, p. 170). For Ruskin's science, the world remained enchanted.

Darwin's last book was, in effect, about worms' defecation, upon which our world is built. Ruskin, alas, increasingly lost his power to function in the disenchanted world that was built that way.

CHAPTER 4

Scientific discourse as an alternative to faith

The enemy of knowledge, as Huxley saw it, was faith: "The man of science has learned to believe in justification, not by faith, but by verification."[1] Huxley's language shapes itself paradoxically, as the negative form of the language of religion; that is, in its often witty and bitter rejection of religion as a method of knowing, it retains the religious structure and the sanction of feeling that goes with it. The fondest "convictions of barbarous and semi-barbarous people" are the convictions Huxley associates with religion: "that authority is the soundest basis of belief; that merit attaches to a readiness to believe; that the doubting disposition is a bad one, and scepticism a sin." Huxley assumes "the exact reverse . . . to be true". The "semi-barbarous" sounds like the John Henry Newman of the *Apologia pro vita sua*, published two years before.

"The improver of natural knowledge" Huxley affirms, "absolutely refuses to acknowledge authority, as such. For him, scepticism is the highest of duties; blind faith the one unpardonable sin" (p. 40). The reversal is "exact," the refusal "absolute," and faith, in the deliberate paradox, becomes an "unpardonable sin." Huxley's language deliberately depends upon the mode it is rejecting. Such reversals provide the form of that "naturalizing" of religion of which James Moore has written so incisively and critically.[2] Huxley is constructing a naturalistic "theodicy," as Moore calls it, in which the justification is established by virtue of naturalism's powers, first, to explain – to make the world even more intelligible than previous ('metaphysical') theodicies had done – and, second, to *change* the world for the better in material ways. The true God is nature, the true worship, science. Moore's argument implies paradox: the secular is the religious.

[1] T. H. Huxley, "On the Advisableness of Improving Natural Knowledge" (1866) *Methods and Results* (London, 1893). p. 41.
[2] "Theodicy and Society: The Crisis of the Intelligentsia," in *Victorian Faith in Crisis: Essays on Continuity and Change in Nineteenth-Century Religious Belief* (London: Macmillan, 1990), ed. Richard J. Helmstadter and Bernard Lightman, pp. 153–86.

Huxley indulges that paradox. In praise of skepticism, doubt, and intellectual openness, Huxley, to Moore's ears, sounds like a dogmatist, aspiring, like any good believer, to the absolute. He believes that 'as our race approaches maturity' it will discover "that there is but one kind of knowledge and but one method of acquiring it" (p. 41). Such faith might be as difficult as Newman's, but it sweeps forward in superb confidence. In its essence, the arguments Huxley made in his lifelong campaign to transfer to science the authority that had until recently belonged to religion, are very close to those being made today by aggressive attacks on the superstitions of religions by scientific and philosophical polemicists like Richard Dawkins and Daniel Dennett, except that these latter try to purge themselves of every last remnant of religion. But Huxley was mounting his argument in a philosophical and critical climate that makes the paradoxical form more understandable, and was participating eagerly in the developing Victorian tradition of attempting to transfer to the world of scientific fact something of the moral and spiritual energy that had previously been associated exclusively with religion. For the Victorians, obviously, abandonment of religion felt like a deep spiritual loss, for which some compensation had to be found. Huxley found it in the science that was displacing religion. His science was designed to keep the world enchanted.

While the substance of his philosophical position has undergone sustained critique for more than a century, Huxley, it has to be remembered, wrote not as a philosopher but as a self-conscious proselytizer for a science that was still struggling to make a place for itself in the culture, and that could only be practiced adequately if it were protected against established intellectual authority. It had to be defined, Huxley believed, in opposition to the religious context in which, as it were, it had incubated during the first half of the century. Such definition constituted not only a crisis of faith; the turn from religion, as Jeffrey von Arx shows in his study of Leslie Stephen's "crisis," entailed a crisis of vocation.[3] The non-Oxbridgean Huxley and the scientific naturalists were not only arguing for "truth", but for the respectability of science as a vocation, for its moral as well as intellectual authority, and – more banally – for the very possibility of making a living at it.

In this light, the arguments of the naturalists have often, recently, been seen as primarily self-serving, the actual epistemological and ethical details of their arguments largely discounted. Frank Turner and Adrian Desmond

---

[3] "The Victorian Crisis of Faith as a Crisis of Vocation," in Helmstadter and Lightman, pp. 262–82.

have demonstrated how thoroughly this aspiration for professional status helped define even the smallest details of Huxley's scientific arguments.[4] But it is no denial of the importance of Huxley's literal arguments to say that his concern for professional status helps account for much of his rhetorical power, nor does that concern undercut the kinds of arguments he makes about epistemology and ethics. I want to insist here that Huxley's rhetoric and arguments require another and, I would hope, more sympathetic look; this is true also for the work of the other naturalists, in particular John Tyndall and W. K. Clifford.[5]

As an imaginative construction aimed at redefining vocation, and getting out from under repressive and failing intellectual and social organizations, the naturalists' vision retains a strong claim to respect. Aware as we now should be of their dogmatic tendencies, we should not diminish the importance of the otherwise obvious fact that central to their method and faith was their opposition to authority and dogma. If part of the counterattack, from Balfour to Shaw to James Moore himself, has been the argument that Huxley is dogmatic in his anti-dogmatism, Huxley nonetheless proffers a way of thinking that resists dogmatism. However

---

[4] Adrian Desmond, *Archetypes and Ancestors: Palaeontology in Victorian England*, 1850–1875 (Chicago, 1984); Frank M. Turner, "Public Science in Britain, 1880-1919", *Isis*, 71 (1980) pp. 589–608; Frank M. Turner, "The Victorian Conflict between Science and Religion: A Professional Dimension", *Isis*, 69 (1978) pp. 356–76. Desmond's brilliant and exhaustive biography of Huxley, published after this essay was originally written, lays out in great detail Huxley's strategies and practices in establishing science as a profession and making sure that like-minded people won the major positions, also suggests, willy-nilly, something of the tenacity and brilliance of Huxley's argumentative style. See Adrian Desmond, *Huxley: From Devil's Disciple to Evolution's High Priest* (Reading, MA: Addison Wesley, 1997).

[5] I am aware that, as Bernard Lightman has shown, the "landscape" of the history of science in the nineteenth century has shifted significantly away from the position that treated the scientific naturalists and the scientific elite as the primary voice of science during the period. Historians such as Desmond and Moore have helped shift the focus on the period, allowing "groups from outside the intellectual elite to emerge from under the shadows cast by the mountainous elevations formerly occupied by scientific naturalism." And the religiously oriented science that dominated in the first half of the century "did not disappear just because Huxley and his allies gained control over many of the important institutions of science." Lightman sums up: "In sum, the power of scientific naturalism, both inside and outside intellectual circles, seems to have been overestimated by the older scholarship. Scientific naturalists and the Anglican clergy were not the only players in the contest for cultural authority." My essay is, however, deliberately aimed, not at denying the significance of the new orientation or at simply replaying the arguments of "the older scholarship," but at affirming the value of the work of the naturalists, which has come under siege in part as a consequence of the recognition that they were not the only, or in some cases, the most important voices of science at the time, and their ideas were not – as many Victorians critical of them also argued – the necessary consequences of a commitment to the value of science. For an excellent discussion of the changes in the "landscape," and a strong representation of other, more popular, voices, see Lightman's *Victorian Popularizers of Science: Designing Nature for New Audiences* (Chicago: University of Chicago Press, 2007), pp. 8–9.

problematic the total commitment to "rationalist" argument might be – and early on William James powerfully critiqued that commitment as epistemologically, morally, humanly inadequate – it is a dangerous move to denigrate rationality of Huxley's sort. Our contemporary scene in which faith so often trumps reason – and "evolution" along the way – provides convincing testimony to the danger. Perhaps not great original thinkers, the scientific naturalists helped create a cultural context in which challenge to authority, demystification, and intellectual scepticism became continuing and healthy tendencies. And that opposition took science and philosophy and culture itself into positions that would eventually lead to the very critiques that have brought many current critics to what I regard as an underestimation of their importance and continuing value.

In their unbridled enthusiasm for science and in their "robustious" rhetoric, the scientific naturalists were often extravagantly optimistic about the possibilities of science and of progress, and unreflecting about the problems their position might raise. They were, as Moore argues, totally unable to entertain the bare prospect of the tremendous ecological calamity that developments in science and technology threaten in our own time to produce. But Huxley was no blind optimist. He came around to resisting the Spencerian version of Social Darwinism, and in *Evolution and Ethics* argued forcefully that human mastery of nature is necessarily limited, that nature will have its way ultimately, and with catastrophic consequences. Huxley's arguments, I want to claim, are morally insightful and historically prescient. There is, for example, more than one way to read the last sentence of his 'Prolegomena' to that book:

That which lies before the human race is a constant struggle to maintain and improve, in opposition to the State of Nature, the State of Art of an organized polity; in which, and by which, man may develop a worthy civilization, capable of maintaining and constantly improving itself, until the evolution of our globe shall have entered so far upon its downward course that the cosmic process resumes its sway; and, once more, the State of Nature prevails over the surface of our planet.[6]

On the one hand, it is possible to emphasize here Huxley's passionate commitment to resisting "Nature," and thus his implicit participation in that Baconian tradition that, in its macho determination to master nature, points to ecological catastrophe. But on the other hand, it is necessary to recognize that Huxley is here responding to a social interpretation of natural selection and evolution that in effect establishes the survival of the fittest as a political principle. And against this Huxley brilliantly and

[6]   T. H. Huxley, *Evolution and Ethics* (London: Macmillan and Co., 1911), p. 45.

courageously stands. The "Prolegomena" is a rejection of eugenics – "there is no hope that mere human beings will ever possess enough intelligence to select the fittest" (p. 34); he is appalled at the idea that those who have power would leave those who do not, those who are not "fit," to starve and die. When he asks that humans resist "Nature," one of the things he means is that humans must resist the blind and stupid amorality of natural processes, the processes which demand of each a thoroughly selfish struggle for survival. While even in a "horticultural" world, a hypothetical world in which civilization is a successfully functioning garden in the midst of the wildness of evolutionary development, "every child born will still bring with him the instinct of unlimited self-assertion. He will have to learn the lesson of self-restraint and renunciation" (p. 44). This is very Victorian. It is also very Freudian. Morality itself, Huxley believed, is a state of art, rather than a state of nature. The insistence on the necessity of altruism, of personal restraint, of recognition of the community instead simply of the self is Huxley's response to the wild affirmations of a social Darwinism that in effect based itself on following the procedures of a Nature, which John Stuart Mill had long before described as committing daily horrendous crimes.[7]

Nevertheless, Moore is certainly also right, in his masterly book on Protestant responses to Darwinism, that the metaphor of warfare between science and religion, so common in Huxley's writing, among others, distorts the complex history of those responses: religion was not by any means uniformly antagonistic to Darwin (or Huxley), and many of those who were first ready to receive Darwin's theory were themselves religious.[8] To make my argument yet more difficult, there is Frank Turner's discussion

---

[7]   For an important discussion of Huxley's thought about altruism in relation to the ideas of modern evolutionary biology and sociobiology, see the essay by George Williams in *Evolution and Ethics: With New Essays on Its Victorian and Sociobiological Context*, ed. James Paradis and George C. Williams (Princeton: Princeton University Press, 1989). Williams discusses how modern evolutionary biologists deal with the paradox in Huxley's argument, that one must fight against nature though one is part of it. Much current discussion points to the development of altruism as part of the process of natural selection. In *Primates and Philosophers: How Morality Evolved* (Princeton. Princeton University Press, 2006), Frans de Waal makes a different case against Huxley, and one with which I am much more in sympathy: that is, that Huxley's insistence the natural condition of human beings is selfish and competitive forces the contradiction at the end of the "Prolegomena," and even contradicts Huxley's own arguments. De Waal, through his animal study and evolutionary theorizing, insists that altruism is built into human nature also. His position is a further development, in fact, of Kropotkin's arguments in *Mutual Aid.* But this important argument moves too far afield from the questions raised in the current essay, and does not contradict the point that *Evolution Ethics*, as a moral document, does important work in resistance to eugenics.

[8]   See, James R. Moore, *The Post-Darwinian Controversies: A Study of the Protestant Struggle to Come to Terms with Darwin in Great Britain and America, 1870–1900* (Cambridge: Cambridge University Press, 1979).

of the movement he has called Victorian "scientific naturalism." Turner's strong analysis and critique of it (and his study of various more or less eccentric scientific or quasi-scientific reactions) belongs in the strong tradition of anti-positivist polemic that has marked much of the philosophy, literature, and cultural history of the last half century. Mincing no words, Turner takes the writing of the great publicists of science, in England – Huxley, Tyndall, Clifford, Spencer, Galton – as demonstrating "the existential intellectual, and moral bankruptcy of scientific naturalism."[9]

That is a hard pill to swallow for someone who has read Huxley and Tyndall and Clifford with a sense of their extraordinary moral energy, with delight at the lucidity with which they expounded the new science, with admiration for their breadth of culture, and with, I must confess, considerable pleasure at the way they were able to slay some of their more retrograde antagonists. Tyndall is clearly right to argue that Huxley, Clifford, Helmholtz, and Du Bois Reymond show remarkable command of a great breadth of literary culture. "Where among modern writers can you find their superiors in clearness and vigour of literary style?" he asks, and I have no answer.[10] One can concede their limits, the validity of William James's extraordinarily humane critique of Clifford, the comic accuracy of Mallock's parody of Tyndall, the scholarly authority of Moore's critique of Huxley, but whatever their inadequacies, the naturalists' work was far more interesting, imaginative, and important than among modern critics it is now usually taken to be. No thinkers were *more* aware of the difficulties of objectivity or of the various ways in which knowledge is filtered through particular consciousnesses. And they were, with the Positivists they often mocked, among the first wave of those Victorian thinkers who recognized how scientific culture, to thrive in the public sphere,

---

[9] Frank M. Turner, *Between Science and Religion: The Reaction to Scientific Naturalism in Late Victorian England* (New Haven, CT: Yale University Press, 1974) p. 36.

[10] John Tyndall, "The Belfast Address", *Fragments of Science*, 2 vols (New York, 1899) 2, p. 199. In his *In Pursuit of a Scientific Culture* (Madison, Wisconsin: University of Wisconsin Press, 1989), Peter Allan Dale allows to positivism (in what may well be the most extensive and important study of nineteenth-century positivism in relation to literature and to the development of modernist and postmodernist theory) its full complexity and richness. His book is not a "defense" of positivism but, with fine-grained analysis, it describes the vagaries of its development and of its influence on the thinkers and writers of the period. He demonstrates that positivist thought was constantly forced to return to the recognition that "imaginary projection" is inevitably a condition of scientific knowledge. The truly imaginary being, he concludes, is "a serious positivist thinker who was unaware of the necessary intervention of the mind's intentional structure between himself or herself and the world as in itself it really is" (pp. 280–1).

had to address as well the emotional, moral, and even spiritual needs of the culture. In this respect at least their work remains important still.

The work of the scientific naturalists may seem a bit more attractive to many who in recent years have watched the effect of religious power in public life, particularly in the United States, where science often must contend against "popular opinion," where evolution is less credited than the Virgin birth, and where the possibility of life-saving work on stem cells is hampered by politicians arguing on dogmatic religious grounds. Turner reminds us, moreover, that the push for science in post-Darwinian years significantly failed: "scientists confronted frustration on all sides" ("Public Science," p. 592). Although our contemporary cultural criticism has tended to view the naturalists as belonging to the dominant new capitalist culture, this is at best half the story. That criticism is a kind of reverse "Whig" history, reading Victorian naturalism from our own current unease. The voices of the new capitalist hegemony, so the reading usually goes, confirmed a version of Darwinism that sanctioned individual enterprise, reduced morality to the physically calculable, disbarred non-material causes, turned psychology into physiology, increased alienation by insisting on the absolute separation of subject and object, and read into the laws of evolution and the conservation of energy justification of unequal distribution of wealth and of social as well as biological superiority.

But there are many other ways to read these things: physiological psychology was certainly a forerunner of modern psychology, and healthily introduced into the study of the human a proper deference to the "body" and its power in shaping human behavior, thought, and feeling. (In recent years, indeed, there has been a salutary and growing exploration of "corporeality" in human affairs, and particularly of the physiological psychology that came to dominate English psychology before Freud.) The introduction of non-material causes into scientific discourse has, recently, produced the non-science of "Intelligent Design." Moreover, the scientific naturalists were hardly all wild social Darwinists (as we have already seen with Huxley), but rather propagated often quite humane interpretations of Darwinian biology. In any case, these kinds of critique are entirely unequal to the complexities of the combats between traditional forms of power, in church and aristocracy, and the aspiration toward meritocracy; it does no justice to the sense of repression felt by the naturalists, or even to the terrible economic difficulties many of the most famous, but particularly T. H. Huxley, had to undergo. It tends to blame naturalist thought for the sins of the economic system that adopted it.

While science was often a handmaiden to technology and not so "pure" as its advocates sometimes argue, Huxley was certainly recalling accurately when he claimed that he would not have remained a student of natural knowledge had he thought that knowledge was only – as he put it in a Carlylean formulation – a "comfort-grinding machine."[11] Science was for Huxley a moral enterprise, but that also meant strong practical applications of its work. That was the way to real social improvement, to real improvement in the quality of life of masses of people, and so it has proved to be, although with other costs we are only now coming fully to recognize. Huxley's commitment to material improvement would seem to connect him to the idea of mechanism, a "buzz word" with Arnold, Carlyle, and others for the unspiritual, the morally banal, the merely pragmatic. But there are other ways to consider the idea of "mechanism." The association with the idea of mechanism not only set science against the highly valued 'organicism' of romantic tradition, but against the Platonic idea of contemplation. Mechanism was managed by mechanics, and the discourse thus was moved from the world of the gentleman to those who worked, to, that is, a lower class: the mechanic has little time to contemplate, and the mechanic belongs at the bottom of the social system, a human who was, socially speaking, a mere machine. Huxley's popularity with working-class groups was no accident.

Writers like Samuel Butler and George Bernard Shaw, among many others, mounted witty and ironic attacks against the naturalists. As early as the 1880s Arthur Balfour, whose two books, *A Defence of Philosophic Doubt* and *The Foundations of Belief,* constituted a very powerful assault on the scientific idea of truth, complained about the intellectual dominance of the scientific naturalists:

Speculation seems sadly in want of destructive criticism at the present time. Whenever any faith is held strongly and universally, there is a constant and overpowering tendency to convert Philosophy, which should be its judge, into its servant. It was so formerly, when theology ruled supreme; it is so now that Science has usurped its place: and I assert with some confidence that the bias given to thought in the days of the schoolmen through the overwhelming influence of the first of these creeds was not a whit more pernicious to the cause of impartial speculation than the bias which it receives at the moment through the influence of the second.[12]

---

[11]   "Improving Natural Knowledge," p. 30.
[12]   Arthur Balfour, *A Defence of Philosophic Doubt: Being an Essay on the Foundations of Belief* (London, 1879) pp. 293–4.

Ironically, Balfour can use precisely the sort of rhetorical move – identifying science with 'faith', finding it governed not by pursuit of truth, but by bias – that the scientists themselves used against their enemies. Huxley's inversion of the language of faith comes back to haunt him here (he died as he was completing his review-refutation of Balfour's *Foundations of Belief*). Given the extravagant claims of the naturalists, Balfour had every right to challenge science as though it had become a faith.

But without descending into the complex and often ferocious contemporary debates about the possibility of a science as pure and disinterested as Huxley imagined, it is important to remember that in these struggles for intellectual and, implicitly, moral authority, Huxley and the naturalists thrust toward the center of cultural power an alternative to traditional society, a deep respect for intellectual merit, a determination to value ideas on the strength of their rational force. The naturalists' pugnacity was not unreasonable in a society that was only slowly and reluctantly allowing them serious professional status, that had traditionally resisted the "mechanical," even in its later secular phases – as so many of the Victorian prophets make clear.

It may be reasonable to prefer the anti-naturalist positions of Balfour, or Ruskin, the conservative ones of Matthew Arnold, or the anti-Darwinian ones of Samuel Butler and G. B. Shaw. It is, however, a mistake not, at least, to consider the fact that the naturalists' arguments were importantly focused on fundamental issues both of knowledge and social organization, and they were almost always intensely humane. Balfour's very shrewd and intelligent criticism and his epistemological skepticism turn him back to readmit the old faith because *all* belief is based on "non-rational" cases.[13] More secular responses get not much further. Ruskin's moral passion and glorious prose simply refuse the epistemological possibilities by denying the usefulness and importance of certain kinds of knowledge that take us below the level of appearances, and his movingly paternal proposals for social reorganization seem wildly out of touch with the world he was addressing.[14]

---

[13] See Christopher Herbert, *Victorian Relativity: Radical Thought and Scientific Discovery* (Chicago: University of Chicago Press, 2001). Herbert discusses Balfour's relativist arguments, particularly in the forerunner to *Foundations of Belief*, that is, *A Defence of Philosophic Doubt*. Herbert emphasizes the radical aspects of Balfour's relativism very effectively. What he does not discuss, however, is the way Balfour (like Newman before him) used skepticism as a way to support a fundamentally conservative intellectual and political tradition.

[14] See in this volume my Ruskin and Darwin paper. Cf., however, Jeffrey Spear's *Dreams of an English Eden: Ruskin and his Tradition in Social Criticism* (New York: Columbia University Press, 1984), which argues that Ruskin's economic theory and practice were, in fact, vital responses to contemporary conditions.

Demonstrating that there are ideological implications to ostensibly disinterested scientific work is only part of the story; what are the ideological implications of its alternatives? The pursuit of disinterest, and the ideal of objectivity and natural observation, were not merely "scientific." Arnold's "disinterest" is a version of John Herschel's, or Huxley's; Carlyle's *Selbsttödung* was a requirement of scientific study; George Eliot's "duty" entailed precisely that refusal to allow interest to interfere with judgment and moral act that we find Huxley urging in essay after essay.[15] The alliance of science with a powerful and morally crude social authority came only when science, having failed to establish its authority on its own terms, allied itself to the nation's military and imperial ambitions. It was not absurd of scientific writers to think of themselves as in the minority, to go out with intellectual six-guns blazing against all forms of authority, imagining the possibility of revolutionizing the moral and social structures of the country.

I want then to affirm that however vulnerable the scientific naturalists were to the kinds of criticism Moore and Turner level at them, they were involved in one of the great imaginative responses to the difficulties of modern culture – as rich and imaginative as, say, Arnold's, or those of the novelists and poets of the Victorian era. And I want to argue that the positions they adopted, however arrogant the formulation might sometimes have been, however implicated in political and self-interested actions for the advancement of new professional power, developed the intellectual strategies for the very critiques contemporary thinkers often use against them. It is surely worth considering how, in the light of the transparent failure of traditional religion and philosophy or even the sages to improve the condition of the ordinary person very much, science could be seen as a genuinely liberating possibility. The battle was part of a class war, and science by and large was used in the interests of the capitalists. But its methods pointed towards the developments of a meritocracy, and implied a far more democratic social order, so that what it affirmed it could also, eventually, negate.

In what follows, I will be looking at the substance, rather than the ideological implications of some of the naturalists' basic arguments. I shall be setting up polarities, which need to be qualified, between traditional assumptions and those to which the naturalists tended – at least by virtue

---

[15] See my "George Eliot's Hypothesis of Reality", in this volume; see also my *Dying to Know: Scientific Epistemology and Narrative in Victorian England* (Chicago: University of Chicago Press, 2002).

of their arguments about science and scientific method. (Tyndall, for example, was so Carlylean outside his scientific work that his moral and social positions seem to belong rather to the sage-like secularization of experience – which often becomes another form of mystification – than to the naturalists' kind.)

These polarities can, crudely, be described in this way:

1) faith in *a priori* knowledge as opposed to "faith" in experience and reason as the source of all knowledge; 2) valuing the spiritual and the timeless as against change and the material (which incorporates the spiritual); 3) commitment to the past as model as opposed to the past as a history of errors to be outlived; 4) belief in a nature hierarchically and purposively organized for the benefit of humankind as opposed to a nature democratically organized, without divine purpose; 5) a world intrinsically meaningful as opposed to one in which meaning is humanly imposed, and in which nature's "usefulness" entails human manipulation of it; 6) confidence in the possibility of objectivity as opposed to a heightened sensitivity to the difficulties of objectivity and of the safeguards required to avoid the distortions of human consciousness and the limitations of human perspective; 7) faith in language as accurately "representing" reality and (consider Carlyle and Ruskin's etymologies) somehow bearing truth within itself (i.e., Adamic language) against a sense of language as an arbitrary tool, not representing reality but useful in allowing manipulation and understanding of it; 8) faith in the humanly satisfying meaning of nature (based on *a priori* belief in the divine organization of nature) as opposed to belief that "objective" investigation may lead to dangerous discovery.

On this latter model "Truth" becomes both an intellectual and a moral virtue, and entails rigorous self-discipline and courage to confront a world inimical to human consciousness. Truth inheres in any study in which scientific method is preserved, and thus serves to protect against any subject matter which might seem, on traditional grounds, immoral.

In addition, as I have already suggested, Victorian scientific naturalism was implicated in its own displacement. The requirement that all knowledge be tested, which often turned into dogmatic denials of alternative models of knowledge or into a philosophically evasive agnosticism, became part of that continuing critique of authority that threatens to subvert all foundationalist thought – including, of course, positivism. So, "scientific method" begins with the refusal of a lie, continues in dogged determination to learn the truth, allows, in the discovery of truth, rational change. Its method is saintly suppression of all interest. Scientific knowledge is beyond prejudice, and claims the authority lost by traditional religion. It is based not in inherited assumptions, but in experience itself, in the confirmation given by a community committed to the same values and procedures, and it looks not backward to a source, but forward, to a development. Such was the official position of the naturalists.

Philosophically, indeed, there are troubles here, but since the primary object of the naturalists was to clear space for free scientific practice, just as Arnold's was to clear space for poetry, they sought to avoid full philosophical elaborations of their position – with the possible exception of Clifford, who died too young to write more than tentative essays on philosophic problems. Particularly, as Turner points out, the naturalists refused confrontation with ontological questions. The naturalists' essential move was against any form of the *a priori*, for, as they saw it, the *a priori* made further discussion impossible; it could be affirmed but not verified, and thus it undercut the whole enterprise of science. But of course, as they also understood, their science could not verify its own initiating assumptions, and hence the Spencerian preoccupation with the unknowable and Huxley's coinage of "agnosticism." Huxley would unabashedly affirm, for example, that "physical science starts from certain postulates," and that, by definition, these are not "demonstrable." One of the postulates is "the objective existence of the material world". We are in metaphysics here, but Huxley does not want to play, and he settles for the view that use of these postulates is justifiable because "expectations logically based upon them are verified, or, at any rate, not contradicted, whenever they can be tested by experience." This may not be the best philosophy, but Huxley knows he is not writing it. Perhaps less excusable is his assumption that "rational order ... pervades the universe." This he does not even affirm as an undemonstrable postulate. Science, for Huxley, is the attempt to discover this order.[16] It is brazen, perhaps, but in effect an essential assumption of science, just as, for Darwin, it was a condition of his scientific work that nothing outside the order of nature be invoked as explanation. If such an invocation were possible, science would be impossible. The *a priori* faith in reason is, in effect, a scientist's practical assertion of what is necessary for there to be any science at all.

Another critical problem was, in effect, the mind-body problem. How could a "body" be moved by a thought? The naturalists were of course aware that an act of will could effect physical change, the raising of an arm, say, or the moving of a foot. Huxley could not understand, nor could Tyndall, what connection there might be between the physical and the immaterial, particularly consciousness (although Clifford struggled toward

---

[16] T. H. Huxley, "The Progress of Science" (1887) in *Methods and Results*, pp. 60–1.

a half-formed conception of "mind-stuff" as a way around the difficulty). This became one of the great issues of late nineteenth-century thought, another version of Cartesian dualism. Huxley and Tyndall settled for the view that one could not have consciousness without parallel physical phenomena. As Tyndall was to put it in his notorious "Belfast Address": "We can trace the development of a nervous system, and correlate with it the parallel phenomena of sensation and thought. We see with undoubting certainty that they go hand in hand. But we try to soar in a vacuum the moment we seek to comprehend the connection between them . . . Man the object is separated by an impassable gulf from man the subject" (p. 295). This impassable gulf did not stop the naturalists from attempting to extend science from study of the inorganic, to study of the organic, and finally to the study of human phenomena, particularly in physiological psychology, which is specifically aimed at connecting consciousness with body.

Taking up the injunction of Comte and Mill, they saw no discontinuity, of the sage-like sort, between material and spiritual. If they did not know what the connection was, they believed there was one, and that belief played a critical role in the whole development of psychology and social science. The rhetorical inversions of Huxley's prose are not merely satirical. They reflect his commitment to find an alternative to the religion whose ideas he rejected but whose values he accepted and whose power is still manifest in his language. The law-driven rational order of the universe, which religion had sustained, but which seemed to stop short at the human, was now to be extended to human organization; the naturalists sought to develop the social sciences on the model of the physical, to seek in human behavior and organization "laws" that would explain and predict – as Herschel, whose astronomy was the model for all science, could predict the movements of the planets. Darwin's efforts to extend "law" to the biological seemed to Darwinians like Huxley to mean the extension of the kinds of laws discoverable in Newtonian physics to human behavior, just the ambition laid out in Mill's *System of Logic* earlier in the century. The differences entailed by a study whose definition required historical, phylogenetic explanation and whose subjects were always unique organisms, was not apparent to Huxley.[17] Surely, given the fundamental intellectual contradiction that supported this move, it is anything but

---

[17]   On this point, see David Hull, *Darwin and his Critics: the Reception of Darwin's Theory of Evolution by the Scientific Community* (Chicago: University of Chicago Press, 1973), pp. 64–74; and Ernst Mayr, *The Growth of Biological Thought* (Cambridge, MA: Harvard University Press, 1981), pp. 36–67.

a symptom of the "intellectual bankruptcy" that Turner called the naturalists' thought. In the context of religious arguments, which insisted that humans were somehow exempt from the orderly structure of the rest of the inorganic and organic world, the move was invaluable, essential to the development of modern psychology and of the social sciences and, more directly, of course, of evolutionary biology.

As a consequence of the rhetorical shift that Huxley and the naturalists were attempting, the authority formerly inhering in religious tradition shifted to their science. The danger was and is that in naturalizing theories that had previously been based in divine sanction, science could also naturalize the prejudices of the culture and reinstate them in theories of racial and sexual superiority. Racism could move from a theologically imposed condition to a scientifically imposed one, and we are all familiar with examples of this development, not least in the Anthropological Society among the Victorians themselves.[18] Nevertheless, the 'method' of science, as formulated by Huxley and the others, always left open, as it leaves open now, the means for undercutting such positions. As cultural critics, Huxley, Tyndall, and Clifford offered refreshing alternatives to Arnold's kind of humanist arguments, which, for all Arnold's breadth of culture, simply took for granted the essential nature of racial difference.

The ideal of Victorian culture tends to have been shaped by Arnold, and by the other great critics of society called "sages." But against that notion of culture, it is worth looking at a more naturalistic one. The struggle to perceive a rational order of the universe is here also very clearly ideological; the failure to recognise the interested elements in ostensibly disinterested study is damaging. Yet the work of E. B. Tylor, in its translation of religious experience into rationally explicable phenomena, offers an interesting example of the kinds of correctives the more existentially alert sages often needed, and of ways in which a radically imperfect scientific method opened new possibilities of value and social organization. Reading *Primitive Culture* now is a curious experience.

If one had wanted to predict how a social scientist would apply the methods of science, Tylor's first chapter would have fulfilled almost all

---

[18]   For a rich and complex treatment of the development of anthropological thought among the Victorians and in relation to modern thinking on the subject, see Christopher Herbert, *Culture and Anomie: Ethnographic Imagination in the Nineteenth Century* (Chicago: University of Chicago Press, 1991). George Stocking, in the most important book on Victorian anthropology, describes how Edward Tylor's seminal work built on the fundamental argument that "the history of mankind is part and parcel of the history of nature." See *Victorian Anthropology* (Chicago: University of Chicago Press, 1987), p. 161.

expectations. It is uniformitarian and evolutionary, and it attempts to apply the methods of natural philosophy to the study of mankind. Thus, Tylor sets to work assuming the "unity of nature, the fixity of its laws," and "the definitive sequence of cause and effect through which every fact depends on what has gone before it."[19] Indeed, although with less affect and aggression, Tylor sounds rather like Tyndall: "To many educated minds there seems something presumptuous and repulsive in the view that the history of mankind is part and parcel of the history of nature, that our thoughts, wills, and actions accord with laws as definite as those which govern the motion of waves, the combination of acids and bases, and the growth of plants and animals" (I, 2). Taking literally the scientific ideal of "law," "regularity," and measurement, Tylor assumes his own capacity for detachment. Needing a "scale," he invents one, as though it were self-evidently in nature; to nobody's surprise, he places Western European civilization at the top, as the standard of measurement. Yet in so doing, he only makes formal the assumptions of all his contemporaries (which is why the scale seemed so self-evident).

Nevertheless, having the idea of a "scale" actually loosens the grip of religious and ethnic complacency at the very moment that it seems to be getting scientific sanction. Tylor's overview of anthropology implies two theories of culture, which distinguish the naturalists and the sages. These were formulated, Tylor argues, in the eighteenth century: the "degenerationist" theory, formulated by Joseph de Maistre, who argued against the "perverse" modern idea that civilization has grown from savagery; and the "progressionist" theory, formulated by Gibbon. Where de Maistre argues that civilization degenerated from a higher stage of culture, Gibbon argues that mankind developed from savage beginnings, from an "abject condition, perhaps the primitive and universal state of man," to a condition from which "it is able to command the animals, to fertilise the earth, to traverse the ocean, and to measure the heavens" (I:33).

For Tylor, as for Darwin, the scientific ideal of "regularity" and the cultural ideal of "progress" are threatened by the possibility of retrogression and of extinction. Yet Tylor, more unambiguously than Darwin, allies himself with the mythos of progression. He even formulates it, as he puts it, "in mythic fashion":

We may fancy ourselves looking on Civilization, as in personal figure she traverses the world; we see her lingering or resting by the way, and often deviating into paths that bring her toiling back to where she had passed by long ago; but, direct

---

[19] Edward B. Tylor, *Primitive Culture*, 2 vols. (London, 1920), I:2.

or devious, her path lies forward, and if now and then she tries a few backward steps, her walk soon falls into a helpless stumbling. It is not according to her nature, her feet were not made to plant uncertain steps behind her, for both in her forward view and in her onward gait she is of truly human type. (I:69)

Even the often gloomy George Eliot, in the famous finale to *Middlemarch*, speaks of "the growing good of the world." But in George Eliot, the disparity between the bleak local narratives and the quasi-religious faith in ultimate goodness becomes evident. Tylor, however, makes the case "scientifically":

In striking a balance between the effects of forward and backward movement in civilization, it must be borne in mind how powerfully the diffusion of culture acts in preserving the results of progress from the attacks of degeneration. A progressive movement in culture spreads, and becomes independent of the fate of its originators [read here Dorothea Brooke's 'incalculably diffusive acts' and Jubal's invention of music]. What is produced in some limited district is diffused over a wider and wider area, where the process of effectual 'stamping out' becomes more and more difficult. Thus it is even possible for the habits and inventions of races long extinct to remain as the common property of surviving nations; and the destructive actions which make such havoc with the civilizations of particular districts fail to destroy the civilization of the world. (1:39)

But the evidence, as Tylor himself often admits, might be read in other ways. Underlying the view is a Spencerian evolutionary model: "the institutions which can best hold their own in the world gradually supersede the less fit ones" (I:69); and this idea of development gives Tylor both the assurance of meaningfulness so essential after the displacement of religious explanation, and the method he needs to make sense of the phenomena of culture. Gradual if locally irregular progress allows for a scale and for a position from which to judge the past, while at the same time it makes a kind of cliodicy, justifying the ways of history to man, making the secularization of experience tolerable.

As with Huxley and Darwin, Tylor finds the present comprehensible only by seeing it historically. One of Darwin's most striking moves was to find the evidence he needed not in the formal functioning of organisms, but in their vestigial and functionless parts. He was fascinated by "mammae in men," for example. Such "vestiges" could only be explained historically, as evidence for an earlier stage of the organism, in which the "vestiges" had been functional. Similarly, Tylor focuses on what he calls "survivals," cultural phenomena with no obvious contemporary function. Their apparent meaninglessness argues a past in which they had performed useful functions. This strategy depends, as Darwin himself was to admit, on a Paleyan assumption "that every detail of structure, excepting rudiments, was of some special, though unrecognised, service."[20] But even if empirically unsubstantiated assumptions could eventually be framed within a rational theory, the world that theory explained was clearly not the one imagined by natural theologians, not designed and intentional down to the last hair of the head. This shift of perspective from the tradition of natural theology, which restricted earlier modes of explanation and, for example, made it extremely difficult to arrive at a theory of evolution, was only one element in the naturalists' alternatives to the humanist idea of culture.

Stocking suggests another in an important essay on Tylor and Arnold. He argues that Tylor's title, *Primitive Culture*, would constitute an oxymoron in Arnold's language. The concept that "primitive" peoples might even *have* a culture begins, though it does not for Tylor fully mean, the idea of cultural relativity – an idea that the Victorian sages rarely entertained. A scale of civilization, after all, implies many different kinds of civilization, even if there is a flat judgment built into the scale. The view, for example, that primitive animism is an early form of science makes the primitive and the civilized dangerously kin. Thus, the ethnocentric Tylor offers an argument that, according to Stocking, "contained at least the germ of cultural plurality": "one way (although perhaps not the most direct) to the idea of different cultures was through the concept of stages of culture. Perhaps more importantly, cultural evolutionism implied a kind of functionalism in the realm of morals and values which, if it was not the same as modern anthropological relativism, was a major step toward it."[21] Gillian Beer argues that Tylor's project was "the recognition of the 'real culture' and the imaginative energy of peoples throughout the world and throughout history."[22] Such a self-consciously comparativist position, based on what Tylor took to be the evidence of the total continuity between primitive beings and "higher" ones, could find no place in Arnold's qualitatively organized scheme of things. Culture is something

[20] Charles Darwin, *The Descent of Man and Selection in Relation to Sex* (1871) (Princeton: Princeton University Press, 1981), I:153. "That all organic beings, including man, present many modifications of structure which are of no service to them at present, nor have been formerly, is, as I can now see, probable . . . each peculiarity must have had its own efficient cause" (I: 153).
[21] George W. Stocking, Jr., *Race, Culture, and Evolution* (Chicago: University of Chicago, 1982).
[22] Gillian Beer, *Darwin's Plots: Evolutionary Narrative in Darwin, George Eliot and Nineteenth-Century Fiction* (London: Routledge and Kegan Paul, 1983), p. 118.

higher than and different from mere civilization; and poor Wragg had no culture.

In the short run, at least, the naturalists won their battles against religious dogmatism; but their most difficult combat came against those, like the writers Turner discusses, with scientific interests of their own, and those, like the sages, who were also secular and oriented toward the arts and literature. Most of the great Victorian sages, however anti-clerical they became, tended to assume some impersonal (if vaguely conceived) power of conscience, spirit, intelligence. Finding the source of value in imagined pasts, secular and divine, the sages tended to view the new with skepticism, if not with outright fear, and therefore paradoxically worked out strategies that would allow them to cling to the institutions and authority they so marvelously criticized. The retailored world that Teufelsdröckh envisions re-embodies traditional values, constraints, and moral order. It is worth noting that their criticism of contemporary culture – particularly Carlyle's – had a strong influence on the decision of several of the naturalists to enter scientific work.

The naturalists' attack on traditional religion is in part an attack on the quintessential degeneration myth, the myth of the Fall. Humanity is not in decline from an ideal golden age, but in progress, by way of science, to a more rational and humane culture. Huxley, at the very end of his life, directly attacked the myth, on both moral and intellectual grounds. How rational can a world be, he asks: what sort of God could have created man "in his own image" and then have allowed him to fall "away from goodness" on the "most trifling temptation"? Huxley adopts a diction self-consciously borrowed from the New Testament as he evokes the cruelty of this conception of the world. As a consequence of the fall "the whole creation travaileth and groaneth in the bonds of sin and misery; now, as ever since Adam and Eve were expelled from Eden, all but a mere fraction of the human race have lived sorrowfully and sinfully, and at death have passed to endless torment."[23] Huxley is more than playfully angry about the idea of so vindictive and unjust a God, and his arguments are rather like those of Charles Darwin, particularly after the death of his daughter Annie. In his *Autobiography*, in a sequence not published until the twentieth century, Darwin wrote: "A being so powerful and so full of knowledge as a God who could create the universe, is to our finite minds omnipotent and omniscient, and it revolts our understanding to suppose that his benevolence is not unbounded, for what advantage can there be in

---

[23] First published in Houston Peterson, *Huxley: Prophet of Science* (London, 1932), p. 326.

the sufferings of millions of the lower animals throughout almost endless time?"[24]

The theory of "degeneration," then, was anathema to the naturalists, but degeneration, of course, need not have been from a literal paradise. It was characteristic of the Victorians to value some pure, authoritative, and immediately apprehended experience; or the Fall might have been from an ideal community, or from language in touch with its experiential sources, or from classical order and balance. Arnold finds an ideal possibility for culture in the Greeks, of whom, Richard Jenkyns argues, he had "an inadequate notion."[25] The Greeks were his myth of culture – balance, order, sanity, health – as medieval Gothic architecture became Ruskin's, with its "savage-ness" and spiritual freedom. The ideas seem radically different, but the resort to a "factual" past as model and authority reflects the same sort of resistance to the new, the same attempt to relocate an older spiritual authority. The corollary of degeneration, the "golden age," lies tacitly in the background of much of their cultural criticism. But the golden age, as Gillian Beer has shown, was disbarred by Darwinian theory. Darwin locates our ancestor in that "hairy quadruped, furnished with a tail and pointed ears, probably arboreal in its habits so unappealing," as Matthew Arnold put it, half-smiling, we hope, "to the sense in us for conduct, the sense in us for beauty." And beyond that unidyllic source lies the true organic origin in unicellular hermaphroditic organisms. On the evolutionary account origins trail no clouds of glory. As Beer puts it, where the biblical paradise should have been we have only an "empire of mollusks." The foundation of truth, once wrested from God, had to be located in some impersonal source. But the "impersonal," outside of God, is without value; and the great quest of nineteenth-century secular culture was for an impersonal authority that could include the normal human preoccupation with "value."

The Cartesian dilemma, as Richard Bernstein calls it, is central to the Victorian debate. Descartes, Bernstein says, "leads us with an apparent and ineluctable necessity to a grand and seductive Either/Or. Either there is some support for our being, a fixed foundation for our knowledge, or we cannot escape the forces of darkness that envelop us with madness, with intellectual and moral chaos."[26] According to Descartes, the human mind,

[24] Charles Darwin, *Autobiography*, ed. Nora Barlow (New York: W. W. Norton and Co., 1958), p. 86.
[25] Richard Jenkyns, *The Victorians and Ancient Greece* (Cambridge, MA, 1980), p. 266.
[26] Richard J. Bernstein, *Beyond Objectivism and Relativism* (Philadelphia, 1983), p. 18.

though limited, has the equipment to know the truth; error results from misuse. The ideal of "self-purification," so dear to the hearts of Victorian thinkers and artists, is part of the Cartesian method. And the quest for some ultimate authority for knowledge through purging of all inherited traditions and the turn to Experience is similarly Cartesian. Descartes wipes out the golden age of knowledge because what we know cannot come to us through "authority." We retreat to the internal "cogito" and construct from there. But once the secular move is made, and the reliance on Descartes' divine source is dismissed, there remains a fundamental dualism.

Like their most obvious antagonists, Huxley and the naturalists shared the terror of "darkness," "madness," and "moral chaos" that would come if no foundation for knowledge were found. Like their antagonists, the naturalists believed that the source was entangled with value: the rational order of the universe is, without question, a good in Huxley's world; and when he asks himself whether he would rather be free, in the theological sense, to choose evil, or be constrained, in the deterministic naturalists' sense, to do what is necessary, he prefers the "necessary" – as long as he can rely on the necessary being a good. Huxley believes, with a conviction beyond ideology, that the clerical view of the world is "bad": it implies an irrational disorder and leads to that worst of sins, ignorance. Better, in the Cartesian dilemma, objectivity and determinism than subjectivity and chaos. Value can be excluded from the surface of the objectivist's thinking because it is deeply bound in the idea of objectivity itself.

In the struggle between the naturalists and traditional religion, the question was not about whether objectivity was possible, but whether it was possible without God. Despite the quest for value-free judgments, the scientists, as the examples of Huxley and Tylor should have demonstrated, were constantly engaged with problems of value; ideas matter ethically too. Further complications arise, however, because the naturalists knew, in spite of their Baconian protestations, that knowledge came in ways not entirely covered by the empiricist formula. The scientists' preoccupation with "imagination," as in Tyndall's famous Belfast lecture, or G. H. Lewes' massive attempt to reconcile science and metaphysics in *Problems of Life and Mind*, is a symptom of widespread recognition that the Baconian method did not adequately describe the complex and irregular procedures of science and that "science" was not as rigorously empirical as its apologists often argued. The great struggles of the Victorians, and of the scientific naturalists and their allies, to view science as an entirely coherent and unified project may well have been mistaken.[27] But they were important and in many ways salutary struggles to establish the credentials of science in a culture still largely dominated by traditional religious authority, and they were critical to the continuing effort to establish that morality itself did not require a religious sanction.

In their struggles to justify the work of science and to formulate its procedures, the scientific naturalists recognized how critical it was to face head on those deep cultural issues that were the subject of the work of the "sages" like Arnold or Carlyle, or Ruskin. The differences are not always stark. Huxley often expresses sentiments we might have expected from Ruskin or Arnold. The naturalists struggled for a science that they believed was, or should be, integral with culture, a power capable of enriching life, not merely materially and quantitatively, but with a sense of history and art and the complexity of social relations. But in rejecting the past as model, the naturalists inevitably questioned standards (morality and taste as well) while they constantly waged war against those who argued that rejection of conventional religion was license for immorality. They lived with an almost puritanical austerity that might have been the envy of the strictest evangelicals even as their inversion of religious rhetoric and their secularization of meaning subverted traditional supports for morality. When Darwin traced the aesthetic sense back to sexual selection, and conscience to the usefulness of social sympathy in natural selection, he wrested those authoritative categories from the absolute. Ironically, while finding their source in natural phenomena, he initiated a tradition the sages could not contemplate, of denaturalizing morality and taste. That is, Art and Morality are not in "nature" but are human developments from anaesthetic and amoral phenomena; human effort has transformed these and given them the same status in nature as physical phenomena.

In modern parlance, the scientists' project was demystification. If they often remystified (as Tylor does) by giving nature *moral* authority, they did not make remystification the kind of high cause evident in Carlyle's

---

[27] Within the philosophy of science there have been important arguments developed in recent years about the disunity of science. One of the most impressive of these arguments is John Dupré, *The Disorder of Things: Metaphysical Foundations of the Disunity of Science* (Cambridge, MA: Harvard University Press, 1993). One of the book's primary theses is "the denial that science constitutes, or could ever come to constitute, a single, unified project" (p. 1). The idea, of course, runs counter to Huxley's view "that there is but one kind of knowledge and but one method of acquiring it". Dupré writes in the twentieth century against the intellectual hegemony of science, while Huxley wrote in the nineteenth, against the intellectual hegemony of the church.

work or in Arnold's wonderful impressionistic catch phrases like "Reason and the will of God," or "Sweetness and Light," or more telling still, "to see the object as in itself it really is." The methods announced by the naturalists would have forced them to criticize many of their own positions.

Some of the richness of the naturalists' position can be inferred from Huxley's part in the great debate with Arnold on Literature and Science, which was in great part about science and education. The consensus has long been that Arnold was the winner. The upholder of culture, concerned with the full human experience, should indeed triumph over the philistine proponent of an exclusively scientific education. Insisting on the "need of humane letters," Arnold connects that word, "humane," with "the paramount desire in men that good should be for ever present to them," and he goes on to argue that humane letters will build the necessary bridge between "the new conceptions" provided by science and "our instinct for beauty, our instinct for conduct."[28]

The unGothic Arnold invokes the Middle Ages against modern science as he tries to explain the function of humane letters. In those days, Arnold says, "knowledge was made to engage . . . emotions . . . powerfully." Even if the religious substance of the medieval vision is dead, the form must be observed. Poetry replaces the religion that science has displaced, and Arnold finds his values by looking backward: "The medieval universities came into being, because the supposed knowledge, delivered by Scripture and the Church, so deeply engaged men's hearts, by so simply, easily, and powerfully relating itself to their desire for conduct, their desire for Beauty" (p. 66). When Huxley looked backward it was to find indications of developments to come, and in essay after essay, reviewing the history of science in European culture, he sees the Middle Ages' preoccupation with the supernatural as an obstacle to knowledge. So much had been lost through the "Dark Ages" that the new scientific men of the Renaissance, "though standing on the shoulders of the old philosophers, were a long time before they saw as much as their forerunners [the ancient Greeks] had done"("Progress of Science," p. 44). The naturalists did not participate in the medievalism that turned so many Victorian eyes to the distant past. Huxley's vision, in good post-Darwinian fashion, is developmental: his interest in history is in origins, not models.

---

[28] Matthew Arnold, *Philistinism in England and America*, ed. R. R. Super (Ann Arbor: University of Michigan Press, 1974).

Arnold's "understanding of science," a recent critic has noted, was "extraordinarily naïve": "he constantly stresses the importance of knowing the results of scientific study, but he seems curiously insensitive to the claims of science as a mode of intellectual culture and thus as an important element in liberal curriculum."[29] He thinks of the natural sciences as mechanisms for gathering facts, some of which develop into new "concepts." But he does not imagine that there is such a thing as "scientific imagination," or that scientific fact might have moral and emotional significance. Neither he nor the other sages could share John Stuart Mill's touching view that "The intensest feeling of the beauty of a cloud lighted by the setting sun, is no hindrance to my knowing that the cloud is vapour of water, subject to all the laws of vapours in a state of suspension."[30]

For Huxley, whatever Arnold might have thought of scientific discourse, knowledge and feeling were not disjunct, and truth was not morally neutral. The scientific (and cultural commitment) to "objectivity" and "disinterest" and dispassion was necessary just because so much is at stake. We must be brave enough, so the rhetoric of all the naturalists goes, to discover the truth and dare to learn what we do not want to know. Despite their perhaps disingenuous bravado, Huxley's arguments were anything but obvious. If some of his aggressively scientistic passages now seem excessive, they justly conceive of the scientist as no mere passive recorder of the way things are – Arnold's view of the scientist at work – but as a visionary, a more convincing sage for his time than the sage himself:

the improvement of natural knowledge whatever direction it has taken, and however low the aims of those who may have commenced it - has not only conferred practical benefits on men, but in so doing has effected a revolution in their conceptions of the universe and of themselves, and has profoundly altered their modes of thinking and their views of right and wrong. I say that natural knowledge, seeking to satisfy wants, has found the ideas which can alone still spiritual cravings. (p. 31)

Huxley steps here directly into the dominant argument of those, like W. H. Mallock, who insisted that there was no way to get from "is" to "ought," from scientific fact to ethical imperative. While philosophically, Huxley may be on dangerous ground, history certainly confirms that the dominance of scientific thought has changed more than the culture's attitude toward the physical world. Moreover, the kind of skepticism that

---

[29]   Robert A. Donovan, "Mill, Arnold, and Scientific Humanism", in *Victorian Science and Victorian Values: Literary Perspectives,* ed. James Paradis and Thomas Postlewait (New York, 1981), p. 189.

[30]   John Stuart Mill, *Autobiography* (1873), ed. Jack Stillinger (Boston, MA, 1969), p. 92.

our contemporary theorists have brought to the idea of objectivity has given more weight to the notion that there is no such thing as untheorized fact, no such thing as fact separate from human needs and interests. If Huxley's arguments were part of that larger polemic to establish the authority of science against more traditional authority, his daring assertion of its "spiritual" in addition to its material value was critical for his own commitment to scientific knowledge. But it is precisely for such views that many humanist historians have condemned the naturalists. Their sin was high valuation of reason and intelligence, the assumption that knowledge is always vitally connected to human values. But their utopianism was an historically comprehensible consequence of the astonishing power of the knowledge the new science was bringing to light. It was, for better or worse, a brave new world, but one that Huxley and his colleagues genuinely believed could extend helpfully to all areas of human experience and work to the improvement of the human condition.

But Huxley was a deeply cultivated man, and one for whom what we now call the "humanities" mattered much. In his debate with Arnold, he was not asking for a purely scientific education. He was responding to a critical failure in English curricula when he wrote, as Lyon Playfair pointed out in his presidential address to the British Association in 1885, that there was "a lamentable deficiency of science education" almost everywhere in England. In the endowed schools, for example, "while twelve to sixteen hours per week are devoted to classics, two to three hours are considered ample for science ... The old traditions of education stick as firmly to schools as a limpet does to a rock; though I do the limpet injustice, for it does make excursions to pastures new."[31]

"Science and Culture" was as daring in its way as Ruskin's "Traffic." In Birmingham, the den of the practical men of practical England, at the opening of a science college, Huxley dared to attack merely "practical" views. With a rhetoric more devious if less thrilling than Ruskin's, he weaves an argument around Josiah Mason's condition that there be "no mere literary instruction and education" at the new college, and ends with an apologia for the languages and the humanities. Arnold's objectives are sound; what is wrong is his view that they can only be attained through exclusively literary education. Huxley in fact smuggles Arnold into the Josiah Mason curriculum, insisting on the importance of "a wider culture

---

[31] Lyon Playfair, "Science and Technology as Sources of Natural Power" (1886), in *Victorian Science*, ed. George Basalla, William Coleman, and H. Kargon (Garden City: Anchor Books, 1970), p. 69.

than that yielded by science alone."[32] The object of scientific education, and of science itself, according to Huxley, is neither prosperity nor education, but, as Ruskin would have been proud to argue, "the enhancement of life." "If the increasing perfection of manufacturing processes is to be accompanied by an increasing debasement of those who carry them on, I do not see the good of industry and prosperity ... The prosperity of industry depends," Huxley tells the founders of the science college, "not merely upon the improvement of manufacturing processes, not even upon the ennobling of the individual character, but upon a third condition as well, namely a clear understanding of the conditions of social life, on the part of both the capitalist and the operative." Nothing could be more sage-like, except perhaps the implicit trust in the ordinary student.

Huxley's lecture is the model of balance that Arnold's is often taken to be. He argues for remediation of an intolerable condition in education, offers a rich vision of the value of humanistic study, and implies a new model, not built on medieval retrospects, of what it might mean to connect knowledge and feeling. While Arnold revealed what should have been disqualifying ignorance of science, Huxley revealed a strong knowledge of the humanities and was willing to risk arguing for Arnold's 'culture' out into the world of social and political action – which, of course, Arnold refused to do, setting 'culture' outside of politics. Of course Huxley and Arnold were friends, and the public encounter, while serious enough, reflects the playfulness of both great writers in their pugnacity. The solemnity with which both are usually read misses the playfulness and flexibility of spirit that made them effective cultural critics if also, perhaps, rather inconsistent philosophers.

Substantively, they agreed far more than they disagreed. Both sought to humanize and broaden the understanding of the society which they mutually regarded as narrow and "philistine." As Huxley wanted to insure that modern languages and literature were part of the 'science' curriculum (for "practical" reasons, of course), so Arnold would allow study of Euclid and Newton and Darwin. Elsewhere, Arnold agreed that science should be part of everyone's curriculum; Huxley is said to have agreed that the Bible should be taught to all students. Despite this fundamental agreement, however, there is a crucial divergence that must be taken into account. Arnold is usually regarded, for better or worse, as a spokesman for rounded culture, for a rich contextual sense of art and human experience, but in his formulaic insistence on beauty and conduct, with its appeal to the

[32] T. H. Huxley, "Science and Culture" (1880), in *Science and Education* (London, 1894), p. 156.

Hellenic or Hebraic past, and with his intense distrust of the complacency of the modern, he remained closed to the widening of the humanist position implicit in Huxley's argument. Arnold looks back, and tends to freeze the past into an ideal; it becomes a point of comparison. Huxley sees the past developmentally, not as a model but as part of the condition that accounts for where we are now. The most profound divergence between the two friends comes, I believe, just here: with all its failures, the constantly transforming present, Huxley would argue, is where value resides.

But finally, the Huxley–Arnold debate is symptom of the critical problem at the heart of the contest to replace traditional humanist and religious authority with the authority of science. Could a science-oriented, secular society satisfy the "spiritual" and "ethical" needs of the new culture? I want to conclude here with a consideration of what it was that led the naturalists to believe they were able to provide a better alternative to the religious vision and to the visions of the more secular sages. The basis of the naturalists' arguments was a kind of "faith" or a cluster of not entirely compatible "faiths" – and this Huxley conceded, if not precisely in these words – in the law-regulated nature of the world, in the adequacy of reason to detect the unity of nature and of scientific investigation. To sustain these faiths they had to look not for philosophical consistency or comprehensiveness, but for pragmatic confirmation. They built their church on assumptions that remained assumptions, and part of their spiritual consolation came from their courageous – this was central to the rhetorical force of their argument – willingness to sacrifice traditional and self-deluding consolation for the sake of making their society better.

But pragmatic effects aside, they opened the way to questioning everything, suggesting that conventions traditionally taken to be inescapably real were in fact arbitrary human constructions. They tended to accept the uniformitarian dogma that knowledge is possible because the world has always worked uniformly, according to laws now in operation, and that ostensibly massive changes and extraordinary phenomena could be accounted for by minute incremental effects of minute causes. *Natura non agit per saltum* was Darwin's watchword, and Lyell's. Knowledge, they believed, can only be achieved when the data of experience are organized into laws and sequences are predictable. Although law did come to replace religion as the guarantor of order in the universe and society, a testimony to God's ordering intelligence, the central naturalist move was to demystify it, remove it from divine intention and locate it in natural regularity. At their most rigorous, the naturalists regarded laws as having no teleological implication. Laws existed in nature as the human formulation of regularity of sequence[33] and such sequence operates by means of uninterrupted cause and effect (cause and effect themselves were often drained of metaphysical implications and understood only as phenomena in constant conjunction). Finally, while Herschel himself understood that "naming" was merely an arbitrary convenience to avoid getting lost in particularities, later science, particularly after Darwin, was leaning imperfectly away from the essentialist view that classification, and its language, are one-to-one representations of the real and absolute distinctions in nature, and was tending to conceive all things as in flux.

The question of what determines the truthfulness of "discovery" in such conditions was the big question of scientific method. Discoveries stick, the naturalists argued, because of their power to connect other "partial generalisations," which explain more than they were intended to explain, and to be subjected to "exact verification" (or, in Popper's later formulation, to be "falsifiable").[34] Scientific truth implied a community of understanding. The truth, finally, lay beyond words, which were to be severed from Platonic essentialism and regarded as conveniences of discussion and ordering, subject only to the rules of language. Truth depended finally on experience. The establishment of this myth of objectivity and positivity, even against the insights implicit in the overt rejection of essentialism and Adamic language, is what gave to science that tinge of orthodoxy that Arthur Balfour and W. H. Mallock assailed. Objectivity belonged to a religious intellectual frame. The Cartesian dilemma becomes most intense at the point at which a divine source of authority "disappears." And thus the strategy of the naturalists in adopting the structure of religious language without its real supernatural and divine referent.

---

[33] See, for one of the most famous examples of this, Darwin's clarification of the metaphor of "natural selection" as quite literally meaning only the regularity of a natural law, which appears in later editions of *The Origin of Species*, ch. iv, and his earlier formulation of the language in the "Introduction" to *The Variation of Animals and Plants under Domestication* (1866), 2 vols (New York, 1900), I:7. For Darwin, laws are merely "the sequence of events as ascertained by us."

[34] It is particularly interesting to note how persistent this view of science has been. E. O. Wilson picks up Whewell's word, "Consilience," as the title of his book arguing for the assimilation of cultural and scientific study in sociobiology. As against the argument of Dupré, Wilson continues to argue for "the unity of the sciences." Wilson defines Whewell's use of the word: "a 'jumping together' of knowledge by the linking of facts and fact based theory across disciplines to create a common groundwork of explanation." E. O. Wilson, *Consilience: the Unity of Knowledge* (New York: Alfred A. Knopf, 1998), p. 8. For a discussion and critique of Wilson's argument, see my *Darwin Loves You: Natural Selection and the Re-enchantment of the World* (Princeton: Princeton University Press, 2006).

Barring language and spirit as "real," the naturalists took the material world as the only real subject of knowledge. Thus, in the demystifying but reductive move that most fully alienated the religious and the humanists, Huxley and Tyndall discussed human life as they discussed physical phenomena; science, as Tyndall put it, attempts "to explain the unknown in terms of the known." He takes as example the excited actions of a merchant who leaps from his chair after reading a letter and makes complicated moves to avert financial disaster. This complex mass of action, emotional, intellectual, and mechanical, is evoked by the "impact upon the retina of the infinitesimal waves of light coming from a few pencil marks on a bit of paper . . . What caused the merchant to spring out of his chair? The contraction of his muscles. What made his muscles contract? An impulse of the nerves, which lifted the proper latch, and liberated the muscular power. Whence this impulse? From the centre of the nervous system. But how did it originate there? This is the critical question, to which someone will reply that it had its origin in the human soul."[35]

Needing to bring behavior within the order of reality recognized by physical science, Tyndall argues that his explanation is better than the conventional religious one, which, in insisting on a willing and free self, implies that there is a "self within the self which acts through the body as through a skillfully constructed instrument." Finally, Tyndall admits, he cannot answer the question, "Whence this impulse?" He cannot discover the connection "between molecular motions and states of consciousness" (pp. 354–5). There are, then, spiritual possibilities, both for Tyndall and for the "agnostic" Huxley, but only if they are not invoked as explanations for material phenomena. In W. H. Mallock's uproarious satiric representation of Tyndall, Tyndall says, "Let us beware, then, of not considering religion noble; but let us beware still more of considering it true."[36] Exposing the metaphysics implicit in our conventional way of talking about "self," and demystifying the language of "spirit" – these were part of the naturalists' programme to make the material respectable in a world whose values were at least professedly "spiritual." That the effort was susceptible to funny satire, in particular from those utterly confident of the authority of traditional systems of value, does nothing to invalidate the effort.

It seemed evident to all of the scientific naturalists that the biology could be assimilated absolutely to a model out of physics. But their

---

[35] John Tyndall, "Science and Man" (1877), *Fragments of Science* 2:353.
[36] W. H. Mallock, *The New Republic* (1877), ed. J. Max Patrick (Gainesville, FL, 1950), p. 42.

attempt to assimilate biology with physics was, at least, premature, although working now out of molecular genetics, the assimilation seems much more likely. Still, as Ernst Mayr believed and argued, "The explanatory equipment of the physical sciences is insufficient to explain complex living systems" (p. 52). Underlying the reductionist moves of the naturalists was the metaphysical assumption, acceptable to humanist and scientist alike, that the world is unified and coherent: there is "but one science about the one real world."[37] Kuhn's theory of scientific revolutions has put this nineteenth-century view in doubt; and Mayr and Stephen Jay Gould have argued persuasively against the view that biology is reducible to physics. The almost comic example of Tyndall's robotic merchant suggests that the naturalists understood that there was a problem. Their strategy was not to yield belief in unity but to confess that they did not understand how it worked. At stake was the possibility of science in a culture that preferred *a priori* authority, and took the idea of the unity of nature as unproblematic.

One of the striking aspects of this problem is that despite the naturalists' triumph over the religious world-view (a temporary one, indeed), and, then, the powerful reaction against the naturalists, continuing from Victorian conservative thought to advanced modern biological thought of the kind that Mayr and Gould practiced and argued for, the questions have not been settled. The development of molecular biology and the discovery of the genome have seemed to change the scientific hierarchy that Mayr rejected and given biology the sort of precision that had seemed to belong entirely to physics. I am in no position to argue the questions that will only be resolved, if at all, through close attention to what science can reveal, but I want to emphasize here the plausibility of the position of the scientific naturalists, a position that has, if in different language and with far greater kinds of material evidence, resumed its importance in contemporary debates, both scientific and cultural. It was not only plausible, but it was part of a strong ethical initiative, an attempt to "naturalize" all of life and thus, as the naturalists thought, give power for change and improvement to people themselves.

Arnold, of course, also urged the importance of "disinterest," and he found his model in Burke. He might, however, have looked to the scientists, who, even when perhaps much too confident about the atomic-Newtonian model of matter, more than conceded that they could be wrong. After all, Huxley's institutionalized science rejected Huxley's

---

[37] Ian Hacking, ed., *Scientific Revolutions* (Oxford: Oxford University Press, 1981), p. 2.

model of the world. As Stephen Toulmin and June Goodfield put it, "the men responsible" for the dogma of classical physics "wished to establish neither a political nor an ideological tyranny and when the time came they refused to shut their eyes to the necessity for fundamental change."[38] Late-nineteenth-century positivism was not, says John Passmore, "an attack on philosophy by arrogant and self-satisfied scientists." Rather, it prepared the way for revolutions in science, "associated with the name of Einstein."[39] Their vested interest was not in particular theories, but in the cultural conditions that allow for free discussion of them. The political and social implications of their commitments are clear, but whatever those implications might be, the naturalists' energy for free inquiry valuably enhanced the possibility of questioning the disinterest even of that move.

Rejection of the naturalists' faith in objectivity in general – the "objective existence of the material," which Huxley affirmed – should not distract attention from the integrity and intensity of the skepticism that for the naturalists was essential to scientific work. The skepticism of positivism and its cousins paradoxically led positivists to raise doubts even about "objectivity," putting the whole idea of it to which they were so committed in peril.[40] Since their enterprise entailed constant testing of the validity of all knowledge, including their own, the scientists had to ask themselves not only what they were knowing but *how* they were knowing it. (This is one of the major reasons that Huxley was so fascinated with Descartes and took him so often as a model.) Preoccupation with method follows from radical skepticism. The struggle to achieve the objectivity many now believe was only another form of mystification implied distrust of the *a priori* as institutionalized superstition, wariness of perception itself as distorted, subject to angles of perspective and limitations of point of view, and disbelief in Adamic language. Science, that is to say, threw everything in doubt, at the same time as it was arguing strenuously that at last a positive method had been found to clear up the endless confusions of philosophy.

Consider how the naturalists handled change, a traditional motif of poetry. Not only did they see that change was continuing and ineluctable, but they had been convinced by Darwin that change was a condition for the production and prospering of life itself. The ideal stability and stasis of

---

[38]   Stephen Toulmin and June Goodfield, *The Architecture of Matter* (New York, 1962), p. 240.
[39]   John Passmore, *A Hundred Years of Philosophy* (Harmondsworth: Penguin, 1967), p. 324.
[40]   See my essay on Positivism, included in this volume, for a consideration of the skeptical nature of positivist thought.

Platonic and Aristotelian philosophy becomes, for the naturalists, a disastrous myth. It would be misguided to minimize some of the unhappy consequences of the new focus on change as it was translated by many naturalists and by much of the culture into the idea of progress. Spencer, Clifford, Tylor, Galton, among others, opened the way for social Darwinism as a real force in social programs. But the distinction between change and progress is critical. While Darwin was adapted to the progressive idea, and much of his writing justifies that adaptation, his theory itself argues not for progress, but only for change. While the naturalists too tended to believe in "progress," they did not in fact assume that all change is in the direction of the better. As Huxley put it in *Evolution and Ethics*, the word " 'Fittest' has a connotation of 'best'; and about 'best' there hangs a moral flavour. In cosmic nature, however, what is fittest depends upon the conditions."[41] The only certain "progress" is adaptation to current environmental conditions. "I believe," says Darwin, "in no law of necessary development."[42] "Natural Selection," he says in his autobiography, "is not perfect in its action, but tends only to render each species as successful as possible in the battle for life with other species, in wonderfully complex and changing circumstances" (p. 90). The emphases on change, instability, and demystifying produced a discourse more complex than any of its arguments or than the dogmatic form it often took. The mixture of messages infiltrated the culture. Yet the naturalists' discourse offered the culture a possibility that it still, on the whole, refuses – to live with the tentative, to risk not knowing, to recognise that action must precede certitude, and, most difficult of all, to understand that there can never be absolute proof.[43]

While holding the line against science and technology, capitalism and democracy, the sages joined religious critics in refusing to be bound by the epistemological limits insisted on by the naturalists. Regarding preoccupation with the material nature of the universe as a kind of moral disease, they rejected an attitude that would risk anarchy in its displacement through reason and experience of an intuitively grasped, historical locus of authority. While scientists were saying that the world was under the reign of law and progressively developing from rude beginnings to higher levels of

---

[41] T. H. Huxley, *Evolution and Ethics* (London, 1911), p. 80.
[42] Charles Darwin, *On the Origin of Species* (Cambridge, MA: Harvard University Press, 1958), p. 351.
[43] All of these qualities were dominant subjects of the major writings of the period – consider Arnold's insistence that action wait for knowledge, or William James' attempt to construct a philosophy that builds action in *before* the kind of certitude scientists and positivists required, or Huxley's own invention, "agnosticism," Spencer's "unknowable," Tyndall's acquiescence in the impossibility of knowing the relation between mind and body.

civilization, the sages were detecting in the withdrawal of authority from the *a priori*, and therefore from clerisy and inherited power, and in the extension of authority to experience and to "observation and experiment," the democratization of nature and the threat of an ultimate disorder.

But with all the ideological and cultural limitations of the naturalists they were at least as committed to a total vision of knowledge and culture as were the sages. As Donald R. Benson has said, "It is more than a passing irony that" the scientific theorists, like Tyndall and W. B. Carpenter, Jevons and Karl Pearson, "should have treated science as an essentially human and even humane activity while the humanists ... resignedly accepted the reductive popular conception of it."[44] When, for example, Huxley was asked to write the opening article for *Nature*, in 1869, he turned to Arnold's own culture hero, Goethe, and offered a translation of some of his aphorisms on nature. Those aphorisms are full of paradoxes – a sense of nature's mysterious refusal to resolve itself into rational human structures. The work is Whitmanesque, yet, as Huxley says, "with a bitter truth in it." Nevertheless, Goethe's vision is progressive. Having described a nature that both gives and takes away, creates life through ingenious modes of death, isolates and unites, completes, but never finishes, he talks of science, in a letter also translated by Huxley, as moving progressively from the comparative to the superlative.[45] Huxley is, of course, pleased with that view, but it is important for our sense of what the scientific methods of the late century were, that he sets it in the context of the moving, gnomic, lyric utterances of the great Romantic poet-scientist.

The humane, intellectual, and moral elements of the writing of the great naturalist-publicists are there in the freshness, clarity, cockiness, and energy of their prose. That the reaction to them was so strong testifies to the power and originality of their vision, if not to its consistency or its philosophic depths. In her brief study of the "scientific movement," as she calls it, Tess Cosslett may take too literally the naturalists' claims for disinterested moral engagement. But she is right that Huxley, Tyndall, and Clifford "insist passionately that science matters unto men ... demonstrate the importance of imagination in scientific thought, and ... present their view of the universe with a Carlylean awe and Mystery."[46] What she does not adequately insist on are the points I want to conclude

---

44   Donald R. Benson, "Facts and Contrasts: Victorian Humanists and Scientific Theorists on Scientific Knowledge", in *Victorian Science and Victorian Values*, p. 315.
45   T. H. Huxley, "Nature: Aphorisms by Goethe", *Nature*, I, 1 (4 November 1869), pp. 9–11.
46   Tess Cosslett, *The 'Scientific Movement' and Victorian Literature* (Sussex, 1982), p. 2.

with here, by looking briefly at the most notorious and adventurous of them – Clifford. I would want to emphasize their role as cultural critics, operating feistily and exuberantly in a context where their excesses were almost parodic responses to traditions of faith and authority. They were intellectual risk-takers, and the excitement of their work is, at this late date, far more in the disruptions than the solutions.

Clifford, for example, was surely a "provincial" in Arnold's scheme of things. His object is to disrupt, and to demystify nature and indeed science itself by depriving idealist or religious positions of their hiding-places in the mysteries of science, or in the limits of empiricist epistemology. And thus his writing is full of abrupt reversals. (The naturalists' inversions of commonsense readings of experience seem to anticipate, at least run parallel to, the Wildean pleasures of paradox that become so prominent in *fin de siècle* literature.) As a mathematician who helped bring non-Euclidean geometry from the continent to England, he was impressed by the evidence that Euclid's axioms themselves, far from being universal or *a priori*, were bound to the here and now. For Clifford, all statements, including those that had been taken to be axioms, are ultimately empirical, contingent on physical conditions: "No maxim can be valid at all times and places for all rational beings," he wrote. "A maxim valid for us can only be valid for such portions of the human race as are practically identical with ourselves."[47] Such a vital recognition of western provincialism is extraordinarily refreshing among Victorian writers.

"Universal statements," he argues, are merely exercises in definition: "the moment we use language at all, we may make statements which are apparently universal, by which we really only assign the meaning of words" (I:390). His sensitivity to the way language works, especially to substantiate abstractions, led him to question almost everything the culture – and science itself – authorized. He cannot allow the idea of law, which, as I have suggested, science had used to replace the banished God, to mean more than perceived regularity of sequence. "Now it is quite true," he argues, "that the word law in the expression 'law of nature,' and the expressions 'law of morals,' 'law of the land,' has two totally different meanings, which no educated person will confound; and I am not aware that anyone has rested the claim of science to judge moral questions on what is no better than a stale and unprofitable pun" (2: 125). While Clifford has what might be regarded as too confident a sense of "fact," he has an equally strong sense of the disguises language

[47]   W. K. Clifford, *Lectures and Essays*, 2 vols. (London, 1910), 2:279.

affords – in science and out – for prejudices. Language harbors for Clifford, as for Derrida, a metaphysic of presence, of which we need constantly to be reminded. "Language is part of the apparatus of thought" but its reference when it aspires to universality is always to itself. The metaphors latent in "law" are only one of many traps for the idealist consciousness.

Clifford's dogmatism is almost always at work against dogma, where inherited authority threatens to close discussion. "It is wrong," says Clifford, "always, everywhere, and for anyone, to believe anything upon insufficient evidence."[48] He releases into his world, through discussion of perception, a giddying stream of relativity, reducing the self to a cable of feeling. Beginning his lecture, "On Some of the Conditions of Mental Development," he asks his audience "what it is that you have done most often during this day." The answer is stunning: "I think you can hardly avoid being drawn to this conclusion: that you have all done nothing else from morning to night but *change your mind*" (1:79). Consciousness exists only in change. Nothing in Clifford's world is stable or univocal and thus nothing can be defined as we normally expect. Character itself is the accumulation of changes, changing in the act of identification. Although Clifford's Tyndallian insistence that all things human are subject to physical laws seems deterministic, his conception of change outreaches that definition. For, as he says, "the character which will roughly represent the law of man's action for some considerable time will not accurately represent that law for two seconds together. No action can take place in accordance with character without modifying the character itself" (1:84–5). Again, to have consciousness "is to have fifty thousand feelings at once, and to know them all in different degrees" (2:20). Elsewhere, he argues that every sensation includes, 'besides the actual message, something that we imagine and add to the message ... not the whole of sensation is immediate experience ... but this experience is supplemented by something else which is not in it" (2:308–9). To explore the implications of these various arguments would take us far into aesthetic theory and into developments in art and thought in our own moment.

What I want to emphasize is the way these arguments reshape common perceptions. Addressed to audiences who were, by all reports, enthralled,

---

[48] 2:175. This assertion is part of what William James calls Clifford's too "robustious" way, and it is clearly key in the great debate with which many of the essays in this book are concerned and that was at the center of Victorian battles over epistemology. What Clifford says here is just what Newman rejects explicitly in his appendix to the *Apologia* on "Liberalism." Obviously, what Clifford says here chimes precisely with what Huxley had to say, and it marks out the naturalists' rejection of religious authority.

Clifford's lectures are designed to destabilize, to turn the world on its head, so that new possibilities, alternatives to traditional notions of faith and order, might come in. Clifford was the Oscar Wilde of the naturalists. In the reaction to scientific dominance at the turn of the century, even in the moving and brilliant critiques by William James, something of Clifford's kind of daring originality has been lost. Lost in particular was that commitment to change normally missing from nostalgic Victorian constructions of bulwarks against anarchy. Clifford threatens that "principle of authority" Arnold sought to resist the constant flux and change manifest in nature and society. Alarmed at the threat, he refuses the risk that Clifford's arguments require and fantasizes a state that would be the embodiment of right reason, a state that would exercise the authority necessary to discriminate true culture, and thus suppress anarchy. A characteristic sage-like passage will serve as a final contrast to the scientist's view of things:

> Great changes there must be, for a revolution cannot accomplish itself without great changes; yet order there must be, for without order a revolution cannot accomplish itself by due course of law. So whatever brings risk of tumult and disorder, multitudinous processions in the streets of our crowded towns, multitudinous meetings in their public places and parks, – demonstrations perfectly unnecessary in the present course of our affairs, – our best self, or right reason, plainly enjoins us to set our face against. It enjoins us to encourage and uphold the occupants of the executive power, whoever they may be, in firmly prohibiting them. But it does this clearly and resolutely, and is thus a real principle of authority.[49]

Of course, the naturalists too insisted that there must be order, and thus the juxtaposition with Clifford is a bit distorting. But it is important to note here how the kind of terror of disorder, characteristic of most of the "sages," leads to certain constrained ways of thinking through which Clifford aggressively breaks. What Arnold says here fairly represents the culture's response to the sort of risks the naturalists were willing to take, at least intellectually. It closes itself to the new, or willingly postpones the new for the sake of order. If we cannot have the ideal, we still must support the state, "might till right is ready." Order and decorum are more important than change.

One of Clifford's essays talks about two qualities of mind, "crystallisation" and "plasticity." The former is the condition of death: "to become crystallised, fixed in opinion and mode of thought, is to lose the great

---

[49] Matthew Arnold, *Culture and Anarchy* (1869), ed. Ian Gregor (Indianapolis, 1971), p. 79.

characteristic of life, by which it is distinguished from inanimate nature: the power of adapting itself to circumstances'(1:116). For Clifford, crystallisation is "propriety." It is reliance on past forms and inherited authority, and it denies the risks and the vitality of movement into an unknown future. He talks of "the immense importance to a nation of checking the growth of conventionalities. Even so important a spokesman for agnosticism as Leslie Stephen sought a scientific theory that would "impose order on the chaos of events."

Near the end of his life Clifford was warmly befriended by Stephen, and certainly shared many of the materialist and agnostic principles that led Stephen to his crisis. He too sought ordering principles. But he plunged recklessly into disorder, risked paradox more pugnaciously than Huxley or Stephen would, "consciously holding [every theory] as an experiment, and being perfectly ready to give it up when found wanting" (1:150). Stephen, von Arx shows, withdrew from politics in the quest for stability and order. In these respects, then, Clifford was probably unique, pushing to their dangerous limits some of the destabilizing implications of science's anti-authoritarian strategies. It is a mistake to ignore these possibilities of the arguments of the scientific naturalists, something far different from the moral and intellectual 'bankruptcy' of which they have been accused. Perhaps we might still learn from them. What Stephen would have been uncomfortable with, what Arnold, leaning back toward the stabilities of an earlier age, could not have endured, can perhaps be summed up in the last sentence of Clifford's essay, printed in fact in Arnoldian italics: *It is not right to be proper.*

CHAPTER 5

In defense of Positivism

No philosophical movement of the nineteenth century engaged more fully the major intellectual preoccupations of the time, and few have been as influential down to the present moment as Positivism. Although Comte was not the only figure whose positivist ideas were disseminated in England,[1] he was the thinker whose systematization of anti-metaphysical scientific knowledge provoked important Victorians like Harriet Martineau, John Stuart Mill, G. H. Lewes and George Eliot to take up "positivism" as a serious philosophy. His ideas became focal points around which positivist programs (and hostility to those programs) constellated, and as Basil Willey claimed many years ago, "Comte is, in a sense, the century in epitome."[2] Twentieth-century positivism was quite a different thing, but many of the issues raised by Comte persist in positivism to this day, and looking at the Victorians' version can help focus some of the critical issues, particularly to do with the relation between fact and value, and the possibility of epistemology being an ethical enterprise (or at least tightly enwound with ethics).

To be sure, even at its height, the "Positivist Society" could count among its London members only ninety-three people. George Eliot, though she composed the Positivist hymn, "O May I Join the Choir Invisible," and was a good friend of Positivists, most particularly Frederic Harrison, would not attend the Positivist Church. T. R. Wright reports the contemporary joke about the schism within the Positivist Society, that "they had come to Church in one cab and left in two."[3] The Comte

---

[1] See Leszek Kolakowski, *The Alienation of Reason: A History of Positivist Thought* (New York: Doubleday & Co., 1968): "It is possible to begin the history of European positivist thought almost anywhere, for many strands we regard as of primary importance in contemporary positivist doctrines had antecedents in antiquity" (p. 11).

[2] Basil Willey, *Nineteenth-Century Studies: Coleridge to Matthew Arnold* (New York: Columbia University Press, 1949), p. 188.

[3] T. R. Wright, *The Religion of Humanity* (Cambridge: Cambridge University Press, 1986), p. 4.

whom Mill ultimately came to criticize and from whom Lewes partly withdrew quite literally transformed his system into a church and projected an authoritarian political structure, more or less on the model of medieval theocracy, and antithetical to Mill's liberal democratic beliefs.

But it is not the madness of Comte's church that constitutes our inheritance from positivism, although that church is only an extreme articulation of the underlying positivist passion that Peter Allan Dale describes (and many hostile to positivism have regarded their reverence for science as something like the moral equivalent of a church). Comte and the Positivist followers believed passionately that a new scientifically-based secularity needed the kind of moral and spiritual passion that was characteristic of religion if society were to sustain itself and progress. Meanwhile, the ideas that led John Stuart Mill to study Comte and support him financially were characteristic of a long nominalist and antimetaphysical tradition. Mill was interested in Comte's phenomenalism, relativism, and anti-essentialism, his denial of the possibility of access to the thing in itself, his insistence on law based not on a theory of causation but of constant succession, his refusal of the *a priori* and of metaphysics, and his historical reading of the development of these ideas. Although, except for the historical theory, these fundamental philosophical positions, as Mill himself noted, were not original, positivism became a productive movement, whose fundamental objectives and methods meshed brilliantly with English Victorian aspirations and anxieties.

Perhaps the aspect of Comte's thought that most attracted Mill – probably even more important than, though certainly consistent with, his epistemology – was his primary objective, the establishment of a science of the human. Positivism – basing itself on science – was founded, that is to say, precisely as an antidote to the corrosiveness of the rationalist/secular/materialist positions that were finding sanction in the increasing successes of science and technology. Comte feared the chaos of his moment, and chose to read it into a progress toward a fuller, positive knowledge. Mill, obviously, had little of Comte's nervousness about democracy and the chaos of conflicting views, but he shared with Comte the faith that human life could be improved by a new, rational study of human behavior – Comte's "sociology." Mill complained in his *System of Logic* that "'the proper study of mankind'" is "the only subject which Philosophy cannot succeed in rescuing from Empiricism," and he sought to generalize the methods successfully followed in the sciences – precisely the project he admired in Comte – in the hope of removing "this blot on the face of science."[4] From the start then, materialist skepticism was allied to the projects of the social and psychological sciences – a condition that might strike a contemporary as ironic given that at this moment such skepticism seems allied precisely to the project of resisting the developments in positivist sociology and evolutionary psychology. What we are watching now, as evolutionary psychology exercises an increasing hold on the popular imagination and makes its reductionist claims about discovering universal aspects of human nature, seems a direct fulfillment of Comte's and Mill's positivist aspirations.

The Comtean Positivist program clearly treated problems of epistemology with moral urgency. The radical synthetic/analytic dualism, the fact/value dichotomy, which so obviously mark the positivist tradition, was partly undercut by Comte's overt ethical energy, an energy that clearly drove all of his epistemological projects. The dominant view is that taking questions of knowledge as questions of morals is simply, as an anti-positivist colleague of mine recently remarked in reviewing my own writing, "a category mistake."[5] This critique, ironically, is itself based on positivist distinctions. Virtually every book discussing positivist thought seems to have to include a discussion of ethics that indicates where the lines might be drawn. The official logical positivist position is that ethical statements represent human construction and that the work of philosophy in the area is to establish "sentences that express connections between observable phenomena (actions and their consequences), and which therefore belong to the positive sciences, particularly to sociology."[6] This is the hard-line positivism that continues to arouse hostility from more interpretative minded social scientists and philosophers, but it makes clear how the fact/value distinction became a crucial tenet of twentieth-century positivism and was at odds with Comte's initiating energies.

One way out of the difficulty, as E. O. Wilson was the most prominent to recognize and argue, was to biologize human behavior entirely, as sociobiology and evolutionary psychology are now trying to do; at the end of that study we would find ourselves with the fulfillment of the ambitions of Comte and Mill to establish a fully scientific study of human

---

[4]   *The System of Logic: Ratiocinative and Inductive* (London: John W. Parker and Son, West Strand, 1856; 1 edn, 1843) II, p. 406. The famous Book VI, is devoted to this project under the heading, "The Logic of the Moral Sciences."

[5]   Hilary Putnam argues strongly against the positivist notion that there are such categorial differences. See his *The Collapse of the Fact/Value Distinction* (Cambridge, MA: Harvard University Press, 2002).

[6]   Richard von Mises, *Positivism: A Study in Human Understanding* (New York: Dover Publications, Inc., 1951), p. 370.

behavior. Ethics does become biology, or vice versa. But the odd point of this development is that while it seems to be sustained by the absolute differentiation between fact and value, the acquisition of fact is always so laden with value that it has borne historically with it precisely that mixture of epistemology and morality that it formally eschews, and that the Comteans built into the church of Victorian Positivism.

Thus, although the logical positivists worked hard to keep knowledge and value in separate categories, positivism, in all of its forms, has usually had a political impetus, and has understood that questions of knowledge were also questions of morals. Comte was explicit about it from the start. The first objective of Positivism with a capital P was to firm up the French Revolution's displacement of the theological and metaphysical orders. In that respect, its project was explicitly revolutionary. It had another face, of course, and that was its attempt, against the disorder created by the French Revolution and the flood of knowledge that followed it, to establish a new and firmer order – that new post-Christian order that Dale talks about. In Comte, this new order reverberates with authoritarian energy. One need look no further than the first chapter of the First System of the "Cours de philosophie positive" where Comte asserts that "The positive philosophy offers the only solid basis for that social reorganization that must succeed the critical condition in which most civilized nations are now living."[7] Comte in effect links the salvation of modern society to a fundamentally anti-democratic ideal of expertise, linking epistemology and political authority explicitly. Thus, while positivism is often regarded as a system that disguises its politics behind its epistemology, its genealogy suggests that its politics were always decidedly overt, not masked.

G. H. Lewes agreed that "a new epoch is dawning, that a new form of social life is growing up out of the ruins of feudalism."[8] Communism, Lewes claims, is a merely political solution to current problems, a "goal" rather than a "path," an object rather than a method. His own solution, at least in 1853, reverberates with Comtean political conservatism, for he argues that full liberty of press, education, and communication "directly tends more and more to become a systematic obstacle to all true social reorganisation" (p. 237). "The present anarchy of politics," he claims, "arises from the anarchy of ideas" (p. 12).

---

[7] Auguste Comte, *Auguste Comte and Positivism: the Essential Writings*, ed., Gertrud Lenzer (Chicago: University of Chicago Press, 1975), p. 83.

[8] G. H. Lewes, *Comte's Philosophy of the Sciences* (London: George Bell, 1890), p. 11.

Mill, consistent even with more recent positivist thinking, would seem to have agreed with Lewes that "all polity is founded on a system of ideas believed in common," and we cannot, "in social problems isolate the political from the moral, the moral from the religious" (p. 12).[9] His theory of government is based on the view that polity is in effect constructed, that is, not a natural thing but built on a system of ideas. Ironically, again, positivism, which in contemporary critiques from the left is seen as reifying things that are really constructed, anticipates the pervasive constructionism of what is often called "postmodern," insisting that all social phenomena, taken by a religious tradition as God-created, are in fact human constructions. Feuerbach trumps Christianity.

And virtually all positivisms assume the priority of intellect in the development of human society. Comte, Mill, and Lewes are children of the Enlightenment conception of social and cultural liberation through developing and increasing knowledge. While all three were forced to confront tension between mind and feeling as part of their serious theorizing about knowledge, and became explicit about the superior power of "Love," or "feeling" (for Lewes, indeed, rationality was only a species of "feeling" – a matter of empirically verifiable biology), all were committed to the idea that, as Roger Smith explains, "The history of science ... provides the key to future progress."[10] In different ways, each of them came to argue not only that the progress of ideas was the condition for social progress, but that ideas were themselves objects of deep feeling – knowledge, politics, morality, religion run into each other.

But Mill, whose passion for knowledge and rationality is equally driven by political ends, takes the positivist arguments and turns them to the interests of liberal democracy. About Comte's own conservative arguments, Mill says, "We fail to see any scientific connection between his theoretical explanation of the past progress of society, and his proposals for future improvement."[11] I need not pause here to recapitulate Mill's famous arguments in *On Liberty* and the essays on the Enfranchisement and the

---

[9] I am grateful to Dennis Patterson for bringing to my attention, however belatedly on my part, the tradition of legal positivism, which at first sight has characteristics strikingly similar to that of "postmodern" constructionism, but which is at the same time faithful to the positivist fact/value dichotomy. Legal positivism's primary position is that law is merely conventional, constructed by social conventions rather than given naturally or representing some abstract Platonic idea of justice. Here is another place where what is often taken in the culture wars as postmodernism's radically disruptive constructionism has its most respectable antecedents in positivist thought.

[10] Roger Smith, *The Norton History of the Human Sciences* (New York: W. W. Norton, 1997), p. 427.

[11] John Stuart Mill, *Auguste Comte and Positivism* (Ann Arbor: University of Michigan Press, 1961; orig., 1865), p. 118.

Subjection of Women, where he insists on the need for something like universal education before there can be a genuinely just society, but the echoes of Positivism are evident throughout. At one point, confronting the counter-argument that he was claiming that knowledge is only possible when there is no unanimity, Mill claims that, "As mankind improve, the number of doctrines which are no longer disputed or doubted will be constantly on the increase; and the well-being of mankind may almost be measured by the number and gravity of the truths which have reached the point of being uncontested."[12] But while Mill's positivism points toward an ultimately unified knowledge to which all intelligent people will have to defer, he is strenuous in his critique of Comte's (and Lewes') rejection of liberal society. He complains angrily that Comte "demands a moral and intellectual authority, charged with the duty of guiding men's opinions and enlightening and warning their consciences; a Spiritual Power, whose judgments on all matters of high moment should deserve, and receive, the same universal respect and deference which is paid to the united judgment of astronomers in matters astronomical." But entrusting such expert authority with institutionalized organized power would, he says, "involve nothing less than a spiritual despotism" (*Comte and Positivism*, p. 98). In effect, Mill's argument against positivism is founded on positivist premises about the fundamental importance of knowledge in political life, and *at the same time* anticipates the ideological critique of positivism that is so marked in our own debates, denying the "unmarked" privilege of scientific authority, or the absurdity of thinking that any given embodiment of scientific thought would exercise power disinterestedly.

Thus, part of the positivist inheritance is the recognition, which is too often taken to be a consequence of post-1960s theory, that knowledge and value are intricately entangled. The hard (and often impassioned) labor of twentieth-century positivists to disentangle knowledge and value is a mark of the intricacy of their implication in each other. At the foundation of the last section of *System of Logic* is the great utilitarian psychological assumption – the greatest happiness principle: "I merely declare my conviction," Mill says, "that the general principle to which all rules of practice ought to

---

[12] John Stuart Mill, *On Liberty* in *Prefaces to Liberty: Selected Writings of John Stuart Mill*, ed. Bernard Wishy (Boston: Beacon Press, 1959), p. 286. This argument, which may not sound particularly positivist, was the fundamental position of theorists of science at the beginning of the nineteenth century. Clearly, this view is closely related to modern reductionism. See John Herschel, *Preliminary Discourse on the Study of Natural Philosophy* (Chicago: University of Chicago Press, 1987; orig. 1830), in which Herschel insists on the primacy of law in the study of nature: laws begin in the minute details of natural fact, and rise to the broad reach of universally encompassing theory.

conform, and the test by which they should be tried, is that of conducive-ness to the happiness of mankind, or rather, of all sentient beings."[13]

Mill's explicitly democratic epistemology is obviously a long way from the epistemology of the Vienna Circle. The logical positivists continued with a vengeance the anti-metaphysical thrust of nineteenth-century posi-tivism. They carried its empiricism yet further, in part because they were alert to the many problems earlier empiricism had encountered – includ-ing its threatened lapse into full scale solipsism and something like ideal-ism that is evident in Karl Pearson's positivism. Sensitive to the hidden metaphysics of language and the enormous difficulty of finding an ulti-mate ground that could move beyond language to the unuttered otherness of the real, the Vienna Circle, turning to intense considerations of lan-guage, was not aberrant in the history of positivism after Comte. Its positivism, an empiricism that pushed toward an ultimate foundation in "protocol sentences," was a logical development from the skepticisms of earlier positivisms.

It is an historical irony, however, that their rigorously anti-metaphysical and nominalist epistemology has in the last decades been associated with reactionary, even fascistic politics. Most of the members of the Vienna Circle, like Carnap and Schlick, were socialists and were driven from Hitler's Europe, while Heidegger, whose philosophy has so significantly affected contemporary left cultural theory, became a Nazi. Michael Friedman claims that "In the European context of the 1920s, logical positivism arose and developed as a powerful revolutionary force, deeply intertwined with the other revolutionary trends (in the sciences, in the arts, in politics, and in society) that made up what we now know as Weimar culture. The logical positivists aimed at nothing less than a total refashioning of phi-losophy as a whole that would definitively end the fruitless, and endless, controversies of traditional metaphysics."[14] (Richard Rorty's quest to end these controversies is surely also an inheritance from the positivists, who, however, thought they could escape those controversies through philoso-phy itself.) I might have lifted this description of the logical positivists for my opening description of Comte's positivism.

Positivism's capacity to sustain its power over those who have tri-umphed in its death is one of its most remarkable features. Larry Laudan's

---

[13]   John Stuart Mill, *A System of Logic: Ratiocinative and Inductive* (London: John W. Parker and Son, 1856), II, p. 539.
[14]   Michael Friedman, *Reconsidering Logical Positivism* (Cambridge: Cambridge University Press, 1999), p. xiii.

Beyond Positivism and Relativism begins with a long section called " 'The Sins of the Fathers . . .': Positivist Origins of Postpositivist Relativisms." There Laudan, no friend of positivism *or* of relativism, argues in detail that what he sees as the failure of postpositivist epistemology – of pure constructivism, of theories of empirical underdetermination, of the view that different conceptual frameworks are incommensurable – is not the result of a break with positivism but of the "fact that it has carried to their natural conclusion several tendencies *indigenous to positivism* itself."[15] Similarly, in his study of the English positivists, Dale discusses the historical continuities between positivism and its ostensible contemporary opposites, like deconstruction. He complains about the "naivete of believing in radical disjunctions and innovations," but perhaps even more importantly, of "the naivete that would oversimplify not only history but also one's present philosophical antagonists in the interests of establishing an easy superiority over beliefs or positions that may never have had any serious exponents" (p. 284).

Friedman begins his study of logical positivism by calling attention to "the very substantial parallels between central aspects of our postpositivist situation and basic elements of the positivists' own philosophical position," and he claims immediately that "far from being naive empiricists . . . the positivists in fact incorporated what we now call the theory ladenness of observation as central to their novel conception of science" (p. 17). Ian Hacking is even more forceful in his insistence on continuities and on the irony of those continuities. "The roots of social constructionism," he claims, "are in the very logical positivism that so many present-day constructionists profess to detest."[16] Stories of positivism's disingenuity, simple mindedness, and death have been greatly exaggerated. If it is our enemy, we had better face our own implication in it.

Almost all of the distrustful and skeptical attitudes poststructuralist theorists have taken up toward knowledge, feeling a kind of revolutionary fervor in their commitments, have a long and often positivist history. Distrust of science and of totalizing narratives and empirical certainty, belief in the primacy of language (and its hidden metaphysics), in the construction of knowledge, in the relative nature of knowledge, in the constructedness of naturalized concepts, in the inescapability of perspective,

---

[15] Larry Laudan, *Beyond Positivism and Relativism: Theory, Method, and Evidence* (Boulder: Westview Press, 1996), p. 6.

[16] Ian Hacking, *The Social Construction of What?* (Cambridge, MA: Harvard University Press, 1999), p. 42.

belief that all facts are laden with theory – all of these have their analogues or sources in the positivist enterprise back to Hume. Positivist theory has always depended primarily on skepticism and negation, perhaps beginning with Hume's quest to find beneath the debris of rationality knowledge that could finally be trusted. Raymond Williams identifies as a defining aspect of all positivisms the attempt to "describe and justify a criterion of reliable knowledge."[17]

But the great heritage of positivism has been in the labor of clearing away, of standing suspiciously over claims to naturalness, reality, and truth, rather than in the establishment of positive truth. Positivism has been most successful in extending and complicating Hume's already deep skepticisms, rather than in achieving what Hume also failed to achieve, the positive affirmations that were supposed to grow out of his negative ideas. The rigorous demands he put on knowledge claims are, in effect, the basis of contemporary postmodern skepticism. Rom Harré has argued that the deep critique of science by many cultural critics is based on what he calls "the fallacy of high redefinition."[18] That is, as critics discover that, for example, empirical evidence is always underdetermined, they argue that science's claim to produce authoritative knowledge is belied. But such a claim depends on a higher expectation for empirical validation than even the positivists were likely to ask for.

The fundamental move of all positivisms is akin to Descartes' establishment of the Great Doubt, the exposure and dismissal of previous errors. Comte historicized that sort of move, arguing that history revealed a progress through error towards positive knowledge, so that it was not Comte but history itself that was producing truth. Huxley, denying all the while any connection to positivism, adopted a fundamental positivist position when he accepted what he took to be Descartes' "golden rule": "give unqualified assent to no propositions but those the truth of which is so clear and distinct that they cannot be doubted. The enunciation of this great first commandment of science consecrated Doubt."[19] Though the hermeneutics of suspicion may have its roots in Marx, Nietzsche, and Freud, it might just as well have been initiated in positivism. Indeed, the most powerful current hermeneutic of suspicion – almost Nietzschean

[17] Raymond Williams, "Positivist" in *Keywords* (New York: Oxford University Press, 1976), pp. 200–1.
[18] Rom Harré, *Varieties of Realism* (Oxford: Basil Blackwell, 1986), p. 5.
[19] T. H. Huxley, "'On Descartes' 'Discourse Touching the Method of Using One's Reason Rightly and of Seeking Scientific Truth,'" in *Methods and Results* (London: Macmillan and Co., 1893), p. 169.

in its boldness – is pretty distinctively positivist, manifested in evolutionary psychology, which begins by hypothesizing the validity of natural selection and adaptation as the explanation of human development and goes on to expose almost all apparent instances of altruism as forms of evolutionary competition.[20] It is true that behind the deep skepticism of evolutionary psychology to all non-biological explanation of human behavior lies a very positive belief in the authority and verifiability of evolutionary facts. The old positivist commitment to fully naturalistic explanation has always entailed some perhaps unadmitted first principle – here, of scientific authority. But there are no knowledge systems or anti-systems that don't begin with some metaphysical assumption, as relativists, for instance, are tired of hearing ("how can you be relativist if you insist that *everything* is relative?").[21]

The deep negativity of the much earlier positivism is clear in Mill's approving representation of Comte's views of what constitutes the fundamental doctrine of a true philosophy:

We have no knowledge of anything but Phaenomena; and our knowledge of phaenomena is relative, not absolute. We know not the essence, nor the real mode of production, of any fact, but only its relations to other facts in the way of succession or of similitude. These relations are constant; that is, always the same in the same circumstances. The constant resemblances which link phaenomena together, and the constant sequences which unite them as antecedent and consequent, are termed their laws. The laws of phenomena are all we know respecting them. Their essential nature, and their ultimate causes, either efficient or final, are unknown and inscrutable to us. (p. 6)

The passage, which lays out the fundamental lines of positivism that make Hacking's or Laudan's view of logical positivism relevant to Comte and Mill as well, is framed entirely by negations: in effect it tells us that we

[20] Debates within evolutionary psychology are much more complicated than this, and I am grateful to Stephen Stich for educating me in some of the more sophisticated debates, particularly about altruism. One of the heated arguments within evolutionary psychology is whether evolution might develop in "group selection," rather than in individual selection. Group selection could allow for a biological basis for "altruism," one of the essential conditions of evolutionary psychology. The best argument for the possibility of group selection as far as I know at the moment, an argument that still has not taken hold in the field of evolutionary psychology, is Elliot Sober and David Sloan Wilson, *Unto Others: The Evolution and Psychology of Unselfish Behavior* (Cambridge, MA.: Harvard University Press, 1998). Two more recent studies develop the argument: David Sloan Wilson, *Darwin's Cathedral: Evolution, Religion, and the Nature of Society* (Chicago: University of Chicago Press, 2002); David Sloan Wilson, *Evolution for Everyone* (New York: Delacorte Press, 2007).
[21] Christopher Herbert, *Victorian Relativity* (Chicago: University of Chicago Press, 2001).

cannot *know* anything except the relations of those things that we cannot know.

Here is strong evidence of the way positivism affirms some fundamental arguments of contemporary skeptical theory. It is certainly anti-essentialist, and in the sense both that it does not believe we have access to the "essence" of things, and that abstract nouns create an illusion of essence that is merely the creation of human methods of perception and ordering. Positivism is – or would be if it were consistent with its own constant principles – always nominalist and depends on a very skeptical view of the workings of the mind and of language. It registers not realities but appearances, not essences but phenomena, not objects but appearances in relation to each other. The logical positivists labored long and hard at finding some mode of verification, often reduced to "protocol sentences," that could stop the endless spirals of skepticism before they did indeed land them in solipsism and relativism. Their arguments could in the end never get them beyond that Humean regularity of sequence that is antithetical to the hidden metaphysics in the language of causality. Like Comte, Mill eschews the word "cause."[22] Science produces laws not from the discovery of hidden causes of things but from the underdetermined evidence of empiricism. Mill does not abandon the word, "law," but in effect redefines it, and with that redefinition in mind, one can see how the intellectual aggressiveness of positivism reflects the deep doubts that make it possible. "All ultimate laws are laws of causation," Mill says, "and the only universal law beyond the pale of mathematics is the law of universal causation, namely that every phaenomenon has a phaenomenal cause; has some phaenomenon other than itself, or some combination of phaenomena, on which it is invariably and unconditionally consequent" (*AC&P*, p. 58). Defining the word "scientifically," Mill insists that "we have no experience of anything which originates or enforces something else" (p. 153). Knowledge can only be derived from the perceived regularity of the sequences of appearances: release a heavy object and it falls every time if we're within the earth's gravity. But there remains the question: what is there to make certain that it will fall next time? That is not what Mill or

---

[22] In fact, Mill keeps the word "cause" as long as it is understood in the sense he insists on: "We may define, therefore, the cause of a phenomenon, to be the antecedent, or the concurrence of antecedents, on which it is invariably and *unconditionally consequent.* Or if we adopt the convenient modification of the meaning of the word cause, which confines it to the assemblage of positive conditions without the negative, then instead of "unconditionally we must say, 'subject to no other than negative conditions.'" (*System of Logic*)

Hume thought of as "necessary knowledge." Science replaces certainty with probability; knowledge derives only from relations.

The next positivist step is a radical skepticism in indeterminacy and even solipsism. Summarizing Mill's position, Leszek Kolakowski points to the way empiricism virtually dissolves the idea of the self: "what is actually given in human knowledge is individual impressions; the cognitive subject is merely a sequence of impressions, and external bodies are never experienced in any other way. The existence of the physical world is reduced to the constant possibility of the impressions we experience" (p. 80). For Mill, the self is reduced to a "permanent possibility of sensation."

One version of "experience" that runs through positivism and emerges forcefully in the work of Mach and of Pearson in England is a pure sensationalism. That is, experience is not some mysterious potent entity. One has no knowledge of the world "out there" but only of one's own sensations; what we call "reality," inferred from "experience," is rather a series and cluster of impressions. A distinction develops between the representation of reality and the reality itself, and positivist skepticism about "reality" can leave the representation hanging out there without anything to represent. One cannot know what is being represented when one experiences nothing but the vibration of the individual sensorium. For Pearson, the whole world, not merely the social world, was constructed by the human imagination – an argument that, as Christopher Herbert has noted, gets very close to Feuerbach's ideas that the Christian God was humanly constructed: "What Feuerbach calls 'theology,' Pearson in effect names 'materialism.' "[23]

Here then even the accusation of positivism's failure to recognize the perspectival nature of all knowledge is misguided (at least in relation to one important version of positivism). Mach's Positivism can allow no knowledge without first requiring awareness of who is experiencing and affirming the facts, or rather laws. As he put it, "there is something all but unexplored standing behind the ego, namely our body."[24] Mach pursues his "analysis of experience" as far as "currently untranscendable elements" will take him, and eliminates "what it is senseless to explore" in order to discover "the complex interdependence of the elements." And he picks up the main lines of positivist thought: "While groups of such elements may be called things or bodies, it turns out that there are strictly speaking no

---

[23] Christopher Herbert, *Victorian Relativity: Radical Thought and Scientific Discovery* (Chicago: University of Chicago Press, 2001), p. 153.
[24] Ernst Mach, *Knowledge and Error*, intro Erwin N. Heibert (Dordrecht: D. Reidel, 1976), p. 8.

isolated objects: they are only fictions for a preliminary enquiry" (p. 9). Mach satisfies himself, finally, by "removing false problems that hinder scientific enquiry ... We offer only a negative rule for scientific research which need not concern the philosopher" (p. 9).

Karl Pearson, in his important *Grammar of Science*, coming near the end of Victoria's reign in 1892, lays out in perhaps more dramatic fashion the negative, as it were anti-philosophic philosophy of the anti-transcendental, claiming, like Mach, that "the outer world is for science a world of sensations, and sensation is known to us only as sense impression."[25] But Pearson takes this radical empirical position to argue that "the arbitrary distinction between outside and inside ourselves is ... merely of everyday practical convenience." "The group of sense-impressions forming what I term myself is only a small subdivision of the vast world of sense-impressions" (p. 80), and finally with Paterian force he argues, "We are cribbed and confined in this world of sense-impressions like the exchange clerk in his world of sounds, and not a step beyond can we get" (p. 76).

This version of positivism makes "experience" an entirely subjective thing. But subjectivity does not establish a firm ego; here it virtually obliterates the "subject," the stable self from which observations and registrations of experience were theoretically made. Kolakowski argues that for the positivists the "self" was "a superfluous hypothesis" (p. 36) and points to its "philosophical destruction of the subject" (p. 131). He argues that this form of positivism, like the philosophies of Husserl and Bergson, asserts that "the world organized by science – regardless of just how the delimiting boundaries are drawn up – is the result of creative human energy, and hence that man is in a way responsible for the 'thing' his scientific thought constructs" (p. 132).

Roaming through the pages of scientific theorizing in the nineteenth century, one feels to be in a kind of echo chamber of postmodern assumptions, though almost always with an affect and a twist that marks the argument as Victorian. So G. H. Lewes does not hesitate to state, boldly, "All knowledge is relative to the knowing mind. This is indisputable."[26] And yet this discussion emerges in the midst of a chapter on "The Certainty of Truths." Lewes is involved, that is, in a distinctive positivist practice, the struggle to pare away everything but what can in fact be known, to cast out vagueness, false assumptions, metaphysical additions.

---

[25] Karl Pearson, *The Grammar of Science* (London: Walter Scott, 1892), pp. 82–3.
[26] G. H. Lewes, *Problems of Life and Mind: First Series, The Foundation of a Creed* (London: Trubner & Co, 1875), p. 80.

"The only rational question," he claims, "is this: Granting that our knowledge of Things never can transcend sensible relations – never can include the modes of Existence which lie outside these relations – are we not to accept the known relations as certainly true and irreversible, because of unknown relations excluded from our expressions?" (p. 80). Oddly, then, we find Lewes here rejecting positivist arguments about the validity of knowledge in order to develop another positivist argument. He rejects the "high redefinition" and in so doing is in a sense less positivist than the critics. Lewes begins with the recognition of the underdetermination of the empirical but refuses to be intimidated by Humean skepticism. If the released object always falls in our experience, are we justified in denying that the law it suggests is not "true and irreversible"? Out of the skepticisms of relativism and anti-essentialism, Lewes outrightly affirms that "It is clearly open to us to attain absolute certainty of relative knowledge; and every identical proposition is an irreversible truth *within the limits of the formulated terms*" (p. 81).

Most of what I have been saying up to now is counterintuitive – positivism as the intellectual parent of deconstruction and indeterminacy. My emphasis on positivist skepticism perhaps has dimmed the obvious fact that, as Kolakowski put it, the positivists were determined to find out if "there is anything absolutely certain in our knowledge, and if so what?" (p. 41). It is partly the difficult intellectual honesty of the positivist enterprise, seeking stability and finding primarily doubt, that gives to its story a kind of historical virtue and makes it worth reconsideration even in the twenty-first century.

Lewes' move from radical relativism to something like an assured (if constrained) realism points to the fundamental difference between the skepticism of contemporary theorists and that of the positivists. For positivists, skepticism has always been the other side of a rigorous demand for precision and certitude; for contemporary theorists it emerges from a distrust of that very demand, and the skepticism works to demonstrate the absence of both precision and certitude, not to open the way to them. Yet contemporary skepticism implicitly depends on the initial positivist demands and criticizes science and rational theories for not being able to achieve them. The positivist goal was (and remains?) the rejection of inadequately tested knowledge in order to find a way more successful than Hume's to a form of knowledge that might finally be trusted. Mill claims that the focus of positivism on experience and the discovery of "constant sequences" were in the interest of prediction, of being able "to control the effect" or at least "to foreknow and adapt ... conduct to it" (pp. 6–7).

Out of the shards and ruins of the old systems of knowledge and with the aid of new methods, new laws of science that seemed on the verge of making sense of the world without metaphysics or theology, nineteenth-century positivists set about building their "Church."

Positivism's negativism has a quasi-heroic quality of the sort that was melodramatically represented in Bertrand Russell's famous whistling-in-the-dark essay, "A Free Man's Worship,"[27] in which he celebrates the pursuit of truth in a world utterly incompatible with human consciousness. The essay smacks of self-pity and arrogance, but in its late-Victorian passion for knowledge and faith in the painful possibility of achieving it, it shouldn't be dismissed as self-deceiving melodrama. There is something that remains attractive in the dogged, often unconvincing refusal of nineteenth-century thinkers to be defeated by what they had themselves wrought through radical, skeptical critique. Carlyle's metaphor, "*sartor resartus,*" works not only for irrationalist late romantics like him, but for positivism itself, a mode of thinking that one might call "rationalist romantic." The ultimate project, as we have seen with Comte, was to be achieved when the old clothes were definitively burned: to reconstruct society by establishing a science of the human. Ironically, it is an idealizing, utopian project, the reverse of what the word "positivism" has been taken to mean.

Positivism's awful contemporary reputation is partly, of course, the consequence of the fact that such utopian/rationalist projects are fraught with danger (and have a nasty history), whatever the initial intentions. Claiming the unmarked position is always threatening. If thinkers in the positivist tradition attempted to displace those who claimed to speak (and thus, irrefutably) with the voice of God, they themselves, even Russell whistling in the dark, tried to speak with the voice of "nature," another figure who cannot be challenged. In the name of nature, a lot of terrible things have been done, things that most of the Victorian iconoclasts who adopted positivist strategies did not recognize or anticipate. Over two centuries, the scary possibilities have proved easier to actualize than the ideal objectives – hence humanists' consistent distrust both of positivism and of its social projects.

The history of this worrying aspect of positivism takes us back at least to Bacon, and certainly into the eighteenth century. James Mill, responding

---

[27] See Bertrand Russell, *Mysticism and Logic* (New York: W. W. Norton, 1929), p. 42. I might note that Weinberg, in his chaper on "God," reproduces Russell's kind of rhetoric, but now without bravado, just an ironic confidence in the moral rightness of disbelieving, of finding no spiritual consolation in a world profoundly material.

to Macaulay's attack on his essays on government, wrote, "The pith of the charge against the author of the 'Essays' [that is, James Mill, himself] is, that he has written 'an elaborate treatise on government,' and deduced the whole science from the assumption of certain propensities of human nature." Mill writes as though he has caught Macaulay in an absurdity. "Now in the name of Sir Richard Birnie and all saints, from what else *should* it be deduced?"[28] Like many of his current descendants, Mill believed in a universal human nature, and believed that one can only develop a theory of politics and society by understanding the realities of that nature. He also anticipated Comte in the belief that social order depended on scientific knowledge. His *Analysis of the Phenomena of the Human Mind* was to show that there could indeed be a science of the human. Comte, of course, made that idea the starting point of his enormous enterprise, and John Stuart Mill undertook to write what might be seen as a prolegomenon to the creation of that science in his *System of Logic*. By the end of the century, Karl Pearson would argue that "good citizenship" depends on scientific knowledge. And in our own moment, the projects of sociobiology and evolutionary psychology only take up once again the earlier ventures toward a science of the human. The continuity of the tradition is striking; the ambitions are the same; the difficulties are the same; the methods change but utopia is an aspect of a continuing stream of positivist thought.

The epigraph to the sixth book of *A System of Logic* is from Condorcet, who seems positivist indeed as Mill quotes him: "If man can predict, with an almost complete assurance, the phenomena whose laws we know … why do we regard it a chimerical enterprise to trace with some appearance of truth the tableau of the future destiny of the human species. The single foundation of belief in the natural sciences is this idea that general laws, known or unknown, which govern the phenomena of the universe, are necessary and constant, and by what reason would this principle be less true for the development of the intellectual and moral faculties than for the other operations of nature?" (p. 404). And while Mill, with characteristic caution, carefully discriminates possible aspects of knowing and confesses the overwhelming complexity of establishing full-fledged "laws" of human nature, he is thoroughly committed to the idea that general laws will be immensely helpful in constructing a science of the human: "Any facts are fitted … to be a subject of science, which follow one another

---

[28] James Mill, *Essays from the Supplement to "The Encyclopedia Brittanica"* (London: Routledge Thoemmes Press, 1992), "The Greatest Happiness Principle," p. 2.

according to constant laws" (p. 418). The problem with a human science is not so much the absence of scientific laws, as the sheer difficulty of gathering the facts. He knows that there is no way he would be able "to foretell," on the basis of law, "how an individual would think, feel, or act, throughout life, with the same certainty with which astronomy enables us to predict the places and the occultations of the heavenly bodies" (pp. 440–1).

Mill seeks, in the second half of the first volume, to analyze the inductive process so that he will be able to establish the "foundation of practical rules, which might be for induction itself what the rules of the syllogism are for the interpretation of induction" (I, p. 309). He seeks to "arrive at a complete theory of the process" of physical science by generalizing and adapting "to all varieties of problems, the methods which [scientists] themselves employed in their habitual pursuits" (p. 309). Well, this is a long way from Feyerabend, and the enterprise is distinctively positivist in ambition. But the ambition, I want to reiterate, is a reflex of doubt and difficulty. Modern critical theory, and the tendency toward negative hermeneutics have become unforgiving of efforts to establish certainties because such efforts tend to be associated (sometimes, but only sometimes, justly) with very non-altruistic, very non-objective graspings for authority and power – with attempts to develop those unmarked positions that give dominance to one position or other because it is deemed to be "natural." But Mill's efforts to outflank what he took as the mystifications of traditional theological authority felt to many to be indeed liberating and expansive.

The extension of science to the human retains to this moment some of its cultural shock value, and in the nineteenth century it was at first perceived as a quite radical enterprise. Secular knowledge made for a refocus from the spirit to the body. Nineteenth-century naturalism made it impossible to ignore the body's connection with whatever it was that made humans human. (In parentheses I should add that ignoring that relation remains a great mistake.) Famously and polemically, the iconoclastic scientific naturalists at times spoke of the body as an automaton, subject to the deterministic laws of current science. Huxley's strong anti-metaphysical bias, which led him into stormy battles with the clerisy, led him also to believe that the mind and the body were thoroughly entangled, and in his pursuit of universal scientific law he could write, in his notorious, "The Physical Basis of Mind," that "all vital action may be said to be the result of the molecular forces of the protoplasm which displays it. And if so, it must be true, in the same sense and to the same extent, that the thoughts to which I am now giving utterance, and your thoughts regarding them, are the expression of molecular change in that matter of life which is the source of our other vital phaenomena."[29] But a naturalistic account of the workings of the mind led to a view that there was no way to disentangle the material "fact" from ideas. This entanglement, which much contemporary cultural commentary takes as distinctly unpositivist, is another part of our positivist inheritance. Rick Rylance quotes Huxley as saying that "The Man who seeks sanctuary from philosophical questions within the walls of the observatory or of the laboratory" will find "the germs, if not the full-grown shapes, of lively metaphysical postulates rampant amidst the most positive and matter-of-fact notions."[30]

Tyndall, perhaps the most notoriously materialist of them all, always backed off at the last minute from a fully mechanical-deterministic explanation of human behavior. In his essay, "Science and Man," he carries the material explanation to the point of the question. He describes a merchant starting up to address some immediate financial danger as he receives frightening news by letter: "This complex mass of action, emotional, intellectual, and mechanical, is evoked by the impact upon the retina of the infinitesimal waves of light coming from a few pencil marks on a bit of paper."[31] For the positivist project, it does not matter much that Tyndall refuses to carry the question into a full-blown science of the human. He seems happy with the mystery at the borders (a trait that W. H. Mallock mocked relentlessly in *The New Republic* [1877]), but his refusal to explain what he believes because of insufficient evidence is consistent with the positivist tradition. Positivism always prided itself on its determination to confess what it could not or did not yet know. But rhetorical humility aside, Tyndall's arguments further the grand positivist project regarding the human as subject to the same sort of scientific analysis that applies, for example, to chemical reactions or heat understood as a mode of motion. The ideal of converging and expanding laws of nature that gradually (and hierarchically) cover everything operates throughout the literature of positivism and of its fellow travelers, from Mill, to Comte, to Tyndall. The laws of nature govern humans as material beings as absolutely and

---

[29]   T. H. Huxley, "The Physical Basis of Mind," in *Methods and Results* (London: Macmillan, 1893), p. 154.

[30]   Quoted in Rick Rylance, *Victorian Psychology and British Culture: 1850–1880* (Oxford: Oxford University Press, 2000), p. 75. From "On Sensation and the Unity of Structure of the Sensiferous Organs." One of the major points of Karl Pearson's *Grammar of Science* (1892), to which I will be referring below, was precisely to try to rid science of its unselfconscious "philosophical postulates," or at least to make scientists aware of them.

[31]   John Tyndall, "Science and Man," *Fragments of Science*, II (New York: Appleton, 1899), p. 32.

deterministically as they govern stars and rocks. Modern reductionism lies ahead.

In the face of the brilliant and moving criticism of these positions by William James, it may seem simply a bad mistake, intellectual and affective, to regard their strengths. James talks ironically of "the rugged and manly school of science,"[32] which sometimes writes "as if the incorruptibly truthful intellect ought positively to prefer bitterness and unacceptableness to the heart" (p. 7). He talks of the "robustious pathos" of their writing, a wonderful phrase that describes perfectly too Russell's later manifestation of the scientistic tendency. And he is particularly hard on Clifford's argument that if one believes anything on "insufficient evidence" it is "sinful because it is stolen in defiance of our duty to mankind" (p. 8). Interestingly, Clifford's positivist commitment mingles epistemology with morality in just the ways the original positivists thought. Yet even James concedes that this positivist insistence on truth at all costs "strikes one as healthy" (p. 8). He does not in fact argue against the passion, or even the pathos, but against the *choice* of passions (which, I claim, are always inevitably at the root of intellectual decisions and choices) and moral directions. He simply argues that it is a mistake to think that once one has rid oneself of wishful thinking, one is left with a residue of pure "intellectual insight." His point is that the wish and the passion are everywhere, even in the austere positivist position. "Our belief in truth itself . . . that there is a truth, and that our minds and it are made for each other, – what is it but a passionate affirmation of desire?" (p. 9). James long anticipates Alisdair MacIntyre in the recognition (and exploitation) of the fact that the epistemological is always implicated in the moral.[33]

Dealing "scientifically" with the human, and purporting to do it as the Victorian naturalists wanted and as current evolutionary psychologists do, is always trouble. The long positivist line that has led to recent efforts fully to biologize the human has opened up potential and historically real ideological sins, and these have all too effectively diverted many critics from attending to what the simplest common sense must affirm, that insistence on the implication of the biological in the condition of being human was a legitimate and important move. And while the intellectual and the passional, as James argues, are always intertwined, the problem

---

[32] William James, *The Will to Believe* (New York: Longmans, 1897), p. 7.

[33] See Alisdair MacIntyre, "Epistemological Crisis, Dramatic Narrative, and the Philosophy of Science," in *Paradigms and Revolutions*, ed. Gary Gutting (South Bend, IN: University of Notre Dame Press, 1980), pp. 54–74.

needs to be recognized as an intellectual one before the questions of ideology can be adequately addressed. That problem can be variously formulated, but one way to do it is by asking whether reductionism is a valid method for the attainment of real knowledge. At the foundations of Positivism lies reductionism. Victorian spokesmen for science were by and large committed to the work of developing the most general laws, gradually to encompass all others, until the complexities of nature, down to human behavior and consciousness, would be reduced to an ultimate intelligible unity.

It is important, coming from the culture side of this debate, not to close out discussion by insisting on the absolute dominance of cultural forces in the study of the human, but to consider what sorts of procedures and materials one would need in order adequately to understand the implication of biology in aspects of human life that have long been believed to be the province of culture. Reductionism assumes the possibility of building block on block, from "neuronal cells" to intricate human social and personal relationships and even, as E. O. Wilson has claimed, into literature and literary criticism. As Richard Lewontin (who obviously has his own ideological axe to grind) puts it in discussing the various attempts to explain the human organism through gene study, "If we had the complete DNA sequence of an organism and unlimited computational power, we could not compute the organism, because the organism does not compute itself from the genes."[34] Lewontin insists that isolated biological conditions cannot account even for the organism, for "it is not possible to ask the question, 'Which genotype caused the best growth,' without specifying the environment in which the growth occurred" (p. 22). While Lewontin attacks this form of reductionism, he does not attack the idea that genes have a lot to do with the organism.

The problem here extends through consideration of the positivists and even of their sociobiologizing descendants: how to address the questions raised by their work not beginning with ideology but with intellectual problems (which may of course have ideological implications from the start). The body, the genes, all do their work in shaping the human. Reductionism has real value, not as an adequate description of the way the world works, but as a great heuristic, the strategy that made modern science as we know it possible. What is, however, certainly wrong with reductionism is what Daniel Dennett (himself no mean reductionist) calls

[34] Richard Lewontin, *The Triple Helix: Gene, Organism, and Environment* (Cambridge, MA: Harvard University Press, 2000), p. 17.

"greedy reductionism,"[35] that is, the tendency to leap to large conclusions from inadequate materials – in the Lewontin description, for example, not recognizing the enormous gap between the raw gene and the trait it is taken to code for.[36]

There are yet other ways in which positivism has left its mark on contemporary thinking. In its pursuit of the human sciences, for example, positivism became a major progenitor of full scale interdisciplinarity, an ideal that now crosses large ideological and epistemological differences. The pursuit of the human sciences entailed crossing the study of the mind with the study of the body and breaking down conventional notions of isolated selves. One of the primary moves that E. O. Wilson makes in his arguments for sociobiology is entirely consistent with this: the study of living things, of beings who have "culture," requires an indisciplinarity that stretches beyond the usual cultural norms – not only the study of history, literature, the arts, and the social sciences, but the physical sciences, ranging from biology through chemistry and even, perhaps, physics.[37] The problem here is not Wilson's commitment to interdisciplinarity

35   "In their zeal to explain too much too fast, scientists and philosophers often underestimate the complexities, trying to skip whole layers or levels of theory in their rush to fasten everything securely and neatly to the foundation," Daniel Dennett, *Darwin's Dangerous Idea: Evolution and the Meanings of Life* (New York: Simon and Schuster, 1995), p. 82. But Dennett is an enthusiast for reductionism, which is clearly his development of the long positivist anti-metaphysical tradition. The reductionist program anchors all knowledge in material fact, and develops from fact into the broad, law-bound theories of the sort that Herschel and other early philosophers of science sought: "In itself, the desire to reduce, to unite, to explain it all in one big overarching theory, is no more to be condemned as immoral than the contrary urge ... It is not wrong to yearn for simple theories, or to yearn for phenomena that no simple (or complex!) theory could ever explain; what is wrong is zealous misrepresentation, in either direction" (p. 82).

36   "Reductionism" is more various and complex than this. I am not at this point ready to pursue the argument, but it is reasonable to argue that the "reductionism" of current sociobiology is not at all the same as the reductionism of positivism. John DuPré has argued, in a very respectful treatment of positivist thought in the midst of a book distinctly not positivist, that "whereas positivist reduction is strictly and intentionally epistemological, contemporary theory reduction, presupposing a structural hierarchy down to microphysics, is thoroughly ontological. Indeed, the microphysical, the basis for contemporary reductionism, was the primary object of positivist epistemological suspicion, and the main target of reduction to the observable," *The Disorder of Things: Metaphysical Foundations of the Disunity of Science* (Cambridge, MA: Harvard University Press, 2003), p. 8. DuPré is pointing to the fact that positivists like Mach refused to accept "atoms," for example, because they were not "observable."

37   In *Sociobiology* (Cambridge, MA: The Belknap Press, University of Harvard Press, 1980), Wilson's language is astonishingly close to Comte's. He talks, in the notorious conclusion of that book, of how sociology is "now in the natural history stage of its development" (p. 299), and he goes on to say that "sociology is drawing closer each day to cultural anthropology, social psychology, and economics, and will soon merge with them" (p. 300). And he makes the expected move, to which Comte could not have gone in his own time, claiming that sociology, for full development, must wait for "neuronal explanation of the human brain" (p. 300).

but his absolute certainty that in any given problem, biology (and its underlying chemistry) trumps the other disciplines. In effect, his interdisciplinarity becomes biological imperialism (as, may I say it, the interdisciplinarity trumpeted in many humanist quarters turns out to be literary imperialism). In its earlier phases, Comte argued for a kind of graduated progress through the disciplines, moving from the "simplest," physical astronomy, through to sociology, the most complex. Although Comte also believed that psychology was a false science, positivism as a more general movement, following out from the work of James Mill, in effect created modern psychology, but a psychology rooted in physiology and, as we have seen with Huxley and Tyndall, molecular physics. The key figures in the development of Victorian psychology, identified by Rick Rylance in his superb recent study – John Stuart Mill, Alexander Bain, Herbert Spencer, and G. H. Lewes – were all either positivists or fellow travelers, whether they adopted the name or not.

Positivism encourages recognition of the mutual dependence of mind and body, indeed of their inextricable connections. Its relentless quest to clear away the rubbish of metaphysics and locate unchallengeable truth required intense consideration of investigative methods, and particularly of perspectival limitations. Questions of truth are inevitably entangled in questions of the functioning of the human mind (the logical positivists put enormous emphasis on language itself – obviously a human construction), and the human mind has a physical location.

I've suggested in my brief allusion to late century sensationalist epistemology the kind of attention to the mind that writers like Pearson and Mach required. No modern theorist has been more subtly investigative of the strategies of human perception, and its limits. Mach's remarkable collection of epistemological essays, *Knowledge and Error*, abjures the sort of large-scale utopian project that I have been associating with positivism, but the book is subtitled, *Sketches on the Psychology of Enquiry*, and it makes an understanding of the perceiver a condition of an adequate epistemology. It entails a mixture of biology, physics, mathematics, and geometry, and theories of perception and imagination. Mach was so extraordinarily sensitive to the peculiarities of consciousness and the multiplicity of facts and sensations, that he stood back from the broadest generalizations to which, on the whole, positivists aspired (and which, from their skepticism, they often resisted). In his efforts to clear away the entangled underbrush of metaphysics and his determination to require empirical evidence, Mach's skepticism even led him to reject the reality of "atoms" because they could not be observed, and Pearson followed him in this respect.[38] Yet his empiricism entailed a reshaping and blurring of the boundaries of knowledge and a refusal to accept traditional disciplinary categories. "Thus," he claims, "there is no isolated feeling, willing and thinking. Sensations, being both physical and mental, form the basis of all mental experience" (p. 17).

Darwin's theory, in any of various interpretations, played an important role in the positivist development of this interdisciplinary project of developing a science of the human. After Darwin it became increasingly difficult to omit biology from psychology. By showing that organisms evolve by natural selection, Darwin in effect was taken to argue that all humans share a common nature – adaptive modes of behavior, adaptive mental qualities, and adaptive emotional strategies. While this argument has culminated in the relentlessly reductionist interpretations of evolutionary psychology, it was already much alive by the end of the nineteenth century. Positivist methodology and Darwinian theory can be taken to have made James Mill's project seem something other than utopian.

For Mach, as for positivist-oriented thinkers throughout the last third of the nineteenth century, the project was "to unite the sciences of nature, life, and society,"[39] and Darwin helped make the connections inescapable. "Thus," claims Mach, "sensations, being both physical and mental, form the basis of all mental experience" (p. 17). Darwinian procedures work as rigorously for mental as for physical activities. Karl Pearson pushes the same project yet further, concluding his *Grammar of Science* with a classification of the sciences that harks back to Bacon and Comte (whose actual classification Pearson dismisses as mere fantasy) and Spencer. Pearson offers a more provisional classification than his predecessors, a more wary and more skeptical one – but the end is similar: to see the connections among all the sciences, to recognize them as part of a larger and ultimately coherent total description of the natural world. Pearson's strategy is skeptical in a great positivist tradition. With proper positivist caution, he offers his classifications as provisional and fragmentary, and laws of nature become accumulations of statistical probability. The conclusion

---

[38]   In his recent major biography of Pearson, Theodore Porter argues convincingly that Pearson was not as deeply influenced by Mach as tradition has had it. He notes for example that "Pearson's arguments for the detachment of man from nature, his alienation from the world that his own mind had produced, placed him also in opposition to Mach." Theodore Porter, *Karl Pearson: the Scientific Life in a Statistical Age* (Princeton: Princeton University Press, 2004), p. 211. Porter also shows that Pearson's early idealism, which led him to doubt the "reality" of the outer world, derived from Spinoza and German idealists before Mach (see p. 64).
[39]   Eichthal to Comte about Herder – correspondence quoted in Lepenies.

to *The Grammar of Science* provides an almost perfect summation of positivist credo and ambitions and skepticism:

Our grandfathers stood puzzled before problems like the physical evolution of the earth, the origin of species, and the descent of man; they were, perforce, content to cloak their ignorance with time-honoured superstition and myth. To our fathers belongs not only the honour of solving these problems but the credit of having borne the brunt of that long and weary battle by which science freed itself from the tyranny of tradition. Their task was the difficult one of daring to know. We, entering upon their heritage, no longer fear tradition, no longer find that to know requires courage. We too, however, stand as our fathers did before problems, which seem to us insoluble – problems, for example, like the genesis of living from lifeless forms, where science has as yet no certain descriptive formula, and perhaps no hope in the immediate future of finding one. Here we have a duty before us, which, if we have faith in the scientific method, is simple and obvious. We must turn a deaf ear to all those who would suggest that we can enter the stronghold of truth by the burrow of superstition, or scale its walls by the ladder of metaphysics. We must accomplish a task more difficult to many minds than daring to know. We must dare to be ignorant. (p. 474)

It would be disingenuous not to mention that all of this high-minded theorizing led, in Pearson's polymathic and important career, to scientific justifications for eugenics. But the historical moment accounts for some of the excess, and, I confess, I find nothing wrong with his basic argument here, nothing that requires the move to eugenics and no inevitable commitment to the eugenics movement he came to lead. It is more than hard to locate in the writing of a figure so important in so egregious a "scientific" movement anything redemptive of positivism. That Pearson took his positivism into eugenics provides a powerful example of why it is that positivism is regarded so negatively among modern cultural theorists. Pearson, who was also something of a feminist and a socialist, to further complicate the easy connection between epistemology and ideology, developed statistics as the stable point from which he could make entirely impersonal, unmarked, readings of human behavior, and get out from under what he saw as the unreflecting metaphysics of science. The ideological disaster of eugenics, which in its early twentieth-century moment seemed to many very left-leaning people a humane application of science to great social problems, should not blind us to the fact that, following Pearson's arguments and his rhetoric, we can understand positivism as an intellectual liberation from conventional constraints, one that, like "postmodern" thought, requires attention to questions of perspective, and, at least rhetorically, intellectual humility.

Beyond Pearson, there lies the development, with intensified Darwinian influence, of sociobiology and evolutionary psychology, which I have been forced to confront here several times already. Here is E. O. Wilson – uncannily echoing Victorian rhetoric – in his famous, and notorious, last chapter of *Sociobiology*: "Let us now consider man in the free spirit of natural history, as though we were zoologists from another planet completing a catalog of social species on Earth. In this macroscopic view the humanities and social sciences shrink to specialized branches of biology: history, biography, and fiction and the protocols of human ethology; and anthropology and sociology together constitute the sociobiology of a single primate species."[40] Wilson's project continues the positivist tradition marked out already by James Mill. He sees evolutionary theory, as Ullica Segerstråle puts it, "as a total explanatory scheme."[41] That is to say, like Comte before him, Wilson believes that the laws of nature apply across all phenomena, including culture, and that those laws can probably be reduced from their variety and complexity to fewer and fewer all-embracing ones. The Comtean echoes ought, I think, to make Wilson nervous – for Wilson, too, the crown of science is a social one, now not sociology but sociobiology.

Wilson's book was greeted, as is well known, by violent attacks, particularly from Richard Lewontin and Stephen Jay Gould. Both distrusted the pure adaptationist program and the argument that human behavior can be explained genetically, which are models of reductionist thought. For Gould, adaptationist science produces only "just so stories." Whatever the details of the conflicts, it is striking how continuous the arguments are with struggles over positivism through the nineteenth century.

The arguments of evolutionary psychology do indeed look like extended refinements of the project James Mill undertook two hundred years ago. Stephen Pinker justifies the program and faces the ideological attacks upon it in his *How the Mind Works*. Pinker sets out to show that there is such a thing as "human nature," as Pearson believed, and as Mill, Comte, and Lewes strongly assumed. He explains that "Natural selection is a homogenizing force within a species; it eliminates the vast majority of macroscopic design variants because they are not improvements." That

---

[40] E. O. Wilson, *Sociobiology* (Cambridge, MA: Belknap Press of Harvard University Press, 1980), p. 271.
[41] Ullica Segerstråle, *Defenders of the Truth: The Battle for Science in the Sociobiology Debate and Beyond* (Oxford: Oxford University Press, 2000), p. 40.

explains, he says, "why all normal people have the same physical organs, and why we all surely have the same mental organs as well."[42] There is something quite Huxleyan in Pinker's aggressive anti-metaphysical and anti-culturalist polemics.

Clearly, with sociobiology and evolutionary psychology, we are at the point of most intense conflict between cultural theorists and thinkers in the positivist tradition. Pinker and other evolutionary psychologists simply sneer at what they call "SSM," the standard social science model, and oppose to it the sheer facts of biological, evolutionarily derived reality. My own inclination is to resist reductionism and the view that all human phenomena must be consistent with the workings of "natural selection." But between the anti-metaphysical energies of evolutionary psychology, which seeks to salvage from the chaos of empirical particularities a stability and a "realism" that allows for scientific understanding of the human mind, and the deep skepticism and relativism of cultural theorizing that seeks to demonstrate the constructedness and the malleability of much that has been taken to be natural, there lies, I believe, another position.

It seems to me that sustained hostility to the positivist tradition has damaged our capacity to come to terms with the harsh unaccommodating actual, which, as Thomas Hardy (and Russell) believed, goes on its ways without reference to humans and their absurd desires, or with any efforts to understand the degree to which and the ways in which human life has been constrained by its physical nature and its physical history. Not every such effort must end with *The Bell Curve.* It has made it all too easy to reject the Victorian aspiration to some sort of coherent understanding of knowledge and of the world and accept aporia and indeterminacy and relativism as the terminus rather than as a set of inevitable obstacles. Settling for the impossibility of getting at the real has the kind of scientific consequences that Intelligent Design has, though the position seems to be precisely opposite. After we have decided that (a) the subject has been created by a great Intelligence or (b) that there is no way to get at the reality of it, there are no more questions to be asked, there is no more work, intellectual or otherwise, to be done.

The positivists recognized the obstacles and tried – more and rather less successfully – to fight through them. Using their corrosively skeptical weapons, we have lost sight of their objectives or have come to regard those objectives as chimerical or ideologically vicious. Let me take the risk

---

[42] Steven Pinker, *How the Mind Works* (New York: W. W. Norton, 1997), p. 49.

of agreeing with the often arrogant Pinker: "A denial of human nature, no less than an emphasis on it, can be warped to serve harmful ends. We should expose whatever ends are harmful and whatever ideas are false, and not confuse the two." Tough positivist talk.

Between that toughness and the enthusiasms of radical skepticism, there might lie the position that several recent thinkers have taken. Philip Kitcher, always a wonderfully sensible critic of philosophical excesses in the realms of science, criticizes what he calls "the-unity-of science" idea. The notion, which lies behind Comte's classification of the sciences, and Mill's and Pearson's view, is fundamental to the science of the nineteenth century and to its positivist apologists. The idea that there are converging laws of nature, that scientists gradually uncover general truths about the natural world that will eventually link in a unified way so that chemistry, physics, astronomy, mineralogy, and so on, will all be linked and so that we can arrive at what Steven Weinberg calls a "theory of everything," was a powerful heuristic in the development of nineteenth-century science. We can see that idea at work in Herschel and Whewell's early studies of science, and we can see it at work as an assumption of all the positivists. "Law" became the presiding gray eminence of Victorian science, and it was in the end to be a law for everything. Conceding that nature must be studied by subdivision into parts, Herschel yet argues: "natural philosophy is essentially united in all its departments, through all which one spirit reigns and one method of enquiry applies."[43]

This broadly held view, Kitcher insists, runs counter to the real history of science, which constantly produces results that do not carry over from one specialized area to another. He denies the Comtean argument that the sciences can be hierarchically unified, and thus seems to undercut the entire positivist enterprise. Kitcher suggests that viewing science from the top down, that is, from laws to particulars, misses the reality that science generally works the other way round, from particulars to laws – that is, to the highest degree of generality possible within the limited areas marked out by the particulars. One needn't delve too far in this sort of argument to see that, in effect, what Kitcher is doing is shooting out from under it the metaphysics that secretly lie in the heart of positivism. That is to say, he uses positivist methods of inquiry and skepticism – methods he explicitly commends as providing models of good reasoning – to demonstrate the inadequacy of the dominant nineteenth-century

---

[43]   John Herschel, *Preliminary Discourse on the Study of Natural Philosophy* (Chicago: University of Chicago Press, 1986), p. 219.

(and indeed twentieth-century) notion of the domain of science.[44] Similarly, John DuPré, in his impressive, *The Disorder of Things*,[45] and Helen Longino, in her recent *The Fate of Knowledge*,[46] move in the direction of pluralism as against a positivist monism. But at the same time, all of these critics reject what Kitcher calls the thesis of global underdetermination – that is, the view that since empirical validation is always less than complete so that inferences from the data always extend beyond what the data can entirely justify, scientific thought is somehow invalidated. All of them are insistent on the power of science to get at something like objective truth. They differ strongly on many issues, but they refuse to allow the gap opened by underdetermination, through which social explanation enters, entirely to upend epistemological validity. The social is essential, but its consequences are not the subversion of science. They find that middle ground that I am suggesting is possible and necessary, and they are enabled to do so in part because of the positivist inheritance that allows them to come to terms with the limits of positivism and the impossibility of the absolute alternatives to them posed by a radical anti-realist constructivism.

So I do not believe, in spite of the death of the word positivism, or its translation into a four-letter word, that the inheritance of positivism or the problems it confronts are gone from current debates, or that many of its more hideous manifestations invalidate all of what every side of current cultural debates has inherited from it. Positivism as a grand enterprise to

[44] See Philip Kitcher, *The Advancement of Science: Science without Legend, Objectivity without Illusions* (New York: Oxford University Press, 1993). Kitcher attempts on the one hand, to destroy the "Legend" version of the history of science, which misses the complexity and irregularities of its movement, and, on the other, to affirm the rationality and progressive nature of science despite the influences of social factors on its epistemological workings. In the end, Kitcher seems to accept a very complicated position compatible with positivism but alert to what might have been called "extrinsic" forces in ways positivists tended not to consider.

[45] DuPré is far less ready than Kitcher to affirm the rational coherence and unity of science. He is, however, committed to a realism that allows for the "recalcitrance of nature," the reality of the world against which scientific arguments can be judged. For DuPré, the only way to be able to locate ideology hidden in scientific judgment is to be in a position to distinguish ideology from incorrect scientific description. He claims that " 'good' science involves inseparable elements of the epistemically and the sociopolitically good" (p. 13).

[46] Helen E. Longino, *The Fate of Knowledge* (Princeton: Princeton University Press, 2002). Like the other two books, this one is concerned with taking into account the effects of sociality on science. The problem for serious philosophers of science who are not ready to take the full skeptical plunge that those have made who find that the social context of science compromises hopelessly its claims to epistemological purity, is to factor the social into the epistemological – and that is a serious move away from positivism. All in different ways work – like Putnam's recent book on the fact/value dichotomy – to deny the view, as Longino puts it, "that the rational and the cognitive, on the one hand, and the social, on the other, constitute exclusive zones or sets of processes and practices" (p. 76).

establish out of the developing revelations of the limitations of secular knowing unity, coherence, meaning, and a good society is, of course, a failed enterprise now. It has left, however, not only a set of tools by which current theorists continue to pursue skepticism to its limits, but with what I continue to regard as an admirable aspiration that cultural theorists tend to distrust because so many of its historical manifestations have ended in things like eugenics. But it is a mistake not to recognize that some of what is most admirable about the Victorians (and some of what is least) bears the burden of the name, positivism; and recognizing that curious admixture, contemporary cultural theorists, often unreasonably labeled "postmodernist," might do well not to assume that there is nothing to be learned from thinkers in the positivist tradition, not to dismiss all bad things as positivist, not to ignore the degree to which they both use its ideas and participate in its struggles down to the present moment.

CHAPTER 6

Why science isn't literature:
the importance of differences

[*The developments in modern literary theory that have produced a radical questioning of the possibility of objectivity, and have turned all written language into discourse, and have insisted on the fictionality of all writing, have also, as a consequence, broken down the borders between fiction and non-fiction. In considering the work and thought of nineteenth-century writers and scientists, it has been necessary to take these critical developments into account and to argue, philosophically and historically, for the importance of the points of view that were held by many Victorian thinkers. In the essays brought together thus far in this book, I have attempted to reconsider the writing and ideas of the Positivists and the scientific naturalists, to see them in relation to their contemporary antagonists and cultural critics. In this essay, which is not directly concerned with the Victorians, I address in terms more recognizably contemporary some of the problems that arise from an extension of the skepticism, already developing among the Victorians, about the possibility of objectivity.*

Although the essay is aimed at contemporary forms of the problems, it seems to me appropriately transitional to the essays about Victorian literature that follow in the next section of this book. Where the previous essays, and this one as well, concentrate on the philosophical and scientific problems, as they are discussed in non-fiction prose, this one addresses our contemporary problems about objectivity by comparing, in a rough-cut sort of way, the work of science to the work of literature (recognizing of course that both terms incorporate vast ranges of difference). The essay attempts to clear the ground, to get a little more practical and a little less theoretical, on the way to a consideration of the work of literature itself. Behind this essay, which flirts with questions of epistemology, as do all the essays gathered in this volume, there lies my commitment to the role of the aesthetic in the epistemological and ethical engagements of the philosophers, popularizers, and scientists. Literature has real work to do, and that work can be best understood by recognizing the distinctiveness of literary practice, as opposed to the practice of non-fiction writers and scientists, always

165

*making overt, presumably testable truth claims.[1] In the realm of the aesthetic
I place this essay here as a kind of transition to the book's final section, which deals
directly with the particular kind of objectivity that literature can achieve –
an objectivity that is not enmired in the sorts of truth claims implicit in every
scientific assertion but that demands attention to otherness irreducible to rules
and laws, to what Derek Attridge calls "singularity." While the subject is
distinctly* not *nineteenth-century culture and literature, the essay in fact
addresses many of the problems that I show the Victorians addressing in the
other essays here, and it suggests that the Victorians' problems continue to be
ours, their solutions to some of them worth re-considering.*]

Does anyone really think science is literature? Do students in Physics
101 ever think they are really in Freshman Comp, or Intro to Lit? If the
New York Times had reported the meeting of the Science and Literature
Society at which this paper was originally delivered, what ironies would it
fashion about the absurdities of scholarship and literary criticism: "Distinguished scholars from all over America joined together in Ann Arbor
last night to hear a literary scholar from Rutgers argue strenuously that
science isn't literature. Nobody laughed – at least not in the Rutgers
Professor's hearing." I construct this hypothetical *Times* story to locate
myself and, I expect, my readers, inside a discourse that is so comfortably
shared by literary critics and theorists that they do not question – perhaps
at times do not even recognize – the *prima facie* peculiarity of some of their
assumptions.

The assumptions I am talking about are three:

(1) All we have is representation (and representation always contains
within it a politics that is disguised and "naturalized").

(2) Thus all knowledge is culturally constructed; "facts" are ideologically loaded representations, not ontologically real phenomena.

(3) All knowledge is thus a play for power not for truth, although it is
often justified in the name of truth.

---

[1] For a discussion of the distinctiveness of literature, from a poststructuralist perspective, with a
strong commitment to the ethical implications both of epistemology and of aesthetics, see Derek
Attridge, *The Singularity of Literature* (London: Routledge, 2004).

Responding responsibly to a work of art means attempting to do justice to it as a singular other; it
involves a judgment that is not simply ethical or aesthetic, and that does not attempt to pigeonhole
it or place it on a scale of values, but that operates as an affirmation of the work's inventiveness . . .
No justice is possible without the singularity of the case – and of the individual standing trial . . . To
act morally toward other persons entails, it hardly needs saying, as full an attempt at understanding
them and their situation as one is capable of; yet both the primary claim of another person upon one
and the final measure of one's behavior lies in the response to, and affirmation of the otherness
which resists that understanding (pp. 128–30).

It would take a better philosopher than me to argue through these assumptions, and I do not want to try. Instead, I want to emphasize their peculiarity, something that, in the comfortable, ragged homogeneity of literary scholars' usual venues is too easy to miss. If these assumptions are held doggedly, we might find ourselves inviting a Shakespeare scholar to do our brain surgery, or a Victorianist to do our rocket science. In addition, unquestioned, these assumptions are likely to undermine the very political and epistemological projects they have often been taken to support. So, beginning at the beginning, I want to assert baldly that even if, when pressed, we cannot adequately define either science or literature, common sense tells us that science isn't literature.[2] "Common sense" may itself be a problematic word. When it's invoked I run for cover since it is a conception that is often used to naturalize socially constructed conditions; but, after all, conflating science and literature is under most circumstances not only absurd but at least as dangerous as many late Victorians and modern commentators think it would be to mistake science for the ideal and absolute authority in all areas of knowledge. If one means by "science" the disciplines of investigating the way the natural world is in as systematic a way as possible, and one means by "literature" the works of the human imagination as it creates its often brilliant, exploratory, and moving fictions, I think we had better keep the distinction, rough and incomplete as it necessarily must be.

I want to begin, then, by calling to mind the conditions that make it something other than a banality to insist at length on the distinction. What characterized most study of science and literature until recently was its preoccupation with the way scientific ideas shaped literary ones. The traffic was all one way, and the whole subject tended to be set within a traditional history of ideas. The scientific texts themselves, even one so available to literary analysis as Darwin's *Origin of Species*, tended not to be read as texts – the most famous exception being Stanley Edgar Hyman's *The Tangled Bank* (1962). That is to say, scientific texts were not "texts," as that word has come to be used in recent critical discourse, but sources. The model was background-and-foreground, and for students of literature,

---

[2] Certainly, some things that have been thought of as "science" have become "literature." One need think only of the conception of "ether" in the nineteenth century. The Ptolemaic scheme similarly has become far more interesting to students of literature than to scientists. The point, quite reasonably made, is that the difference between science and literature often if not always depends on what the culture decides is "true" at the moment. I am therefore not willing to rely entirely on "common sense," while at the same time I do not think it safe to ignore it.

important works of science were "background." For students of science, important works of literature were, at best, what they are now – diversion. That model implicitly separated the worlds of art and the worlds of knowledge, and at the same time it implicitly affirmed the intellectual authority of science over literature.

The background/foreground model is now notoriously, and appropriately, in disrepute. We recognize that the *Origin* is no more and no less a text than, say, *Middlemarch*, and Gillian Beer has shown how Milton and Shakespeare might have helped shape Darwin's scientific imagination.[3] The denial of binary categories like science/literature, according to which study tended to be organized, is, of course, one of the characteristic marks of poststructuralist thought. Important as that earlier tradition of study of science and literature has been, new perspectives on the relationship have given a new seriousness to the subject. Both science and literature are now seen as cultural artifacts, developed in a medium – intellectual, social, political of almost infinite complexity of interdependence and relationship. Moreover, even so primitive and common-sense a notion as that of "fact" has lost its innocence. Common sense may resist, but facts are not out there, hard, intractable realities to which human reasoning must bend, but constructions of human reasoning. All facts are theory-laden – they are not prior to the operations of meaning-making but meaningful texts themselves. This view is not new, although emphasis on it has intensified in these poststructuralist years. Willam Whewell, as early as 1838, following Immanuel Kant, could say that "there is a mask of theory over the whole face of nature . . . "[4] In the postmodernist view, what is mistaken as natural may be culturally constructed so that the "fact" can only be made "background" or "source" if its textuality and the system of thought and language that makes it possible are ignored. As Mary Hesse has put it,

the imperialism previously claimed for natural science in the empiricist tradition has now turned in some quarters into its opposite, namely an assimilation of natural science itself to something approaching the hermeneutic critique. This critique comes both from philosophers of science dissatisfied with logical empiricist accounts of the structure of science and from historians of science who have

---

[3] See Gillian Beer, *Darwin's Plots* (London: Routledge and Kegan Paul, 1983), and her essay, "Darwin's Reading and the Fictions of Development," in David Kohn, ed., *The Darwinian Heritage* (Princeton: Princeton University Press, 1985), pp. 554–7.

[4] William Whewell, *History of Scientific Ideas. Being the First Part of the Philosophy of the Inductive Sciences*, 2 vols. (London: John W. Parker & Son, 1858), p. 46.

been brought to question the theory of a 'demarcation' of science from other attitudes to and theories of the natural world, in the light of the similarities and continuities between 'science' and 'pre-science' or 'non-science' that can be found in its history.[5]

Foucault's archaeology, not strictly responsible for this new imperialism, is the best known articulation of the attitudes that led to it. His popularity among literary theorists is an indication of how widespread is the rejection of the science/literature binary. Thomas Kuhn's *Structure of Scientific Revolutions*, no matter how much it has been displaced and refuted, helped open up to the study of the history of science the extraordinary possibilities of noninternalist explanation. Discontinuity was as much part of Kuhn's original conception as it was of Foucault's, and part of the threat of Kuhnian theory was that in its rejection of the positivist model of scientific method, it made it possible to consider elements out of the rest of culture, even irrationalities, in the procedures and developments of science. If scientific authority is dependent on the dominant paradigm within the scientific community, something else besides direct reference to nature is going on when science accepts some evidence and rejects other. In some ways, Foucault and other so-called "poststructuralist" theorists have only followed out the implications of positivist thought itself in elaborating the implications of the view that scientific proofs, like all empirical evidence, are underdetermined. This view has opened the way to reflection on the nature of the scientific community, even to an anthropology of science, and on the systems of thought into which ostensible "fact" is fed. Foucault argued that history of science artificially constructed a continuum in time, an internally developing and cumulative sequence of discoveries, while it excluded as anti-scientific everything that resisted the sequence or that fell beneath the level of consciousness. Thus, he thrust science into a whole set of contemporaneous discourses, all of which, at the deepest level, were governed by the same codes and systems. The cultural "episteme" that Foucault posited was in a sense a large scale "paradigm."

What matters here is that Foucault made scientific knowledge a function of a kind of cultural unconscious and ripped it from the bosom of rationality into the worlds of discourse and of power. I don't mean to suggest that Foucault has himself mattered a great deal to historians and

---

[5]   Mary Hesse, *Revolutions and Reconstructions in the Philosophy of Science* (Bloomington: Indiana University Press, 1980), p. 169.

sociologists of science but to indicate a way of thinking that has determined the subject of this essay. It has become legitimate, and in some places necessary, to explain science in terms of the nonscientific. Kuhn found a sociological dimension to the history of science. For him, and for Ludwik Fleck thirty years before in the *Genesis and Development of a Scientific Fact*,[6] facts are not phenomena revealed but ideas that are constructed as much socially as intellectually and that depend on the dominant point of view of the scientific community (and often quite clearly on broader prejudices of the wider culture to which the scientists belong).

There are of course strong antagonists to the idea that sociology has anything to do with the real history of science, but it should go without saying that in sociology and in literature the dominant view now is that science needs to be understood as a social construction; all knowledge is socially constructed. As Steven Shapin, one of the most interesting scholars associated with the Edinburgh "strong programme" of the sociology of knowledge, has put it: "If scientific representations were simply determined by the nature of reality, then no sociological accounts of the production and evaluation of scientific knowledge could be offered."[7] But, as Shapin points out, "the underdetermination of scientific accounts of reality and the 'theory-laden' nature of fact-statements are both quite widely accepted"(p. 159). Under the pressure of these sorts of critiques and analyses, the standard nineteenth- and early twentieth- century conception of the distinctiveness and authority of science breaks down. That standard notion is still held, if unsystematically, by the culture at large and by most practicing scientists.

That is, to summarize, science is distinguished (1) by the "objectivity" and "rationality" of its procedures, and the disinterest of its practitioners; (2) by its rigorous requirements of verification, by replication of results; (3) by the universal validity of its conclusions; (4) by its capacity to represent adequately a nonverbal and nonsymbolic reality. Unlike literature, its results are (5) progressive, the cumulative acquisition of new knowledge of the real world by means of observation and experiment, developing (6) to the generalized level of natural laws. And unlike literature, the results of science are not affected by rhetorical manipulation of arguments (which

---

[6] Ludwik Fleck, *Genesis and Development of a Scientific Fact* (Chicago: University of Chicago Press, 1979 [1935]).

[7] Steven Shapin, "History of Science and its Sociological Constructions," *History of Science* 20 (1982), p. 159.

would introduce an element of irrationality) nor by the social contexts from which it emerges, nor by the psychology or personality of the experimenter. Science explains the world and by virtue of its uncovering of universal laws is predictive as well. But the subversion of almost all of these apparently distinctive qualities has made it increasingly reasonable to regard science not as the antithesis to literature, but as another form of it. On the positivist model, observation was prior to theory. As Peter Galison has recently shown, on the post-World War II antipositivist model, theory has epistemological priority over observation – all observation is not only theory-laden but strictly theoretical. Galison makes clear that both positivist and antipositivist positions are universalist, positing a unified method for all science regardless of place and time; and he urges a new, third model, which takes into account material culture (the place of instrumentation in science, for example) without devolving into another reductivist determinist system.[8]

Regardless of this developing concern with the material in the study of science, the currently dominant antipositivist position within the institution of "literary" study takes textuality as the condition of all knowledge. In this view, since knowledge is culturally constructed and the merest fact theory-laden, the fullest knowledge of science comes with an understanding of the means of representation – the language by which the cultural is naturalized or, as it is often put, "mystified." Formerly subordinate to science and scientific fact, literature in the textualist dispensation is almost imperialistic – it takes all discourse, that is to say, all knowledge, for its province. An understanding of that knowledge entails an understanding of how the knowledge was constituted. As Howard Horwitz, in a brilliant article on the new historicism, has put it, "Instruction in the mediation of representation – language and literature study – suddenly seems essential to comprehending the working of subjectivity and social relations."[9] Horwitz is talking about history, but in at least this version of the poststructuralist view of things, science is as fictional, as constructed, as history. The relations of literature and science now entail not foregrounding and backgrounding but the analysis of the ways science represents, the exposure of its

[8] Peter Galison, "History, Philosophy, and the Central Metaphor," *Science in Context* 2 (Spring, 1988): pp. 197–211.
[9] Howard Horwitz, "'I Can't Remember': Skepticism, Synthetic Histories, Critical Action," *The South Atlantic Quarterly*, 87 (1988), p. 792.

subjectivity and contradictions, the exploration of its rhetoric, its meta-phors, its implicit narrative structures.[10]

When pushed far enough, these procedures, often stimulating and polit-ically alive, lead to some odd and sometimes deeply uncomfortable posi-tions. It has been difficult enough deciding what literature is: Terry Eagleton has effectively used our inability to define literature as a ground for his own reading of literary history and for his own overtly political critical theory.[11] The transformation of science into text is a transformation into literature. From the point of view of practicing theorists, then, science *becomes* liter-ature. There is a great virtue to this idea in so far as it allows critics of language and culture to *read* scientific texts for the way they use language, for the way they participate in or resist the culture – in fact, just *as* literature. Keeping in mind that the text has other functions and other kinds of read-ers, interested not in the cultural drift but in the systematic coherence of the evidence and the argument, such cultural criticism of scientific texts seems to me both fascinating and valuable. But once the "science is literature" argument is well established in its full sense, it becomes too easy to say that everything is a fiction. All distinctions are obliterated by that discovery; it becomes too easy to lose the obvious point with which my argument began, that science is somehow different from literature after all, and that only very strange people would work themselves into a position from which any distinction becomes impossible.

---

[10]   There is, of course, an enormous literature on this kind of reading. The best known practitioner is Bruno Latour, whose *Laboratory Life* (London: Sage, 1979), written with Steve Woolgar, has become a classic of its genre. Greg Meyers' *Writing Biology* (Madison: University of Wisconsin Press, 1990) offers impressive readings of the language of journal articles, grant proposals, and other strictly professional, "scientific" documents. Among the many other books that address these issues in various ways, I call attention to a few representative and important ones: Barry Barnes, *Scientific Knowledge and Sociological Theory* (London: Routledge and Kegan Paul, 1974); Charles Bazerman, *Shaping Written Knowledge: Essays in the Growth, Form, Function, and Impli-cations of the Scientific Article* (Madison: University of Wisconsin Press, 1988); Donald N. McClos-key, *The Rhetoric of Economics* (Madison: University of Wisconsin Press, 1985); Steven Shapin and Simon Schaffer, *Leviathan and the Air-Pump: Hobbes, Boyle, and the Experimental Life, including a translation of Thomas Hobbes, Dialogus physicus de natura aeris by Simon Schaffer* (Princeton: Princeton University Press, 1984). Feminist critiques of science, its epistemology, its procedures, its exclusions, its constitution of the feminine subject, have proliferated recently. Evelyn Fox Keller's *Reflections on Gender and Science* (New Haven: Yale University Press, 1985) is perhaps the most impressive still in its exploration of the way scientific language and methods implicitly exclude the feminine, although Keller is careful to argue for a realist position and to support scientific method. In this connection, see Clifford Geertz, "A Lab of One's Own," *New York Review of Books*, November 8, 1990, pp. 19–23.

[11]   Terry Eagleton, *Literary Theory* (Oxford: Blackwell, 1985), p. 215: "The present crisis in the field of literary studies is at root a crisis in the definition of the subject itself. That it should prove difficult to provide such a definition is, as I hope to have shown . . . hardly surprising."

Paisley Livingston describes the phenomenon this way: "having understood that, in relation to one view of science, literary and humanistic knowledge is nothing but a series of gratuitous worldviews, the literary scholar returns the insult, declaring that scientific knowledge too is nothing but a worldview . . . that is, that scientific knowledge is a myth."[12] There is a large and growing unease, on the part of people otherwise strongly sympathetic to the ideological implications of poststructuralist critiques of scientific knowledge, about the impossibility of using those critiques to authorize any knowledge.

One of the most important expressions of this unease, and one of the most rhetorically powerful, is a now classic essay on the question of "objectivity" and feminism by Donna Haraway. Haraway is, of course, fully aware of how the idea of "objectivity" has been used to naturalize what is socially constructed and to deny precisely the experience and knowledge of women by disguising its male face behind claims for universality. Nevertheless, she says, "the further I get in describing the radical social constructionist program and a particular version of postmodernism, coupled with the acid tools of critical discourse in the human sciences, the more nervous I get."[13] The difficulty, as she puts it, is that she had set out "wanting a strong tool for deconstructing the truth claims of hostile science by showing the radical historical specificity, and so contestability, of every layer of the onion of scientific and technological constructions, and we end up with a kind of epistemological electroshock therapy, which far from ushering us into the high stakes tables of the games of contesting public truths, lays us out on the table with self-induced multiple personality disorder." The trauma results in part from the enforced recognition that the tool she has found not only works on hostile subjects, but on oneself. One hasn't a leg to stand on. The cost of obliterating differences is manifest for feminists. For them the unmasking of objectivity led, says Haraway, to "one more excuse for not learning any Post-Newtonian physics and one more reason to drop the old feminist self-help practices of repairing our own cars. They're just texts anyway, so let the boys have them back" (p. 578). The point is surely not to readopt the conventions of scientific method that had helped disenfranchise women in the first place: Haraway attempts to work out a way to replace traditional "objectivity" with a sense of the way all knowledge is situated, locally.

[12]   Paisley Livingston, *Literary Knowledge: Humanistic Inquiry and the Philosophy of Science* (Ithaca: Cornell University Press, 1988).
[13]   Donna Haraway, "Situated Knowledges: The Science Question in Feminism and the Privilege of Partial Perspective," *Feminist Studies* 14 (1988), p. 577.

I will not follow her arguments here; but what I want to emphasize is her recognition that the acid tools of semiotic, hermeneutic, deconstructionist, Foucauldian critique threaten to deconstruct and demystify not only the present culture's conception of the natural, the true, the authoritative, and the scientific, but *any* conception of them. Is it the case that the only way to avoid the historical consequences of claims for objectivity is to deny the possibility of any of those qualities that the concept of "objectivity" importantly if often misleadingly purported to describe; is it the case that to keep science from performing its political tricks it is necessary to deny the concept of science itself? One possibility could be to reduce all debates about knowledge to combats at arms – in the manner recommended and practiced by Stanley Fish – affirming that all knowledge is culturally constructed, that all truth claims are ideological, and that's fine and let's see which ideology wins. This extreme position conflates the sociological, the epistemological, the rhetorical. One can demonstrate convincingly that the other side is disguising ideology with universalist claims; but self-evidently (and it is often part of the rhetorical strategy to concede this – without, however, giving up one's case) one cannot step back and avoid the demonstration that one's own demonstration is equally ideological. The problem is how to preserve the antifoundationalist positions without reducing all debate to irrational combats at arms.

While many thinkers do avoid the Fishian combat at irrational arms (Richard Rorty is an obvious example), a full antifoundationalism must run the danger of becoming metaphysical itself. The claim that all scientifically realist claims to authority are ultimately metaphysical is itself ultimately metaphysical. The critical question for students of science and literature is how to mediate between the total obliteration of distinction between the two and the old positivist assertion of absolute difference. Once again, Haraway's formulation of the problem seems useful:

So, I think my problem, and "our" problem, is how to have simultaneously an account of radical historical contingency for all knowledge claims and knowing subjects, a critical practice for recognizing our "semiotic technologies" for making meanings, and a no-nonsense commitment to a faithful account of a "real" world, one that can be partially shared and that is friendly to earthwide projects of finite freedom, adequate material abundance, modest meaning in suffering, and limited happiness.

Such a science without Faustian pact is in some ways more difficult to achieve than the universalist science that sells its soul to the devil. It requires an extraordinary and perhaps impossible balance, a tentativeness that keeps all aspirations to knowledge from becoming aspirations to power as well. The temptation, for those steeped in the Faust myths, who have read Marlowe, Goethe, and Mary Shelley too much, is – if choice must be made – to prefer radical historical contingency to what Haraway calls a "faithful account of a 'real' world."

Complete contingency has its difficulties, too. For example, Joan Scott, the fine deconstructionist/feminist/historian, has spoken of the "ultimate futility" of "resting arguments for social change on claims to objectivity."[14] While I am committed to Scott's feminist objectives, I find myself stymied by paradoxes. Clearly, the feminist sociologist whom Scott criticizes in a review offers arguments no more "objective" and "gender-free" than those of her opponents, and Scott is surely correct to seek another kind of response to the naturalizing of gender differences that is fundamental to much social science. "I don't think," says Scott, that "denying the 'reality' [note this word in quotation marks] of gender distinctions is an effective way to advance discussion. Those distinctions are part of the reality [no quotation marks] we confront, not only in social science research, but in institutions and organizations as disparate as schools, churches, families, and the *New York Times*." The two uses of "reality" mark a crux: why does the second "reality" denoting the way social science works – carry the weight of what can only be called objective authority, while the first "reality" does not?

The question re-emerges: what authorizes truth statements such as this? The science/literature dichotomy has got to be reimagined, to be felt along the finger tips just as Scott feels the reality of the socially enforced gender differences whose workings she is committed to understand. I take it as one of the primary functions of students of the relations between science and literature to attempt to reconstruct the difference implied in the subject as it is named: science/literature. Having understood the ways they are like each other, we need to avoid the reductiveness of identity and try to figure out the ways in which they are not. And the project should be partly in the interest of working out Haraway's "problem," which ought to be everyone's: how to reconcile a sense of radical historical contingency with a "faithful account of a real world." A sense of difference will, or ought, to strengthen those special literary skills of semiotic and rhetorical analysis which should be brought to bear on science, which is not concerned with those skills. And perhaps equally important, a sense of

---

[14] Joan Scott, "The Pitfalls of 'Scientific Feminism,'" *Tikkun* 4 (2, 1989), pp. 90–2.

difference will do something to ease the aspirations to intellectual imperialism of much literary theory. If we claim all "texts" as our province and
all things human as "texts" we turn everything into literature and thus
have nothing to learn that is not already literary.

I want to talk about differences because differences are the condition of
relationships; if there are no differences there is only identity. "Otherness,"
one of the things that literature can teach, gets lost in textuality; if we turn
to science, imagined as a process that is not merely text, we open ourselves
to an other that we cannot manipulate with rhetorical strategies. It might
strengthen us if we could learn from science and not merely assimilate it,
and consider more seriously what could be that hard unaccommodating
actual to which writers like George Eliot and Henry James felt the need to
defer. Finally, I want to speculate about the nature of the differences and
the implications of difference for the work of theorists, critics, sociologists
of science, philosophers. Since I will avoid trying to come up with any more
precise definition of either science or literature than the vague one with
which I began, this might seem particularly presumptuous.

I begin, for the purposes of argument, by accepting the view that
science, like everything else within the discourse of our culture, is "constructed," and thus by not being able to categorize or define differences
between science and literature. I am in fact convinced that science as text
can be literature – but its status depends on nothing intrinsic to itself, only
on what sorts of questions the student chooses to ask of it. On the other
hand, it is impossible not to notice, as John Limon suggestively points out,
that while I could not become a scientist without many years of training, a
literate scientist could write novels and criticism tomorrow and might be
successful at it.[15] How come? While I have been insisting here on the
difference between science and literature and may seem to be implying
that literature has nothing to do with knowledge, I do not of course mean
that. Literature can be a means to situated knowledge, can be an opening

---

[15] This essay was written just before the "outbreak" of the science wars, that culminated in the
famous Sokal hoax of the journal, *Social Text*. In the major text of the offensive against cultural
study of science, or even cultural mention of science, the book of Norman Levitt and Paul R.
Gross, *The Higher Superstition*, the authors make a strong point of saying that scientists could
easily take over the literature programs, but the literary people had no hope of taking over the
science programs. The assumption of course is that there would be no loss. Literary study is for
amateurs and science is for professionals. In fact, the authors are probably right, that virtually no
literary scholars could teach serious science courses. The implication, that people outside of science
should have nothing to say about it, suggests something of the imperial attitudes, perhaps on both
side of the "wars." The asymmetry, however, does not imply that scientists could handle literature
well, or that literary scholars have no right to consider science in culture.

to other, scientific forms of knowledge; and – if we mean by literature literary-critical procedures – it provides us with a conception of how language works, how meaning is constructed, that becomes an essential part of our intellectual equipment in a world pervasively textual.

But I have implicitly distinguished science from literature in terms of knowledge because I do want to insist that literary knowledge is, by and large, different from scientific knowledge. Not, of course, absolutely. Perhaps not even intrinsically. But in effect, certainly. Literature (if not also literary criticism) resists systematization, tests our abstractly conceived ideas against the rich texture of experience, and is more concerned with the singular than the general. In the comparison of literature and science, the appropriate analogue, though not exclusively or even usually what is meant, is between science and literary criticism. Presumably, science is a study of the natural world as criticism is a study of literature. So literature is the "subject" of criticism and "nature" is the subject of science. That being the case, the question would be, is science different from literary criticism? Most scientists I know wouldn't have trouble with the question!

Let me begin here by raising the question of textuality. It would probably take many scientists by surprise to know that their primary activity was the production of texts, in the same way that literary critics produce texts. Darwin loved the study of nature, experimenting with flowers, studying the anatomy of barnacles, watching earthworms. He hated writing. Many of the most interesting philosophers of science find their way out of some of the critical problems of realism and representation by insisting that the primary activity of scientists is in the laboratory. One of the most subtle and satisfying of these philosophers, Ian Hacking, rejects "the false dichotomy between acting and thinking" which produces, on his account, "notions of incommensurability and transcendental nominalism." The harm, he says "comes from a single-minded obsession with representation and thinking and theory, at the expense of intervention and action and experiment ... I study experimental science, and find in it the sure basis of an uncontentious realism."[16]

Hacking finds the debate about realism/antirealism empty and irresolvable, and he thus turns, for a fuller sense of reality, to "intervention." Moreover, while he can rehearse all the arguments about observation as theory-laden, he insists that "a philosophy of experimental science cannot allow theory-dominated philosophy to make the very concept of

[16] Ian Hacking, *Representing and Intervening* (Cambridge: Cambridge University Press, 1983), p. 131.

observation become suspect." He accepts and then dismisses the textual-izing of "fact" by insisting that all observation is theory-loaded: "if you wanted," he says, "to call every belief, proto-belief, and belief that could be invented, a theory, do so. But then the claim about theoryloaded is trifling." So he argues, "the fact that observing depends upon theories has none of the anti-rational consequences that have sometimes been inferred from the thesis that all observation is theory-loaded" (p. 185). That is real, Hacking insists, which he affects or is affected by, and he turns to con-sideration of what goes on in the laboratory, where effects can be created.

Rom Harré, in different ways, insists on viewing science not as a rep-resentational text but as an activity: " 'science,' " he says, "is not a logically coherent body of knowledge in the strict, unforgiving sense of the philos-ophers' high redefinition, but a cluster of material and cognitive practi-ces"; "it is an activity: it is something people do."[17] Not, of course, that criticism isn't something people do; but criticism is always verbal. Only if one takes the idea that all observation is theory-laden as nontrivial can one assimilate laboratory activity to literary activity. Turning the experience of the laboratory into texts does, indeed, open science to the full semiotic critique; but that activity is, as Harré argues, only a very small part of scientific activity. "Experiment," says Hacking, "is not stating or reporting but doing – and not doing things with words"(p. 173). There is no way to, no need to decontextualize. But short of acquiescing in a world that is a steady fog of identity, it is necessary to distinguish among words, test tubes, cyclotrons, and different degrees of theory – full-scale scientific theories, general and unsystematic cultural assumptions, anticipatory guesses, etc. Hacking argues, through many impressively elicited historical examples, "that much truly fundamental research precedes any relevant theory whatsoever"(p. 158).

Philosophy of science needs history of science, should in part always be history of science, because history almost always breaks down totalizing theories through examples that don't fit. History of science in this respect would make a valuable contribution to literary theory, requiring local and particular understandings of potentially reductive arguments, like that which affirms the theory-laden nature of all observations. In any case, science has to be discriminated from texts, even if scientific "texts" are fair game for semiotic and sociological and literary analysis. The question is, what does one find out through such analysis; and I would argue that one finds out a lot but does not get adequate epistemological explanations

---

[17]   Rom Harré, *Varieties of Realism* (Oxford: Basil Blackwell, 1986), p. 6.

of the scientific results. So whatever is the answer to the question of whether science is different from literature when taken from the point of view of epistemology, the best answer is clearly what my scientist friends would claim when we view the question from the point of view of practice: yes, very. It is not only that the subject of the two disciplines is different, unless we want to equate literary texts with nature (which can, of course, be done by asserting that the only nature we know is constructed – "a text" rather than a brute reality). Even given that "nature" is very much a human conception, there are the simple brute evidences that scientists' manipulations of "nature" produce bombs, internal combustion engines, computers, while critics' manipulation of texts produces more texts.[18]

I am not trying to develop any elaborate theory of differences; if anything, I am offering up for reinspection banalities which may have seemed to have lost their significance. While there have been superb studies, like Shapin and Schaffer's *Leviathan and the Air-Pump*, for instance, showing that traditional notions of replication don't really work as positivist theory required, there is simply no science without an affirming or resisting community. Larry Laudan has impressively argued that thus far no school of philosophy or sociology has developed arguments adequate to the explanation of both scientific consensus and scientific disagreement. He finds also that the arguments for any form of scientific realism (and he includes Richard Boyd, Hilary Putnam, and W. H. Newton-Smith in his judgment) are both incomplete and inconsistent and cannot in any way account for the "success" of science.[19] The epistemic problems with which he deals continue to worry philosophers of science, and I am obviously not going to resolve them. But even the most cogent critique of traditional views of scientific "success" – and in Laudan's case that includes an argument that the boundaries between science and philosophy are arbitrary – needs to come to terms with the fact both of scientific achievement and of its methods for determining success.

These, again, have no parallel in literature. The preoccupation of science is with its current literature. That is, in its concern with the validity of current research and its aspiration to resolve as yet unsolved problems, it is

---

[18]   A colleague of mine takes issue with this point, insisting that there is plenty of evidence that critical texts have important physical consequences. Of course: that is why the contest over contextualizing of science evokes such intense feelings. But again a distinction can be made between the way words are used and the production of those words. For example, ecological theories can produce results in the use of pesticides, or the depletion of the rainforests. Science and technology construct their arguments out of the manipulation of materials with the direct aim of further manipulation.

[19]   Larry Laudan, *Science and Values* (Berkeley: University of California Press, 1984).

not much interested in how it got to where it is. The stories science tells are usually about "nature," rarely about its own past. Great scientific texts are only interesting in so far as they are still the last word in one or another aspect of contemporary research, which is one of the reasons that period-icals are more important than books to practicing scientists. John Limon argues that perhaps the one axiomatic distinction between science and literature is that science has no history.[20] Whereas in literature, Milton, Shakespeare, Chaucer, Homer, Dante, Plato, etc., remain living classics – with what Limon calls an "independent existence," taught and retaught, criticized and analyzed over and over, in science the subject is always nature now. Limon quotes Kuhn's well known essay on science and art: "Unlike art, science destroys its past." Literature and criticism alike remain interested in what critics like Dryden, Johnson, and Arnold said, but the work of earlier scientists whose problems have been solved or whose answers have been displaced does not enter into the work of the laboratory. Literature's preoccupation with the past, its indifference to a conception of itself as "progressive," is one of its fundamental differences from science. It is consequently also far more self-reflexive, engaged with its own procedures as subject rather than means. The very powerful equip-ment it has developed for the analysis of all texts, scientific ones included, is an outgrowth of its own self-preoccupation. Self-reflexiveness, histor-icity, textuality – these are some of the characteristic marks of literature.

Obviously, the boundaries between literature and philosophy or science are tentative and wavering. We have, I hope, learned too much in these past decades to allow ourselves to feel comfortable with absolute demar-cation. And certainly, I am not claiming difference in order to reinstate priority and the background/foreground model of relationship. But the very power to demystify science's traditional claims to absolute authority in the area of knowledge depends on keeping clear what is distinctive in criticism. Such clarity provides the tools to explore the textuality of science without denying its difference. I would hope, also, that it would encourage a little humility in the face of other kinds of knowledge – scientific knowl-edge, which constitutes perhaps the most extraordinary (and dangerous) creation of the human imagination over the last three centuries.

In exploring the relations between science and literature, theorists are unlikely to be able to construct "a theory" of those relations that can be very helpful or apply in all cases. Any such theory would itself be

---

[20] John Limon, *The Place of Fiction in the Time of Science* (Cambridge: Cambridge University Press, 1990), pp. 8–10.

universalizing in ways cultural critiques have taught us to resist in the first place. But more decisively, the relations between science and literature are too various to systematize. Writers engage with science at second and third hand, using it selectively, without full knowledge of the complexities of its findings. They admire, or not, resist or not, unselfconsciously or self-consciously absorb, distort, simplify, imply alternatives, despair, rejoice, ignore. But critics of science and literature need to keep in mind the variousness and incompleteness of writers' and scientists' interrelations. I hope constructivist and antifoundationalist theory is not incompatible with deep respect for those aspects of science not subject to the imperial constraints of language. Science, as perhaps the greatest achievement of the Western imagination, needed and still needs the demystifying that has emerged from history and sociology of science, and from the critical theories of poststructuralism. But the aim of those most deeply concerned with the relations between science and literature, science and culture ought to be like Haraway's: to reconcile a sense of radical historical contingency (so much the province of literary theory and criticism) with a "faithful account of a real world" (a task that only science and literature together can achieve).

PART III

Literature, secularity, and the quest for otherness

CHAPTER 7

Realism

In undertaking to write about "realism" in a broad, summary way, I recognize that I can bring very little fresh news. I have made my own arguments about it in a book now more than twenty-five years old – *The Realistic Imagination* – and it seems merely redundant to repeat the arguments I made there, although I know no way of writing about realism without reverting to at least some of them; and since the publication of that book a large critical literature about realism has continued to grow, suggesting that realism has struggled back, though in a considerably weakened form, and under the scrutiny of very skeptical eyes, to some of the respectability that it lost, at least among highbrow writers, early in the twentieth century. What credit it had by the mid-twentieth century seemed to have been exhausted entirely by the radically anti-realist arguments of modern literary theory after the 1960s, when the very notion of representing "reality" in any credible way was taken as reprehensible (perhaps ideologically dangerous) naïveté, or simple bad faith. For the modernists, Virginia Woolf's marvelous and famous essay, "Mr. Bennett and Mrs Brown," brilliantly dramatizes the aesthetic (and psychological and even moral) inadequacy of realist attempts to register in all their particularity things as they are as opposed to finding ways into interiority and the mysteries of the self.

For the postmodernists, some of the animus against realism can be traced in J. Hillis Miller's two important essays on George Eliot's *Middlemarch* and one on Dickens' *Sketches by "Boz"*,[1] each of which meticulously argues, though in different ways, that reading these texts literally as coherent representations of reality misses almost entirely the way the

---

[1] J. Hillis Miller, "Narrative and History," *ELH*, 41 (1974); pp. 455–73; "Optic and Semiotic in *Middlemarch*," in *The Worlds of Victorian Fiction*, ed. J. H. Buckley (Cambridge, MA: Harvard University Press, 1975); "The Fiction of Realism: *Sketches by Boz, Oliver Twist*, and *Cruikshank's Illustrations*," *Dickens Centennial Essays*, ed. Ada Nisbet and Blake Nevius (Berkeley: University of California Press, 1971), pp. 85–153.

language of the books works and the ultimate impossibility of realistic representation. Neither of the famous Victorian, insistently realist texts turns out to be really realistic. Nor can any literary text be. Beyond the epistemological problems, realism, it is also often suggested in recent discussions, at least in its manifestation in English, is always an act of "containment," an effort at "naturalizing," and thus no disinterested rendering of things as they are but imaginations of ways of keeping things under control, fashioning them so as to exclude their disruptive possibilities. The contradictions and impossibilities that epistemological questioning exposes turn out to have large social and ideological implications, and from the perspective of most recent theory, not good implications.

I do not want to fight the old fights again in part because they are old news and in part because I agree in significant part with all the critiques but find that in resisting what I would take to be a very common-sense notion of realism that they try to demystify, they inadequately appreciate the distinctive and great virtues of realism and the interest and complexity of its workings. If it be true that realism as a full representation of the real must fail in any absolute sense, given the nature of the medium itself and the inevitable limits of human knowing and perspective, there are ways in which the efforts of realism – so brilliantly analyzed by Auerbach as a strong democratizing force with roots as deep as the Bible and Homer, and so strongly defended by Lukács – continue to matter and require not passive recording but strenuous art. Once the necessary demystifying takes place; once the limits of the mode are laid bare; once the epistemological and ideological problems and disguises are recognized, realism remains an important, even a necessary mode of literary art.

Given, however, the vastness of the topic and of the debate, I would like here, after laying out some of the general grounds of the conversation about realism, to consider a few of its important, characteristically recurrent elements. And I will try to do this by taking most of my examples from a single novel, *Vanity Fair*, a novel that has managed to survive the aesthetic and ideological wars as both an eccentric and an exemplary realist fiction. I want not to explicate the book, but rather to look at some exemplary fragments that can help suggest the limits, the problems, and the power of nineteenth-century English realism. Bringing the discussion down from broad generalities about epistemology and ideology through a close look at exemplars of realistic technique and subject matter (like close looks at any rich and powerful text) can tell us a lot about what makes realism interesting and important still beyond the difficulties that mark most commentary upon it.

I

To begin, then, with the general, "realism" is a word that begs so many questions that it seems, at first, and at second and third thought, almost absurd to try to talk about it as though it were possible to define it adequately or develop a coherent set of statements about it. It is not simply that literary "realism" descends from a strange, even paradoxical history with which we are all at least glancingly familiar, moving from what might well be called an absolute idealism that posits the reality of universals (and the implicit unreality of the particulars that we would now identify as the real) to an empiricist argument that posits the only knowable reality as that which we can acquire from "experience," and, in the late form of logical positivism, to a dismissal of Platonic universals as "nonsense." Realism is in its very nature a paradoxical form. The more strenuously empiricism pushes against an epistemology that makes ideas more real than matter, that insists on (divinely) inherited knowledge, that gives first place to intuition and imagination, the more clear it becomes that realism always, more or less surreptitiously, still depends on the mind as much as on "external nature." Perhaps ironically, therefore, realism has always tended to contain (in both senses of the word) idealism of some form or other, threatening to slide into what emerged in its late nineteenth-century manifestations as an almost absolute solipsism, Pater's thick wall of personality through which no real voice ever pierces. "Experience," it turns out, is always of one's sensations not of the things out there that supposedly trigger them. The external turns out to be internal, and realism's increasing turn to interiority, to throwing the drama inside, as Henry James put it, is in one sense an epistemological inevitability, although of course there are less philosophical and literary forces at work in the novel's turn to individual consciousness as primary subject.

The paradox of realism's implication in idealism is matched by another one: realism, rather than being, what it sometimes has given itself to be, an anti-literary mode, or at least a mode that depends not on literary tradition but on the way the world is, is of necessity a thoroughly literary mode. The urge to reality takes shape, consistently, in response to literary precedent, to the "cloud-borne angels ... prophets, sibyls, and ... the heroic warriors" against which George Eliot in the famous Chapter 17 of *Adam Bede* sets "an old woman bending over her flower pot." The realist novel is similarly antagonistic to the romantic heroines whom Charlotte Brontë exposes as empty vessels, and to the romantic resolution in marriage that Thackeray deromanticizes in Dobbin's marriage to Amelia. In every gesture toward the real, in every mock-heroic simile, from Fielding through Thackeray and Trollope, there is an echo of some literature that has imagined a very different reality. The satirical denial of early, often quixotic, literary modes becomes a kind of signature of realism, which then in its very mockery invests the old literary forms with a new importance and marks its own anti-literary procedures as self-consciously literary. The literariness is a mark of realism's necessary self-consciousness, but it tends to be driven by a strong moral impulse (as well as an aesthetic one). For the realist, there is a lot at stake in getting it right, in telling the "truth," and it is no accident that realism tended to be the dominant narrative mode of a Victorian England in which perhaps the greatest of all virtues, greater than sexual propriety, was truth-telling. Observing things as they are, even with quasi-scientific detachment, displaces false representations with authentic ones, and forces us, as readers, out of the kinds of delusions that lead to moral disaster – Don Quixote's, or Emma Woodhouse's, or Emma Bovary's, or Pip's, or even Amelia Sedley's, for she, though innocent, makes a fantasy of her lover and then husband, and, were it not for good old Dobbin, would permanently have ruined her life and the lives of others around her.

Lurking in the workings of realism is an element of earlier kinds of narratives, exemplary tales, for example, or allegory, what Michael McKeon has described as a "pedagogical end," that is, the teaching of precept by example.[2] As McKeon points out, that pedagogical end becomes less central to narrative in the long history of realism, but among the Victorians, it is clear that while overt pedagogy is increasingly abjured – George Eliot claims that she will not let her stories lapse "from the picture to the diagram" – the pedagogical end is absorbed into a decades long parable that demonstrates, both in form and in subject matter, the ethical importance of telling the truth and of finding it out. These things, says George Eliot half mockingly about the famous looking glass metaphor in *Middlemarch*, are a parable. Realism, then, even as it struggles out from the traditions that helped found it, is paradoxically an attenuated form of a distinctly non-realistic narrative practice.

Realism's giddying self-contradictory condition is confused yet further by the fact that it has one consistent commitment, the very hard work of trying to reach beyond words to describe the way things are. This work must be in constant process and always unstable because the way things are

---

[2]   See Michael McKeon, ed., *Theory of the Novel: A Historical Approach* (Baltimore: Johns Hopkins University Press, 2000), p. 610.

is subject to historical transformation of the culture's understanding of the way things are, and because it must be inflected by an awareness of how different things look from different perspectives. What holds realism together in its flexibility and changefulness is the fact that despite the paradoxes it is always also committed to the common-sense notion that what we see – not our words or our ideas – is "really there," that the physical world is not a Cartesian dream but is really real, as opposed to being constituted of mere ideas or individual sensations – or romantic quixotic distortions. Realism, in this connection (still, however, allied to empiricist philosophy, though not systematically) is the commitment to register the external real and then (or at the same time) the interiority that perceives it and distorts or penetrates it.

The argument that, as Rosalind Coward and John Ellis put it, realism treats language "as though it stands in for, is identical with, the real world," and treats the signifier as identical to a (pre-existent) signified[3] is at most only partially true, but even if it were true, it need not have the consequences much post-structuralist theory implies. That is, realism's effort to stand in for the world can hardly be an unselfconscious, a naïve and self-deceived mode of narrative. Realism makes the difficulties of the work of representation inescapably obvious to the writer; it makes inevitable an intense self-consciousness, sometimes explicit, sometimes not. No writer attempting to reach beyond words can fail to be struck by the work words do, by the obstacles they put up to transparency, and therefore no such writer can fail to recognize the degree to which the creation of illusion is an essential feature of the realist process. Realism *is* an illusion, just as representational art is illusory, finding ways to suggest depth and three dimensions on a two dimensional canvas, finding strategies by which to create the sense of light, as the impressionists did, just by *not* making the brush strokes look like the thing being represented (except from certain viewing perspectives).[4]

In his innovative and important book on Jane Austen, William Galperin describes Austen's narrative practice, conventionally taken as realistic, as being in the very texture of its language conscious of itself and designed to resist mere passive recording of the way things are, or are conventionally taken to be. And although Galperin treats Austen's best

---

[3]   See McKeon, p. 595.

[4]   See Elizabeth Deeds Ermarth, *Realism and Consensus in the English Novel* (Princeton: Princeton University Press, 1983). Ermarth discusses at great length the development of perspective in European art and shows, among other things, how "realism is built not on naïve assumptions about how reality can be directly represented but by cultural consensus."

writing as more a critique of realism than "realistic" in any of the dominant senses in popular discussion of it,[5] it seems to me that what he describes so effectively in Austen is a central characteristic of almost all interesting realist practice and does not exclude Austen from the realism that followed upon her work among the Victorians, but puts her dead center. While of course there are many "realist" novels that seem simply to plunge in, tell their stories, describe their little (or not so little) worlds and worry not at all about the nature of the perspective from which the story is to be told, or the problematic nature of the reality being described, on the whole realistic fiction is required to think about itself a great deal. If the world of the novel is to be represented as real (itself, of course, an oxymoronic condition), the first thing that has to be got straight is the difference between "reality," whatever we decide that is, and a work of literature, and the degree to which what is represented is being shaped by the author. That is to say, the realist novel has got to face the fact that it is a fiction, that it is made up – something that Thackeray does strenuously, if erratically, in *Vanity Fair.*

It is hard for me not to recur in this connection to a telling line of Northrop Frye's that I found fundamental to my earliest thoughts about realism: "The realistic writer," Frye claims, "soon finds that the requirements of literary form and plausible content always fight against each other."[6] This is both self-evident and in some ways radically subversive of any pure realist enterprise, Biffin's, for example, in Gissing's *New Grub Street.* His vast and ambitious work in progress, "Mr. Bailey, Grocer," will be, as Biffin himself knows, virtually unreadable, a record of everything in the life of "Mr. Bailey," an austere, endless representation of all the details of an ordinary life, the "ignobly decent," as he puts it. Biffin describes how he would, for example, represent the banal conversation between two lovers he hears in the street: "I am going to reproduce it verbatim without one single impertinent suggestion of any point of view save that of honest reporting. The result will be something unutterably tedious. Precisely. That is the stamp of the ignobly decent life. If it were anything but tedious it would be untrue."[7] (As a student, I was taught that this way of imagining art entailed the "fallacy of imitative form," the mistaken view that art consists in precisely duplicating the form of the world it is describing.

[5] William Galperin, *The Historical Austen* (Philadelphia: University of Pennsylvania Press, 2003), pp. 44–87, in particular.
[6] Northrop Frye, *Fables of Identity: Studies in Poetic Mythology* (New York: Harcourt, Brace, 1963), p. 36.
[7] George Gissing, *New Grub Street* (London: Penguin, 1985 [1891]), ch. 10, p. 74.

Modernist theory, deeply self-conscious about "form," rejected realism in part because, like Biffin, it seemed to ignore what Frye describes as the "requirements of literary form.")

In a way, it is a cheat that Gissing finally allows Biffin actually to complete the manuscript – how could he ever have reached the end of these tedious registrations of the real? When Frye talks of the tension between literary form and plausibility, he is implying a fundamental tension in all realist texts, one that often manifests itself as a tension between focus on character and interest in plot. Biffin's realist novel will have no plot. Trollope distinguishes his own work from the "sensation novel," a subgenre in which the workings of plot and the discovery of how it will come out tend to create the driving energy. But for Trollope, the true work of the novel is "observation," and the true interest of the writer (and the readers) is in the characters. He argues that it should not matter if the reader knows the whole story. In reading a sensation novel, one is concerned to find out what will happen next, how the mysteries will be resolved, but reading a Trollopean, realist novel, one finds that the pleasure of the experience has little to do with the plot, which can seem an arbitrary authorial imposition on the narrative rather than intrinsic to the life and characters it is representing; the pleasure is just in the interest that develops in the representation of verisimilar objects and characters.

Although retrospectively, it is easy to think of nineteenth-century realist fiction as sometimes plot heavy (not so, for the most part, with Trollope), it is characterized more significantly by a sort of "detailism" – an intense registration of the particulars of the material world that the protagonists inhabit – and novels devoted to details, context, and character give less the illusion of manipulation than those in which what will happen is the driving force of the narrative. In so far as the duality holds (and Trollope argues that it is artificial and that all novelists in the end must work at both poles), detailism and representation work toward plausibility and away from form, plot works toward it. Thus, on the one hand, one has the "large, loose baggy monsters" of which James complains, and on the other, one has the stunning formal precision of *Wuthering Heights*, which meticulously organizes and balances events and sustains itself through the energies of romance. Nineteenth-century realism, as we can understand it today, leans toward the scrupulous construction of social and historical context, and to the life of characters within that context. In its fullest form, Biffin's "Mr. Bailey, Grocer," it produces the most artless art, the least regardful of the requirements of literary form.

But this tendency of realism to formless and plotless representation of what can be observed and of character further compounds the paradoxes at the heart of the realist enterprise, for in order to write such a boring, realistic, heroless, plotless novel, Biffin must sustain the most austere, the most ascetic artistic commitment, giving his life to the writing of a book whose authenticity guarantees that it will be a commercial failure. But given the distinction between art and realist representation, narrators must remain alert, perhaps not to the potential tediousness of their work but to the difference between what they can narrate and what is out there to be narrated. Biffin could never, really, have finished that book just because Frye is right. The plausible has no beginning and no end.

Such problems of representation require that the realist novel think, first of all, about the question of perspective. The great mid-nineteenth century developments in free indirect discourse come, of course, in realistic fiction, and come precisely because of the felt inadequacy of strictly omniscient representation of "reality" – among other things, the danger of a voice too authoritative, too un-Biffin-like in determining the readers' judgments and understanding; and because of the necessary doubts authors might have about the power of omniscience really to be omniscient, or of the novel to contain all that is out there to be represented. Free indirect discourse is an ingenious compromise between first person narration, whose limits and unreliability have been part of novelists' problems since *Pamela*, and full omniscience. And free indirect discourse has turned out to be the best mode by which an author can, as it were, disappear, and give the impression that what unfolds on the page simply happens without his (or her) intervention or help. On the other hand, it allows interiority without subjecting the reader to the full bias of the characters' desires and prejudices and without the falsity of representation of thought that comes registered inside quotation marks, as though the mind works precisely in the rhetorically imposing way that stage representation requires. Moreover, free indirect style encourages the reader to be an active participant in the narrative rather than a passive receiver of "fact" and judgments and thus further gives the sense that the narration is like life, in which there are no omniscient narrators to help us decide what to think about what we experience. The narrator is, to be sure, there in the third-person perspective of passages of free indirect discourse, and a writer like George Eliot can occasionally interject an implicit judgment in the midst of such passages, as happens often with "poor Rosamond," or even "poor Dorothea," but characters whose consciousness is so recorded have the widest space in which to open themselves to the readers' judgments. Free indirect discourse is a remarkably devious invention in that it is extremely good at creating the illusion that consciousness is being rendered without authorial intervention, and that the language is the strictest representation, Biffin-like, of the workings of a real character's mind.

Omniscient narrations are far less illusory. If on the one hand, they can be described as monologic as opposed to dialogic, constrained by a single consciousness rather than revelatory of the free play of alternative voices, they still have the virtue of not fully disguising the presence of a narrator, and in realism, one would take it, openness about the fact of the presence of a narrator makes a narration more "true," if, from the point of view of literary modernists, less artistically effective. There is a certain irony that Henry James, who was so self-consciously creating and theorizing the "art" of the novel, was so strongly committed to sustaining its illusions that he required the writer to delude readers into believing that they were in direct contact with the real. Consider how upset James gets at Trollope's habit of admitting he is writing a novel right in the middle of a novel – "He took a suicidal satisfaction in reminding the reader that the story he was telling was only, after all, a make-believe."[8] The worst sin a realist artist can commit, apparently, is to confess (truthfully and therefore realistically?) that he or she is making up a story.

Ironically, however, it is possible to think of the naïve Victorians as more sophisticated about novel theory than James himself, for the various ways in which they comment on their narratives has something of the postmodern about it. That is, they create their worlds while being intensely and often explicitly self-conscious about the medium through which they are doing it, and worrying not at all that the efforts at illusion will be undercut by overt exposures of the devices by which the illusion is being created. Who, among novel readers, does not know he or she is reading a novel? In the long run, it is not clear whether Jamesian modernism or Trollopean Victorianism is more "realistic," but it is also not clear which requires greater art.

II

There is no novel more self-conscious (and perhaps inconsistent) about the fact of its illusionism, about the difference between the claims of art and the claims of plausibility, about the inadequacies of omniscient

8   Henry James, "Anthony Trollope," *Essays on Literature; American Writers; English Writers* (New York: The Library of America, 1984), p. 1, 343.

representation in the efforts toward authentic representation of the real, than *Vanity Fair*. The narrator's representation of himself as a puppet master and of the characters as puppets is well known. But the narrator also appears as an "I" in the book, someone who, we are told quite late, has actually met Becky in Germany. If the characters are puppets, they are odd puppets, or it's an odd narrator; it becomes necessary, for any sort of consistency, to think of "puppets" as a metaphor, although, famously, there is a concluding vignette in which the "author" is in fact putting real puppets back in a box. Yet the narrator not only meets these puppets in Germany, but some of them provide him with information he needs to tell the story. Early on, in yet another guise, the narrator asks, "as a man and a brother," "to step down from the platform, and talk about" the characters he has been introducing.[9] And in a move that might be recognized from Scott's *Waverley*, he pauses to tell "us" – and the "us," the readers, are very much part of the text – in what other ways "we might have treated this subject," and he goes on to describe other literary forms that he has, on consideration, rejected (ch. 6). In the role of omniscient narrator, he sometimes abdicates, but then selectively loses, his power to know every-thing, claiming that he is unable to tell us what have been the motives of his characters. If any narration can be taken to be unstable and incon-sistent, the narration of *Vanity Fair* is it.

The inconsistency is both created and compounded by the fact that *Vanity Fair* is a persistently ironic book. In the great Cervantean tradition, and in keeping with Thackeray's earlier work and the original title of the novel, "Pen and Pencil Sketches of English Society," *Vanity Fair* satirizes almost everything, using literary devices to counter literary devices, exploding conventional ways of writing a novel, even ending on a note that pulls the rug out from under any of us who, led by the conventions of comic romance, or comic realism, expect and wait hopefully for the mar-riage of Dobbin and Amelia. When that marriage comes, the possibilities of romance are long since gone, and even a touch of bitterness enters the prose:

He has got the prize he has been trying for all his life. The bird has come in at last. There it is with its head on his shoulder, billing and cooing close up to his heart, with soft outstretched fluttering wings. This is what he has asked for every day and hour for eighteen years. This is what he pined after. Here it is – the summit, the end – the last page. (ch. 67, p. 804)

---

[9]   William Thackeray, *Vanity Fair: A Novel Without a Hero* (London: Penguin, 2003 [1848]), ch. 8.

The climax, then, arrives as the book announces (metaphorically) that it *is* a book and we are on the last page. As literature and life are conflated and comment on each other, the satire edges toward contempt, and its intensity raises the stakes. It is not only Amelia who makes an unsatisfactory bride, but marriage as an institution is implicated, and perhaps more seriously yet, the marriage plot itself is called into question, as well as the conventions of formal closure.

Part of the irony of the passage is that just as it is announcing it has arrived at "the last page," it is developing the conventions that will dominate realism. That is, it creates its reality by satirizing conventional literary form. The genre of realist fiction, which in England began and was sustained for the most part by the comic tradition that concludes the drama in marriage, increasingly tends to treat marriage not as an ending but as a beginning. Thackeray helps, boldly, to initiate this change: Becky marries Rawdon early on and the book explores many marriages with an ironic, one might almost say, embittered, tone. Twenty-five years later, George Eliot would make the very substance of perhaps the greatest English realist novel two marriages – that between Dorothea Brooke and Casaubon, which happens within a few chapters of the start of *Middlemarch*, and that between Rosamond and Lydgate, which happens not much later. The drama of James' *The Golden Bowl,* a book that is at once closely tied to the traditions of Victorian realism and distinctly modernist in mode, really begins with the marriage of the Prince to Maggie Verver.

Thackeray's ironic comment on Amelia and Dobbin's marriage has large implications for the form of realist fiction, but it has also a biting ethical energy to it. It is not only a reaction to the obvious fact of the anguish of Thackeray's own marriage. It is angry more broadly about romantic illusion; it is angry about conventions of representation that take romantic love seriously. It is contemptuous of the happy ending, for it is clear that the requirements of literary form rub hard against the requirements of realistic representation as Thackeray understands the real. Any ending within a self-consciously realist text is going to be arbitrary; there can be no real conclusion. But Thackeray intimates this without allowing his book to answer to realism's potential shapelessness, for he uses the conventional ending even as he satirically employs it to undercut the convention.

The ending of *Vanity Fair* is, however, certainly an illusion. Becky Sharp, the "villainess" (who for many readers – significantly for the implications of Thackeray's book and for realism – is the real heroine of the book), lives outside the punishment that poetic justice would require, and despite the fact that there is a strong implication that she has murdered Amelia's brother. Her life goes on beyond "the last page." And another and different sort of novel begs to be written, Biffin-like, or perhaps James-like, exploring the interiority of a Dobbin who clearly no longer loves his wife but is gentle and good to her, and of an "Emmy" who knows this is the case. In refusing the satisfactions of closure, Thackeray is implicitly affirming the importance of the realist enterprise; in rejecting the comic ending and the possibility of a satisfactory conclusion ("Which of us is happy in this world?" the book's final paragraph asks), Thackeray is, with some fatigue, turning away from the literary forms that in fact give spine and structure to his own enormous book. Thackeray arrives at what might be seen as the ultimate attitude of the realist, something like contempt for the impossible enterprise and for the fantasies to which it aspires.

Thackeray's very individual, somewhat tired and disillusioned relation to his writing can be taken as a useful metaphor for the tendencies of realism. In so far as the realist aspires to tell the truth, both author and reader must be perpetually disillusioned, for it is impossible not to be aware of limits to both transparency and comprehensiveness. What I said in an earlier work seems still to the point of realism now: "to take seriously any set of particulars is to falsify."[10] Inclusion implies exclusion. The focus on any character or set of characters, any object or set of objects, implies a denial of the importance of the characters or objects not described, but for Thackeray and the realists, implicitly, every object and every character is worthy of attention. To follow out the democratic impulse that Auerbach detects as fundamental to the development of realism would be to move to a narrative in which there are no focal figures but every figure would gather the fullest sympathetic and imaginative attention. There is, then, a moral implication to these kinds of exclusions, as, for example, when the narrator notes how doctors would pay more attention to Amelia's son, Georgie, than to others: "did they sit up for the folks at the Pineries, when Ralph Plantagenet, and Gwendoline, and Guinever Mango had the same juvenile complaint? Did they sit up for little Mary Clapp, the landlord's daughter, who actually caught the disease off little Georgie?" (ch. 38, p. 451). Significantly, these "characters" appear nowhere else in the novel; they are other novels not written, of which the author, who will not write those novels, wants to remind us. As the narrator of *Middlemarch* forcefully does

[10] George Levine, *The Realistic Imagination: The English Novel from Frankenstein to Lady Chatterley* (Chicago: University of Chicago Press, 1981), p. 154.

remind us, there are other sensibilities than that of our hero or heroine: "Why always Dorothea?" That is the realist question, thick with ethical implications, and it is a question that in other ways, Thackeray is always asking.

Theme and form, in realism, play into each other – the questions of how much of reality can be represented, about whether reality can ever be represented at all, are thematized in *Vanity Fair* as they often are in other realist texts. But virtually every page plays out, in one way or other, problems that characteristically emerged in nineteenth-century realist fictions – problems clearly related to what Franco Moretti describes, following Karl Mannheim, the collapse of status society.[11] Formal changes in literary narrative were as tied closely to the economic and social transformations that were changing the face of England through the eighteenth and nineteenth centuries. Michael McKeon has argued that "questions of truth," epistemological ones, or "questions of virtue," social ones, had everything to do with the generic instability that helped produce and sustain the realist novel as a form. We can see in *Vanity Fair* that Thackeray is indeed worrying questions of virtue, for it implies reconceptions of the most fundamental categories of being – of religion and individuality and selfhood and privacy and public life and education and class. Most critically, as Moretti suggests, "the world of work changes at an incredible and incessant pace" (p. 4), and it was hard to be a "realist" at the time without making the question of the protagonist's vocation critical to the drama. In a genre addressed to a new middle-class audience, the question was less whom will I marry than what can I do. "What can I do?" echoes remarkably among the protagonists of a large number of Victorian novels. Although Thackeray focuses in his novel on a world aspiring to the condition of aristocracy, much of the narrative depends on the fact that Becky Sharp must make a living. She tries to make it the old way, by marrying up, but she just misses and thus for hundreds of pages her story is devoted to her quest for money, a quest that leads to those two brilliant virtuoso chapters on "How to Live on Nothing a Year."

The other side of the question of vocation is the question of inheritance, which had a long life in pre-realist genres, and which oddly but

---

[11] For an indispensable discussion of the *Bildungsroman* as the characteristic form of the early nineteenth century, see Franco Moretti, *The Way of the World: the Bildungsroman in European Culture* (London: Verso, 1987), p. 4 and *passim*. The *Bildungsroman* is perhaps the most important subgenre of realist fiction. In describing the ways in which "youth" is reconceived and redramatized, particularly in relation to work, Moretti provides an excellent overview of the nature of English realism as well.

significantly survives well into the history of nineteenth-century realism. Inheritance in Victorian novels is often the key to the crossing of classes, which is one of the central themes of Victorian fiction. Becky counts on inheritance in the first half of the novel and worries about what "to do" only after it's clear that the inheritance will not come her way. Amelia spends much of the book living with the consequence of being disinherited. All of these issues are entangled with questions of class and vocation just because they are manifestations of the new instability of class status, as, in the reshuffling of the orders of power in nineteenth-century society, money and class came to be fundamentally separate categories, even while the fundamental attitudes of a hierarchical society remained in place.

It is no accident, again, that one of the founding novels of modern English realistic fiction, *Pamela*, the heroine of which Fielding recreated as the maid-heroine Shamela, is a pre-Becky. But the narrative of crossing classes is also the narrative of "Virtue rewarded," a phrase that has formal as well as ethical implications. Implicitly, the narrative of middle-class realist fiction will be one that issues finally in the rewarding of virtue, which means, in formal terms, that the right woman marries the right man, and all discord and injustice is resolved in the comic ending.

All of these almost obsessive preoccupations of realist fiction, their relation to the ethical, their relation to the practice of accurate representation, and their relation, finally, to literary form, cause a fundamental crisis in realist practice. This crisis, which, I would argue, leads to realism's constant formal transformations – the place of marriage in the narratives, for example, or the shift to focus on characters' interiority, or the move away from comic to something like tragic form – is a peculiarly secular one. The problems with which the realist novel engages are, as the title "Vanity Fair" suggests, secular problems. The realist novel is predominantly a secular form, in which the implicit order of the world, inferable from traditional comic and tragic and epic forms, can only be achieved in worldly terms. The achievements of traditional comic form depend on an implicit faith that justice and meaning are built into the world, and the imbalance and hierarchical nature of the social order could be justified by a sense of the reality of the transcendent and a world beyond. Virtue could be rewarded because virtue *was* rewarded in a just and divinely ordered world; success could go with comic conclusions because success was not contaminated by worldly corruptions. But almost all of this was slowly, inexorably changed and complicated by the development of new economic and social orders in which money was displacing class status as the chief mark of success, and in which money was increasingly conceivable apart from class status. Such a transformation could not help but have powerful effects on the nature of literary genres themselves, and could not help but be central to a literary genre that self-consciously sought to represent the modern world as it really was, as opposed to the traditional and legendary world that had made the substance of earlier literatures.

Conceiving a world in which money displaces class, and in which social status is fluid, the realist novel becomes fundamentally secular. The critical question for protagonists becomes how to get money, although that question is frequently displaced and disguised. In the story of Fred Vincy in *Middlemarch*, we have an encapsulated form of the kind of problem with which realistic fiction persistently engaged. For Fred begins life assuming an inheritance that he does not get. One kind of life-narrative immediately transforms into another: what is it that Fred can do to earn the money he will need to survive and succeed (and win his beloved's hand)? *Middlemarch* makes the subject of his narrative, then, the question of work itself. And while in *Vanity Fair* we have no such focus on work, in fact Becky's story anticipates the pattern (though as a woman her story is somewhat different, and she seeks money through love relations).

Money becomes the pivot, implicit or explicit, on which nineteenth-century realist fiction turns. Certainly, whatever the ostensible issues, there can be no success in the world of Victorian realism without money, however disguised its sources are. Absence of money is the fundamental fact of Amelia's story after the death of George, and all the pathos and tensions of that story depend on money's absence. But when the question of virtue is tied to the question of money, the realist novel is faced with ethical (and formal) problems that it often tries to evade. It is one of the ironies of English nineteenth-century realism that while money is essential for success, and therefore for the comic ending, the quest for money (beyond what is necessary for survival, and sometimes even then) is unequivocally a mark of shame, corruption, evil. Outside of the novels of Anthony Trollope, this apparently excessive generalization is almost universally true. The essential question, often not articulated, but suggested powerfully, for example, by *Vanity Fair*, is how it can be possible for a protagonist to sustain the moral virtues that the culture admires and at the same time achieve success. The realist novel is persistently driven to imagine such figures, and with very mixed results.

The concepts of intrinsic virtue and of some ultimate possibility of moral justice depend on the sense that moral order is built into the world and that, in the long run, worldly troubles are compensated for in the light of divine oversight and presence. The world, otherwise, is both an ethical and aesthetic catastrophe, rather like what John Henry Newman believed the world without God to be:

To consider the world in its length and breadth, its various history, the many races of man, their starts, their fortunes, their mutual alienation, their conflicts; and then their ways, habits, governments, forms of worship; their enterprises, their aimless courses, their random achievements and acquirements, the impotent conclusion of long-standing fact, the tokens so faint and broken of a superintending design, the blind evolution of what turn out to be great powers or truths, the progress of things, as if from unreasoning elements, not towards final causes, the greatness and littleness of man, his far-reaching aims, his short duration, the curtain hung over his futurity, the disappointments of life, the defeat of good, the success of evil, physical pain, mental anguish, the prevalence and intensity of sin, the pervading idolatries, the corruptions, the dreary hopeless irreligion, that condition of the whole race, so fearfully yet exactly described in the Apostle's words, "having no hope and without God in the world," – all this is a vision to dizzy and appall; and inflicts upon the mind the sense of a profound mystery which is absolutely beyond human solution.[12]

What Newman describes in this exhausting, breath-taking catalogue of the conditions of this world is Vanity Fair itself – a vision to dizzy and appall. Many Victorian realists, perhaps most brilliantly and strenuously George Eliot, tried to imagine into the secular world the sort of moral order that Newman here describes as impossible. Thackeray's response to this horrific vision is to make comedy and satire but, beyond that, to leave each of us corrupted and, as the narrator concludes, unsatisfied.

Despite many more or less realist narratives that seem to affirm the most pious and religiously correct visions of reality, the realist novel was, like *Vanity Fair*, a fundamentally secular enterprise, rendering a world like that which Newman describes while resisting the idea that it presents "a profound mystery which is absolutely beyond human solution." *Vanity Fair* is a good representative of nineteenth-century realism just because it so doggedly insists on confining its narration to the doings of "Vanity Fair." While the very determination to do that and to invoke Bunyan's place can reasonably enough suggest the possibility of a divine if hidden presence in the world or at least of a genuine piety, Thackeray's novel treats religion as it treats commercial culture – it is simply a fact of this lower world and

---

[12]   John Henry Newman, *Apologia pro vita sua: Being a History of His Religious Opinions* (Oxford: Oxford University Press, 1967 [1864]), ch. 5.

plays into the narrative as it affects such things as inheritance. Certainly, the book's clergy are totally worldly figures. Its preoccupations, however, with class, with commercial success, with social climbing, with "how to live on nothing a year," with hypocrisy, and with inheritance are secular to the extreme. The narrator closes the door on Amelia's prayers because, he claims, these are not the province of Vanity Fair, but it would be no stretch to suggest that Thackeray himself closed off a representation of that kind of piety just because it would change the nature of the novel itself (and perhaps might be merely sentimentally tedious).

III

To follow up on this question of the secularity of the novel and to conclude this all too general argument, I want to take off from a line of Becky's that might help focus the problems of realism I have been discussing. In chapter 41, she pauses to reflect as she rises toward the high point of her career, just before her audience with the king himself, and she thinks about the way in which the entirely virtuous Lady Jane, having inherited a large sum of money, conducts herself. "I think," thinks Becky, "I could be a good woman if I had five thousand a year." The omnipresent, though rather elusive narrator then comments: "And who knows but Rebecca was right in her speculations – and that it was only a question of money and fortune which made the difference between her and an honest woman" (p. 490).

This seems innocuous enough, that is, just a little piece of Becky's cynicism and a little piece of Thackeray's irony. But Becky's comment might, if taken in another way, represent a fundamental conflict in realism's conception of character and of its relation to the scrupulously detailed and historically precise world in which characters in realist fiction move. And the narrator's comment might, ironically, be taken as quite literal.

So there is a double irony here. The first, of course, is the narrator's commentary on Becky's reflection, which seems to imply that qualities of character do *not* depend on circumstance. But the more telling irony is that the narrator's ironies might not be ironic at all. Realist practice, throughout its literary life, is to insist on the context in which characters move, on the details I've mentioned before, on history, on social context. That super text of realism, *Middlemarch*, for example, is subtitled "A Study of Provincial Life." Here the question of secularity looms large, for realism is the mode that reads character into the conditions of ordinary life, the life of Vanity Fair, and makes drama of their apparent everydayness, of their problems in making a living, of their relations with their neighbors, of the things that they have and want, of their domesticity. Every character in a realist novel must be read in relation to the circumstances of his or her life.

Vanity Fair is, for much of its length, particularly careful to describe the circumstances and, with characteristic irony but with great significance, makes much of what happens in the story dependent on the great historical moment of Waterloo and the defeat of Napoleon – Amelia's father loses his fortune because of the war; Amelia loses her husband in it; and the book is careful to test the quality of its major characters against the event, without ever directly representing it (a world-historical event and therefore beyond the borders of a domestic realist narrative). Becky emerges from Waterloo as something of a Napoleonic figure, but it is also clear from earlier information we get about her that who Becky is depends partly on where she comes from, who her parents were, what class she belongs to, what possibilities are open to a young woman without wealth, and of course what is going on in Europe at the time she comes of age. Part of what evoked disgust from many readers of *Vanity Fair* was just the cynical sense it intimated (even while resisting it with ambiguous ironies) that Becky is at least partly right and the narrator is not being ironic.

Even if we are to take the narrator's comment as ironic, aware that the novel shares the cultural revulsion from the idea that character is not integrally and permanently itself, that it is not either intrinsically virtuous or intrinsically evil, and that money can be determining even of goodness, Thackeray's way of handling the issues, of observing as a good realist should, raises questions. His narrative reveals what he may be ironically disparaging in his comment on Becky's thought. Becky's way of thinking about virtue, which many readers did in fact take as Thackeray's, was repellent to many, some of whom found the book truly disgusting and morally repulsive.

On the other hand, when George Eliot made pretty much the same point in another way and as a central theme of her novels, she was, by and large, taken with the greatest seriousness and respect. One of the most famous lines in all of George Eliot's novels comes near the end of *Middlemarch*, when she asserts, "For there is no creature whose inward being is so strong that it is not greatly determined by what lies outside it" ("Finale", p. 821). This is Becky in a more solemn, less personal mode! The fact that George Eliot's novels, like a large proportion of realist novels, have no intrinsically evil people in them (except perhaps Grandcourt in *Daniel Deronda*) is a reflection of this sense of character. Mr. Farebrother, the gentle and generous clergyman in *Middlemarch*, tells

Dorothea: "character is not cut in marble – it is not something solid and unalterable. It is something living and changing, and may become diseased as our bodies do" (ch. 72, p. 724). The bad guys in George Eliot's fiction, like Tito Melema in *Romola*, or even Arthur Donnithorne in *Adam Bede*, go bad because of circumstance, or at least partly because of circumstance. It is true that realism, as it is manifested in Thackeray and George Eliot, tends to hold on for a long time to a sense of an intrinsic self that may be pushed and strained by circumstance but that is nevertheless whole and integral. But all strong realists understand that circumstance can become decisive. And thus Becky's reflections, which ought to be further evidence of her corruption and the shallowness of her moral sense, take on great significance for realist texts, including *Vanity Fair*. She writes like a novelist in many parts of the book, and here she is even thinking like a novelist, a realist, secular one.

Nor is it an accident that Becky's reflections take her to money as the determining circumstance. Becky acknowledges (and has always acknowledged) to herself what the society won't admit, that virtue is somehow closely tied to money, and that money is the key element in the secular world. The focus on money, in fact, is the firmest mark that realist fiction is fundamentally secular. The fluidity of money is the counterpart to the new fluidity of "status" in the worlds represented by nineteenth-century realist fiction; its power to corrupt corresponds to the vision of the material world that Newman shows us. It is, in a way, what displaces an ordering god, for it is the condition of success, the condition of the happy ending. The difference is that realist novels either avoid confronting the ways in which money works to build success, or exonerate its protagonists from concern for money by allowing them to inherit it (and thus not dirty their hands in its acquisition), simply to have it all along, or to show along the way that although they have it, they really don't care for it and would never compromise themselves to retain it.

A roll call of representative Victorian novels will make clear how broadly this argument applies. Even Jane Eyre inherits out of the blue the money that gives her the power to save Rochester and to aid her cousins, and she gives away most of it. Pip, in *Great Expectations*, who has been corrupted by money, can only be redeemed by risking all of it, losing all of it, in order to save the life of his benefactor; Margaret in *North and South* inherits the money that she wants to give to Thornton, and their declaration of love is in fact based on her renunciation of her money for him; Little Dorrit achieves happiness only because she is bankrupt, and Clennam can accept her for the same reason. The heroes of Victorian novels are notoriously weak and ineffectual, like Clennam, largely because a strong hero would have to be shown in the capitalist game of successful pursuit of money, where Scrooge-like figures are more likely to be in control. Becky Sharp might have been portrayed as another kind of heroine, someone who having led a difficult and penurious childhood struggles up to success, say, like Jane Eyre. But Becky is allowed to be seen pursuing money, and in the shadiest of ways, and that pursuit marks her as the wicked mermaid, the "monster" whose "hideous tail" is under water. Against Becky's betrayal of Rawdon as she milks Lord Steyne of everything she gets, the novel juxtaposes Amelia's solitary struggle for money enough to give little Georgie the most elementary things. The absence of money forces her to give up Georgie to his grandfather, Mr. Osborne. For both women, money is the critical need but the juxtaposition sets up the limits of what relation to money is morally sustainable.

The work of the realist, to represent things as they are, and in this case the workings of an economy that is ruthless and selfish, the secular order in which money is the essential condition both for survival and for power, leads to a recognition, built into the very title of Thackeray's novel, that things as they are do not include the moral and just distribution of rewards. Vanity Fair does not allow very often for the form of comedy (except as comedy is structured around ironies), does not provide those resolutions in union and community that are normally marked by the marriage and the marriage plot, but perhaps most important, does not allow active people to avoid the contamination and even corruption that engagement with the economic order entails. Hapless and affectionate as Amelia is, her sentimental passion for Georgie, as it causes strains with her mother and father, is itself morally strained. That most early nineteenth-century realist texts tend to end with marriages that are the clearest form of the distribution of justice possible often strains the commitment to probability that is part of the realist project. That *Vanity Fair* in effect mocks this tradition makes part of its power as a representative of the realist impulse. Unlike, say, *Villette*, in which Lucy and M. Paul do come together, if even for a very brief moment, *Vanity Fair* allows for no happy marriages: Becky and Rawdon, Amelia and George, Amelia and Dobbin provide, in the end, no sense of justice or order.

But in the 1840s *Vanity Fair* was unusual. If David Copperfield's first marriage was inadequate, the second, with Agnes pointing upward, will be just right. Adam Bede and Dinah finally come together despite Adam's mistaken fascination with Hetty Sorrel. These endings suggest an ultimate meaningfulness in a secular world that seems marked by Newmanian disorder and meaninglessness, and for the most part, in the comic tradition of early nineteenth-century realism, the world, though threatening, does not get malicious, or indifferent.

It is a commonplace of modern reception of Victorian fiction that Victorian novels are marked by often extravagant and barely plausible coincidence. Isn't it a remarkable coincidence that Jane Eyre, on the verge of death, stumbles upon the house of cousins? Isn't it a coincidence that Casaubon in *Middlemarch* dies just at the point at which Dorothea was preparing to throw away her life for him? Isn't it a coincidence that Margaret Hale inherits money from her father's friend in time for her to save Thornton's factory? Isn't it a coincidence that Little Dorrit loses her money just in time to save Clennam? Isn't it a coincidence that Lucy Snowe is rescued in *Villette* by the family that first took her in in England? Isn't it a coincidence that Daniel Deronda turns out to be Jewish after all, and thus can satisfy both his future wife, Mirah, and her messianic brother?

Vanity Fair, on the other hand, doesn't rely on coincidences. And this is, I would argue, because the book is so doggedly determined to see the secular world as Newman sees it. It doesn't make sense. It doesn't satisfy. Coincidence can be the instrument of the providential plot, and without providence coincidence is simply implausible. The struggle of the secular novelist to build comic plots depends upon an assumption that the world intrinsically does make sense, but without God to provide the meaning missing from strictly secular conditions. Thus, most of the early Victorians tend to intimate a religious order somewhere behind the disorder of the world, Dickens most famously in the religious imagery of *Little Dorrit*. Coincidences function rather like the *dei ex machina* of early literary forms, but gods are not allowed.

This order increasingly breaks down as realist fiction continues to explore the possibilities available to the ignobly decent, as Biffin would have it, in an intensely capitalist society. One way I have found to read the tensions that this struggle produced for the very form of Victorian fiction is through the lens of Max Weber's theory laid out in *The Protestant Ethic and the "Spirit" of Capitalism*. While that theory has been rethought and criticized since its first publication, it doesn't for my purposes matter very much whether it correctly diagnoses the relation between religion and capitalism in the nineteenth century. I want to suggest that a significant proportion of English nineteenth-century novels test out the Weberian thesis before the fact. For Weber argues that the ascetic virtues that Calvinist religion required turn out to be precisely the virtues that are required for success in a capitalist economy. One of the central features of the "Protestant spirit" that Weber discusses is just that it shares the Victorian novel's distrust of money. Ironically, the Protestant spirit is financially successful in large part because practicing Calvinists did not work to get money, to acquire luxury, to make their lives easier, but because work and self-sacrifice were intrinsic to the Protestant calling. "Work while it is day," says Carlyle, referring to John: 9:4, "for the night cometh in which no man can work." So in a Weberian narrative, the most successful capitalist would turn out to be like the protagonists of Victorian novels, that is, uninterested in money, perhaps contemptuous of it, but interested in the work itself. In a Weberian scenario, then, success and virtue are two faces of the same coin.

George Eliot makes a gesture at this way of thinking about "success" in the character of Caleb Garth, in *Middlemarch*. Caleb is a capable and generous man who loves his work but cares not at all for money and is distrustful of those who pursue it. He makes of the word "business" an almost sacred icon. And he makes a great success of his work. In his life, at least, virtue and secular success come together, and he is clearly to be read as a model. But I think it no accident that his work is, in effect, pre-capitalist. More important, Caleb's story is almost a side bar in a novel that carefully plots the failure of piety, and even of talent, because of the pull of money. The true ascetic, the true pious Protestant who rules with a kind of moral despotism over Middlemarch, is Bulstrode, whom Caleb distrusts, and who is successful in a Weberian way, but who in the end is absolutely corrupted. Realist novels in effect test Weber's thesis and in forcing a detailed attention to the lives and methods of its central characters, consistently dramatize the incompatibility between true piety and self-denial and worldly success. There is virtually no reconciling virtue and successful work in the new economy, and Dickens famously explores and elaborates this polarity, as in the character of Wemmick, in *Great Expectations*, who is in effect two different people, the inhumane man who works for Jaggers, and the loving son who makes his home his castle. These tests of characters' engagement with money and power make it increasingly difficult for the realist novel to sustain the comic form it held onto so long in England.

Although reconciliation was for the most part impossible, there are plenty of realist novels that try it. Dinah Mulock Craik tries it in *John Halifax, Gentleman*, taking for her protagonist a rags to riches hero who is utterly perfect both as a worker and as a man. It is an unusual book among the Victorians because it not only attempts to portray an active and a good man, but takes the risk of describing, at least a little, the nature of the work that earns him success. The more a realist novel delves into the details of money matters, the less successful it is in representing wholly or largely virtuous protagonists. "There is something almost awful in the thought of a writer undertaking to give a detailed picture of the actions of a perfectly virtuous being," says Henry James of *John Halifax*. "If Miss Mulock had weighed her task more fairly, she would have shrunk from it in dismay."[13] Other Victorian writers struggled with the problem. Few dared to invent such a character as Halifax, but largely, I think, because moral perfection in characters is incompatible with the realist project of finding subject and form in the ordinary. Realism, as *Vanity Fair* makes abundantly clear, keeps the world historical and the truly heroic offstage; it is a world in which everyone is compromised in one way or other, as realist writers consistently took compromise to be the condition of normal existence. Thus the attempt to reconcile the protestant spirit to capitalism, so brilliantly affirmed by Weber, has a very hard time of it in the world of realist narrative, when characters are forced to face the moral consequences of each of their choices and readers expect satisfying closure.

The movement in late Victorian fiction from comic to tragic form in realism is then only partly the result of the influence of French realism on the English. It is an almost inevitable consequence of a fundamentally secular reading of the world in which, inescapably, money becomes the condition for protagonists' success. Hardy, for example, was hostile to naturalism, but wrote novel after novel in which the ingredients of class struggle and the problem of work figured as importantly as in earlier Victorian novels. But in not a single book does he represent a strong male figure who manages to remain both successful and virtuous. The world of Victorian realism turns upside down in Hardy as he self-consciously imagines his characters in a world that is so totally secular that it almost becomes, at times, demonic. "The President of the Immortals," for example, presides over Tess's fate, so that even at this late date in the history of nineteenth-century realism the ironic tradition in realism is at work, and the doubleness of its implications remains. Rejecting the possibility of the transcendent and of the ideal – in fact, plotting his stories, like that of Angel Clare, around the disastrous consequences of attempting to live the ideal – Hardy keeps the very literary and ideal qualities of realism alive. Tess is after all a "pure woman," and the President of the Immortals is a modern version of God.

---

[13] Henry James, *Essays on Literature: American Writers; English Writers* (New York: The Library of America, 1984), p. 845.

Realism, throughout its history in the nineteenth century remained an ambivalent and often self-contradictory mode. It was consistent only in its determination to find strategies for describing the world as it was, and inconsistent, of course, if only because every artist's conception of what the world was differed and the world changed from moment to moment, generation to generation. But it was consistent, too, in worrying ethical issues around the developments in contemporary economy and society, and so it regularly failed to find a satisfying way to represent an active and virtuous protagonist who achieves success without being corrupted along the way. It struggled to reconcile success and virtue, but was too honest as a literary mode to accomplish that easily. Its commitment to close observation of the details of society and the context in which characters move helped destabilize the conception of selfhood and character on which the Victorian novel built its greatest successes. In the world of realism, as in the world that Darwin was representing to his culture, everything is in flux, including character.

Thackeray's *Vanity Fair* is most interesting in its anticipatory exploration of realism's problems, problems both ethical and aesthetic, problems of perspective, of narrative voice, of characterization, and of the consequences of the relation between character and context. What contemporary readers found disgusting and disturbing about its worldliness are some its most interesting virtues, its concession that we are all compromised and partly corrupted by money, its implication that behind the secular world there is no force for order and justice, its refusal of the happy ending because it will not reconcile success and merit (or not quite), its delicious indulgence in the things of this world, and its cynicism that powers its satire.

Reconciling probability and literary form in a world gone secular is ultimately the greatest challenge to the realist sensibility. Hardy, resisting the label of naturalist or realist, argued that his books were not at all "reality," but pursuits of the design in the carpet. In the ambiguous status of realism, it should be enough to say that it remained throughout its long career a very literary mode, one which even now often tries to disguise its literariness and one that must remain partial in its representations, and therefore vulnerable to the kinds of critiques I invoked at the start of this essay. But it is a mode that by virtue of its commitment to getting it right is in constant flux, changing its conception of the real with the movement of time, reimagining character and even selfhood – in an enterprise in which Becky herself participates – both in the context of the social conditions in which it must live and through the kinds of experiments with interiority that mark its history from Austen, to George Eliot, to James, to Woolf and Joyce. Its very weaknesses, its failure, for example, to imagine strong male protagonists, or its tendency not to consider the details by which protagonists do make money and achieve power, its exploitation of coincidences to achieve what a thorough pursuit of probability could not – these and others are also marks of its remarkable aspirations and indications of its extraordinary achievements, as well.

Let's say that whatever its limits and its ideological complicities, realism is always interesting, whether it be Mr. Bennett's or Mrs. Brown's, or Biffin's.

CHAPTER 8

Dickens, secularism, and agency

It would be silly and demonstrably untrue to argue that the novel is an inevitably secular form. Religion, in a myriad of ways, gets affirmed in a myriad of novels. And yet the novel as a form tends to resist the pressures put upon it by many writers to transcend the limits of the "secular" world. Fully fleshed narratives demand the kind of details that embody and flesh out ideas and faiths and inexplicable spiritual mysteries. The Victorian novel, written in the midst of culture-wide conflicts about just such matters, tends toward the secular even as it insists – as it so often does – on the providential order of things. In constant tension between the conventions and intentions of its worldliness and its entirely understandable aspirations beyond the worldly, Victorian fiction, I want after all to argue, is a secular form if ever there was one.[1]

To make a clinching case for this proposition, it would be necessary to treat in some detail a wide variety of Victorian fiction well beyond the

[1] In this paper there won't be time for anything like a full discussion of the idea of secularity. Part of what I mean by it is belief that all of experience must be recognized as non-transcendental, as operating entirely in terms of the natural world, without miracles or supernatural interventions. This is the "epistemological" aspect of it, and the one that will get most of my attention here. But beyond this, I mean something like what Charles Taylor describes in his essay, "Modes of Secularism" (Rajeev Bhargava, ed., *Secularism and its Critics* [Delhi: Oxford University Press, 1998], in which he – a believing Roman Catholic – sees secularism as a kind of moral imperative in the modern world, one that allows for the extraordinary range of beliefs among people and that makes possible democracy, a social organization that is not governed by any one of those myriad beliefs but is willing to acquiesce, in order to make civilized life possible, in an "overlapping consensus" on culture-wide decisions about the particulars of ordinary and social life, on the law, and rules of social behavior. The secularism of the Victorian novel that I am discussing descends from a broad complex of things, philosophical (empiricism) and economic and cultural, but in the commitment to realism that followed from these things it moved inevitably toward the secular. Realist representation of society and individuals, self-consciously made the ideal by writers as diverse as Dickens, Thackeray and George Eliot, which always registers "mixed conditions" and insists on plausible causal explanations of events and behavior. Like scientific uniformitarianism and the actualism of Lyell and Darwin, it tends to expel excess even when it most values it, and in this respect certainly moves clearly in the direction of Taylor's ideas. For the most recent, authoritative and fullest analysis of "secularism," see Taylor's new book, *A Secular Age* (Cambridge, MA: Harvard University Press, 2007).

established canon and take into account the enormous popularity of religiously inclined narratives: Dinah Mulock Craik might then have to figure as
importantly as Charlotte Brontë, Mrs. Oliphant as Thackeray, Maria Corelli
as Trollope. One would have to confront Newman's two novels, *Callista* and
Loss and Gain. But any study of this problem would also obviously require
close attention to Dickens, and particularly to his most overtly religious
novel, *Little Dorrit.* So it will be with a brief discussion of *Little Dorrit* as
an initial test case for my broader argument that I will conclude.

I

Most mid-twentieth century critics, reacting to denigration of the Victorians by early modernists, came to them accepting the cliché that all of
Victorian England was undergoing a crisis of faith. We were attracted to
them – despite the shift in aesthetic expectations that called all things
Victorian into question – just because we could see how their culture
had opened the way toward an expanding and richer secular society.
The kind of criticism that has dominated in recent years has forced us
to qualify much of this initial enthusiasm for the Victorians. But for many
of us now, become somewhat cynical twenty-first century intellectuals, it
has been more than a little shocking to discover that in America more than
a century later, the thinking of skeptical Victorians (be it Mill or Darwin
or George Eliot or Leslie Stephen) is still controversial, even inflamma-
tory. The jury of popular opinion, in twenty-first century America at least,
is in, and the Victorian skeptics are out. It is in response, in part, to my
shock at that discovery that I, a child of Victorian skepticism – though a
child no longer – began to worry the question of secularism itself. Might it
have been a mirage, after all? Does a position that had seemed, perhaps to
historically naïve eyes, so inevitable and at the same time so epistemologically necessary, so aesthetically engaging and even ethically imperative,
turn out to have been either unreal or culturally ineffectual or both?

Our view that Victorian culture was on the fast track to secularism gave
us a distorted sense of that culture and was based largely on the reading of
a select group of intellectuals. There at the gateway was Carlyle thrashing
about in his "everlasting No," and John Stuart Mill deep in depression,
while George Eliot was soon to refuse to go to church with her father and
brother. And there at the far end of the century was Herbert Spencer
doggedly systematizing the world according to a theory of equilibrium,
and the brilliant scientific naturalists like T. H. Huxley, John Tyndall, and
W. K. Clifford being cockily iconoclastic, and of course there was Leslie

Stephen making his agnostic's apology. All of these famous instances point to a culture from which religion seemed to be being driven almost daily, and despite some very impressive rear guard actions like those of W. H. Mallock or William Balfour, driven successfully to secularity.

But if the perspective of philosophical radicals and overwrought intellectuals has been somewhat deceptive, the novel, a medium that reached well beyond the class of intellectual radicals, is another matter entirely. I want to argue here that it becomes a kind of battleground in which the developing conventions of the form itself often resist the pressures of the moral and sometimes explicitly religious energies that drive the narrative. The Victorian novel aspires overtly to represent the ordinary (even as we realize that the very concept of the ordinary is constrained by the contingencies of time, place, and perspective) and to give voice to the common experience of common people leading ordinary lives, outside the realm of the intellectual avant garde. Its strategies, from Dickens' satirical assaults on forms of cultural and governmental pomposity, to Thackeray's mock-epic similes, to George Eliot's transformation of St. Teresa into Dorothea Brooke, are deflationary and, as we all know, domesticating. Its concern in all arenas is not the strictly rational but the richly experienced – it was the Victorians who gave our culture the first big pre-Freudian dose of the Unconscious, and who transferred the powers of Romantic poetry into realist narrative. That being the case, the Victorian novel was full of piety, its plots largely providential in shape even when the author is explicitly secular, and it is frequently constrained and structured by explicitly (or inexplicitly) Christian values, pointing Christian morals with occasionally repellent ease. Although there are plenty of instances in which skepticism or even deconversion is dramatically central, for the most part it would have been difficult to infer from the Victorian novel as a whole that secularism was on the march.

But despite the piety, the novel as a form, having developed for a century with the development of the new bourgeoisie and capitalism, was intrinsically secular. Many years ago, Barry Qualls definitively traced the parallels between Victorian narrative and the Puritan tradition, suggesting that the novelists were "determined that their words could still lead 'Christian' of the latter day to the Celestial City."[2] But, as Qualls argues, Dickens (and implicitly others) "finds quite impossible Carlyle's assertion that 'God lives,' that there is a transcendent reality behind the world of

---

[2]   Barry Qualls, *The Secular Pilgrims of Victorian Fiction* (Cambridge: Cambridge University Press, 1982), p. ix.

appearances" (109–10). Inspired in part, as was the "spirit of capitalism," by a Calvinistic ethic, the novel made its way in the secular world with ease and was part of the spirit of capitalism's energizing force. The Victorian novel, as Qualls showed, even secularized, as it utilized, the tradition of emblem and symbol through which the transcendent might be glimpsed in a secular world.

That the novel was intrinsically secular is certainly not entirely news, but in what ways, given its frequently religious directions, might that have been so, how did it exercise a secularizing and compromising pressure on religious ideals, and how might that pressure have been extended to resist even the religious inclinations of its practitioners, exposing dramatically the contradictions built into the development that allowed the Protestant ethic to become a condition for the spirit of capitalism? The novel's determinedly detailed and accurate look at the new industrial and capitalist society – even as it frequently mystifies the relation between the system as a whole and the difficult fates of the novels' characters – puts pressure on the providential narratives bequeathed to it by Christianity, creates characteristic tensions and instabilities as it tends to move from comic to tragic structures, and implies alternate modes of value. Worldliness and other-worldliness do not make comfortable bedfellows there. Secularity was not simply an epistemological argument of the radical intellectuals, but a way of living and imagining the moral life within the day to day world. In so far as it did take hold, it had to do so as William James understood that religion itself resisted it – that is, not on strictly rational, epistemological grounds (of the sort that James denigrated in the iconoclastic writings of W. K. Clifford), but on the grounds of deep feeling, deep emotional need, and a kind of Pascalian, pragmatic bet.

I focus then on the recognition implied in the novel, both in its earlier comic forms and its later more ambivalent and tragic ones, that a fully naturalized world is one in which the Christian virtues that religion and Western culture had affirmed are, however desirable and admirable, only fragilely sustainable and easily corruptible or compromised; the fully religious narrative and resolution can, in the novel, be best, and almost exclusively realized in death. The realist novel needed something like the "Nemesis" George Eliot invoked so often to imagine the possibility that virtue would be rewarded, vice punished. And the natural world was the world, as Thackeray had rendered it, of *Vanity Fair*. If providence is to make itself known in that world, it can come only at the point of leaving it; to imagine a narrative of development and action in which merit is appropriately – even if only roughly – rewarded, in which the condition of virtue is compatible with the conditions of Vanity Fair, or in which uncorrupted virtue is even possible – as in Mulock Craik's *John Halifax, Gentleman* – entails a fundamental violation of the rules of the novel, of the canons of plausibility. It mattered not how religious the novelists were, the novel's world is a secular one, and in the novel, Victorians, and certainly Dickens, resisted and explored the consequences of that fact. Extremes appear, of course, as in *John Halifax*, and there are even invocations of potentially supernatural agencies, but in the end the Victorian realist novel, even so extravagant a one as *Wuthering Heights*, moves toward compromise and recognition of the impossibility of the ideal. The failure of Victorian secularism, and of the "free thought" that, through the last quarter of the nineteenth century, worried the possibilities of naturalism, agnosticism, and atheism, can be understood in part through the movement of realistic fiction from comic to tragic form, the movement from a sense of the compatibility of the natural world with moral order, to a deep recognition of their incompatibility. From *Pickwick Papers* and *Oliver Twist* to *Little Dorrit* and *Our Mutual Friend*, Dickens enacts something like that movement,[3] struggles imaginatively and almost heroically with it as he attempts to imagine a place for decency and love in a world that promises no rewards for them; and the strains evident in his resistance to raw secularity are an impressive indicator of a culture-wide sense of the social and moral contradictions built into the partnership of otherworldliness and capitalism.

Steven Marcus had it exactly right when, in a casual comment in his chapter on *Oliver Twist*, he noted that "Dickens was of course a Christian ... which is to say that, living when he did, his involvement with Christian culture was by nature profound, passionate, contradictory and, as frequently as not, adverse."[4] Distinctly not one of the Victorian philosophical radicals, Dickens was, unequivocally, a Christian, despite his passionate hostility to some forms of evangelical and institutional Christianity. Angus Wilson, some years after Marcus' remarks, made the point even more strongly: Dickens, he says, "is Christian not merely in the

---

[3]   In *Charles Dickens: The World of his Novels* (Cambridge, MA: Harvard University Press, 1959), J. Hillis Miller lays out something of this argument in his very first chapter, on *Pickwick Papers*: "The crucial event of the novel is Pickwick's discovery that transcendent power and goodness are no longer immanent in the world" (p. 35). And he goes on to say that the critical question with which Dickens would then be wrestling for the rest of this career was "How is a person who cannot withdraw going to avoid being destroyed by the evil forces in the world?"
[4]   Steven Marcus, *Dickens: from Pickwick to Dombey* (New York: Basic Books, 1965), p. 68.

formal sense of the word; in profound ways the Christian religion makes sense of his work."[5]

Nor is there any gainsaying the fact that Dickens' culture was pervasively Christian. "That Victorian Britain was ... a society remarkable for the extent and intensity of its religious life is," claims Gerald Parsons, "scarcely open to question." Frank Turner, introducing a volume on the Victorian crisis of faith, points out that while there were indeed a great number of deconversions, often movingly described in autobiographies and novels, and much rich and complicated discussion of questions of faith, "Victorian faith entered crisis not in the midst of any attack on religion but rather during the period of the most fervent religious crusade that the British nation had known since the seventeenth century, indeed during the last great effort on the part of all denominations to Christianize Britain."[6]

Turner's argument is substantiated by a considerable body of historical work. Callum Brown's *The Death of Christian Britain* argues persuasively that Britain did not really become secular until the 1960s. Too many scholars, Brown argues, "have failed to perceive the robustness of popular religiosity during industrialization and urban growth between the 1750s and the 1950s."[7] Gerald Parsons provides some astonishing statistics on the number of churches built and of ministers added during Victoria's reign, and shows that the Victorians supported what he calls "a bewildering diversity" of voluntary societies and agencies, all reflecting "the vitality and passion of Victorian religious life" (p. 6). As Richard Altick indicated almost fifty years ago, "it would be futile even to try to estimate how many copies of religious and moral works of all sorts were distributed in Britain in the nineteenth century."[8] To take just one small example, by 1867, the S.P.C.K. alone was distributing 8 million tracts a year, and the Religious Tract Society 20 million. "Few are the nineteenth-century autobiographies which fail to contain, among the lists of their authors' early reading, a substantial proportion of religious works, biographical, historical, homiletical, exegetical, reflective" (p. 108), so that, Altick goes on, "Religious literature was everywhere."

Dickens' novels are recognizably expressions of (and reactions to) the resurgence of popular religion not so much institutionally but experientially, personally – an inheritance from both Romanticism and the powerful

---

5 Quoted in, Dennis Walder, *Dickens and Religion* (London: George Allen and Unwin, 1981), p. 1.
6 Frank Turner, "The Victorian Crisis of Faith and the Faith that was Lost," in *Victorian Faith in Crisis*, ed., Richard J. Helmstadter and Bernard Lightman (London: Macmillan, 1990), p. 11.
7 Callum Brown, *The Death of Christian Britain* (London: Routledge, 2001), p. 195.
8 Richard Altick, *The English Common Reader: A Social History of the Mass Reading Public, 1800–1900* (Chicago: University of Chicago Press, 1957), pp. 108; 101–3.

evangelical movements at the start of the century. The "personal," Brown claims, "is intrinsically wrapped up with language, discourses on personal moral worth, the narrative structures within which these are located" (p. 195). The "tracts" Altick discusses are certainly part of this discourse, but so too are the popular narratives, the industrial parables of writers like Harriet Martineau, the moral fables of Hannah More, and, yes, the novels of Dickens. The moral framework was certainly Christian, usually explicitly so.

It is the clear presence of Christianity in Dickens' work, the fact that Wilson is right in arguing that "religion makes sense" of it, that makes the question of secularity in the novels particularly interesting. Whatever their extravagances, Dickens' novels, like those of most of his contemporaries, bind themselves to the conventions of probability and, implicitly, to the priority of the "real." His defensiveness against charges that he was not realistic is notorious. "There are such men as Sikes," he asserts in his Preface to *Oliver Twist*; and as to spontaneous combustion, we all remember his insistence in his preface to *Bleak House*, "I shall not abandon the facts until there shall have been a considerable Spontaneous Combustion of the testimony on which human occurrences are usually received."[9]

The novel as a form has from the start made drama of the relation between worldliness and religion, and for the larger part of its early history in the eighteenth and nineteenth century produced comic endings consonant with but distinctly not the same as the providential plot inherited from the Puritan tradition that it attempted partly to defy, partly to emulate. As Leopold Damrosch has argued, "'the faith of the reader' that Fielding invokes is a belief in plausible events, not miracles."[10] The

---

[9]   See George Ford, *Dickens and his Readers* (Princeton: Princeton University Press, 1955), pp. 129–55, for an excellent discussion of Dickens' views on probability in fiction. While Dickens was criticized harshly in his own time for his failures of probability and for the extravagance of his prose and the flatness of his characters, he saw himself as simply investing reality with the extravagances of art. While Ford wants to show that Dickens' strenuous public defenses of the reality of his novelistic treatments put him in an awkward position and belied his own artistic commitments, he also shows that Dickens did indeed see himself as committed to representing reality precisely, with an excitement that no other writer might achieve. He was committed, that is, to the romantic side of familiar things.
[10] Leopold Damrosch, Jr. *God's Plot and Man's Stories: Studies in the Fictional Imagination from Milton to Fielding* (Chicago: University of Chicago Press, 1985), p. 283. Damrosch argues that there was a major Puritan influence on the development of the novel, which, as a form, he sees as having tested out alternative religious positions. Here is his major point: "The relevance of Puritanism to the novel does not really lie in particular doctrinal points … [but] rather in the peculiar power, as a basis for fiction, of a faith that sees human life as a narrative invented by God but interpreted by human beings" (p. 4). Damrosch wants to insist on the presence of Christianity in fictional narratives. My argument, rather, is that the pressures of secularity increasingly tested and strained the providential narrative. The compromise by which the novel acts out Weber's thesis about religion and the rise of capitalism forces it increasingly to recognize the incoherence of a religious view with a commitment as well to worldly success.

conventions of comic fiction took precedence over the conventions of divine intervention. But whatever the literary convention, even in the work of a less literary and more pious writer like Richardson, virtue and worldly success were certainly not fictionally incompatible. It is not simply religion that makes sense of Dickens' works, but more interestingly yet, the tensions in them between a wished for Christian ideal and a pervasively secular imagination. This tension, fundamental to the whole development of the novel in England (and, with a nod toward Max Weber, to the development of middle-class society in Europe), contributes significantly to the peculiar quality of Dickens' books, to the characteristic tensions in them, those produced not only by the plot and the conflict of characters, but by theme and structure, all of which often seem, particularly in the late novels, close to spinning out of control.

Dickens' is only the most extreme example of the way in which the novel can combine a self-evident relish for life (as in his encyclopedic mastery of the texture of contemporary urban life, manifested in his virtuoso representations of the material world, the objects that fill it in shop windows, houses, and streets, its food, its mud and fog, its narrow alleyways and stinking rivers, its pleasures in the popular arts) with a not quite fully articulated aspiration toward moral ideals clearly based in Christianity and gesturing toward a transcendent reality that might some-how redeem the abundant disorders of modern England. The doubleness is intrinsic to the novel as a form, which, largely through its fascination with material particularities, in effect blocks access to the transcendence it can nevertheless attempt to intimate.

In a footnote, Marcus quotes a passage from Calvin that can suggest the difficulty of this combination of worldly and ideal features. "The mind," Calvin writes, "is never seriously excited to desire and meditate on the future life without having previously imbibed a contempt of the present. There is no medium between these two extremes; either the earth must become vile in our estimation, or it must retain our immoderate love" (quoted on p. 164). Dickens' hatred of such Calvinist world-hatred gives life to many of his novels. But full of just that immoderate love, his books are also catalogues and dramatizations of the fascination and dangers of the world's vileness. His novels seem to belie the Calvinist dualism even as they make it comprehensible. Fagin and Quilp and Squeers and Pecksniff and Heep and the Smallweeds and Krook make an astonishingly wicked and delightful Rogues' Gallery. And the gallery of angels is set against it, filled as it is with extravagantly good, innocent, dying children or, more usually, miraculously innocent and self-sacrificing women, Little Nell, and

Esther, Lizzie Hexam, and Little Dorrit the best known of them. None of these hates the world; each of them, however, has somehow managed to make personal desire for worldly things secondary to the desires of others. In a bitter moment in *Little Dorrit*, registering Amy Dorrit's absolute sacrifices to her father, the narrator comments on William Dorrit's self-involvement by noting that "No other person upon earth, save herself, could have been so unmindful of her wants."[11] That kind of embittered hostility has its parallel in the ferocious anger at selfish worldliness that pervades *Our Mutual Friend* and much of the later Dickens. William Dorrit has none of the charming fascination of Quilp or even of Fagin. He is at best touchingly contemptible, like Casby (who is at least comic) or Fascination Fledgeby of *Our Mutual Friend.*

II

How then does the intrinsic secularity of the novel form sustain itself even as it dramatizes or overtly expresses sincere religious commitment; how does the genre itself trump the content? I want to come at this point indirectly by developing an analogy with the science that was contemporary with the growth of the Victorian novel, both because its commitment to register the natural world empirically parallels the novel's dominant commitment to realism, and because it was largely in the hands of practitioners and theorists who were themselves religious and did not think of their work as incompatible with their religion. The question, in a way, was whether the form of scientific experiment and thought, determined by a basically empiricist epistemology, would be compatible with the scientists' own religious commitments. Most of the founders of the British Academy for the Advancement of Science in 1832 were members of the clergy. Charles Lyell was not a clergyman, but he was Christian enough to resist almost to the end the naturalist evolutionism of his young disciple, Charles Darwin. What is perhaps most striking about this (aside, of course, from the fact that Darwin learned much of what he believed about scientific method and theory from Lyell) is that the theoretical foundation of Lyell's argument was that science could only be successful if it were absolutely naturalistic. The fundamental principle of *Principles of Geology* is an axiom for all modern science: to understand any natural phenomenon one must confine consideration to laws recognized as *verae causae,*

---

[11]   Charles Dickens, *Little Dorrit* (London: Penguin, 1971 [1857]), p. 274.

that is, true causes, recognized now to be in operation. James Hutton, according to Lyell, finally set geology in the right direction because he was the first to attempt "to dispense entirely with all hypothetical causes, and to explain the former changes of the earth's crust, by reference exclusively to natural agents."[12] Hutton showed, claims Lyell, that "all past changes on the globe had been brought about by the slow agency of existing causes" (p. 630).

In a letter to a friend written while he was working on *Principles*, Lyell explains that his book,

> will endeavour to establish the *principle[s] of reasoning* in the science; and all my geology will come in as illustration of my views of those principles, and as evidence strengthening the system necessarily arising out of the admission of such principles, which, as you know, are neither more nor less than that *no causes whatever* have from the earliest time to which we can look back, to the present, ever acted, but those *now acting*, and that they never acted with different degrees of energy from that which they now exert.[13]

If there has never been at any time in any place any cause not now in operation, there were no miracles, God could not have created the world as the Bible describes him to have done, no supernatural intervention in this world is conceivable. Scientists might well be religious, but their science required of them that they make "reference exclusively to natural agents."

Perhaps the most prominent scientist of the time, John Herschel, in his still fascinating *Preliminary Discourse on the Study of Natural Philosophy*, lays out the methods by which a genuine science might be practiced, and begins by rejecting the complaint that religion and science are incompatible. No, he claims, that can't be right: "Truth can never be opposed to truth."[14] We can and must continue scientifically looking for scientific answers, but we may be certain that those answers will never conflict with true Christian doctrine. In effect, the claim is that if there is a god (no doubt for Herschel), his works must be manifest *in* the world, and that scientific scrutiny of that world will reveal him.

There would come a time, most obviously with Darwin and the extension of naturalistic description to the human, when the doctrines of Christianity and the laws of science would seem so obviously in conflict

---

[12] Charles Lyell, *Principles of Geology*, Vol. 1 (Chicago: University of Chicago Press, 1990 [1830]), p. 61.
[13] Cited by Martin J. S. Rudwick, ed., *Principles of Geology*, I, pp. xii–xiii.
[14] John Herschel, *Preliminary Discourse on the Study of Natural Philosophy* (Chicago: University of Chicago Press, 1987 [1830]), p. 9.

that one truth would have to yield to the other.[15] And it is striking, in reading Darwin, to notice how insistent he is that any *single* "fact" inconsistent with his explanations would be, as he says eight or so times in the *Origin*, "fatal to his theory." The introduction of a single non-naturalistic event or cause would mean toppling the book's entire argument. Only naturalistic explanations were acceptable, and they had to obey Lyell's actualist principles. If religion were to survive this development in science, which increasingly claimed to be able to describe all of the natural world, it would have to do so in a non-natural space. To find that space one would almost have to be the Calvin that Marcus quotes, that is, reject the material world. Where might one find such space in the Victorian novel? How about in the unvisited spots that Thackeray so carefully closes off in *Vanity Fair*? As Amelia goes to pray the day she leaves home to marry George, the narrator asks, "Have we a right to repeat or overhear her prayers? These, brother, are secrets, and out of the domain of Vanity Fair, in which our story lies."[16]

Although few of the great scientists of that era were Calvinists, most of them were religious, just as most of the novelists were religious – in their way. And it is the commitment to religion that makes so clear the generic secularity of their science. This is perhaps even better inferred from William Whewell's contribution to the Bridgewater Treatises. These apparently last gasps of natural theology – until our recent flirtations with "intelligent design," alas – insistently claim that the natural world gives evidence of its creator. But Whewell, perhaps the most original thinker about science in the first half of the nineteenth century, is very cautious about what constitutes a legitimate scientific argument. He invokes Bacon as saying that "the handling of final causes ... mixed with the rest in physical inquiries, hath intercepted the severe and diligent inquiry of all real and physical causes ... to the great arrest and prejudice of farther discovery."[17] For

---

[15] The argument persists into the present, many scientists insisting that they can work in science, in evolutionary biology or any other field that might implicitly challenge a biblical narrative, and remain religious. The position taken among the Victorians has been revived in particular by Stephen Jay Gould, who talks about "two non-overlapping magisteria." Leave unto science the things that are natural, to God the things that are of God – that's the point – and Gould is comfortable with this analysis. But of course, literal Christians, among others, will not accept any scientific assertion that seems to contradict the word of the Bible. See Gould's, *Rocks of Ages: Science and Religion in the Fullness of Life* (New York: The Ballantine Publishing Group, 1999). On the other hand, there are spokespeople for science, like Richard Dawkins and Daniel Dennett, for whom religious belief is simply unintelligible in the light of the way science sees and satisfactorily describes the world. The most popular of the recent works in this genre is Dawkins' *The God Delusion* (New York: Houghton Mifflin, 2006).

[16] William Makepeace Thackeray, *Vanity Fair* (London: Penguin Books, 2001 [1848]), ch. 26, p. 298.

[17] Cited in *Astronomy and General Physics Considered with Reference to Natural Theology* (London: H. G. Bohn, 1852; 1833), p. 303.

Whewell, this means that "final causes are to be excluded from *physical inquiry.*" We are not "to assume that we know the objects of the Creator's design, and put this assumed purpose in the place of a physical cause." Intent on defining what is specifically scientific, he argues that "the physical philosopher has it for his business" to explain the physical world according to the laws of nature, and that it is only "through this philosophical care that our views of final causes acquire their force and value as aids to religion" (pp. 304–5). Religion can follow from science, Whewell thinks, but cannot be inside the science, which is generically constrained to adhere strictly to the laws of the physical world.

Max Weber, a century later, approaches the subject in a manner very different from Whewell's, but with results just about the same. "That science today is irreligious, he claims, "no one will doubt in his innermost being, even if he will not admit it to himself." But with exactly the same kind of commitment to the responsibility of science to keep within the confines of natural explanation, he adds: "science 'free from presuppositions' expects . . . no less – and no more – than acknowledgment that *if* the process can be explained without . . . supernatural interventions, which an empirical explanation has to eliminate as causal facts, the process is to be explained the way science attempts to do. And the believer can do this without being disloyal to his faith."[18]

Interestingly, it is the commitment to piety among scientists that helped open the way to some of the critical tensions between science and religion. Natural theology takes the evidence of the natural world as the proof of God's existence. It was common, even usual, that those who argued for natural evidences of the creator believed also in revelation and even miracle. Bishop Butler's subtle and careful arguments about using the analogy of nature as evidence are part of a large argument that includes – in effect, begins with – belief in revelation. But once the field of natural theology is established, it is obliged, in itself, to demand of natural phenomena that they be clear evidences of divine creation. And it was just this move that John Henry Newman, so subtle and careful a thinker on this matter, rejected. As A. Dwight Culler puts it, he "cared less for Paley . . . than he did for Darwin."[19] Culler quotes Newman as saying that Natural Theology he had "ever viewed with the greatest suspicion." It has a tendency, Newman thought, with great prescience and insight, "if

[18] Max Weber, *The Protestant Ethic and the Spirit of Capitalism* (Los Angeles: Roxbury Publishing Company, 1998 [1930]), p. 27.
[19] A. Dwight Culler, *The Imperial Intellect* (New Haven: Yale University Press, 1955), p. 267.

contemplated exclusively, to dispose the mind against Christianity, because it speaks only of laws and cannot tell of their suspension, that is, of miracles" (pp. 267–8). Newman's reasons for distrusting Natural Theology are complex, but it is clear that he recognized that its tendency was to level Nature and God. The true evidences of religion are not naturalist at all, and God is not just what Newman brilliantly called "the natural world with a divine glow upon it" (p. 268). Once the natural world is given priority in the argument, there is trouble for religion, even if the intent is to show that the natural world is evidence of divinity.

Hugh Miller was of another mind, and I turn to him briefly here because he conveniently formulates the condition I am trying to get at. That brilliant and pious stonecutter geologist believed that science would in fact yield conclusions not only consonant with religious belief but fully confirmatory of it. But he chastised Victorian clergy for being "a full age behind the requirements of the time" as they continued to build their arguments for god on metaphysics. He warned them as early as 1850 that there was coming what he called "a battle of the Evidences," and that battle "will have as certainly to be fought on the field of physical science."[20] The novel too is a battleground of evidences, and a similar difficulty arises – probability and mimesis ought to reveal a divinely ordered world inside a providential plot; but probability and mimesis always threaten to fail to do this. Miller is ready to stake his faith on the evidences of God's presence he will find *in* nature. But at this point, the genre takes control of the argument, and it always remains possible that the evidence will not point to the divine despite Miller's confidence that science cannot be disruptive of fundamental Christian beliefs, or despite Dickens apparent confidence, evident in the very friendly treatment of the *Origin* in both *Household Words* and *All the Year Round,* that science will not be incompatible with his ideal values.

---

[20] In a fascinating discussion of the nature of evidence for the existence of the creator in nature, Hugh Miller takes a strong scientific stance and attacks clergy for lingering in metaphysics when the true evidence must be derived from nature itself. Miller argues that "ere the Churches can be prepared competently to deal with it [*that is, with the current arguments for development, which Miller sees inevitably to lead to atheism, even if not atheistic in intention*], or with the other objections of a similar class which the infidelity of an age so largely engaged as the present in physical pursuits will be from time to time originating they must greatly extend their educational walks into the field of physical science. The mighty change which has taken place during the present century, in the direction in which the minds of the first order are operating . . . seems to have too much escaped the notice of our theologians . . . it is in the departments of physics, not of metaphysics, that the greater minds of the age are engaged . . . The battle of the Evidences will have as certainly to be fought on the field of physical science, as it was contested in the last age on that of the metaphysics." Hugh Miller, *Foot-Prints of the Creator, or, The Asterolepis of Stromness* (Boston: Gould and Lincoln, 1851), pp. 43–5.

Where scientific discovery constantly put pressure on religious explanation, the novel's secular epistemology put pressure on religious interpretations of life and morals. It tests piety's forms and conventions in large part by forcing readers to recognize the full personal engagement of the pious and the moral in the details of ordinary life. The novel is then the perfect venue for George Eliot or Trollope's worldly and sympathetic representation of clergy and of people of faith for it does not require either the author's or the reader's acquiescence in the faith so sympathetically registered. It is obviously no accident that George Eliot's first fictional works were about clergy, about true believers who are seen as humans subject to human desires and mistakes. Dickens often does the reverse, tries to expose the clergy as sweaty, greedy, hungry, selfish beings who exploit religiosity for their own interests. Ironically, however, such satiric attacks on the clergy are more likely to indicate some sort of serious belief in the realities of religious views than George Eliot's compassionate treatment. The anger of the exposure suggests that Dickens wants to believe in the religious purity of the ideals these clergy merely exploit. But the exposure secularizes as fully as the sympathy does. There is no necessary connection in fiction – perhaps also in life – between goodness and belief. The tensions between the secularity of the form and the religious, even transcendental objectives the narratives may try to suggest, parallel the problem of religious science depending for evidence on naturalistic phenomena.

The tension between secularity and religion in fiction might be further illuminated by Max Weber's views about the relation of religion to modern capitalism and to the diffusion of scientific rationality and authority through European culture. "Scientific progress," he claimed, means "that if one but wished one *could* learn" at any time anything one wanted to know about "the conditions under which we live."[21] The consequences of this development he labeled "disenchantment," the recognition that there are "no mysterious incalculable forces" (p. 139). In this respect, willy-nilly, the work of Lyell and Whewell, two men determined to save religion from the potential encroachments of science, was radically secular, and in Weber's sense, disenchanting. Their work theorizes and argues for foundational principles of science, principles that are entirely naturalistic, and suggest, as Weber puts it, that "one can, in principle, master all things by calculation." Some novels, one would think, certainly many of Dickens', are

---

[21]   Max Weber, "Science as a Vocation," in *From Max Weber: Essays in Sociology*, ed. C. C. Gerth and
       H. Wright Mills (Oxford: Oxford University Press, 1946), p. 139.

almost designed to resist this view, narrative being a mode that forces us out of the merely rational and abstract and requires our engagement with particulars. But as Dickens turns to particulars and gets Sissy Jupe to oppose compassion for individuals to a general, averaging, rationalizing sense of overall benefits, he is resisting science not with the transcendent but with the value of individual feeling. Think only of Louisa Gradgrind sinking to the ground at her father's feet. The alternatives to Gradgrind's disenchanting calculations are not metaphysical ideas or intuitions of divinity but the circus: "People mutht be amuthed." The secularity of rationality is opposed by the secularity of personal feeling.

Certainly, the tradition of Calvinism that Marcus invokes lies some-where behind this movement toward the valuing of individual conscious-ness, and the novel was a form that did much to sanction the replacement of doctrinal and institutionally supported religion by its insistence on personal consciousness and personal belief. But fictional commitment to the validity of personal feeling might also be traced back to philosophical and at least quasi-scientific roots. The connection of the realistic enterprise with the development of empiricism was long ago classically established by Ian Watt, who, as Michael McKeon has succinctly explained, connects the development of "formal realism" with "a parallel innovation in philo-sophical discourse, and these he connects, in turn, with a set of socio-economic developments at whose center are the rise of the middle class, the growth of commercial capitalism" by way of 'individualism' – that is, "in . . . validation of individual experience."[22]

Weber's theory of disenchantment was linked to that other connection of great importance to the development of the Victorian novel – "the connection of the spirit of economic life with the rational ethics of ascetic Protestantism" (p. 27). At the end of *The Protestant Ethic and the "Spirit" of Capitalism,* Weber almost lyrically and elegiacally (although he might have been appalled by my adverbs here) discusses what happens when, as in America,

the spirit of religious asceticism . . . has escaped from the cage. But victorious capitalism, since it rests on mechanical foundations, needs its support no longer. The rosy blush of its laughing heir, the Enlightenment, seems also to be irretriev-ably fading, and the idea of duty in one's calling prowls about in our lives like the ghost of dead religious beliefs. Where the fulfillment of the calling cannot directly be related to the highest spiritual and cultural values, or when, on the other hand,

---

[22]   Michael McKeon, *Theory of the Novel: a Historical Approach* (Baltimore: Johns Hopkins Uni-versity Press, 2000), p. 382.

it need not be felt simply as economic compulsion, the individual generally abandons the attempt to justify it at all. (p. 182)

As I have suggested already, the argument that the spirit of capitalism depended upon a Protestant ethic implies a familiar narrative: virtue rewarded. The providential narrative. When Fielding rewrote Richardson's *Pamela* as a sham he was identifying one of the central problems of the novel form that was to grow inside the new capitalism: is it possible to be piously virtuous and to achieve worldly success? What is it that constitutes success in the novel world? Is it possible, in the world so described, to be successful and not have money? If money is a moral disaster, the embodiment of material values, the equivalent of Boffin's dust heaps, can one acquire it without morally dirtying the soul? If so, the form of Weber's narrative becomes comic, which is the characteristic form of early realist fiction. But this passage about modern America suggests what the problems with the form, the form of Jane Austen and Walter Scott in their very different ways, were to be. Reward tends finally to be fully dissociated from virtue, which, along with the religion that sanctioned it, becomes a mere cover for self-interest and greed.

III

The modern novel almost generically worries out these problems. It is a commonplace that money and class, from Defoe, Richardson and Fielding through the whole of the nineteenth century, are central preoccupations of the realist novel, both thematically and formally. The *Bildung* narrative, which figures so importantly in the development of the nineteenth-century novel, frequently entangles an inevitable romantic plot with a plot of vocation, so that money and romance will often become aspects of the same problems. This is obvious enough in the most famous examples, as in *Pendennis* and *David Copperfield*, but even where vocation is not so strictly at stake, as early as Jane Austen, comic resolution entails the marriage of Knightley and Emma, for example, as the material conditions of their lives suggest is appropriate; and Fanny and Edmund will replay the *Pamela* story, with interesting variations and emphasis on the question of poverty. Yet the *opposition* of romance and money is one of the starting points of the modern novel, even though Richardson almost immediately came under fire for secretly making money the real motive of apparent virtue. Writers ever after have tried

to avoid the possibility of interpreting their very moral romantic protagonists as hypocrites who are in it for profit.

Yet as the novel committed itself to the most authentic possible
registration of the details of the sorts of lives their readers were ostensibly living, it became particularly difficult to imagine behavior leading
to material success that is not tainted by acquiescence in a society built
on the profit motive. It is true that a large proportion of Victorian
novels avoid direct representation of the nature of the work the protagonists do that earn them their living; moreover, the novels will often
suggest that it is not so much the system, but its abuse that causes the
pain and injustice so meticulously and compassionately reported.
Nonetheless, the novels have to confront the reality of the injustices
and the suffering if they are to engage at all with the poor and the
working classes.

In the interpretation of novels in which virtue is rewarded, one
might claim that hypocrisy and cynicism have vied for dominance.
In the novelistic battle of the evidences, the realist tradition puts the
ideal on the defensive. Active and decisive protagonists are particularly
dangerous figures for novelists, for how might a heroically decisive
figure convincingly be shown to fight his way with full consciousness
toward success and *not* be exposed as complicit in an economy operating ruthlessly in pursuit of profit? Weber provided a narrative that
explains how success in business might be understood as a symptom
of religious virtue and compatible with the most ferociously aggressive
capitalist behavior; in fiction, this sort of development tends to be
transformed into something like fairy tale, as in *Pamela* or its virtual
opposite, *Tom Jones*. When asked why "money should be made out of
men," Benjamin Franklin's father quoted to him this passage from
Proverbs: "Seest thou a man diligent in his business? He shall stand
before kings" (xxii, 29). As Weber put it, "earning money within the
modern economic order is, so long as it is done legally, the result and the
expression of virtue and proficiency in a calling" (pp. 53–54). But Tom
is revealed to be a great inheritor of wealth; Pamela manages to catch
Lord B. Neither earns the wealth in business or trade. The providential
plot enters realist narrative in such a form, though with the wry ironies
of Jane Austen, the romantic enthusiasm of Scott, or the romantic and
Puritanical seriousness of Dickens.

Yet there seem to be some striking confirmations of Weber's thesis in
the representation of hard working figures in the novel, and the whole
celebratory, post-Carlylean moralizing of "work" that emerges in many

novels suggests that working success – not gratuitous inheritance or fortunate marriage – might indeed be tied to virtue. Perhaps the most famous instance is George Eliot's reverential portrayal of Caleb Garth, in *Middlemarch*. His invocation of "business" as an almost divine incantation is, of course, designed to emphasize the distance between work, a virtue in its own right, and money, the worldly reward for that virtue. Caleb is obviously entirely interested in the former and utterly regardless of the latter. He risks ruin because of his personal affection. But it is difficult not to grow a bit cynical. Caleb's hard and faithful work is rewarded in the novel, after all; that success, only partly consistent with what George Eliot shows us about how people fare in Middlemarch, seems tied to her desire to believe and demonstrate that Caleb's very Calvinist virtues of self-denial, efficiency, promptitude, and skill will eventually bring secular success. At the same time, the novel punishes Lydgate for his worldly self-indulgences and makes of Bulstrode a virtual caricature of the Weberian spirit only to ruin him too – but only because he has not been honest.

Thus, while the economic history that Weber theorizes reveals a culture in which a rejection of worldliness, systematic self-repression, and hard work, might yield worldly rewards, the novel, often playing out this very story, could rarely manage it untroubled. The strain in George Eliot's imagination of a "Nemesis" that somehow is built into a fully secular world is apparent in the very self-consciousness with which she manages appropriate punishment for Bulstrode, for example, or appropriate rewards for Caleb. The secular vision makes it very difficult to accommodate providence or to imagine the neat fit between moral virtue and temporal success, and this is particularly true when the protagonist is active and decisive. The opposition between material success and virtue is a consistent theme of Victorian fiction, even where virtue is, indeed, rewarded materially.

The uneasiness of nineteenth-century novels with their own heroes is a characteristic of the genre itself, and seems largely a consequence of this opposition and the tension it produces, sometimes inside the narrative, sometimes in the narrator's relation to the story. It is characteristic of the form of the modern novel in England, taking off, say, from *Pamela*, running through the heroes of the Waverley novels, hovering over the Dobbin-Amelia relation in *Vanity Fair*, and emerging full-blown in the whole run of Dickens' novels. Thackeray, in his preface to *Pendennis*, famously laments that "Since the author of *Tom Jones* was buried, no writer of fiction among us has been permitted to depict to his utmost power a MAN."[23] The post-Waverley protagonist is himself a symptom of the battle of the evidences, the possibility of ideality countered by the apparent inevitability of more or less radical compromise. Only by keeping the protagonist outside the action can the ideal be saved, although the novel then leaves us with a figure distinctly unheroic, after all. Scott famously noted, in his anonymous review of his own work, that "a leading fault in these novels is the total want of interest which the reader attaches to the character of the hero." These figures are, Scott argues, "very amiable and very insipid sort of young men."[24] Scott's explanation of this effect is much to the point: "His chief characters are never actors, but always acted upon by the spur of circumstances, and have their fates uniformly determined by the agency of the subordinate persons" (p. 240). In the world of the Victorian novel, it is almost always best *not* to act, although the great Carlylean injunction, derived from John, 9:4, with its strong residue of Calvinism, to which so much Victorian literature pays obeisance, is to "work while it is day, for the night cometh in which no man can work."

But when characters are driven entirely by forces beyond their control, they are relieved of moral responsibility. So Carlyle's injunction, often taken as central to Victorian culture, is constantly troubled in the novels themselves. Novelists need the success of their protagonists to bring off their comic endings, but they are hard pressed to imagine ways, within the textured representation of middle class life and economy, to represent it without radically compromising the protagonists' moral integrity. Ideal moral behavior is for the most part dramatized as incompatible with success within the new economic system, or, more frequently, the incompatibility is disguised by investing women – who have to remain outside the economic system – with ideality and focusing on flawed male protagonists who must mature. It is a lot easier to represent Esther Summerson as tirelessly active, than it is to represent John Jarndyce, who flees at the slightest indication of an "east wind," as active.

Notoriously, the really interesting characters in much Victorian fiction tend to be the villains. While Franco Moretti rightly points to the way the English *Bildungsroman* resists "experience," and is in a certain sense a

---

[23]   William Makepeace Thackeray, *Pendennis* (London: J. M. Dent, 1959 [1848–50]), I, p. xvi.
[24]   Ioan Williams, ed., *Sir Walter Scott on Novelists and Fiction* (New York: Barnes and Noble, 1968), p. 240.

sustained "fairy tale,"[25] he perhaps underplays the degree to which the tendency to return to an established order and to confirm the sometimes imperiled identity of the protagonist is put under extreme pressure by the representation of a social and economic order that is anything but ideal. That order surrounds the protagonist and the story, and threatens to turn the narrative – certainly in the last quarter of the nineteenth century – from the traditional romantic-comic fairy-tale ending to something bleaker and more difficult. While in the English novel, the *Bildung* tends in fact to reward the weak and flawed protagonist with the usual comic happy ending in romance, just because it refuses to show him battling directly for success, it almost invariably raises questions and doubts and suggests possible darker alternatives that in the end it will avoid.

By the time of Hardy the problem was out in the open, and in *The Mayor of Casterbridge* he dramatizes the price of action, just as he severs the connection between morality and success. With him, the situation tended to be reversed, and there was no possibility of narrating convincingly the protagonist's weakness and innocence and virtue without also tracing some sorts of crucial failures in the social and economic worlds. Wherever the Protestant ethic drove successful capitalists, the narrated story of life inside the economy, inside "vanity fair," kept the divine hand out and registered some rather seamy doings. The "fairy tale" that makes Moretti so uneasy must finally stop working because the difference between ideal virtue and the reality of the mixed conditions that realism always registers become too great.

Although women characters too, in the conditions of nineteenth-century realism, must suffer compromises, as, for example, most obviously, the over-idealistic Dorothea Brooke, or the very practical Jane Eyre or the carefully self-abnegating Lucy Snowe, they are rarely threatened by the kind of corruption intrinsic to ambition in the economic system. Women characters can be unequivocally good, and can import into their behavior

---

[25] Franco Moretti, *The Way of the World: The Bildungsroman in European Culture* (London: Verso, 1987). See Moretti's entire discussion of the way the English novel differs from the Continental in its treatment of youth, development, and possibility. He emphasizes the English novel's failure in fact to deal with the mixed conditions that radically compromise moral choice and that make any notion of a decisive and unambiguous ending virtually impossible. From one point of view, he writes, the *Bildung* tradition in England gives us "but one long fairy-tale with a happy ending, far more elementary and limited than its continental counterparts" (p. 213). The implication of his argument is that my own general argument here would work better with the continental novel, and I believe that is true. But the English novel is also, willy-nilly, a fully secular form no matter how traditional many of its devices may be, and part of what is most striking about the English novel is just the tension the best of them produce between the obligatory romantic-comic resolution and the possible alternatives it has, in various ways, so carefully averted.

the ideals of the truly religious life because, through most of the century, they have only a tightly constricted place in the economic system; yet they must live in novels with men, and must be subject to the critique implicit in the famous "But" with which Arthur Pendennis arrived at the romantic-comic conclusion of his story. The "but" intimates the realities that Moretti says the English novel largely avoids. It embodies – with a sort of Thackerayan fatigue – the secularity that imposes itself on the most religious aspirations of the English novel. The "but," Pen explains, "will come in spite of us." "I will whisper to you when you are on your knees at church," it says. Laura, the angel in the house of this novel, exclaims, "Pen, you frighten me" (II, p. 343). The "But" marks a refusal to accept the fact that, as Pen puts it in just the next paragraph, "some of you seem exempt from the fall." "Some of you" are of course women. "But" is the secular caveat and the mark, also, of the characteristically weak protagonist of nineteenth-century fiction. It registers the fact that nobody is exempt, in particular not the weak and wavering hero. It becomes the word for the inevitable compromise that secularity entails.

Secularity and money, in the new capitalist economy, go hand in hand, and money is the key material object of a large proportion of Victorian fiction. Before turning finally to *Little Dorrit*, it will be useful to emphasize again how pervasive in mainstream nineteenth-century fiction are these secular symptoms and motifs, and how bound up they are with the novel's mode of shaping both its protagonists and its plots. Perhaps the most obvious and central text for the argument is *Vanity Fair*, a book that is all about money: its two brilliant chapters on "How to Live Well on Nothing a Year" become a kind of field guide to how money works through all levels of society. It's not pretty. But the most powerful, disturbing and significant passage for an understanding of the importance of the subject to the form comes in an almost throwaway line of Becky Sharp: "I could be a good woman if I had five thousand a year" (p. 490).

The revulsion with which *Vanity Fair* was received in some quarters might well have been focused on this point. It is easy enough, taking the high moral line, to see this as the clearest sign of Becky's villainy, but of course that is not how Becky's claim works nor how Becky is imagined. Becky's argument challenges the notion that character is intrinsic, free, and spiritual in nature, and suggests that it is deeply involved in the material, in the very sorts of context upon which realistic fiction has always focused. The idea is both subversive of the fundamental moral and transcendental values towards which the religious imagination aspired and a sensible inference from the realist novel's preoccupation with context.

Social and historical context puts character under pressures that undercut, or threaten to undercut the assumption that virtue is unconditional, independent of the contingencies of time and place.[26]

The most famous example in Dickens of a narrative that denies the contingency of character is *Oliver Twist*, which has about it something of the fairy tale not so much because Oliver turns out, if you'll forgive me, to be a rich bastard after all, but because, notoriously, none of the world he has lived in has rubbed off on his language, his manners, his emotions, his ideas.[27] While the book shows powerfully how *other* characters in the novel are shaped and threatened by their environments, its comic form depends upon its protagonist's uncontaminated innocence and resistance to context. Against this sort of narrative refusal to make context count in characterization, we have, for example, George Eliot's grinding insistence on the importance of the medium in which people live and her rigorous tracing of the way character and behavior are shaped by it – if Lydgate hadn't been in need of Bulstrode's money, he would have behaved very differently; he wouldn't have been compromised; he wouldn't have had to settle for a money-making career of no moral or cultural consequence. George Eliot manages this without the cynical ironies implicit in Becky's claims. She simply builds it into the novel form itself. Money and character, in the main tradition of the realist novel, *are* mutually dependent, even as novelists often struggle to resist what their narratives demonstrate.

Money may be a dirty business, but almost nowhere in the world of the realist novel can one do without it. The realist novel will not let a serious writer wrest characters entirely loose from social context, and fundamental material needs. So in Charlotte Brontë's novels money matters almost as centrally as in Dickens or in George Eliot, but with a difference. Consider

---

[26] It is interesting to note how critical the notion of "personal identity" is to religious belief in immortality. When Bishop Butler addresses the issue he begins with an extended chapter on "personal identity," demonstrating philosophically that we are objectively self-identical. It is not merely a matter of self-consciousness. Butler attacks the idea that "Personality is not a permanent, but a transient thing . . . that no one can any more remain one and the same person two moments together, than two successive moments can be one and the same moment." *The Analogy of Religion, Natural and Revealed; to which are added two brief dissertations; on Personal Identity and on the Nature of Virtue; and Fifteen Sermons* (London: George Bell and Sons, 1882; 1736), p. 331. Becky's argument about the way in which context would change her nature is, implicitly, a step toward the idea that identity is contingent, not permanent.

[27] Moretti claims that this is in effect the implication of the entire tradition of the *Bildungsroman* in England. He sees Tom Jones as a figure utterly unaffected by his experiences: "they are mere digressions . . . and they will never shed a different light on, nor force Tom from, the straight and narrow path of asexual *childhood* love. Contrary to *Wilhelm Meister*, in the English novel the most significant experiences are not those that alter but those that *confirm* the choices made by childhood 'innocence'" (p. 182). For a fuller discussion of this problem, see the essay on "Realism" in this volume.

Jane Eyre's attitude toward money. Her first conversation, after she is rescued from starvation and exhaustion, includes her angry reproach to Hannah, the serving woman: "if you are a Christian, you ought not to consider poverty a crime."[28] And when she learns that she has inherited £20,000, she unhesitatingly determines to share it. Her explanation to St. John Rivers, newly discovered as cousin, is equally revealing: "It would please and benefit me to have five thousand pounds; it would torment and oppress me to have twenty thousand pounds; which, moreover, could never be mine in justice, though it might in law" (ch. 33, p. 329). Despite her principles and her generosity, Brontë emphasizes Jane's practicality, letting Jane admit that £5,000 would "please and benefit me." In this respect she is at least apparently different from Dickens' saintly heroines. She guides her relation to money very strictly by her sense of "justice" and of merit. But there is no nonsense about its irrelevance. The central crisis of the book, Jane's wandering after leaving Rochester, could only have happened because Jane had no financial resources. The cheating, if we may call it that, is that Jane stumbles on the household of her own cousins and then can inherit enough money to keep her going.

The first point to be noted is that while a protagonist, even a woman, may indeed acquire wealth, it can only be without direct effort to obtain it; the second – and in a matter of inheritance this is particularly difficult – is that having money must always be justified by merit. Lingering behind the virtually instinctive, traditional revulsion from money and pursuit of it in Victorian fiction, we spy that almost inevitable providential plot, after all. Inheritance is one of the very few means by which realist characters can escape the radical compromises inside the new social order that pursuit of success implies. Jane's effort to link money to merit both participates in and resists this aspect of Protestantism.

Usually recognized grudgingly as a secular necessity, money almost always provokes the Victorian novel to the verge of a moral and nervous breakdown. (This obviously is not true for Anthony Trollope, who is outspoken about the virtue of money, the superiority of people who have it – at least for the sake of entertainment.) Unease about money is evident in *Jane Eyre*: it is the motivating force of the plot of *Little Dorrit*. Novels, with some regularity, need to find ways to allow sympathetic protagonists to have money, as quietly as possible, of course, and on the basis of merit, but need also to demonstrate money's power as *radix malorum* in the hands or minds of others. The great test of Bella Wilfer in Dickens'

---

[28] Charlotte Brontë, *Jane Eyre* (New York: W. W. Norton, 1971; 1847), ch. 27, p. 270.

Our Mutual Friend is to measure her reaction to Boffin's feigned miser-liness. At the point at which feeling triumphs over money, she becomes worthy of the status of heroine and of marrying the bland, virtually non-existent John Harmon, and acquiring the money anyway. But the whole novel dramatizes very clearly that financial success in modern society is virtually unattainable through merit alone.

When money falls into the hands of protagonists it has to work over-time to become something other than it is, or to disappear. My example here is Elizabeth Gaskell's *North and South*. As an industrial novel, it would seem to have much more on the table than a romance and a comic ending in marriage, particularly as the title itself insists on the thematic centrality of social context. The entire novel builds, of course, to the happy ending that will come with the marriage of North and South, of Thornton and Margaret. And yet, almost as in a parody (one can imagine Oscar Wilde handling the scene), the moment of romantic revelation and under-standing is a matter of business. Thornton, the one entirely honorable industrialist, goes bankrupt just because he refuses to risk his workers' money on a speculation. Margaret, at the last, has come into money, so that roles are reversed, and the woman is in the dominant worldly posi-tion. In the crucial last scene, there is no love-making or approach to love-making. For Margaret, the newly acquired money matters only as a means to assist the man she has discovered she loves. "If," she says to Thornton, "you take some money of mine, eighteen-thousand and fifty-seven pounds, lying just at this moment unused in the bank, and bringing me in only two and a half percent. – you could pay me much better interest." We understand that Thornton would never accept a gift of the money, and thus Margaret offers it in the form of a loan that would ostensibly profit her. But of course Thornton reads right through the business and takes it as an offer not of money but of love: his voice was "hoarse and trembling with tender passion, as he said, 'Margaret!'"[29] The love story and the economic story are one. Thornton responds, one would have to infer, not to the money but to the fact that Margaret is offering it. And yet it takes no cynical reading to realize that the money is everything, just as it is being understood as nothing. It has to be there for the romance to work. And yet if we read the story with attention to the question of the relation of financial success to merit, we need to realize that the industrialist who merits worldly success cannot get it through merit – only through love; and the woman who has the money has got it with no hand in

---

[29] Elizabeth Gaskell, *North and South* (London: Penguin Books, 1970; 1845), ch. 52, p. 529.

industry and commerce at all. It is mere chance, not merit, that gives to Margaret an inheritance that will allow the manufacturer/lover to resume an honorable pursuit of material success. The novel's troubled relation to money and worldly success continues here in a peculiarly convoluted way, registering the purity of its protagonists by allowing them the success that worldly engagement could not provide them.

IV

Radix malorum est cupiditas

I turn at last to *Little Dorrit*, in which the tension between the religious and the secular is thematically and formally central, and the motif that most fully embodies the tension is money itself: almost all of the major moments of the book show money marking the lives of the characters. The preoccupations and problems I have noted as characteristic of the novel as a genre are prominent: the pervasiveness of money as energizing force, guilt accruing object, and point of concern; the centrality of a weak and indecisive hero; and an elaborate plot forcing itself toward some comic harmony but strained intensely toward the possibility of matching merit, virtue, and reward. Arthur Clennam is almost the quintessential weak hero whom Scott described, about which Thackeray complained, and around which a striking proportion of nineteenth-century novels spin. The final union of the lovers depends upon money, as much as does the final union in *North and South.*

In *Little Dorrit* Dickens seems both more overtly religious and more self-conscious about secularity than he had ever been before. In one of his working notes he wrote, "Set the darkness and vengeance against the New Testament."[30] At this point in his life and career – as many commentators have noted – Dickens strenuously cultivated a New Testament sensibility that emerges in the language of his books and of his correspondence and public lectures. The apparent thrust of *Little Dorrit* is, as Dennis Walder has put it, "to show that one can free oneself from the imprisoning forces associated with a narrow Old Testament faith of stern self-denial and wrathful vengeance by means of the broadly redemptive, loving spirit of the New" (p. 179). But the religious intensity runs parallel to the increasing disgust Dickens himself expresses for the social and material conditions of contemporary England. The religion, then, is paralleled by a

---

[30]   Quoted in Peter Ackroyd, *Dickens* (New York: HarperCollins, 1990), p. 778.

marked world-weariness, even world abhorrence, that has about it something of the Calvinist severity and anger that, at the same time, he is attacking angrily through analysis of the demoralized character of Arthur Clennam and of the relentless vengefulness of his mother. The famous prison imagery entails a quasi-religious vision of the world as secular prison: "Far aslant across the city, over its jumbled roofs, and through the open tracery of its church towers, struck the long bright rays, bars of the prison of this lower world."[31]

Self-evidently, it is in this prison of the lower world that everything in the novel must unfold, and the novel is consistently troubled by a determined registration of this prison as repulsive and destructive, while it is particularly outraged by the austere and world-hating religion exemplified by Clennam's mother. Religion and secularity constantly play off against each other, for the raw secularity of the bleak imprisoned world is recognizable here only in the language that religion itself provides. Moreover, throughout the novel, biblical allusions comment on the degraded and degrading secularity of the realist world. The aspiration to a transcendent vision struggles with an entirely secular understanding of how the world, at least the social world that Dickens chooses to describe, works. One might say that *Little Dorrit* dramatizes the necessary compromise between Dickensian New Testament ideal (and as Moretti suggests, the characteristic ideal of the English novel) and the secularity his commitment to realist probability entailed.

The problem was to find a way to squeeze into the secular surfaces of the book some intimation of spiritual possibility. The dreary and ugly world into which Clennam moves on a representatively dreary Sunday are evidences of real fatigue and disgust, as is the surrealistically charged description of the area around Clennam's old home, to which at the start he makes his sad pilgrimage. Moving through some of the "crooked and descending" streets, he passes the "mouldy hall of some obsolete Worshipful Company," and the "illuminated windows of a Congregationless Church," and then "warehouses and wharves, and here and there a narrow alley leading to the river, where a wretched little bill, found drowned, was weeping on the wet wall" (ch. 3, p. 70). The corruption of the propped up house, in the midst of these squalid evidences of decay and death, gives a rough sense of the underside of the world the novel describes with so much satiric contempt, in fancier areas of the city. Where, in the midst of these realistically and symbolically described manifestations of a world

[31] Charles Dickens, *Little Dorrit* (London: Penguin Books, 1971; 1857), II, ch. 30, p. 81.

rotting away in its sheer materiality, might there be glimpses of true spirit and transcendence?

It is obviously in the figure of Little Dorrit that Dickens tries to gives us such a glimpse, and here most obviously can be felt the strain of trying to imagine transcendence in a world in which religion itself has become secular, and to do so in a way that will satisfy the secular and realist constraints of the novel form. A victim of the economic system from the start, Amy is born into just such physical and moral conditions as Clennam finds around and in his old home, but in a literal prison, the Marshalsea. While Clennam is trapped inside the sordidness and decay emblematized in his sad secular pilgrimage, Amy Dorrit is somehow immune to the material and psychological conditions in which she grows and lives: "Worldly wise in hard and poor necessities, she was innocent in all things else. Innocent, in the mist through which she saw her father, and the prison, and the turbid living river that flowed through it and flowed on" (ch. 7, p. 118). She is imagined as deeply *of* the material world, as any character in a novel with realist claims must be; but Dickens figures her also as untainted by the turbid flow of secular time, by its materiality, its hard and poor necessities.

As the anti-Becky Sharp, impervious to secularity's demeaning pressures, Little Dorrit strains the limits of the genre and is even, on occasion, allowed the voice of transcendence, as when she preaches the divine mercy that the book's last chapters attempt to embody:

O Mrs Clennam, Mrs Clennam ... angry feelings and unforgiving deeds are no comfort and no guide to you and me. My life has been passed in this poor prison, and my teaching has been very defective; but let me implore you to remember later and better days. Be guided only by the healer of the sick, the raiser of the dead, the friend of all who were afflicted and forlorn, the patient Master who shed tears of compassion for our infirmities. We cannot but be right if we put all the rest away, and do everything in remembrance of Him. There is no vengeance and no infliction of suffering in His life, I am sure. There can be no confusion in following Him, and seeking for no other footsteps, I am certain. (ch. 31, p. 861)

Such preaching is uncharacteristic of the always self-effacing Little Dorrit. The book knows all too well, not least in the determined creation of its almost saintly heroine, that nobody in the secular world, the only world the novel knows, is able to follow this injunction unfailingly, not even Amy herself, who for one brief moment earlier on had railed against the injustice done to her father, and throughout the narrative has nurtured a not entirely repressed secular love of Arthur Clennam, who notes at last, in his own weakness, when Amy comes to help him in the Marshalsea, that she "looked something more womanly" (II, ch. 20, p. 826).

Juxtaposition of the two women almost makes a morality play, Amy the religious counterpart to Mrs. Clennam's Calvinist and hate-filled religiosity. When Amy asks Mrs. Clennam to "remember" those latter and better days, the days that lie outside secularity, she can only remind the reader that the book cannot trespass on such places except in the imagination of its titular heroine. As the novel winds down, the religious imagery and influence grow more intense, diffusing even to the point of softening the inexorable Mrs. Clennam, who rises, "as if a dead woman had risen" (II, ch. 30, p. 853), and shows for the first time understanding and compassion for both Amy and Arthur, although she keeps the secret of Arthur's birth, and thus of her own shame. It is not beside the point that Amy's last dramatic act within the novel is a morally ambiguous one, although of course it is also designed to heighten even further our sense of her deference to secular promises: she burns the evidence that Arthur is not Mrs. Clennam's son, and thus keeps him forever in the dark.

Within the tradition of comic realism to which *Little Dorrit* marginally belongs, the providential plot works out again, but it is radically compromised. Although worldly success is not allowed, the success that is allowed is distinctly, explicitly in this world. As what seems like a self-conscious anti-*Pamela, Little Dorrit* does not reconcile merit and worldly reward. The religious imagery continues, virtually concluding at the marriage "with the sun shining on them through the painted figure of Our Saviour on the window" (p. 894), but the intimation of life and transcendence lives only in the image, not in the narrative itself.

The story twists and turns to provide reasonable explanations for effects that seem designed to appeal to forces outside the realm of mere plausibility. It is in the very straining of the plot that the tensions between the religious and the secular are most evident. For everything about the story, from Clennam's return to the collapse of his mother's house describes what would seem a natural movement toward decay. Only some movement from beyond the natural could change this direction. The constant movement of degradation – like the mud around Mrs. Clennam's house, the decay that the dominion of the Barnacles guarantees to an ailing nation, the disasters produced by the Merdle bubble enticing everyone, from William Dorrit to Pancks to Arthur Clennam, to pursue unmerited money – is counteracted by Dickens' pursuit of something else at work that will be redemptive at last.

The major redemptive event in the book is the marriage of Arthur and Amy. And that depends entirely on the withdrawal of money from their connection. Only through such straining could the comic tradition of English realism be sustained inside conventions of probability and verisimilitude. It required a plot more complex and confused than any in Dickens' work to achieve the form of providential order. To write the final installments of the novel, Dickens had to summarize the previous action in his notes, almost as the contemporary reader still has to do in the reading.

Mary Poovey's comments about *Our Mutual Friend* might be applied as well to *Little Dorrit*: "on the one hand, the novel struggled against the modern disaggregating of domains by insisting that economic behavior not be freed from a moral analytic; on the other hand, *Our Mutual Friend* betrays the anxieties generated *by* this disaggregation."[32] Weber's theory can be invoked again to help explain the tensions here, tensions that can be traced throughout Victorian fiction. The moralizing of money matters is consistent with the idea that the "Protestant spirit" was at the heart of a developing capitalism. But in *Little Dorrit* there is a difference. We do have Merdle's famous financial bubble, a financial success built on speculation and falsity rather than self-abnegation and honorable hard work, with the inevitable consequences. And we have a figure like Casby, who radiates a false charity around his brutal grasping for money, or, more extensively, like Gowan and the entire Barnacle family, for whom work is anathema and demeaning: "how not to do it" is the perfect anti-capitalist formula, as it is also the perfect anti-Calvinist formula. Dickens' deep hostility to these kinds of self-interested and lazy indulgences in wealth runs parallel again to the very Old Testament attitudes that he condemns so mercilessly in Mrs. Clennam. These figures confirm the corruption that comes with an unmoralized or a falsely moralized relation to money and worldly success.

But there is, finally, no moralizing money. In the later Dickens, there is simply no touching money without being dirtied. While, on the one hand, survival in secular society depends on the possession of at least some money, and only moralized money can begin to be consonant with the virtue required of Dickensian protagonists, on the other, it is virtually impossible in Dickens to find a way to acquire money that is not fatally

---

[32] Mary Poovey, *Making a Social Body: British Cultural Formation, 1830–1864* (Chicago: University of Chicago Press, 1995), p. 156.

tainted. Pip's moral redemption in *Great Expectations* depends on his losing the fortune Magwitch would bestow on him. Money has real value only in its absence. "I have no use for money," Amy passionately exclaims to Clennam. "I have no wish for it" (ch. 29, p. 828). But the book is obsessed with money nevertheless, and its workings are registered with an almost Thackerayan attentiveness. It is obviously not irrelevant that Amy's first effort after Clennam's visit to the Marshalsea is to prevent him from making any more of those euphemistically disguised "tributes" to her father.

The difference here from Poovey's description of the tensions in *Our Mutual Friend*, is that in *Little Dorrit* even the moralizing of money is not enough. Although there is plenty in Dickens and in most of the great novelists of the period to support Weber's thesis, *Little Dorrit* will have nothing of it. Here, it is not that people must be honorable with their money; it is that they must renounce it entirely to be morally saved. Money is the key emblem of that corrupt and depressing secularity that Dickens describes so powerfully and with a quite awful grasp of living detail. It is the circulating material that makes for moral decay, that draws even the finest away from the ideal aspirations that Little Dorrit preaches in her speech to Mrs. Clennam. Only Daniel Doyce embodies unequivocally the Protestant ethic in his relation to work, and it is marked by his fundamental lack of interest in money. He delegates all money matters to Clennam as he applies all his energy and ingenuity to his work. The result, in the decadent nightmare of English culture, is that Doyce has to go out of the country to get anything done. When Clennam loses Doyce's money, Doyce is not upset.

By the end, what stands between Arthur and Amy is only the Dorrit money. The virtuous protagonist cannot accept the virtuous heroine's merely fortuitous wealth. And thus the final love scene, if that's what it might be called, is in effect a mutual and joyful renunciation of money. The irony is that, even if upside down, the relationship depends entirely on money, on Clennam's early guilt that something is owed to the Dorrits, on the attempt to discover the source of William Dorrit's debts, on the attempt to recover his inheritance, on Amy's inheritance and loss of wealth. Money is everywhere. Love and personal commitment become possible only through a kind of negotiation in which money is entirely banished.

As in the final scene between Thornton and Margaret, the proposal (this time on the part of the woman) comes not with an expression of overt affection, but with a discussion of money. The joy of the scene is worldly loss. The excitement is in Amy's eagerness to tell Clennam, another bankrupt protagonist, that she is penniless: "Do you feel quite strong enough to know what a great fortune I have got?" she asks. "I have been anxiously waiting to tell you. I have been longing and longing to tell you" (ch. 34, p. 885).

There is a touch of playfulness here, as there isn't in *North and South*, and just because Amy is confident in her poverty and certain that not having money will win her loved one. "You are sure," she asks Clennam, "that you will not take it [that is, her wealth]." "Never," the honorable Clennam necessarily replies. Laying her face down on Clennam's hand in a gesture she could not indulge if she were wealthy, Amy joyfully exclaims: "I have nothing in the world. I am as poor as when I lived here." But there is a difference, too. Thornton, ever the strong male, takes the initiative and exclaims "Margaret" at Margaret's offer of a loan. Dickens' scene gives no words to Clennam, ever the passive figure, even here. He sheds "manly tears" (what else), but it is Amy who takes the initiative in a way distinctly uncharacteristic of Dickensian or Victorian heroines in general. She begins again, clasping his hand, "Never to part, my dearest Arthur; never any more, until the last" (ch. 34, p. 886). Although Amy relies on Clennam's former expression of a wish that he had recognized that she was a woman earlier (ch. 29, p. 829), and although she swears absolute submission, Amy is positively aggressive. She can be so because she is penniless. The most convincing and touching aspect of Little Dorrit's character throughout the novel, as she is made to embody Dickens' sense of a reality beyond the secular, is her unmistakable secular love for Clennam. Real joy, it turns out, is itself secular.

For Dickens' project in *Little Dorrit* to succeed it was necessary that virtue and social and economic success be separated. The cruel conditions of the life that Dickens so intensely describes makes it impossible for him to imagine that the world is really accommodated to virtue. Earlier novels, even *Bleak House*, allow the sort of happy ending that brings virtue together with some kind of worldly success, but in *Little Dorrit* it feels as though it is too late; what is worldly is inevitably implicated in corruption. As Poovey argues, "taking money literally, as a good and an end in itself, leads to the literal commodification of human beings" (p. 166). The very initiating energy of the plot implies just this idea. When Arthur returns to see his mother for the first time, he is driven by a guilt that he is only justified in feeling because of his understanding of money itself. "In grasping at money and in driving hard bargains," he says to his mother, "someone may have been grievously deceived, injured, ruined" (ch. 5, p. 88). Little Dorrit thus enters his life as a victim of money. The implication of this initiating energy of the plot is that the only life to be trusted is outside the economy. And in the novel there is virtually nothing outside the economy, except, perhaps, Little Dorrit herself. Virtue may be rewarded, after all, but only when money is transformed into other forms of non-material wealth: "I never was rich before," Little Dorrit exclaims to Arthur.

Unlike Becky Sharp, the book implies, Amy's character would be no different if she were rich. On the European tour, wealth makes her unhappy because she misses the opportunity to assist her father that poverty had afforded her. With Oliver Twist, one feels a touch of authorial naïveté about the boy's innocence in the midst of an actively corrupting environment. But when Dickens makes Little Dorrit a literal "child of the Marshalsea," he self-consciously affirms the possibility of a spiritual condition in which social context – the bread and butter of realism – is irrelevant to character. The final love scene, enacted in the Marshalsea, the purest symbol of the constraints and corruptions of the dominant economic system, strains probability just because in its resistance to traditional novel form and to the idea of a secularity that is consistent with Christian morality, it insists so doggedly on a religious ideal.

Secularity triumphs nonetheless, if a secularity chastised and modified by the experience the book narrates. Money is indeed the root of all evil; and because it is so, despite everyone's – even a saint's – need for it, the realist protagonist loses virtually all powers of agency. And the supreme example of this loss in Victorian fiction is just "nobody," that is, Arthur Clennam. In Clennam, a version of Scott's "insipid" hero, Dickens' overtly thematizes the weakness that, from Scott through the whole tradition of the Victorian novel, is more or less disguised by good nature, good intentions, good looks. "I have no will," says Clennam, right at the start (ch. 2, p. 59). His story ought to be a Pip-like *Bildung* of the development of the will. His is to be a redemptive pilgrimage, and the book's narrative as a whole is designed to affirm the New Testament vision of mercy and altruism in the midst of the dark materiality of the ordinary world, and the vengeful teachings of Calvinism.

Criticism has long regarded Clennam, in his unusual interiority, to be an autobiographical surrogate for Dickens himself. But there is no Dickensian energy in Clennam, and were it to appear, it would necessarily manifest itself as a moral violation, like any action in a world so manifestly corrupt. Clennam must be the post-Scott insipid hero trying to *do* something. He insists, to the horror of the Barnacles, on wanting to "know," as a condition for being able to act justly. And his pursuit of the Barnacles for knowledge of the source of William Dorrit's debts is about all that he can do as an actor, an agent, without compromising himself. At least there is virtue in struggling hopelessly against secular inertia and selfishness. But, in his weakness, the great system entangles and corrupts him. Not only does Dickens emphasize what other novelists often tried to disguise, the weakness of the "hero," but he dramatizes that weakness through the soliloquies in which Clennam sees himself as "nobody."

Like the protagonist of many a Bildungsroman, Clennam asks himself repeatedly, "what he was to do henceforth in life" (16, p. 231). "What can I do?" is an echoing refrain in Victorian fiction. Little Dorrit gives him a vocation, as Mirah, for example, gives Daniel Deronda – another though quite different indecisive young hero. Clennam, however, acts independently really only once, and investing via Pancks in the Merdle bubble forces him into debt, into consequent repercussions that reduce him finally to the Marshalsea and a near fatal illness. Where Deronda finds a nation to establish, Clennam sinks back and is saved by his poverty.

Through the contortions of the plot and the weakness of the hero, the novel finds a way to conclude pointing toward a New Testament mercy that might ease the pain of this prison of a lower world. But it is a resolution for two. There are casualties everywhere else, most particularly in Amy's family. Father and uncle die together; Fanny is stuck in a stupid marriage she arranged for all the wrong reasons; Tip dies. The natural narrative of decay and decline is played out everywhere in the novel but in the lives of the protagonists. They escape because they have renounced the conditions of survival in the society that the novel has so persuasively and repulsively described.

Little Dorrit develops extravagantly basic tensions present in almost all Victorian fiction, particularly in its attempt to reaffirm the possibility of transcendence in so radically fallen a world. The last pages are dominated by Dickens' transformation of the rays of the sun from the prison bars of this lower world earlier in the book to rays that carry with them the image of "Our Saviour" from the stained glass windows of the church. And the wonderful, deeply moving last paragraph of the book is preceded by the moment when the lovers stand at the portico of the church looking at the street "in the autumn sun's bright rays." It is as though the sun is not a prison but an invitation to new life. But the possibility of a truly new life outside this lower world is intimated by Dickens only in images. The power of the last paragraph lies in its resolute, utterly necessary return to that world. And the key phrase is "went down."

Each sentence of the last paragraph reiterates that phrase. There are no "latter and better days" here, but only the lower world. And the novel resolves itself powerfully just because it can only generate a hope for such days, while it accedes to the condition of all novelistic, of all life – the condition of being "down" here. Formally, the ending of *Little Dorrit* retains the quality of the "happy ending" that is the mark of the early modern realist novel. But of course, it is a happy ending manqué, in that there is not only no longer any question of material reward for the good protagonists, but the happiness depends entirely on the absence of such reward. Ironically, the last paragraph is one of the few critical places in the novel where money doesn't figure prominently. Yet there is a kind of evasion that allows Dickens and the novel to slip into the attitudes towards work and money that mark the "Protestant ethic."

We know from the preceding chapter that Clennam will go back to work for Doyce, will be given a second chance. And we know, as Meagles describes it, that Doyce is flourishing overseas, "directing works and executing labours over yonder, that it would make your hair stand on end to look at. He's no public offender, bless you, now! He's medaled and ribboned, and starred and crossed, and I don't-know-what all'd, like a born nobleman. But we mustn't talk about that over here" (ch. 34, p. 891). Dickens' unwillingness to show Doyce active and prosperous in England is not simply an aspect of his ironic attack against English bureaucracy and Barnacalism, though it is certainly partly that. He simply has no way to dramatize the acquisition of wealth that is not radically compromised, and so Doyce's success happens off stage, abroad. Doyce's enterprising, active life is precisely not the life that might constitute material for the protagonist of a Dickens novel. But he can be invoked here as a means by which Clennam can gain access to money without himself being tainted by it. Given the novel's commitment to social and contextual precision, no character, not even Clennam or Little Dorrit, can get on without money. The novel cannot finally reconcile the polar opposites – as they are established in the work and largely inherited from the novel form itself – of secularity and religion, of ethics and money.

But, like its protagonists, the book does what it can do, given the fact that it must necessarily "go down." We can't quite be sure about how Amy and Arthur will be able to sustain their integrity in a world populated, as the last grim and wonderful sentence tells us, by the "noisy and the eager, and the arrogant and froward and the vain," fretting and chafing and making "their usual uproar."

So the novel does not let Dickens off the hook, but he, for the most part, takes advantage of the pressures, intimating the possibility of the transcendence that lies behind the secular but most importantly dramatizing the limits of secularity – no redemptive acts, no heroism, only "a modest life of usefulness and happiness," lived in a world where some few people benefit briefly from that modesty and usefulness, but where the "arrogant and the froward and the vain" remain in command, and it is sufficient even for the best of us to live.

CHAPTER 9

The heartbeat of the squirrel

Have you ever held to your ear a living sparrow, or finch, or warbler and heard its heart beat? Have you ever felt the almost terrifying lightness of those creatures, who, out there at the feeder or among the trees, seem substantial enough? Everything changes once you've done it, as I have done it. The warmth in the feathers could only signify life; but I stilled the bird between fingers whose power I had never imagined before that moment. Each finger weighed orders of magnitude more than the bird, and any one of them might have killed it. I was terrified that in my awkwardness I *would* kill it. Holding a thing so wild and wildly different helpless in my hand, I felt disoriented and awed. That first time I listened to a warbler's heartbeat *my* heart in hiding stirred for the bird. I couldn't guess how many times a second its heart beat, but it seemed that no thing, even in my imagination, could live at so intense a pace. And although the rapping, almost whirring, of the heart was slightly muffled by the layer of delicate feathers, probably heavier than the bird's bone structure, its sound came to me as a roar of energy out of control, more rapid than any machine. The energy was life itself; the bird was overwhelmingly alive.

I've since learned that a house sparrow's heart at rest beats at the rate of 460 a minute. And this bird, smaller than a house sparrow, trapped in my fingers, however helplessly still, was *not* at rest. Confronted with so violently insistent a life in so fragile and feathery a body, I felt that I had found the Darwinian sublime. Darwin spent his life discovering differences, in awe at little things, at pinhead-size barnacles, and worms and bees and ants; and with the bird warm, vital, still at my ear, I experienced that awe viscerally and may even have been hearing the roar that lies on the other side of silence.

That little bird, with whom I became, briefly, so intimate, made all birds yet more strange and beautiful to me. It announced its utter difference simply in the act of being. I've since learned that such birds weigh about ten grams and that they have big hearts for their size (they need them to circulate the blood adequately to sustain them through long flights), and when I see a common bird at my feeder, a house sparrow, or a cardinal, or a titmouse, I think often about that roaring heart while the bird appears to display itself for my admiration of its colors, of its dexterity, almost as though it were ready for Hallmark cards to turn it into a silently pretty and humanly friendly object. But the memory of that heartbeat leaves every bird I see, each with its extraordinary, sublimely intense life, absolutely inaccessible to me and absolutely other. And that encounter with their otherness makes them more, not less, important to me, more liberating, more real. It liberates from the insistent selfness of me. It is an opening, and a mystery.

William Galperin, the distinguished scholar of Romantic literature, seemed to be speaking directly to that experience when he remarked at a literature conference that the closer we look at a subject, the more irreducibly other it becomes. The one thing that roaring heart taught me unequivocally (I not being an absolute solipsist) is that those birds are not me, absolutely not me, and that their behavior has nothing to do with being pretty for people, though one can guess that it has a lot to do with attracting or frightening away other birds. The closer I held it to my ear, the more particularly I could see its feathering and hear its amazing heart, the less possible it became to assimilate it to my way of being. It was an emotional effect, but it was also rather like reading a book with deep attention, or looking intensely at a painting: every inch, every instant is a surprise, a jolt that displaces the self even as it transforms it. I imagine it's rather like the work of good science, as the enormous complexity of the ordinary begins to emerge from what had seemed entirely normal. One learns how things work, to be sure, but with Darwinian awe, as when he talks of the hive making instinct of the bee. "One must be a dull man who can examine the exquisite structure of a comb, so beautifully adapted to its end, without enthusiastic admiration."[1] Of course, Darwin was interested in figuring things out, and he figured out a lot of things, but while he thrillingly imagined the biological connection between human and bee and made Victorian guesses about the reasons for their behavior, he never truly figured out what it was like to be a bee, and never got over the wonder of it.

There is a famous essay by Thomas Nagel, "What is it like to be a bat?" that might help us understand Galperin's apparent paradox, my experience of the bird's heartbeat, George Eliot's squirrel, and the culture of Victorian fiction.[2] My sense of the absolute otherness of the birds

[1]   Charles Darwin, *On the Origin of Species* (Cambridge, MA: Harvard University Press, 1964), p. 224.
[2]   Thomas Nagel, "What is it like to be a bat?" *Philosophical Review*, 83 (October, 1974), p. 435–50.

corresponds to Nagel's philosophical imagination as, by way of bats, he considers the relation between subjectivity and objectivity, between matter and thought.

Nagel denies that any "objective" knowledge of the biological nature of a being – such as the knowledge of the bee's habits at which Darwin marveled – can answer the question, "what is it like to be that being?" It is impossible, on Nagel's account, to move from material, objective fact to consciousness. "At present," he claims, we have "no conception of what an explanation of the physical nature of a mental phenomenon would be." That the bee builds its storage spaces in the form that will take the largest quantities, or that the sparrow's heart is beating 460 times a minute tells us nothing of what it is like to be either bee or sparrow. All we can do is project into the sparrow what *we* would feel like if *our* heart were beating that fast, but then we are not outside ourselves, not objective – we are saying what it would be like *for us* if our hearts beat that fast, not what it is like for the sparrow. The awe we feel, the sense of the sublime that the overwhelming speed of the heart produces, is conditioned by the fact that we live with hearts that beat much less rapidly, not by the subjectivity of the bird. And, Nagel says, until some absolute new breakthrough in studies of subjectivity comes along, we will never know what it feels like to be a bat, to be a sparrow, or to be Mr. Casaubon.

That last is my personal extrapolation from Nagel's argument, for Nagel is primarily interested in the disconnection between the material and any subjective consciousness. He notes that

There is a sense in which phenomenological facts are perfectly objective: one person can know or say of another what the quality of the other's experience is. They are subjective, however, in the sense that even this objective ascription of experience is possible only for someone sufficiently similar to the object of ascription to be able to adopt his point of view – to understand the ascription in the first person as well as in the third, so to speak. The more different from oneself the other experiencer is, the less success one can expect with this enterprise. In our own case we occupy the relevant point of view, but we will have as much difficulty understanding our own experience properly if we approach it from another point of view as we would if we tried to understand the experience of another species without taking up *its* point of view.

The difficulties, as we follow Nagel's arguments, seem insuperable: how is it possible to know real "difference," to enter the consciousnesses and the feelings of the bird, or the bat, or the squirrel, or another human being, like the very different Mr. Casaubon? Yet I read and care about literature because I want to know what it is like to be a bird or a bat or a bee or even Mr. Casaubon, and I want to know what it is like not to be me. Literature at least *tries* to defy Nagel's argument, or, as Nagel doesn't try to do, to make us feel the power of that full otherness he claims belongs to every organism of whom it makes sense to say there is something that it is like to be it. That is, for me, there are two fundamental aspects of literature that make it (and bird watching) irresistible – its defiant effort to create a sense of what it is like to be an other; and its powerful affirmation of the unknowable reality of the other.

Much modern criticism finds hypocrisy or self-deceit where Victorian writers were ostensibly aiming at sympathy and openness. Indeed, if modern criticism's cynicism about sympathy were entirely justified, it would mean that the project of Victorian moral realism was merely deceitful, self-deceitful, or self-congratulatory. If it is right that Victorians' engagement with otherness is simply (or complexly) an affirmation of the self pretending to care or deceiving itself into believing it cares, our best relation to the Victorian novel is probably, as Lennard Davis long ago argued, resistance.[3]

By now we all know the story well, of how Victorian realism was in the end anything but disruptive, and D. A. Miller's *The Novel and the Police*[4] has become the locus classicus for the argument that however resistant and subversive Victorian novels might seem to be, a close look always reveals the controlling police (metaphorical or real) at work. On Miller's account, however beautifully sympathetic it usually is to the particular qualities of the novels, the Victorian realist novel nails us to ourselves, providing a handbook to comportment in the newly bougeoisefied Victorian culture.

It is certainly true that, as William Galperin tries to show in his brilliant recent rereading of Jane Austen's novels, realism is deeply deceptive, if not ultimately outrageously dishonest in attempting to convey the idea that it represents the real adequately while leaving out vast chunks of reality inconvenient for its narratives. It dishonestly allows readers to feel a new breadth of tolerance and openness while quietly reinforcing their old prejudices. Allowing the happy union of Emma Woodhouse and

[3] See Lennard Davis, *Resisting Novels: Ideology and Fiction* (New York: Methuen, 1987). Davis begins by confessing that he is a lover of novels, but in this book he is "attempting to be an enemy of the pleasure of reading" (p.2). He goes on to explain that "in seeking resistance to the novel, I will be developing the idea that the novel is to culture as defenses are to individuals" (p. 2).

[4] D. A. Miller, *The Novel and the Police* (Berkeley: University of California Press, 1988). The work of the Victorian novel, Miller argues, "is to confirm the novel-reader in his identity as 'liberal subject,' a term with which I allude not just to the subject whose private life, mental or domestic, is felt to provide constant inarguable evidence of his constitutive 'freedom,' but also to, broadly speaking, the political regime that sets store by this subject" (p. x).

Mr. Knightley and confirming Knightley's moral judgments and vision, it fends off frank encounters with otherness. The central example Galperin uses here is Miss Bates, that verbose and sadly secondary old maid in *Emma*, who hovers about the margins of the protagonists' concerns. Galperin finds in Miss Bates intimations of an otherness which the realism of Jane Austen's novel largely skirts, a range of possible realities almost entirely neglected by the other characters and, outside of Miss Bates, by the narrator herself.[5] Miss Bates's tedious, wordy babbling is tolerated out of mere politeness by the characters, but more important, is noticed largely as sad, distracting noise by readers, who recognize Miss Bates's importance only as she becomes the butt of Emma's accurate but unkind joke and thus paves the way for the necessary union and comic ending of the novel.

I differ with Galperin only in what this means about realism: for him, the example of Miss Bates is evidence of the inadequacy, indeed the fraudulence of "realism" as it demonstrates its deceptive, indeed dangerous incapacity to represent reality. For me, it is the fullest expression of realism as against the inevitable formal constraints of literary work. Miss Bates gives readers a taste of "that tempting range of relevancies" that good narrators must, it would seem, ignore. "We do not expect people to be deeply moved by what is not unusual," writes George Eliot. Miss Bates is no more unusual than a squirrel, and it is her very sad ordinariness that makes her vulnerable to Emma's gibe. The sparrow with the heart beating at 460 thumps a minute is as banal as anybody's backyard or most city streets. "That element of tragedy which lies in the very fact of frequency, has not yet wrought itself into the coarse emotion of mankind; and perhaps our frames could hardly bear much of it."

I want to emphasize here not simply the very fact of frequency, the ordinariness of Miss Bates, the banality of Casaubon or of the young Fred Vincy, but the squirrel's heartbeat. The common animal, the squirrel, serves well, as does the pesky, ever present house sparrow I invoked at the start. The imaginative leap George Eliot wants her realism to take is the leap by which one comes to know what it is like to be a squirrel. At times we sentimentalize squirrels, and I have seen lots of people laying out peanuts for them, as if, poor things, they were starving and helpless

---

5   William Galperin, *The Historical Austen* (Philadelphia: University of Pennsylvania Press, 2003). Miss Bates, Galperin says, gives us a point of view other than that of the narrator, and she "is a powerful, and one could argue progressive, counter to the novel's 'other' hysteric, Mr. Woodhouse" (p. 191). "What cannot be denied," says Galperin, "is that without Miss Bates, the partialized view of reality that Austen herself is routinely charged with endorsing in her seemingly narrow conceptions of social life and decorum would appear even more partial than it is" (p. 193).

without human aid. But anyone who has watched squirrels at work knows that they are truly wild, utterly regardless of any human constraints (this is particularly hard on people who feed birds, the way I do), extraordinarily adaptive, ferociously tenacious, and their hearts beat almost as fast as some birds', 130 to 450 times a minute. The squirrels turn our gardens into the wild, resist domestication, and are as unknowable as my songbird or Nagel's bat. On George Eliot's account, if we knew what it were like to be a squirrel, if we recognized the needs and pains of its life with the intimacy she tries to provide us in her treatment of, say, Dorothea, or Lydgate, we would die. A condition of our survival is not knowing. A condition of our moral being is an effort to know.

Animals are almost the perfect test of the possibility of achieving the kind of imaginative self-transference that the ideal of Victorian moral realism implies. Nagel's evocation of the bat wildly twisting through one's living room suggests rightly enough that sense of frightened distance between the "us" and the "them"; and animals, like my little bird or George Eliot's squirrel, while not so obviously not-us, are almost absolutely not us. Squirrels are harder to know than Casaubon. And Victorian fiction certainly acts the part of a literature that is full of ostensible feeling but that manages that feeling by assimilating the animal to human purposes. Harriet Ritvo's wonderful books on taxonomy and animals provide overwhelming and fascinating evidence that animals, in Victorian society (and I expect it is not much different for our own) serve very social and ideological purposes. For me – as lover of that alien heart-thumping bird – they become then something of a depressing experience despite their brilliance, or perhaps because of it. For what she shows, in chapter after brilliant chapter, is the way nineteenth-century culture "used" animals, turned them almost always to social purposes. Her wonderfully titled first chapter, "The Nature of the Beast," tells us not about the nature of the beast – according to Nagel a non-starter – but about humans' changed relations to the beast as nature became increasingly tamed and animals thus decreasingly threatening. *The Animal Estate* shows us animals serving to represent the moral hierarchies of human society, to confirm humans' superior status, to justify and celebrate the expansion of the empire. Animals, Ritvo reminds us, "never talk back."[6]

---

[6] Harriet Ritvo, *The Animal Estate: the English and other Creatures in the Victorian Age* (Cambridge, MA: Harvard University Press, 1987). See also, *The Platypus and the Mermaid, and other figments of the Classifying Imagination* (Cambridge: Cambridge University Press, 1997).

Thus, while it is certain that urban Victorians had a much fuller experience of animals than modern city dwellers do, and while their streets were full of horse manure, and even urbanites might breed chickens and pigs at home, the animals were domesticated and tamed and either humanized or eaten or beaten or hunted or all of the above. There were zoological exhibitions and there were the menageries that Ritvo has discussed, but those turn out to have been places in which "the conquests of . . . more fortunate countrymen" were symbolically celebrated, or where visitors came to feel part of the empire's triumphs. One looks hard to find encounters with animals that register the integrity of the animal itself. Domestic animals, of course, were bred to satisfy the needs of their masters, and it took a Sikes, fleeing police and the searching mobs, to drive a Victorian dog away from his master.

Characteristically, Victorian literary animals reflect the needs and values of their owners. So Diogenes, the more or less untamed dog in *Dombey and Son*, "scrambling" to his window to see Carker approaching, tells us all we need to know about Carker, for, in spite of "all soothing," Diogenes "barks and growls, and makes at him from that height, as if he would spring down and tear him limb from limb."[7] And here is how Florence is introduced to the clumsy bad tempered dog: "'Come then, Di! Dear Di! Make friends with your new mistress. Let us love each other, Di!'" said Florence, fondling his shaggy head. And Di, the rough and gruff, as if his hairy hide were pervious to the tear that dropped upon it, and dog's heart melted as it fell, put his nose up to her face, and swore fidelity" (ch. 18, p. 280). Or consider how, in *Lady Audley's Secret*, Alicia's dog responds to the otherwise almost universally loved Lady Audley: "The Newfoundland rolled his eyes slowly round in the direction of the speaker, as if he understood every word that had been said. Lady Audley happened to enter the room at this very moment, and the animal cowered down by the side of his mistress with a suppressed growl. There was something in the manner of the dog which was, if anything, more indicative of terror than of fury, incredible as it appears that Caesar should be frightened of so fragile a creature as Lucy Audley."[8] That's all we need to know about Lady Audley. But what do we know about Caesar in all his Newfoundland dogginess?

Literature works at the illusion that you can get outside of yourself by getting you inside characters ostensibly alien to you, distant from you. The act of knowing what it is to be something else is also an act of not being

---

[7] Charles Dickens, *Dombey and Son* (London: Penguin Books, 2002), Ch. 22, p. 349.
[8] Mary Elizabeth Braddon, *Lady Audley's Secret* (New York: Dover Books, 1974), ch. 14, p. 70.

oneself, of, for a moment, shaking oneself loose from the absolute and apparently inescapable egocentric predicament. Wanting to know what it is like not to be me is the corollary of wanting full sympathetic understanding of something that is not-me. But it is not quite the same thing. There's an epistemological question here, a question that haunts Victorian realist fiction, and it's an ethical one as well. It's the "Why Always Dorothea" question, compounded by the problem of whether it's at all possible to know anything else. It's the question about Mr. Casaubon's "equivalent center of self." I take this *kind* of question to be the critical point of Victorian realism, and I take that point to have the moral force George Eliot accorded to it. But they are really two different questions: one, can we imagine other people's ways of being with a sympathy or, better, an empathy that allows us to feel them as though we are they? Two, can we recognize the absolute otherness of other beings and accept it without attempting to assimilate the otherness into us, without making it an aspect of ourselves, a part of the habitual selfness of our own being?

Let us take for granted what some would want to argue, that the great achievement of Victorian realism is precisely this power of imagining what Nagel says we can't know, what it is like to be – a Casaubon, a Sikes, a Mr. Merdle, a Eustacia Vye, even a Grandcourt, and of course a Maggie Tulliver, a Little Dorrit, a Tess Durbeyfield. And let's, for the sake of this argument, grant that we can even know what it is to be one of those animals, who seem so preternaturally human, Diogenes, and Caesar, and Mrs. Merdle's parrot.

The second question I've posed rarely gets asked, implicitly or not, in Victorian literature, or perhaps in any literature; it barely seems to get recognized as a possible question.[9] Realism's preoccupation with understanding other consciousnesses, blossoming through the nineteenth century into full scale psychological novels that begin to make realism itself seem unrealistic, requires elaborate strategies for knowing the other, strategies that assume knowability in the first place, and do not stop with Nagel's notion that one cannot know what it feels like to be a bat – or a complex human being thoroughly different from oneself. The best of us are well-wadded with stupidity, and so George Eliot assumes that

---

[9]   In an interesting discussion of the ethics of literature, Derek Attridge addresses both kinds of recognition of otherness very usefully: "To act morally toward other persons entails, it hardly needs saying, as full an attempt at understanding them and their situation as one is capable of; yet both the primary claim of another person upon and the final measure of one's behavior lies in the response to, and affirmation of, the otherness which resists that understanding." Derek Attridge, *The Singularity of Literature* (London: Routledge, 2004), p. 129.

intelligence and moral sympathy will open to us a world so multiple, so complex, so full of pain that we could not endure it. We manage by not hearing the squirrel's heart beat and we focus our attention on "this particular web" of narration that excludes many other worlds full of life. It is interesting and important, I think, that George Eliot uses an animal, the squirrel, to represent that which we do not know, which we can barely imagine, barely dare to imagine.

George Eliot's squirrel is like my bird. We are all well-wadded with stupidity, not only the kind of insuperable stupidity that Nagel's essay attempts to describe, but the stupidity of an egoism that keeps us stupid so that we won't die of the roar. As narrator, George Eliot chooses "this particular web" over "the tempting range of relevancies called the universe." It is perhaps the only way to write a novel, but that of course begins to call into question the idea of realism. If we were to listen to the squirrel's heart beat we would be in touch with something equivalently real, "an equivalent center of self."

I am guessing that those birds with the astonishing hearts have equivalent centers of self also, but it's only a guess, of course. It's an ethical bet. The bird and that damned squirrel devouring all the feed I've set out for the birds matter as much as I do. That is, from their point of view in so far as their point of view is knowable at all. I really can't know what it is like to be one of those animals, though Victorian realism tends to simplify the job by humanizing them. What is important, however – and here we move just a step beyond where George Eliot felt obliged to take us – is that we feel the reality of the not-me that the bird might be taken to be, that we recognize it as part of that tempting range of relevancies. Perhaps we can't after all even know what it's like to be Casaubon or any other human either, but the work of Victorian realist literature is in large part to battle the solipsist model. Is there a way, with sad Gwendolen Harleth at the end of *Daniel Deronda*, to recognize that our horizons "are but a dipping onward of an existence with which [our] own was revolving"?[10] Beyond that, can we register that "existence" with something like joy (as I registered the beating of the songbird's heart), without really knowing what it is, as Dickens can know what Diogenes is, or Mary Braddon can know what Caesar is?

I do not want for an instant to minimize the project and achievement of the Victorian realism that aspired to know the other and the different, to make us feel what it is like to be a Casaubon or any of the host of

---

[10]   George Eliot, *Daniel Deronda* (Oxford: Oxford World Classics, 1984), ch. 69, p. 689.

characters that give Victorian fiction its peculiar distinction. But I want to argue beyond that first great achievement of Victorian moral realism that the greatest Victorian fiction aspires to the recognition and honoring of *unknowable* others. The most prolonged and intense struggle, manifesting itself in remarkable new ways to explore consciousness, to discover the other, *be* the other, through free indirect discourse brought to a new peak of artfulness by Henry James, or stream of consciousness, which became so important early in the twentieth century. But there was and always would be a residuum of otherness that will not bend to explorations of consciousness. The greatest Victorian fiction reaches beyond its own deep humanity to the recognition of other, unknowable realities. It is the ultimate end of realism, an end that seems to drive realism outside of itself but that, even as it goes to produce other forms, remains allied to the realistic imagination. We may be well-wadded with stupidity, but we know that the squirrel's heart is beating irrelevantly to our stories, to the realism that makes it into narrative; and that recognition of the reality of the irrelevant is the ultimate end and rarely achieved object of realism.

Nothing could do more to deflate our hopeless and inescapable egocentrism than to follow George Eliot's line into this second level of anti-egoism. Several years ago, Andrew Miller gave a talk that cited Kierkegaard's *Sickness unto Death* describing despair as the condition of man's being nailed to himself. I am not a Kierkegaardian but I sometimes think of the inescapability of selfhood, and of Victorian realism's rigorous efforts to open out to a not self that is not *only*, not *merely*, sympathy, but a profound recognition of existences with which the self is revolving – hearing that roar of the birds and the squirrel's heart – if only at moments, of course. All the time would be too much, and we would die of that roar, as George Eliot warns us.

As I seek, with George Eliot's determination, to come to understand Casaubon's otherness, his sensitivity to pain and shame, his anxiety and jealousies and meanness, or whatever he might be feeling that escapes even the narrator's judgment of him, I want to be able to value him not as he serves as stand in, say, for my sense of myself, my worst self, and not as the petty villain over whom we want our favorites to triumph, but rather as a reality of difference, another world whose presence I must register, and whose distinctive not-me-ness can give me my deepest sense of reality.

Victorian realism became the dominant literary mode of its time because it promised entrance to other worlds, not mere fantasies, which are clearly human projections, but "the real thing." It promised to break through the limits of individual consciousness to reveal the reality of other lives. While it gave dignity (or at least publicity) to the details of its readers' lives by setting them in the center of narratives about more or less ordinary people,[11] while it confirmed or affirmed for the first time the value of the quotidian, while it transformed the ordinary into satisfying human drama, it also threatened at every moment to violate the quotidian complacency by intimating realities we had not known or had ignored. The greatest realist works aspire to be uncomfortable. We all know that Victorian realist fiction almost always resolves into a comfortable balance of virtue and justice, but I want to insist here that in the process of doing so it frequently imagines, in a way that becomes permanently threatening, realities that remain to trouble our happy endings because they cannot be assimilated to ourselves.

Darwin anthropomorphized and in fact did some of his most interesting work by virtue of seeing animals as having human qualities. His theory is the titanically anthropomorphic theory of all theories: we are all, humans and all living things, of one literal family. His theory of sexual selection, as I have argued elsewhere, depends on the projection of human values and desires into animals like peahens and pheasants. But the response of a Victorian audience sufficiently enamored of animals to hamper seriously British science's efforts at vivisection for scientific purposes, was horror at the idea that they too might be descended from the animals they otherwise cared for so much. These responses fully justify Ritvo's studies of how animals were absorbed into the social and cultural ideals of the humans who captured, studied, destroyed (and occasionally loved) them. The enormous difficulty evident in Victorian fiction of allowing animals their own intrinsic natures had much to do with the terror of finding oneself an animal after all.

Moments in which animals, as animals inaccessible in Nagelian ways, emerge are in fact rare in Victorian fiction. But, occasionally, one can find them elsewhere – in Melville's *Moby Dick*, for example, where the dumb white whale cannot even answer to Ahab's idea of evil; or in Faulkner's story, "The Bear," as it appears in *Go Down Moses*. The old bear becomes a

[11] In her most recent book, *How Novels Think*, Nancy Armstrong argues that the novel as a form in effect created the sense of individuality that we all take for granted, imagined protagonists as individuals capable of shaping their own fates, responding to constraints. The novel and the development of the "modern subject" are one. Skeptical about the nature of the "individual," arguing that the "individual" is a figure created by and naturalized by the novel, Armstrong sees the danger of the exclusions of alternative possibilities of imagining the individual and the self, and the often damaging effect individualism has had historically, socially, culturally. Once again, the emphasis is on the large ideological dangers of the novel. See *How Novels Think: The Limits of Individualism from* 1719–1900 (New York: Columbia University Press, 2005).

condition of Ike McCaslin's growth to maturity, an initiation rite: "I will have to see him" (p. 204), the ten-year-old says to himself. These are stories of human rituals, but they depend on the living reality of whale and bear; maturity is registered as the recognition of absolute otherness. The confrontation with these great beasts teaches humans how to recognize and respect that otherness. Culturally speaking, such stories, built on respect for wildness and the nonhuman, are probably historically consequent upon the widespread taming of the wilderness and domestication of animals, or caging them. But they insistently, thematically, require the sort of respect for difference implied by George Eliot's squirrel, but more scarily because they are dangerous. On the most literal level, all of this must also have to do with the nature of America, with its remaining wildernesses, and with a broad range of animals still dangerous and out in the wild. But most important, for the purposes of this argument, is that both these stories in effect accept Nagle's view of whether one can know what it is like to be a bat, and they turn it to the anti-egoist energies that was the grand ideal of Victorian realism.

Ike as a child growing to manhood relinquishes completely to the wilderness. He removes the taint of his last connection to civilization, the watch and the compass, and he gets lost. Only then, refusing fear but obviously in danger, does he see the bear, in one of the great moments of American literature. "It did not emerge, appear: it was just there" (p. 209). There is no panic, no rush on either side. It is a moment that one won't find in Victorian literature, and yet it achieves something that, as I see it, lies at the far end of the Victorian realist ideal – the imagination of two creatures recognizing and respecting their mutual reality, and passing each other quietly. Each grows as a consequence, or at least, the boy grows, achieving that sense of an existence revolving with his own that might be taken as threatening but that, requiring and evoking respect, passes quietly on.

It is striking, however, that such moments appear in narratives that, formally speaking, utterly reject the conventions of Victorian realism. Crudely put, Ike's story, like *Moby Dick*, is a romance, a narrative that works itself out in a ritual that leaves behind it all the conventional explanatory force of cultural and social context. In realist narrative, animals will, almost inevitably, be absorbed and adapted, as Ritvo shows they were adapted historically, to human ends, and they will absorb the projections of human feelings and desires that the Bear and the whale resist.

But if one looks, one can find in the corners of much Victorian fiction some intimations of the sort of reality intimated by the Bear and the

Whale, though of course not with such massive and ritualized power. The Miss Bateses, marginalized and perhaps only tempting relevancies, emerge often, sometimes with thematic deliberation, sometimes not. Barbara Hardy long ago argued that "there is something wrong with a critical account of a novel which mentions only those details and images which fit into a symbolic series or a codifiable moral argument."[12] And while she was after other game, the point holds true in particular for those instances, in largely realist novels, that resist meaning, the encounters with things that lie on the outskirts of this particular web. Thomas Hardy is to the point here, for while his novels are usually very highly formalized, there are moments that register just the animal difference that has such powerful symbolic force in romance. There is that moment, for example, in *Tess*, somehow deeply moving and profoundly non-human, when Tess, walking through the fields toward the sound of Angel Clare's "strumming of strings," in a kind of exalted sensuous rapture, "went stealthy as a cat through this profusion of growth, gathering cuckoo-spittle on her skirts, cracking snails that were underfoot."[13] It's a remarkable and beautiful passage and obviously has direct thematic relevance to Tess's sensuality and to her obviously sexual attraction to Angel, but at the same time it offers us more than we need, in particular, it offers us a reality to which Tess does not attend, the lives of those snails whose shells she was cracking underfoot, the living slugs that she brushed past (who knew that slugs produced slug-slime?) and insect secretions. In her own self-enclosed passion, Tess does not recognize the existences with whose world she is revolving, and while all of that in the passage contributes to the extraordinary sensuosity that drives Tess, it evokes another world for which Hardy's narrative cannot stop, but whose existence is part of our discovery as we read. Not exactly Moby Dick, to be sure, but one of those grace notes, often integral to full realist work, that allows us once again to ask, why always Dorothea, or why always Tess.

There is an even more striking instance (in fact several instances) in *A Pair of Blue Eyes*. In one of those amazing scenes of Hardy's in which spies are spying on spies who are spying on . . . Hardy describes the meeting of Stephen's friend Knight with Elfride in a gazebo at night:

The scratch of a striking light was heard, and a glow radiated from the interior of the building. The light gave birth to dancing leaf-shadows, stem-shadows,

[12]   Barbara Hardy, *The Appropriate Form* (London: The Athlone Press, 1964), p. 13.
[13]   Thomas Hardy, *Tess of the D'Urbervilles* (New York: Oxford World Classics, 1988), ch. 19, p. 127.

lustrous streaks, dots, sparkles, and threads of silver-sheen of all imaginable variety and transience. It awakened gnats, which flew toward it, revealed shiny gossamer threads, disturbed earthworms. Stephen gave but little attention to these phenomena, and less time. He saw in the summer-house a strongly illuminated picture.[14]

For what, I asked myself when I first read it, do we need those gnats and earthworms and spider webs? It is obviously the Hardyesque beautiful and I wouldn't have surrendered the paragraph for the whole plot, but it's important that Stephen noticed none of this astonishing life, aroused by the main characters' actions. Nor does Mrs. Jethway, who is similarly spying on Elfride. There is a life beyond the narrative, insisting on its life, giving life to the book that doesn't really need it. Hardy is the most insistent of the Victorian novelists on the life that exists outside the range of the protagonists' consciousness, and here he evokes a whole world utterly indifferent to the complex love relations being woven and unwoven. Now of course, not even this passage asks us what it is like to be a gnat or an earthworm (though we can remember how Darwin played music to earthworms). But it does make us profoundly alert to other forms of life than ours that, even in their minuteness, diminish our own importance by not caring about us.

But for me, the most forceful parallel in Victorian fiction to the great American romance encounters with the wildly non-human energies of animals is, of all things, Heathcliff, in *Wuthering Heights*. Unlike some recent criticism that reads Heathcliff, legitimately, into history and race relations, I want for a moment to consider why it is that despite the fact that he is ruthlessly cruel, and even hangs puppies – realist animals – Heathcliff is so romantically forceful a figure. It is not that he looks like Laurence Olivier, or even that as a child he was abused by Hareton, but that he is, finally, utterly incomprehensible, as is the first Catherine. Right from the start, even the dense Lockwood thinks, "I bestow my own attributes over-liberally on him."[15] Almost the first scene is of a barely domesticated dog, a "ruffianly bitch," and two "grim, shaggy sheep dogs" that go after Lockwood. It matters to my point that they are not even given names. Heathcliff and Catherine are passionate figures whose passions are equally unnamed and unexplained. They are marked, Heathcliff completely, Catherine partially, by their utter incompatibility with realist narrative subjects. The book refuses to explain where Heathcliff comes

[14] Thomas Hardy, *A Pair of Blue Eyes* (London: Macmillan, 1975), ch. 25, p. 267.
[15] Emily Brontë, *Wuthering Heights* (London: Penguin Books, 2003), ch 1, p. 6.

from; it refuses to explain where he goes or how he becomes successful after he flees the Heights; it refuses even to attribute motives of revenge to him, though those are clear enough; but certainly it refuses to explain the excesses except in that they have something to do with his non-sexual passion for Cathy. Here is one of those books in which, while it is easy to project motives into the figures, motives are refused, explanations withheld. Heathcliff is simply a powerful, dangerous figure whose action might mark him as a villain in a Scott novel, perhaps, but whose villainy is not even explained as villainy but leaves him, for generations to follow, enormously attractive. *Wuthering Heights* is a romance. The wildness is juxtaposed with the convention, with Lockwood's trivial romanticizing, with Nelly's assumption of normal moral values, with Isabella's misguided romanticizing, with Edgar's aspiration to domestic decency. Heathcliff is a kind of Moby Dick, though with malice aforethought. He represents, in a way, the danger that engagement with an utterly unknowable other always entails. He thus steps outside both the conventions of Victorian narrative and, for the readers, the limits of the self nailed to the self.

I take this excess to be the outer limit, the ultimate ideal, of Victorian realist narrative, even as it deliberately exploits and rejects the dominant conventions by which Victorian realism tries to imply the possibility of knowing the other and to anthropomorphize and domesticate. Victorian realism tries hard to explain things and through explanation to get us out of ourselves. There's little space in it for dangerously unknowable forms of life, and so it perhaps makes sense to close here, after circumventing the topic of Victorian animals for quite a while, with another not quite Victorian animal, D. H. Lawrence's "St. Mawr."

No need here to get into Lawrence's peculiar sensuous mysticism, or even to deal with some of what I regard as pretty absurd commentary in this short novel about the absence of real men in the modern world. But I do want to emphasize that in order to do the work he thinks needs to get done in relation to Victorian realism, Lawrence has recourse to a particularly difficult and powerful horse, St. Mawr. The horse cries out to be taken as a symbol, just as the great white whale did. It doesn't like to be touched; it refuses to respond to the decadent Rico, the protagonist, Lou's, husband. It does Lou's work by throwing Rico off and wounding him and thus opening the way for Lou to leave. But like the bear and the whale, St. Mawr is both distinctly a protagonist and *not* human, not, in being whatever it is that he is like, part of the plot, and he disappears from the story toward the end. What is required is the sort of intelligent and profoundly physical attention that Lewis, the groom, and Phoenix, his

American-Indian counterpart, give him. "I don't know one single man," says the protagonist Lou, "who is a proud living animal."[16] St. Mawr is a proud living animal.

To be such is to step outside of Victorian fiction and outside Victorian realism. As much as the story, *St. Mawr*, is a parable of the decay of maleness and of modernity itself, it is also a critique of Victorian realism (in which, it is important to remember, the male protagonists are notoriously weak and indecisive), and it takes a dumb, proud horse to justify the critique. Lawrence is tired of "mind," as is Lou, of course. When Lou's mother counters, "Man is wonderful because he is able to think," a distinctly Victorian view of things (p. 48), Lou replies, "But is he?" Men and their thinking are "paltry," she claims. Thinking and physicality are, in Lawrence's view, mutually dependent, and thinking that is not paltry does not require words at all.

So Lawrence does not try to "explain" St. Mawr. He is dangerous to conventional people, to people who talk endlessly about ideas or behavior or things. To escape the general rot of chit chat and triviality, the conventional life of moral placing, Lawrence substitutes a *Noli me tangere* – nobody among the good guys in the book wants to be touched. What is essential is a retreat into solitude – "retreat to the desert," says the narrator – for purification and resistance. The horse's very silence recommends it to Lawrence. But of course, the narrative that describes *St. Mawr* is outside the realm of realism, critiques it more overtly but with the same sort of intensity and contempt that Emily Brontë employs. The realist world is dead; the only life is in the horse, and it is valuable just because it cannot be explained in terms that would work in realism. "I love St Mawr," says Lou, "because he isn't intimate. He stands where one can't get him. And he burns with life" (p. 49).

That was how I felt when I held that bird, whom I *could* touch literally but whom, in some fuller sense, I could not touch at all. Of course, when one reflects on this imagination of utter difference, of impenetrable not-meness that can't be assimilated, one is in the end still using for human and even personal purposes the animal that requires of realists, and of romantics like Lawrence and, I hope, of us all – the bird, the squirrel, the gnat, the whale, the bear, the horse – the fullest respect for its difference and its reality. It was hard for the Victorians to let go of the selves they wanted to transcend. They could only do it in moments, and Lawrence, in loving the horse, could only do so by assimilating it to the self that needed transcendence. But the Victorians, and Lawrence – we too – are only human.

---

[16]   D. H. Lawrence, *"St Mawr" and "The Man who Died"* (New York: Vintage Books, 1953), p. 50.

CHAPTER 10

Real toads in imaginary gardens, or vice versa

I believe that at the heart of Coetzee's manner, his style, his themes, there is a fundamental insistence on, a passionate demand for the real. Nobody, of course, is more self-conscious about the nature of narrative, about the fluidity with which words and things pass into each other, about the complexities of writing, or about the elusive and literary character of the real. Nobody is more quietly self-reflexive, more preoccupied with the problems of art and writing. Derek Attridge is obviously right to focus on the way the narratives in *Elizabeth Costello* are preoccupied with "what it means to commit oneself to a life of writing."[1] In Coetzee's recent novel, *Slow Man*, Elizabeth Costello appears as a character who, Bartleby-like, moves in on the main character, Paul, who thinks that she is watching him simply to get material for a novel; we watch her and him, sensing that it is all a novel that Costello is in fact writing under the hand of Coetzee, but compellingly engaged with what lies beyond words. It is dizzying in a Borgesian way.

But there is a sequence in *Slow Man* that focuses a particular and growingly important aspect of Coetzee's art and that might be taken as a central quality of what makes writing and life matter. It has to do with animals, a subject that since the publication of the lecture/essay, "The Lives of Animals," has been recognized as a particular and sometimes perplexing preoccupation of Coetzee, even in novels that seem to have little to do with them. Costello is urging the protagonist, Paul, to act, to make a choice, "do something." Paul cynically but convincingly responds, "so that you can put me in a book?" To which Elizabeth answers, "So that someone, somewhere *might* put you in a book."[2] Such a passage, while seeming to urge the importance of action as opposed to language, or

---

[1] Derek Attridge, *J. M. Coetzee and the Ethics of Reading* (Chicago: University of Chicago Press, 2004), p. 200.
[2] J. M. Coetzee, *Slow Man* (New York: Viking, 2005), p. 229.

action as a condition for language, is giddying in its self-reflexiveness because here, engaged in ethical battle, are two figures *in* a book, one whose life extends back into *another* book composed largely of lectures that Coetzee was supposed to give in different venues and that might have been expected to be non-fiction, but were not.

Coetzee plays with "reality," and expectations about it, but certainly writes as though the fictional is our best way into the real. The most striking aspect of the passage is Costello's way of trying to convince Paul to act: "Consider: somewhere in a jungle in Maharashtra State a tiger is this very moment opening its amber eyes, *and it is not thinking of you at all!*" (p. 229).

For Coetzee language and action and being and not-being are intricately and always inseparable. The exchange between Paul and Elizabeth is far too complicated and fluid to be centered on this one image, but it is the intensity of the image – the "amber eyes" of the tiger – that most vividly catches attention; and it is surely related to a passage in the last chapter of Coetzee's *Elizabeth Costello*, the Kafkaeasque "At the gate." When pressed in her last hearing before the board that is to decide whether Costello is to pass into the eternity that lies, apparently, on the other side of the "Gates," to say what she believes, she offers this stunning and, it would seem, half mad response: "What do I believe? I believe in those little frogs." The "little frogs" emerge when the torrential rains after the scorching droughts of rural Victoria subside and leave behind "acres of mud." "At night," she says, "you would hear the belling of tens of thousands of little frogs rejoicing in the largesse of the heavens. The air would be dense with their calls as it was at noon with the rasping of cicadas." The frogs, she says, are always there, but underground in dry season. Costello describes how they live down there, and how they die, as "their heartbeat slows, their breathing stops, they turn the colour of mud."[3] It is a characteristically beautiful and terrible Coetzee passage in which Costello is uncharacteristically, as she admits, open and florid. She recalls her childhood encounters with those frogs, "some as small as the tip of my little finger, creatures so insignificant and so remote from your loftier concerns that you would not hear of them otherwise. In my account, for whose many failings I beg your pardon, the life cycle of the frog may sound allegorical, but to the frogs themselves it is no allegory, it is the thing itself, the only thing." "What do I believe? I believe in those little frogs." Frogs and tigers. Things in themselves. Minds unlike ours, unnoticed and unnoted except as allegories for us. Allegorically imagined but not allegorical. It is not the

[3] J. M. Coetzee, *Elizabeth Costello* (New York: Viking, 2003), pp. 216–17.

allegory that Costello believes in, though she has implied it. Blake's tiger burning bright is not only insistently real: it is fundamentally unrelated to its allegorist.

Of course, there is no escaping the allegorical energy of fiction, and certainly not of Coetzee, who makes of "Before the Gate" a strangely allusive and literary chapter. It is impossible to ignore the non-realist aspect of the narrative in which the protagonist seems to be called to account before the ultimate Judge, in a narrative that obviously (and overtly) imitates Kafka, who is mentioned several times, but also the most fundamental Western myths of Judgment. In this context, the "animal" seems to be translated into something that belongs to human consciousness and that thus helps the writer, the human, make sense of the world. And yet the fundamental fact of the almost unintelligible world is the absolute difference of the animal from the human mind that conceives it, a difference that gives Costello a model for a kind of writing that struggles to *avoid* allegory, the translation of other things, other lives, into the work of human consciousness. Earlier realism was also not strictly allegorical, but one of the key differences with Coetzee is how immediately foregrounded the question is. Costello self-consciously tries not to make the animals she talks about signify anything but themselves – how successfully she does that is open to question, if only by Costello herself.

Coetzee and Costello struggle toward the not-self, toward the paradoxical imagination of intense life and otherness. It is something like this unimaginably different thing toward which Costello aspires that gives its fullest ethical force to Coetzee's painful and often pained commitment to a life of writing. We all recognize the astringent, brilliantly uninflected prose, the austere pellucid narration that marks almost all of Coetzee's work. It is a prose that makes of his realism something decidedly different from that of the Victorians. If both of them are deeply concerned with ethical problems, and problems of feeling, the Victorians make the feeling part of the style and the overt subject of the "representation" of things. In Coetzee (and clearly in the writing of Costello) the feeling is rigorously excluded (in the interests, one suspects, of a yet deeper and more difficult feeling). One can hear in Costello's austerity something of the passion for access to the not-self, the lambent eyes of the tiger awakening and not thinking of him at all. (Even the idea of "access" is inadequate to the effort, which seems to be directed toward the imagination of a reality that lies beyond any of the self-preoccupations of the human and toward, therefore, the most complete ethical – and epistemological – achievement, which would be simply to know that there is a deep reality that we don't, cannot, and perhaps must not know.) The fullest achievement of the realist, which Attridge has reminded us Coetzee always is (no matter what else he is) is his own disappearance – the vivid absorption into absolute otherness. Of course, there is something oxymoronic about the whole enterprise, something else, I believe, that Coetzee fully understands and tries to work out in different ways in different narratives.

Attridge has talked about the fusion of the ethical and the literary in Coetzee's work. That is right, and the fusion happens particularly just in the sort of images I have cited from his last two books. "It is because of the indifference of those little frogs to my belief (all they want from life is a chance to gobble down mosquitoes and sing; and the males among them, the ones who do most of the singing, sing not to fill the night air with melody but as a form of courtship, for which they hope to be rewarded with orgasm (the frog variety of orgasm, again and again and again) – it is because of their indifference to me that I believe in them."

The ultimate condition of objectivity is one's own irrelevance to what is known. The passage is obviously self-contradictory in that even in insisting on that indifference and difference Costello is anthropomorphizing, as the frogs *want* to sing and "gobble." Costello writes as though she knows what the frogs want, while wanting to know that she doesn't. And yet of course it is the only way to register the difference, to show them wanting *not* us, to show them not thinking about us, to show them being unselfconscious and merely animal and having only the "frog variety" of orgasm. No doubt the character Costello and Coetzee himself understand this contradiction. Costello apologizes for making her argument in what she calls "a lamentably literary" (p. 217) sort of way.

To make this argument about what I take to be an absolutely central quality of Coetzee's work, though I have based it so far only on a couple of metaphors, it might be useful, if perhaps a bit irregular in a piece of *literary* criticism, to relate a little anecdote of my experience in meeting Coetzee, an anecdote that might help to make sense of his preoccupations with what is not relevant to his protagonists, and in particular with animals; it might help make sense, as well, of Coetzee's profound ethical and aesthetic commitment to absolute otherness. Several years ago, I was invited to speak at a conference designed to inaugurate a new humanities center at Dartmouth. The featured speaker was to be J. M. Coetzee, and I was eager to hear him and perhaps meet him. As we walked into the auditorium for the occasion, I turned to a friend and asked whether he thought this would be a "real lecture" on the humanities, as the title in the program suggested, or whether it might be, like "The Lives of Animals" lecture I had recently read, a story, though the story had been delivered originally as a lecture of Coetzee's. After the usual sort of academic introduction (brilliantly imitated in the "novel," *Elizabeth Costello*), Coetzee was presented and began without prelude or flourish or explanation, "She had not seen her sister in twelve years."

The startling unlecturelike sentence, quietly unremarkable, clearly shocked the audience and tore it out of the conventions of lecture-going to which – virtually all academics – we were entirely habituated. (Attridge reports the same experience when he went to hear Coetzee deliver "The Lives of Animals" lecture.) It was hard to know how to listen. We were not getting a lecture, but a story. But were we? Given current literary/theoretical complexity and expertise, we might well want to break down the hard distinction between lecture and story. Lectures are also fictions, one might claim, rhetorically different but in the end telling a kind of documented story after all. The effect on the audience made clear that everyone understood the difference – it was felt rather than theorized. But there must also remain a sense of difference in that the lecture makes truth claims and a story does not (yet, of course, it might work the other way around, too). The lecture may be wrong, and untrue in that sense, but for the most part we know that it is an argument, or an exposition, and it is engaged beyond the limits of its prose in some rhetorical invasion of a non-verbal world. The speaker intervenes directly in an argument. The story teller, Elizabeth Costello claims, is simply describing. "I do imitations, as Aristotle might have said." Yet in the story Coetzee read to us in place of a conventional lecture, it is impossible not to take seriously an overwhelming conviction that Elizabeth Costello's sister, Blanche, or Sister Bridget, means what she says. And what she says is acerbic, virtually an attack on the audience gathered to listen to Coetzee. The fiction is in a real garden, or so it seems. And it feels as though the fiction is pushing against the real, making it be yet more real by tearing away at the disguises and fictions and conventions that have made the event possible.

The audience listened with far more strained attentiveness than lecture audiences normally give, and took Sister Bridget's searing and painful attack on the humanities like a series of body blows, as if Sister Bridget weren't a fiction at all. Although they are deadlocked in antipathetic visions of the world, Bridget and Elizabeth share the same straightforwardness, the same austerity, the same willingness to say things unpleasant to listening ears, but without venom or violence, if anything with a sense of being compelled to speak the truth and of almost wishing it weren't she telling it. Listening with excitement and fascination to Coetzee quietly reading his story, I could imagine then what it must have felt like to be in the audience when Elizabeth Costello gave her "lives of animals" lecture at Princeton, or was it Appleton College?

It is hard to capture the quality and effect of detachment that marks Coetzee's prose representing these women. There, for the opening of a humanities center intended to celebrate and extend the work of the humanities, Coetzee dispassionately mouths the words of a speaker who says flat out, I "have no message of comfort to bring to you, despite the generosity of the gesture you have extended to me. The message I bring is that you lost your way long ago . . . The *studia humanitas* have taken a long time to die, but now, at the end of the second millennium of our era, they are truly on their deathbed. All the more bitter should be that death, I would say, since it has been brought about by the monster enthroned by those very studies as first and animating principle of the universe." The monster she names is "reason, mechanical reason" (p. 123).

Sister Bridget's rejection of secular literature circles around the mutual quest of the humanities and religion for the *word*. She knows, as Elizabeth knows, that in writing we seek the "word." The original humanists sought what she calls "the True Word, by which they understood then, and I understand now, the redemptive word." Elizabeth Costello, like her sister, seeks the word, and one might even say, the redemptive word, even though it might be a *different* word, and she persistently renounces belief. But for her the redemptive word always implies a self and self-consciousness that keeps her and us from the real thing, the real tiger and the real frog. As a writer, her job is to find the words that get us as close to that real thing as possible. The act is both aesthetic and ethical, one might say that it would be as close as Coetzee might come to the redemptive, in the worlds he describes that are so desperately in need of redemption, and so certainly without it.

When Coetzee stopped reading, the moderator acted as though we had just heard a normal lecture and invited questions. It was a difficult moment. Coetzee's answers were barely answers at all. It is as if he were as Elizabeth Costello was to be later, "At the Gate." It seemed as though he knew nothing about the story he had just read, about the characters in it, or about what Sister Bridget had said. It seemed as though he believed nothing. It was as though he wasn't there. There wasn't much use in pursuing the usual pattern of academic lectures, and we all adjourned. Though I rarely do such a thing, I made a point afterwards of approaching Coetzee as we were all having the requisite drinks and snacks. I was embarrassed but put to him how stunning and moving I had found his presentation, and – perhaps because I was a man of an age – he engaged me in what felt to me to be a personal and deeply felt conversation, largely about aging, and he promised to send me yet another Elizabeth Costello talk, the one on realism, that opens the book with this telling sentence: "There is first of all the problem of the opening, namely, how to get us from where we are, which is, as yet, nowhere, to the far bank" (p. 1). The book then begins with Elizabeth Costello, "in the far territory, where we want to be." Coetzee did indeed send me that essay, first published I think in *Salmagundi*. I was touched that he remembered. It was important to me and I am convinced he knew that and therefore acted on it. He had given me the feeling, which I bear with me to this day, that he is a man saturated with the sense of the other, a good man, a man strained to work out the terrible seriousness of committing himself to the life of a writer, which means seeking always, somehow, impossibly, to know what it is to be that tiger with the lambent eyes to whom he is nothing.

That of course is merely a personal experience. But it took me back to the first thing I had read by Coetzee, "The Lives of Animals," now chapter four of *Elizabeth Costello*. How is it, I thought, that animals figure so ferociously in Coetzee's work? There is another stunning point of faith in "At the Gate," when Costello recalls an episode in the *Odyssey* in which in the kingdom of the dead, Odysseus, following the instructions of Tiresias, "digs a furrow, cuts the throat of his favourite ram, lets its blood flow into the furrow." That episode "always sends a shiver down her back." And as she reflects, she thinks, "she believes most unquestionably in the ram, the ram dragged by its master down to this terrible place. The ram is not just an idea" (p. 211). It is a real ram in an imaginary story. Costello believes in the ram as she believes in the frog that she knew when she was a child and in the tiger that she imagined.

And then there are the animals in *Disgrace*. Of all things, a story about a disgraced and sexually compromised professor, which in most contemporaries' hands, say those of Philip Roth, would carry us in very different directions of self-examination, perhaps sexual comedy, perhaps staged battles against aging, in Coetzee's hands takes the protagonist to work in an animal shelter. For Coetzee, the deepest ethical, aesthetic, and epistemological questions are linked with animals, those unknowable others whose reality his prose, like Elizabeth Costello's passionate attack on the use of animals for food, strains to find. At that point in her lecture that arouses the greatest hostility, Elizabeth compares the experimentation on and slaughter of animals to the work of the Nazi concentration camps. "Fullness of being," she says, "is hard to sustain in confinement." The devastating work of reason is most devastating in its work on "creatures least able to bear confinement," "in zoos, in laboratories, institutions where the flow of joy that comes from living not *in* or *as* a body but simply from being an embodied being has no place." And "the particular horror of the camps," she says, "is not that despite a humanity shared with their victims, the killers treated them like lice. That is too abstract. The horror is that the killers refused to think themselves into the place of their victims . . . They did not say, 'I am burning, I am falling in ash,'" (p. 79).

After such a line, we are left almost gasping. The ultimate condition is to be transformed utterly into the non-living. Yet we are left too with the human, with the consciousness that creates, allegorizes, and eats animals. And the end of *Disgrace*, in its stunningly clipped and powerful focus on David Lurie's work at the animal shelter, movingly suggests what, after all, cannot, in words, be communicated: the terrible reality of the being of the tiger and the frog. David thinks of a young dog, not quite ready, one would have thought, to die. He knows he can save it for a while, but he knows as well that sooner or later he will have to bring it to its death. He thinks, there will be a time "when he will have to bring him to Bev Shaw in her operating room (perhaps he will carry him in his arms, perhaps he will do that for him) and caress him and brush back the fur so that the needle can find the vein, and whisper to him and support him in the moment when, bewilderingly, his legs buckle; and then, when the soul is out, fold him up and pack him away in his bag." And then he *does* carry the dog to Bev: "'Come,' he says, bends, opens his arms. The dog wags its crippled rear, sniffs his face, licks his cheeks, his lips, his ears. He does nothing to stop it. 'Come.'"

The very last lines of this almost unbearable concluding chapter, which follows on a book in which Lurie's daughter is brutally raped, are directly to the point of those real rams, and tigers and frogs in imaginary gardens: "Bearing him in his arms like a lamb, he re-enters the surgery. 'I thought you would save him for another week,' says Bev Shaw. 'Are you giving him up?' 'I am giving him up.'"[4]

This awful surrender is the fullest realization of utter difference. The trusting, licking, loving animal goes to his death out of the mercy he does not want and that David Lurie does not want to give. The personal surrender by David is part of what is entailed in coming at last fully upon another. Of course the terrible irony of this passage is that the dog, unlike the tiger, is indeed thinking about him. So compounded with the act of recognition is the act of betrayal.

---

[4]   J. M. Coetzee, *Disgrace* (London: Penguin Books, 1999), p. 220.

Coetzee is never easy. As Attridge says, he is not trying to get himself off the hook by having Elizabeth Costello and Sister Bridget take the blame for positions he holds. Costello and Bridget are, precisely, the not-Coetzee to which his work aspires. The works as a whole are not making arguments but feeling the full consequences of the arguments in human relations, human feelings, "passions," for which Costello learns the board is really looking. (Not epistemology, but aesthetics, one might say.) In one of the particularly fascinating sequences in "The Lives of Animals," Costello attacks the argument of Thomas Nagel in his famous essay, "What is it like to be a bat?"

Costello argues that Nagel "is wrong" to think that in order to know what it is to be a bat, "we need to be able to experience bat life through the sense modalities of a bat." But, she says, "To be a living bat is to be full of being; being fully a bat is like being fully human, which is also to be full of being," and to be full of being is "to live as a body-soul. One name for the experience of being is *joy*."[5] Costello argues, in her austerely, almost coldly passionate way, that surrendering to the difference, seeing only the difference, is a step toward extermination camps. "The question to ask should not be: Do we have something in common – reason, self-consciousness, a soul – with other animals?" (p. 79). We must begin with a recognition of the fullness of being.

Costello knows what Coetzee knows, that the real redemptive work is not in belief but in finding the word that will get us to those animals. That, one might say, is the work of literature. That is particularly the work of realist literature. Regardless of the abstractions of epistemology, regardless of the possibilities of objectivity or the force of rational argument, against which Elizabeth Costello struggles to find appropriate defenses, literature tests out the ideas against experience and affirms the fullness of life, and its value. It is the work of finding the redemptive word, a work that can never be completed but can never be ignored. It is Coetzee's work. He knows, in the words with which he chooses to invent and imagine his world, that the animals – the dogs, the frogs, the tigers – are there, and that they matter at least as much as he does.

---

[5] See my discussion of Nagel's essay in the preceding chapter, "The heartbeat of the squirrel." Unlike Costello, I largely accept Nagel's argument, but ultimately agree that literature (and I focus of course on realist literature) deliberately defies the merely rational argument that the other can't be known. In the end, Costello is, of course, right that there is an ultimate similarity in all living things, the sense of "fullness of being," and in so far as there is that similarity Nagel is wrong to insist on absolute difference. The ethical point, in any case, is that beyond the mere possibility of knowing, there is the responsibility, first, to try to know, and second, to recognize the other's fullness of being and its similarity, in that respect, to us.

Epilogue

The conventional reading is that "realism," certainly in the Victorian and late-Victorian mode, buckled to radical critiques and, by the beginning of the twentieth century, gave way to various experimental literary modes and to a widely shared sense, among the finest writers, that the strict representation of reality was both impossible and – in the mode of Gissing's Biffin – unutterably tedious. Mr. Bennett, with his realist representation of the surfaces of things, cannot read Mrs. Brown. Moreover, the possibility of in fact "representing" the real seemed more and more remote, in particular, insofar as the approach was literal. The human mind, human perceptions, human feelings, desires, and needs, get in the way of seeing things as in themselves they really are. As far back as Kant it had become clear that we could never know the thing in itself, but rather, at best, as Pater put it, only the thing as in itself it seems to me to be.

Modernism and post-modernism experimented with various forms of non-representational, or symbolist, or fantastic forms of art, from Dada to cubism, to the theater of the Absurd. Postmodern theory dramatized and speculated on the self-referentiality of all language and of all art. The apparent "innocence" of the Victorians would never be recovered and was not lamented because, as cultural theory increasingly has demonstrated, the innocence disguised – perhaps also from the artists themselves – the ideological work their literature was doing.

But there are other ways to read this history, most particularly by beginning with the impressive sophistication of the Victorians themselves, their own awareness of the tricks and strategies of consciousness, their own worries about the possibility of objectivity and, its concomitant in literature, the possibility of knowing the other. What complicates and yet makes look naïve much of the Victorian work in literature and art, was the often overt moral impetus. So, as many of the essays in this book have insisted, epistemology for the most sophisticated Victorian thinkers was entangled with ethics; and art, in its efforts to "see the object as in itself it really is," was struggling toward a culture of compassion and fellow-feeling even as, out in the streets and markets, things were moving in the other direction.

Realism was not *only*, as much contemporary criticism sees it, a more or less surreptitious way to propagandize for the new economic and social order and affirm the possibility of the good life in the new system; it was also, and intensely, an effort to break through the philosophically recognized limits of knowing, and the theoretically inevitable assertion of what Dickens often called "Number one." There is often a remarkable tension between the implications of the resolutions of novels – those necessary more or less happy endings and shapings and reshapings of experience that threatened to move out of control into meaninglessness – and the effect of the very texture of the novels. Many of them, like the great massive works of the later Dickens, or like *Middlemarch*, or almost always the novels of Thackeray, threaten us with their details, with their explorations of multiple minds in multiply complex situations. The endings are *not* inevitable. As people used to say about travel, it's not the pleasure of being there, but the pleasure of getting there that is most valuable. And getting there, in Victorian realist fiction, is to be confronted with great masses of material, not all of which – as I have quoted Barbara Hardy as saying – can be squeezed into the dominant themes and patterns.

And yet, there is a sense in which *everything* in literature must be allegorical. It registers things, places, animals, even people, in a way that signifies – that means something other than what it is, and, in particular, means something to humans about what it means to be human, and about how the human relates to a world that seems *not* to be human at all. Even the act of understanding, or attempting to understand the other – the other person, the other living creature – is also an attempt to assimilate that other to the self, or, more altruistically, to transform the self by entering into the other. Perhaps "allegory" is not quite the right word, but certainly things, people, animals, in literature always resonate with significances beyond what they are and related to what *we* are. In so far as the simplest definition of "allegory" applies, it might be possible to take all literature as allegorical – for "allegory," writes Ian Fletcher, "says one thing and means another."[1] Metaphor works that way. Metonymy works that way. Realism, metonymic at base, even then in its commitment to represent things as they are and to tell the truth, absolutely, works by suggesting relevancies and connections that are *not* stated.

---

1   Angus Fletcher, *Allegory* (Ithaca, NY: Cornell University Press, 1964), p. 2.

Among the Victorians, the struggle to get to know the other was pervasive – it was, in effect, the basis of the realist literature that dominated
the literary scene. But realism, deeply imagined, always tends to run up
against the impossibility of knowing, the absolute otherness of the other,
and much of the revulsion against realism in the early twentieth century
had to do with the growing intensity of this sense – the strange and often
frightening unknowability of the world. The extraordinary labors of
explorers of consciousness, like Henry James, or Virginia Woolf, or James
Joyce, or even, in his way, D. H. Lawrence, have deep roots in the realism
they seemed to be rejecting.

Realism as a literary mode falters when it runs up against the unknowable, and the moral effort of Victorian realism is deeply troubled by the
encounter. And yet one of the great achievements of what I take to be the
ultimate realist impulse is the capacity to register (I worry here about the
word "represent") the reality of the unknowable other *and* to continue to
care – to allow threatening and incomprehensible difference its value and,
as it were, its privacy. In much aesthetic theory, encounters of this kind are
encounters with "the sublime." The sublime is the condition of the utterly
unknowable, or rather, of the human confrontation with it. Paul de Man,
discussing Kant's treatment of the sublime, says that "No mind, no inside
to correspond to an outside, can be found in Kant's scene. To the extent
that any mind or judgment are [*sic*] present at all, they are in error: it is
false to think of the sky as a roof or of the ocean as bounded by the horizon
of the sky."[2] Later, he argues that "The dynamics of the sublime mark the
moment when the infinite is frozen into the materiality of stone, when no
pathos, anxiety, or sympathy is conceivable; it is, indeed, the moment of
a-pathos, or apathy, as the complete loss of the symbolic" (p. 127).

Arrived there, we find realism nowhere. And yet, of course, it is everywhere. The sublime, in its stunning freezing materiality, beyond human
feeling, is registered by humans with awe and fear and wonder just as it
banishes conventional feeling, achieves what de Man calls "apathy."
There is the ultimate double-reverse, as it were, in the artist's aspiration
to the sublime, or frightened confrontation with it. That is, it banishes all
the ordinariness with which realism is most concerned and that evokes all
the domestic and distinctly human feelings that give such power to a book
like *Middlemarch*, and at the same time ends up – as art – serving human
purposes again, even some of those moral purposes that modern literature
had seemed to leave behind to the Victorians. That is, the great moral (and

2   Paul de Man, *Aesthetic Ideology* (Minneapolis: University of Minnesota Press, 1996), p 127.

epistemological achievement) of this confrontation with the absolute otherness of the other is the power or determination to respect (too mild a word
in the context of the discussion of the sublime) and value, not to assimilate
or destroy it – not to translate it into something transcendental that
requires our worship and a sense of divine order beyond what, to us mere
mortals, can be understood.

Realism, resisting (and succumbing to) allegory with every word, but at
the edge of the sublime abyss, with its secular, ethical, and epistemological
energies, seeps back into the modernist and post-modernist enterprise, and
bears the Victorians' moral burden.

Index